The Moral Metaphor System

The Moral Metaphor System

A Conceptual Metaphor Approach

NING YU

Great Clarendon Street, Oxford, OX2 6DP,
United Kingdom

Oxford University Press is a department of the University of Oxford.
It furthers the University's objective of excellence in research, scholarship,
and education by publishing worldwide. Oxford is a registered trade mark of
Oxford University Press in the UK and in certain other countries

Impression: 1

Published in the United States of America by Oxford University Press
198 Madison Avenue, New York, NY 10016, United States of America

British Library Cataloguing in Publication Data
Data available

Library of Congress Control Number: 2021952883

ISBN 978-0-19-286632-5

DOI: 10.1093/oso/9780192866325.001.0001

Printed and bound by
CPI Group (UK) Ltd, Croydon, CR0 4YY

Contents

Acknowledgments

The year 2020 was the 40th anniversary of the publication of George Lakoff and Mark Johnson's monumental book *Metaphors We Live By* (1980). This book of mine is meant to be a humble tribute that I hope to pay to Lakoff and Johnson, and to their seminal work, small-sized as is, for its massive and lasting impact on the academic world, with thousands and thousands of citations, not only in linguistics and philosophy, but also in many other disciplines proximally or distally related.

Thirty-three years ago, I had the opportunity to read *Metaphors We Live By* for the first time. Six years later, I embarked on my own journey of metaphor research, focusing on Chinese, my native language, sometimes in comparison with English. On this journey, I have had the honor, privilege, and pleasure of interacting closely with, and benefiting directly from, many great scholars in the field, including Lakoff and Johnson themselves. I would like to thank, from the bottom of my heart, all of them, too many to mention individually by name here.

However, I do want to single out two of them, Ray Gibbs and Zoltán Kövecses, because they deserve my very special thanks. I was extremely fortunate to get to know them in person upfront on my journey, and have had their friendly company all along. Their guidance and assistance have helped me enormously at various junctures of the road. Their scholarship has permeated the flesh and blood of my own.

I also want to express my profound gratitude to the two anonymous reviewers for Oxford University Press (OUP) for their invaluable comments and suggestions, and to the editors at OUP, Julia Steer, Vicki Sunter, and Joy Mellor, as well as the production team, for their professional assistance and technical support.

The ideas of this book started to emerge in three of my earlier journal articles, all published in *Metaphor and Symbol* (Taylor and Francis Group):

1. Yu, Ning. 2015. Metaphorical character of moral cognition: A comparative and decompositional analysis. *Metaphor and Symbol* 30(3): 163–183.
2. Yu, Ning. 2016. Spatial metaphors for morality: A perspective from Chinese. *Metaphor and Symbol* 31(2): 108–125.

3. Yu, Ning, Tianfang Wang, and Yingliang He. 2016. Spatial subsystem of moral metaphors: A cognitive semantic study. *Metaphor and Symbol* 31(4): 195–211.

As listed above, the third article was written with two co-authors. At the time of collaboration, Tianfang and Yingliang were still MA students, but they are now PhD candidates, at The Pennsylvania State University. I want to thank them for their contribution, and am especially happy to see their intellectual growth since then.

Lastly, I want to extend my heart-felt gratitude to my wife, Jie (Lily) Huang, a librarian at the Penn State Libraries. I could never imagine having finished this book without her professional informational assistance as well as essential logistic support at home.

Penn State-University Park
September 2021

List of Figures

List of Tables

1

Moral cognition and embodied metaphor

Introduction

1.1 Conceptual metaphor theory: Morality and metaphor research

Morality is an eternal subject for human inquiry into what it means to be human, concerning the fundamental human judgment on what is good or right in contrast to what is bad or wrong, in the enhancing of human wellbeing. Our moral cognition, which consists of cognitive processes and mechanisms involved in making moral judgments based on our moral values and principles, allows us to make such judgments on human character and behavior, or intention and action, distinguishing between right and wrong, or good and evil, in moral choices and decisions, and regulating interpersonal relations and interactions in social life. As a social concept, morality refers to abstract values and principles in our social life, which lack concrete referents existing in the physical world that we can experience with our perceptual senses. We, therefore, conceptualize morality using metaphor (e.g., Denham 2000; Haggerty 1997; Harley 1993; Johnson 1993; Noonan 1988; Ross 2011). As is argued, metaphor is a powerful cognitive tool for understanding abstract social concepts (e.g., Landau, Robinson, and Meier 2014; Maasen and Weingart 2000). In effect, as Gibbs (2020: 1) put it recently, "metaphor is everywhere in human life", and it "bursts forth in most every discourse domain, is seen in virtually every language and culture that has been studied, and, quite important, is evident in many facets of human expressive action".

Metaphor research is one of the central topics in cognitive linguistics, which is a theoretic paradigm for the study of language as an integral part of cognition and culture (e.g., Lakoff 1987a; Lakoff and Johnson 1980, 1999; Langacker 1987, 1991; Talmy 2000; see also Croft and Cruse 2004; Evans 2019; Geeraerts and Cuycken 2007; Kövecses 2006; Ungerer and Schmid 2013). The most influential cognitive linguistic approach to metaphor, metonymy,

The Moral Metaphor System. Ning Yu, Oxford University Press. © Ning Yu (2022).
DOI: 10.1093/oso/9780192866325.003.0001

and figurative language in general is known as conceptual metaphor theory (CMT) (e.g., Barcelona 2000a; Dirven and Pörings 2002; Fusaroli and Morgagni 2009; Gibbs 1994, 2017; Kövecses 2000, 2005, 2015a, 2020; Lakoff and Johnson 1980, 1999; Lakoff and Turner 1989; Littlemore 2019; Panther and Radden 1999; Panther and Thornburg 2003; Panther, Thornburg, and Barcelona 2009; Sullivan 2013; see also Dancygier and Sweetser 2014; Kövecses 2010). In fact, CMT is acclaimed as "the dominant force in the contemporary world of interdisciplinary metaphor studies" (Gibbs 2009: 14). According to CMT, metaphor is primarily conceptual in nature, and it is an essential mode of thinking, or a "figure of thought" (Lakoff 1986). In CMT, a conceptual metaphor is defined as "a cross-domain mapping in the conceptual system" (Lakoff 1993: 203). As such, conceptual metaphors are manifested in metaphorical expressions, which are linguistic expressions, such as words, phrases, and sentences, as well as multimodal expressions more broadly, such as co-speech gestures, sign languages, and static and moving images (e.g., Cienki and Müller 2008; Forceville and Urios-Aparisi 2009; Taub 2001; Wilcox 2000). Metaphorical expressions, linguistic or multimodal, are the surface realization of their underlying cross-domain mappings, or conceptual metaphors. Gibbs (2014: 19–20) summarizes the development and achievement of CMT in the following passage:

> Since 1980, several hundred cognitive linguistic projects have demonstrated how systematic patterns of conventional expressions reveal the presence of underlying conceptual metaphors. These studies have explored a large range of target concepts and domains (e.g., the mind, concepts of the self, emotions, science, morality and ethics, economics, legal concepts, politics, mathematics, illness and death, education, psychoanalysis), within a vast number of languages (e.g., Spanish, Dutch, Chinese, Hungarian, Persian, Arabic, French, Japanese, Cora, Swedish), including sign languages and ancient languages (e.g., Latin, Ancient Greek), and have investigated the role of conceptual metaphors in thinking and speaking/writing within many academic disciplines (e.g., education, philosophy, mathematics, theater arts, physics, chemistry, architecture, political science, economics, geography, nursing, religion, law, business and marketing, and film).

Furthermore, Gibbs (2017: 5–7) outlines CMT's broad scope of impact as follows: CMT has made important contributions to (i) a new way of thinking about linguistic structure and behavior as a significant part of cognitive linguistics' program; (ii) the understanding of the pervasiveness of metaphorical language and thought across a wide range of cognitive domains and cultural and linguistic environments; (iii) the alteration of our scholarly conception of the relationship between language and thought with its claim about abstract thinking being based partly on metaphorical mapping; and (iv) the study of embodied cognition as a leading force in the "second revolution" of cognitive science.

Though exceptionally productive ever since it began to rise in popularity 40 years ago, CMT has its own limitations as an approach to metaphor research that has received many critiques and criticisms both within and beyond cognitive linguistics (see, e.g., Cameron and Low 1999; Cienki and Müller 2008; Deignan 2005; Glucksberg and McGlone 1999; Haser 2005; McGlone 2007; Murphy 1996; Ritchie 2013; Semino 2008; Steen 2011; Vervaeke and Kennedy 1996; see also Gibbs 2009, 2011, 2014, 2017; Kövecses 2008, 2017b for evaluations or responses). In a series of publications, Gibbs (2009, 2011, 2014, 2017) has made a most comprehensive evaluation of its weaknesses as well as its strengths, and issues and controversies that have been identified and raised regarding CMT. As he points out, the most general question about CMT is whether the presence of metaphor in language necessarily indicates anything about the way people ordinarily think (Gibbs 2014). Specific criticisms of CMT include the following points (see Gibbs 2014: 20–24):

(i) *Isolated constructed examples*: Far too many of the linguistic analyses presented in favor of CMT are based on isolated examples often constructed by the research analyst.

(ii) *Limitations of the individual analyst*: Linguistic analyses of conceptual metaphors are based on an individual linguist's own intuitions that may be theoretically motivated.

(iii) *Lack of explicit criteria for metaphor identification*: CMT analyses rarely provide explicit criteria about either how to identify linguistic metaphors in language or how to infer conceptual metaphors based on different groupings of metaphoric discourse.

(iv) *Issue of falsifiability and need for nonlinguistic evidence*: CMT is unfalsifiable if the only data in its favor are linguistic expressions, thus relying on circular logic when arguing for underlying conceptual metaphors with linguistic evidence only.

(v) *Ignorance of other factors*: CMT ignores other alternative possibilities, such as cultural, ideological, and linguistic factors, in its accounts of metaphoric thought and language.

(vi) *A reductionist approach*: CMT is far too reductionist in its account of verbal metaphor, reducing the consideration of novel poetic language to static conceptual metaphors that are grounded in recurring embodied experiences and even neural processes.

In light of these criticisms, Gibbs (2014: 31–32) calls upon CMT scholars to put CMT on firmer empirical ground. They should, among other things, (a) be more explicit about the ways they perform their linguistic analyses of language to infer conceptual metaphors; (b) seek to integrate their findings from linguistic analyses with those obtained by corpus, behavioral, and neuroscience-based research methods; (c) better articulate what empirical hypotheses and experimental predictions arise from more linguistic analyses of metaphor; (d) explore alternative explanations for the data collected in support of the theory; and (e) be more open about what it cannot accomplish simply because no single theory may be capable of explaining all aspects of the complex phenomena that are metaphorical language and thought. Looking back, we can say that CMT scholars and practitioners have made considerable progress in all these areas.

In the past decades, CMT has argued that our moral cognition is partly metaphorical, emerging in part from a complex system of conceptual metaphors for the understanding of moral principles and values (e.g., Johnson 1993, 1996, 2014; Lakoff 1996, 2004, 2006a, 2006b, 2008b; Lakoff and Johnson 1999). Lakoff and Johnson (1999), the founders of CMT, assert that this complex metaphor system for morality contain clusters of metaphorical mappings for conceptualizing, reasoning about, and communicating our moral ideas. That is the reason why morality is one of the common target domains of conceptual metaphors (Kövecses 2010).

This line of research on the metaphorical nature of moral understanding started with Johnson's 1993 book *Moral imagination: Implications of cognitive science for ethics*, in which he argues that metaphor is pervasive in our moral reasoning, lying at the heart of our imaginative moral rationality. Different moral metaphor systems have been examined along this line of research. Their source concepts, in my view, can be characterized loosely as falling into three broad conceptual domains, or domain matrixes as combinations of domains (Croft and Cruse 2004): (i) the financial and commercial domain, (ii) the familial and social domain, and (iii) the bodily and physical domain. These are discussed briefly below.

The financial and commercial domain

The moral metaphor system grounded in the financial and commercial domain is known as the Moral Accounting Metaphor (see, e.g., Johnson 1993: chapter 2, 1996; Lakoff 1996: chapter 4; Lakoff and Johnson 1999: chapter 14). This moral metaphor system focuses on the aspects of MORAL INTERACTION among people in the "moral book" and construes them as records of COMMERCIAL TRANSACTION in the accounting book. This general metaphoric mapping entails numerous submappings, such as those between wellbeing and wealth, moral deeds and commercial commodities, moral debt and financial debt, moral credit and financial credit, justice and fair exchange, and so forth. Thus, for instance, our moral acts toward others increase their wellbeing, putting them in moral debt to us and giving us moral credit. As Johnson (1996: 55) puts it, this moral metaphor system "gives rise to a pattern of reasoning about our duties, rights, and obligations" and, on the basis of it, "we reason about what is fair, and our moral discourse reveals this underlying conceptual metaphor system" (e.g., *In judging him, **take into account** all the good things he has done. I'm holding you **accountable** for her suffering. All her sacrifices for others surely **balance out** the bad things she did. I **owe** you a favor for that good deed. I'll make you **pay** for what you did!*). It is suggested that the Moral Accounting Metaphor is realized in a few basic moral schemes—Reciprocation, Retribution, Revenge, Restitution, and Altruism (see, e.g., Johnson 1993: chapter 2; Lakoff 1996: chapter 4; Lakoff and Johnson 1999: chapter 14)—which all elaborate on the notion of "balance" in the accounting book. According to the Moral Accounting Metaphor, "justice is the settling of accounts, which results in the balancing of the moral books" (Lakoff and Johnson 1999: 296).

The familial and social domain

Morality from the familial and social domain is known as being rooted in the Strict Father and Nurturant Parent models of the family, first proposed by Lakoff in his 1996 book *Moral politics* to account for ideological differences between conservatives and liberals in U.S. domestic politics. That is, the two political orientations of conservatism and liberalism were proposed as being ultimately based on different models of the family. Conservatism is grounded on the Strict Father family morality, whereas liberalism is based on the Nurturant Parent family morality. Thus, political liberalism and conservatism hold different views of morality because they are based on different family models that organize moral metaphors in different ways, giving priority to certain metaphors and downplaying others. For instance, the Strict Father model gives top priority to moral authority and moral strength, whereas the Nurturant Parent model places more emphasis on moral nurturance and moral empathy. According to Lakoff and Johnson (1999), human morality might be based on models of the family for two reasons. First, children's moral sensibility and moral understanding are first formed within their families. For young children, therefore, morality is just their family morality. Second, children's moral education largely stems from their family situations. Massive social influences on their subsequent development of moral values get filtered through their family morality. Lakoff and Johnson's (1999: 313) hypothesis about moral understanding is that models of the family "order our metaphors for morality into relatively coherent ethical perspectives by which we live our lives". That is, morality in general is conceptualized metaphorically as some form of family morality. This metaphorical conceptualization gives rise to the Family of Man Metaphor, by which people ought to treat each other the way they treat their family members (see Lakoff and Johnson 1999: 317).

The bodily and physical domain

The source concepts of moral metaphors in this domain are usually derived from our bodily, or sensorimotor, experience in the physical environment. Moral metaphors of this type often refer to the moral character of individual people or of society as a whole (see Johnson 1993, 1996). Johnson (1996: 57–60) discusses some basic metaphors for morality that can be categorized as belonging to this type:

(i) MORALITY IS HEALTH and IMMORALITY IS SICKNESS
    Since moral evil is a *disease*, we must *quarantine* those who are immoral so that we are not exposed to their influence. We must keep ourselves *clean, pure*, and *protected* from moral *infection*.

(ii) BEING MORAL IS BEING UPRIGHT
    When we are morally *healthy* and *strong*, we can stand *upright* against evil *forces*. Morality is thus a struggle to maintain moral *strength* and moral *balance* so that we can stay *in control* to resist immoral *forces* and do not *fall* into evil ways.

(iii) BEING MORAL IS BEING IN THE NORMAL PLACE

Moral ends are the *places* we should strive to reach, and being moral is going *where* you ought to go. Deviance is immoral because it can take people away from the right *path* and lead them *astray*. Also, if things are out of their normal *place* or moral *order*, society will *break down* and cease to *function*.

(iv) MORALITY IS LIGHT and IMMORALITY IS DARKNESS

Moral *darkness* is a threat to our basic wellbeing, with evil being a *dark force*. The *darkness* of evil makes people incapable of seeing the good and knowing what is right and wrong. The *dark side* in people threatens to overcome the *light* in them.

As illustrated above, the moral metaphors of this type are really grounded in the nature of our bodies and how they function in the physical world.

Lakoff and Johnson (1999: 290) argue that cognitive science, especially cognitive semantics, "gives us the means for detailed and comprehensive analysis of what our moral concepts are and how their logic works", and that "our cognitive unconscious is populated with an extensive system of metaphoric mappings for conceptualizing, reasoning about, and communicating our moral ideas". While asserting the metaphorical nature of moral understanding, Lakoff and Johnson (1999) also ask the question: Is all morality metaphoric? Their answer is no. As they suggest, there is nothing inherently metaphoric about "basic experiential morality" as aspects of human wellbeing. Nevertheless, "there is no ethical system that is not metaphorical" (p. 325). Lakoff and Johnson also raise the question of whether metaphorical concepts are universal. They indicate that the empirical research has not yet been carried out to make that determination, but the evidence available thus far suggests that they are very good candidates for universal moral concepts.

As reviewed above, the CMT research shows that our ethical values and principles are rooted metaphorically in our embodied and socioculturally situated habitation of the world (see, e.g., Johnson 1993, Lakoff 1996, Lakoff and Johnson 1999). This claim, framed within CMT, has inspired or motivated a growing body of research on the metaphorical nature of social cognition in general, and of moral cognition in particular. The disciplinary areas involved include, but are not limited to, business discourse research (e.g., Koller 2005); history (e.g., Slingerland 2011); religious studies (e.g., Howe 2006; Massengill 2008; Meier and Fetterman 2020; Nazar 2015; Slingerland 2004), public health care and medical research (e.g., Diekema 1989; Ferentzy and Turner 2012; Hanne 2015; Wurzbach 1999), political science (e.g., Abdel-Raheem 2014; Bougher 2012; Holman 2016; McAdams et al. 2008), philosophical research (e.g., Cady 2005; Campbell 2013; Coeckelbergh 2010; Courte 1998; Fesmire 1999, 2003; Klaassen 1998), and especially social psychology (e.g., Landau 2017; Landau, Meier, and Keefer 2010; Landau, Robinson, and Meier 2014; Meier and Robinson 2004; Meier, Robinson, and Clore 2004; Meier et al. 2007; Sheikh, Botindari, and White 2013; Sherman and Clore 2009; Zhong and House 2014; Zhong and Liljenquist 2006).

Thus, for example, CMT is applied to religious studies for the analysis of religious discourse. In her book-length study, Howe (2006) applied the tools of conceptual metaphor to biblical hermeneutics, analyzing 1 Peter as an exemplar of Christian moral discourse. Her goal was to employ conceptual metaphor analysis to explain how modern readers make sense of Scripture, and her claim was that conceptual metaphor, grounded in basic embodied human experience, plays a crucial role in the creation of meaning in Christian moral discourse. Another study applying the CMT approach to moral metaphors in religious discourse is Massengill (2008), which explored the way in which moral metaphors are utilized in such religious discourses as prayers, liturgies, and other worship resources prepared for religious services. The author focused on the conceptual metaphors with such source concepts as FAMILY, JOURNEY, and PHYSICAL GROWTH, which serve as conceptual building blocks for different moral systems. These conceptual metaphors also have their horizontal and vertical variants, which may represent different moral orientations in the construction of the larger moral worldviews. For instance, God and humans are invariably framed in a vertical relationship whereas humans have a horizontal relationship among themselves (see also Meier and Fetterman 2020). The author also found that the metaphorical structures of religious language for worship may differ from those contained in political discourse as proposed by Lakoff (1996).

In contrast to religion, concerning human mental wellbeing, conceptual metaphor research has also been carried out to investigate morality and ethics in medicine and health care, which are concerned with human physical wellbeing. From a physician's point of view, Diekema (1989: 23) studied medical professionals' language from which he discerned various metaphors that "pervade" their conceptual systems, shaping their perceptions, their thoughts and feelings, and ultimately their behavior. For example, a prominent set of conceptual metaphors that construes medicine as a business with more specific mappings between hospitals and marketplaces, medical services and commodities, patients and consumers, and physicians and business employees. With such a cognitive model composed of conceptual metaphors shared by medical professionals, medicine would then become a service to be purchased, the success of physicians would be defined by the gross financial profit, and the best delivery of medical care would be judged by the balance sheet and the bottom line. Diekema (1989) argued that reflection on such metaphors and willingness to be self-critical are important aspects of physicians' ethical responsibility.

Another example is Wurzbach's (1999) study applying CMT to the study of moral metaphors in nursing. In this article, the author traced the salient conceptual metaphors for morality that have affected nurses' moral perceptions, values, and responsibilities through different stages of history, paralleled by the changes in social trends and contexts. For example, in the first half of the twentieth century, the dominant metaphor was a military one, when nurses were trained like soldiers, highlighting nurses' ethical virtues as loyalty and obedience to authorities. In the 1960s and 1970s, accompanied by the women's movement and a general questioning of authority (be it the authority of parents or husbands, doctors or hospitals), the military metaphor transitioned to a new moral metaphor that emerged with the new orientations in ethical values. The new one was the legal metaphor of advocacy, with which the fiduciary relationship between attorneys and clients is mapped onto that between nurses and patients. Nurses have the moral responsibility to defend the rights of their patients, supporting patients' goals rather than the goals of hospitals or doctors. The author argued that different moral metaphors of nursing provided moral principles and values that guided nurses in their practice and, for that matter, nurses could not afford to follow moral metaphors without reflection. This study showed that nursing practice had been affected by the changes of dominant moral metaphors in the profession. It is exactly what Lakoff and Johnson (1980: 3) meant when they said that metaphor is "not just in language but in thought and action".

All these examples illustrate how conceptual metaphors play an essential role in shaping and structuring moral cognition. In the next section, I discuss the CMT view on the emergence of conceptual metaphors and its relationship with the embodiment hypothesis in cognitive science, an interdisciplinary field where a number of disciplines such as anthropology, artificial intelligence, linguistics, philosophy, psychology converge and overlap for the study of the mind and cognition.

1.2 Metaphor, body, and culture: Embodiment

At its very inception, CMT places much stress on the "experiential bases of metaphors" (Lakoff and Johnson 1980: 14–21). Thus, Lakoff and Johnson (1980: 14) argue that conceptual metaphors, which structure our conceptual system to a considerable extent, are not arbitrary, but grounded "in our physical and cultural experience". While they emphasize the importance of "direct physical experience", they also point out that:

> what we call "direct physical experience" is never merely a matter of having a body of a certain sort; rather, *every* experience takes place within a vast background of cultural presuppositions. ... Cultural assumptions, values, and attitudes are not a conceptual overlay which we may or may not place upon experience as we choose. It would be more correct to say that all experience is cultural through and through, that we experience our "world" in such a way that our culture is already present in the very experience itself.
> (Lakoff and Johnson 1980: 57)

That is, according to CMT, the experiential basis of conceptual metaphors is both bodily and cultural. On the one hand, metaphors are motivated by and grounded in the body and bodily experience, extending body-based meaning and inference into abstract thought through systematic conceptual mappings from bodily-based sensorimotor source domains onto abstract target domains (Johnson 2007; Johnson and Rohrer 2007; Lakoff 1993). On the other hand, such metaphorical mappings do not arise from within the body alone but emerge from bodily interactions that are to a large extent defined by the cultural world (see, e.g., Kövecses 2005, 2015a). This is because the bodily experiences that form the source domains for conceptual metaphors are themselves complex social and cultural constructions, which set up specific perspectives from which "aspects of embodied experience are viewed as particularly salient and meaningful in people's lives" (Gibbs 1999: 154).

In my chapter titled "Metaphor from body and culture" in *The Cambridge handbook of metaphor and thought* (Gibbs 2008), I argue that conceptual metaphors emerge from the interaction between body and culture.

> While the body is a potentially universal source for emerging metaphors, culture functions as a filter that selects aspects of sensorimotor experience and connects them with subjective experiences and judgments for metaphorical mappings. That is, metaphors are grounded in bodily experience but shaped

by cultural understanding. Put differently, metaphors are embodied in their cultural environment.

(Yu 2008: 247)

It is worth noting that the CMT claim for conceptual metaphors emerging from the interaction between body and culture should be viewed as being embedded in a larger academic context and intellectual movement in which the notion of "embodiment" attracted a growing interest in cognitive linguistics (e.g., Brenzinger and Kraska-Szlenk 2014; Frank et al. 2008; Kraska-Szlenk 2020; Lakoff and Johnson 1999; Lakoff and Núñez 2000; Maalej and Yu 2011; Sharifian et al. 2008; Yu 2009a, 2009b; Ziemke, Zlatev, and Frank 2007) as well as cognitive science at large (e.g., Berdayes, Esposito, and Murphy 2004; Csordas 1994; de Vega, Glenberg, and Graesser 2008; Gallagher 2005; Gibbs 2006; Johnson 1987, 2007, 2017; Krois et al. 2007a; Rowlands 2010; Shanahan 2010; Shapiro 2011; Vallet et al. 2016; Varela, Thompson, and Rosch 1991; Weiss and Haber 1999). As Krois et al. (2007b) point out, the concept of embodiment provides a way to link scientific and humanistic disciplines. In fact, the meaning of the term *embodiment* has also been "stretched in different directions" (Strathern 1996: 196), especially because it is now a common theoretic construct used in a wide variety of disciplines. There exist different theories of embodiment, often highly divergent from one another, and sometimes having very little in common (Rohrer 2006, 2007; Violi 2003, 2008).

The term *embodiment*, as suggested by the root of the word itself, has to do with the body as the existential ground of the mind. That is, embodiment, as the very essence of human existence, is really about how the body is related to the mind in human experience in the physical and cultural world, and how this relationship affects human cognition. Scholars in cognitive science have put forward a variety of programmatic tenets for the embodiment paradigm regarding the fundamental role of the human body in the workings of the human mind, including, for instance, the body grounding the mind, the body extending the mind, the body enacting the mind, the body informing the mind, the body schematizing the mind, the body shaping the mind. They have also proposed different embodiment tenets for the study of the relationship between body, mind, and culture: namely "the body in the mind" (Johnson 1987), "the culture in the mind" (Shore 1998), and "the culture in the body" (Maalej 2004, 2008). All of these are important theses for the exploration into the embodied nature of human cognition and socioculturally situated nature of human embodiment (Frank et al. 2008; Ziemke, Zlatev, and Frank 2007).

In Yu (2015b), I characterized the notion of embodiment as emphasizing the role of the body in grounding and framing cognition within the physical and cultural context. In contrast with the Cartesian mind-body dualism, the embodiment hypothesis claims that the body actually shapes the mind (Gallagher 2005). Such a mind is therefore embodied in that it is crucially shaped by the particular nature of the human body, including our perceptual and motor systems and our interactions with the physical and cultural world. However, the mind is not shaped universally because the body itself may take different "shapes" in different cultures in the first place. While the body is an intimate reality to us, with basic physical structures, functions, and experiences common among all of us, the notion of "body", however, is a multifaceted concept that is culturally constructed, meaning quite different things across cultures, or even within cultures over history (see Yu 2009a: 12–28). Cultures may construe the body and bodily experiences quite differently, attributing different values and significances to various body parts and organs and their functions. Various cultural construals of the body and bodily experiences may motivate different schematizations and conceptualizations, which give rise to varied perspectives in the understanding of human inhabitations and functions in the world (Yu 2015b; see also Gibbs 1999; Kövecses 2005, 2015a; Chapter 7 of this book).

For example, different cultures in the world may vary in viewing which part of the body plays the central role in a person's mental life. Thus, there is a need "to look for the mind inside the body" across various cultures (Sharifian et al. 2008). Sharifian et al. (2008) took it as their central aim to contribute to the knowledge of various cultures' conceptualizations of how such mental functions as feeling, thinking, and knowing are related to particular parts of the body as is reflected in their respective languages, trying to identify synchronic variation and trace diachronic development. It was found that the major loci of the mind are the abdomen region, the heart region, and the head or brain region. The three types of conceptualizations of the mind can therefore be labeled as "abdominocentrism", "cardiocentrism", and "cerebrocentrism", respectively. As the studies presented in the chapters of the book show, the "abdomen-centering" languages include Basque, Indonesian, Kuuk Thaayorre, and Malay; the "heart-centering" languages include Chinese, Japanese, and Korean; and the dualistic "heart/head-centering" languages include Dutch, English, Northeastern Neo-Aramaic, Persian, and Tunisian Arabic.

A contrastive case is found, for instance, between Western and Chinese cultures in terms of the conceptualization of "person". The Western conceptualization of "person" is dualistic in that a person is "split" into two distinct and separate parts: the body and the mind. This mind-body dichotomy defines

Cartesian dualism, which has been the dominant philosophical view in the West for hundreds of years. The mind-body dualism is also conceptualized and expressed metonymically as a dichotomy between head (i.e., HEAD FOR MIND or LOCATION FOR ACTIVITY) and heart (i.e., HEART FOR BODY or PART FOR WHOLE), with the former being the center of thought and the latter the seat of emotions. In contrast to the Western dualistic view, Chinese culture takes on a more holistic view that sees the heart as the center of both emotions and thought. According to the traditional Chinese conceptualization, therefore, although a person also consists of two parts—the body and the heart (i.e., 身 shēn "body" and 心 xīn "heart"), these two are however not separate, the latter being an integral part of the former. In the Chinese conceptualization, the heart is traditionally regarded as the central faculty of cognition, which unifies all cognitive and affective aspects of a human person, such as mental, intellectual, rational, moral, emotional, dispositional, and so on (see Yu 2009a, 2015b). The contrast outlined here characterizes two cultural traditions that have developed different conceptualizations of person, self, and cognitive agent.

In a general sense, the term *embodiment* attributes a more active and constructive role to the body in human cognition. As Lakoff and Johnson (1999) have argued, our mind is embodied in the profound sense that the very structure of our thoughts comes from the nature of our body. In his book titled *Embodiment and cognitive science*, Gibbs (2006: 1) states that in cognitive science, embodiment refers to "understanding the role of an agent's own body in its everyday, situated cognition", namely how our bodies influence the ways we think and speak. He outlines the following as the embodiment premise:

> People's subjective, felt experiences of their bodies in action provide part of the fundamental grounding for language and thought. Cognition is what occurs when the body engages the physical, cultural world and must be studied in terms of the dynamical interactions between people and the environment. Human language and thought emerge from recurring patterns of embodied activity that constrain ongoing intelligent behavior. We must not assume cognition to be purely internal, symbolic, computational, and disembodied, but seek out the gross and detailed ways that language and thought are inextricably shaped by embodied action.
>
> (Gibbs 2006: 9)

Gibbs suggests that the key feature here for understanding the embodied nature of human cognition is to "look for possible mind-body and language-body connections" (p. 9) as formed in the interaction between the body and the physical and cultural world. He goes on to characterize the relationship between body and culture and the diversity of cultural meanings attached to the body. As he suggests, the body system offers insightful analysis for understanding cultural systems because physical environments in which people and their bodies move are imbued with culture. The body is appreciated for its symbolic properties as people instill cultural meanings into bodily processes and activities. Culture does not just inform, but it also constitutes, embodied experience. Many embodied experiences are rooted in sociocultural contexts. This does not imply that people in various cultures have different physiologies, but only that they weigh their embodied experiences differently in how they interpret their sensorimotor interactions in and with the world around them. It is therefore important to explore the linkages between embodiment and cultural meaning (Gibbs 2006: 36–39).

In sum, this section has highlighted two theses of CMT in particular and cognitive linguistics in general. First, metaphors emerge from the interaction between body and culture. Second, embodiment is socioculturally situated. My goal as a cognitive linguist is to study language as a window to cognition and culture, or cognition at the cultural level. My focus in this monograph, however, is on the area of morality. In the next section, I discuss how moral cognition, as part of cultural cognition, can manifest itself in language, and how linguistic description and analysis can lead to the revelation of cultural cognition, including moral cognition.

1.3 Moral cognition, cultural cognition, and language

Despite the growing body of conceptual metaphor studies in the field of cognitive linguistics, it seems, research into metaphorical understanding of morality in languages has been surprisingly scarce, in comparison with studies of emotion and time metaphors, for instance. Even studies that address the metaphorical nature of moral cognition in English aimed more at critical analyses leading to philosophical, ideological, or political insights, rather than at the display of the moral metaphor system as manifested in the language per se.

This book presents a cognitive linguistic study of moral metaphors in the CMT framework. I study conceptual metaphors for morality as manifested linguistically and, to a much more limited extent, multimodally in English and Chinese, attempting to contribute a comparative perspective on the research topic of moral imagination through metaphor. My focus is on the linguistic manifestation of moral metaphors in these two languages. To this end, my primary task is to expand the investigation of the "range" (Kövecses 2010: 183–184) of fundamental moral metaphors, that is, the range of possible source concepts for MORALITY and IMMORALITY as target concepts. These two concepts, along with their adjectival forms, MORAL and IMMORAL, represent the bipolar valence of moral opposition. Of course, the English words *morality* and *moral* also have a neutral sense, relating or referring to the whole domain, semantic or conceptual.

In tackling this book project, I hope to shed some light on the metaphorical nature of moral cognition and how it is systematically manifested in language. In other words, I hope to contribute to the construction of a "language-based folk model" (Kövecses 2015b: 271) for morality, as it is composed of folk theories of morality. "Folk theories, as opposed to expert theories, are naïve nonscientific understanding of the world by lay people for their everyday purposes" (p. 271). Since the folk model is language-based, thus shared by the speakers of a linguistic community, it is also what is referred to as a cultural model of morality. Cultural models are cognitive representations and configurations of knowledge (i.e., cognitive models) about a certain field that are rooted in individual minds but collectively shared by members of a cultural group and, as such, they are taken-for-granted and often out-of-awareness, but play a central role in their holders' understanding of the world and behavior in it (see, e.g., Bennardo and de Munck 2014; Holland and Quinn 1987; Kövecses 2005; Ungerer and Schmid 2013).

That is, cultural models pertain to cognition at the cultural level, or cultural cognition (e.g., D'Andrade 1989; DiMaggio 1997; Frank 2015; Quinn and Holland 1987; Sharifian 2008, 2009, 2017). As Sharifian (2017: 3) characterizes it, the notion of "cultural cognition" affords an integrated understanding of cognition and culture as they relate to language and offers a multidisciplinary understanding of cognition that moves beyond the level of the individual mind. While cultural cognition is inevitably rooted in the minds of individual members of a cultural group, its elements, however, are not equally shared by the members of that group; instead, they are heterogeneously distributed so that the members of the group show variation and differences in their access to and internalization of their community's cultural cognition. In other words, individual members' cognition can never capture the totality of their shared cultural cognition. Furthermore, "cultural cognition is dynamic in that it is constantly being negotiated and renegotiated across generations and through contact between speech communities" (p. 3).

At this point, a question to ask is: What is the relationship between cultural cognition and language? I ask this question in order to highlight the relevancy of linguistic studies to moral cognition. Sharifian (2017: 5) has the following to say about the pivotal role of language in recording and transmitting cultural cognition:

> As a central aspect of cultural cognition, language serves (in the words of wa Thiong'o, 1986) as a "collective memory bank" of the cultural cognition of a speech community. Many aspects of a speech community's language are shaped by elements of cultural cognition that have prevailed at different stages in the history of that community and that have left traces in subsequent linguistic practice. In this sense, language can be viewed as a primary mechanism for "storing" and communicating cultural cognition, acting both as a memory bank and a fluid vehicle for the (re-)transmission of cultural cognition.

To study the interaction between language, culture, and cognition, Sharifian proposes a theoretical and analytical framework of "Cultural Linguistics", which explores the relationship between language and cultural conceptualizations (Sharifian 2015, 2017). Cultural conceptualizations as more specific instantiations and functions of cultural cognition encompass three particular instances: namely, cultural schemas, cultural categories, and cultural metaphors. According to Sharifian (2017: 7), cultural schemas are "beliefs, norms, rules, and expectations of behavior as well as values relating to various aspects and components of experience"; cultural categories are "those culturally constructed conceptual categories (colors, emotions, attributes, foodstuffs, kinship terms, events, etc.) that are primarily reflected in the lexicon of human languages"; and cultural metaphors are "cross-domain conceptualizations grounded in cultural traditions such as folk medicine, worldview, or a spiritual belief system". The necessity of studying language in the understanding of cultural conceptualizations consists in the following observation that cultural conceptualizations are realized in language.

> Language plays a dual role in relation to cultural conceptualizations. On the one hand, linguistic interactions are crucial to the development of cultural conceptualizations, as they provide a space for speakers to construct and co-construct meanings about their experiences. On the other hand, many aspects of both language structure and language use draw on and reflect cultural conceptualizations.
>
> (Sharifian 2017: 5)

As reflected in this dual role that language plays in relation to cultural conceptualizations, the mutuality here is that cultural conceptualizations underlie and motivate the use of human languages and, conversely, features of human languages encode or instantiate culturally constructed conceptualizations. Given the strong linkage between cultural conceptualizations and language, it makes good sense, therefore, to study cultural conceptualizations, and cultural cognition more generally, through close examination of language.

In essence, what I study in this monograph is moral cognition at the cultural level, or cultural cognition in its moral subcase. More specifically, I study metaphorical conceptualizations of morality as parts of cultural cognition, or cultural conceptualizations of morality through metaphor. A linguistic approach is a natural choice.

1.4 The moral metaphor system: Three subsystems

With respect to the experiential grounding of moral metaphors, it has been observed that the range of possible metaphors for morality is fairly restricted, and all of them appear to be grounded in our experiences of wellbeing, especially physical wellbeing (Lakoff and Johnson 1999). Thus, for instance, morality and immorality are conceptualized in terms of "light" and "darkness", or "cleanness" and "dirtiness"; a moral or immoral person is conceptualized as being "healthy" or "sick", or "strong" or "weak"; and the moral character of a person can be "high" or "low", or "pure" or "polluted" (Johnson 1993, 1996; Lakoff and Johnson 1999). Lakoff and Johnson's (1999) findings come from their study of the moral metaphor system as manifested in the English language. The question that comes along with the findings is whether or not conceptual metaphors for morality found in English are culture-specific, widespread, or universal. Lakoff and Johnson (1999: 311) note that, since the source domains of these conceptual metaphors cluster on "basic human experiences of wellbeing", they "define a large part of the Western moral tradition" and, furthermore, "they are not unique to occidental culture" and some of them may very well be candidates for universals. Nevertheless, as they point out, the "cross-cultural research has not been done yet to determine whether any of them are truly universal" (Lakoff and Johnson 1999: 312).

As a metaphor researcher who is particularly interested in the interplay of language, culture, and cognition, I set out on this book project with the following central goal in mind: that is, to contribute to the discovery of potential commonalities that define human moral cognition in general, as well as to the detection of possible differences that characterize distinct cultures concerning moral cognition. Again, what I am trying to probe into is moral cognition at the cultural level as reflected in language, in this case, English and Chinese. More specifically, my objectives for this study are fourfold:

(i) to outline the linguistic patterns in the English and Chinese moral talk via a systematic description of linguistic data;

(ii) to analyze the linguistic data so as to find out if the linguistic patterns so produced reflect the putative conceptual patterns, formulated as conceptual metaphors, hypothesized to exist in English and Chinese on the basis of preceding studies as well as personal observations;

(iii) to shed light on moral cognition at large from a comparative, cross-linguistic perspective for potential universals and variations at both linguistic and conceptual levels; and

(iv) to contribute to the CMT literature in general both theoretically and methodologically.

According to cognitive linguistics, "language is taken to be a good guide to uncovering the content and structure of our conceptual system" (Kövecses 2015b: 270). It is hoped that the findings of my linguistic study can lead to further hypotheses for future studies.

A study of this nature, ideally, should probe into as many languages as possible. In reality, however, individual researchers' knowledge of languages is limited, especially considering the fact that there are as many as over 6,000 different languages spoken in the world. For my study, I focus on two languages that I know relatively well, English and Chinese. By "Chinese" I refer to the standard Chinese language also known as "Mandarin Chinese", but not to the exclusion of occasional dialectal usages. Chinese is my first or native language whereas English is my second language as well as the language that I utilize chiefly for academic purposes. It so happens that these two languages have the most speakers in the world, and that they are not genetically related to each other in any way, even though isolated elements, especially in lexicon, can be found and attributed to borrowing through the history of language contact, mainly in modern times. Other than individual researchers' limitations in the knowledge of languages, the breadths and depths of individual research projects are limited as well, constrained by the capacity and time which individual researchers have to carry out particular research projects. Fortunately, scholarship is always accumulative in nature. My study is built on preceding studies in the field, and my hope is that this study, with its findings worthy or significant enough, can serve as a starting and reference point for similar or different studies in the future that will broaden and deepen the scope of my study on English and Chinese, and that, moreover, will extend and expand this kind of study to other languages and cultures, and to other kinds of studies in neighboring disciplinary fields. In this way, a more complete picture of moral cognition and language will unfold, with my study being one piece of the puzzle.

Moral metaphors may be analyzed as forming different systems depending on different clusters of target and source concepts involved in metaphorical mappings. For my current study, I concentrate on the target concepts MORAL and IMMORAL and those source concepts from the bodily and physical domain, or domain matrix, which is the third one of the three source domains that I discussed in section 1.1. The conceptual metaphors formulated with the source concepts from this domain are usually utilized to describe the moral character of individual people or society at large. Following the CMT tradition, the present study attempts to outline this moral metaphor system, especially its major clusters of conceptual metaphors, based on primarily linguistic evidence from both English and Chinese and, to a much more limited extent, multimodal evidence from the corresponding cultures (see Chapters 6 and 7).

While a unified and coherent one, this system, in my opinion, can be analyzed as consisting of three major subsystems as three clusters of conceptual metaphors, whose source concepts are from the domain of bodily experiences in the physical world. These conceptual metaphors are formulated in contrastive categories with bipolar values for the target concepts MORAL and IMMORAL. Thus, for instance, a person can be morally "beautiful" or "ugly", "clean" or "dirty", or "high" or "low".

At the linguistic level, the source concepts are represented by semantically antonymous words. For the lack of better terms, the three subsystems are named in a shorthand fashion as "Physical" (e.g., BEAUTIFUL vs. UGLY), "Visual" (e.g., CLEAN vs. DIRTY), and "Spatial" (e.g., HIGH vs. LOW). Although termed and differentiated in a three-way distinction chiefly for the purpose of systematic analysis, the three subsystems are obviously not separate, but merging into one another and embracing a common core, as a unified whole of moral metaphor system (see section 6.5). They are unified into a whole as illustrated schematically in Figure 1.1, by the three circles overlapping one another and sharing the same center. In reality, that is, what is physical appeals to vision and exists in space, what is visual has spatial dimensions and physical substance, and what is spatial has visual consequence and physical existence.

In other words, no one can exist without the presence of the other two. When I use one term to name one subsystem, it only means that the angle of the triangle represented by that term is *in* the focus, or the "spotlight", whereas the other two angles represented by the other two terms are *out of* it (with different focuses represented by different circles), but it is all three angles linked by all three lines that form the triangle as an inseparable whole. Besides, "Physical" is higher up in the triangular relationship because it is a more general concept than the other two. As suggested above, this term is used more narrowly to refer to the existence and substance of physical objects including living organisms.

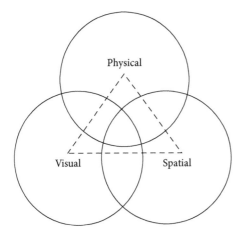

Fig. 1.1 The three subsystems of moral metaphor system under study

Together, being physical, being visual, and being spatial are the properties of what is "concrete" in contrast to what is "abstract", as well as what is "sensorimotor" in contrast to what is "nonsensorimotor". We can crown the three subsystems of moral metaphor system under study with three general metaphoric formulas:

(i)   MORALITY IS PHYSICALITY
(ii) MORALITY IS VISUALITY
(iii) MORALITY IS SPATIALITY

The three general metaphors, again formulated in a shorthand fashion, can be characterized as existing at the domain level, and they can therefore be called "domain-level metaphors", according to the "extended CMT" (Kövecses 2020). The extended CMT (i.e., extended from Lakoff and Johnson's "standard CMT") holds the view that conceptual metaphors exist at multiple levels: the image-schema level, the domain level, the frame level, and the mental-space level, ranging from the most schematic to the most specific (Kövecses 2017a,

2020: chapter 4; see also section 2.7). The three domain-level metaphors summarizing the three subsystems of moral metaphor system will be studied in depth in Chapters 3, 4, and 5, respectively.

As displayed in Figure 1.1, the three subsystems of moral metaphors arise from three overlapping categories and linked dimensions of our embodied experience. Vision is a salient physical function of our body that is itself a living physical object, an organism, which operates in and interacts with the spatial and physical environment all the time. Every day, we undergo experiences, positive or negative, as we work our way through space and time, moving from one location to another, interacting with one object after another, socializing with fellow human beings individually or collectively, and feeling changes in our body from one condition to another. All these embodied experiences, physical, visual, and spatial, work their way up via metaphor to contribute to our understanding of and reasoning about morality. In this process, the three overlapping categories and linked dimensions of our embodied experience serve as the source domains from which source concepts are drawn and mapped onto the target domain of MORALITY. It is in this way that the moral metaphor system under study partially constitutes and structures our moral cognition.

As suggested above, this moral metaphor system as clusters of conceptual metaphors has its source concepts from the domains of bodily and physical experience. I exclude from my study other moral metaphor systems rooted in, for instance, familial, social, religious, or financial realms of life, such as moral authority, moral order, moral nurturance, moral empathy, moral balance (in the Moral Accounting Metaphor), and so on. Those moral metaphor systems have already been studied in depth and detail in the literature (see, e.g., Johnson 1993, 1996; Lakoff 1996; Lakoff and Johnson 1999: chapter 14). Since the source concepts to be studied in this monograph are the major ones constituting the three subsystems, I do not root out other possible source concepts, major or minor, that can be placed in the three subsystems. Thus far, however, the English and Chinese evidence, from the preceding studies in the literature and from my own research, seems to converge on the ones in the three subsystems to be studied. Those ones are, therefore, the focus of my study.

In this study, I see the moral metaphors under analysis as forming a system with three subsystems, characterized and categorized by the kinds (physical, visual, or spatial) and levels (more schematic or more specific) of concepts, source and target, involved in the metaphorical mappings. It therefore takes a systematic approach to a full description and a thorough analysis of this system. This is what I aim to achieve in the chapters that follow. Each moral metaphor is examined in relation to other moral metaphors in the same sub-system, and each subsystem is investigated in relation to other subsystems in the same system. In so doing, I attempt to suggest at least some hints at how moral metaphors as a distinct system may relate to and interact with non-moral metaphors in other metaphor systems (see Chapter 6). So conceived, my study is characterized by two keywords: *system* and *systematicity*. The for-mer refers to the fact that metaphors (conceptual and linguistic) are connected in networks; the latter refers to the need that metaphors should be studied in networks. That is what this monograph is about, with the examination of a moral metaphor system as part of the effort to study metaphor from a holistic and systematic perspective.

At this point, I would like to make a caveat early on. This is a study of con-ceptual metaphors for morality. We should always bear in mind, however, that conceptual metaphors, no matter how widespread, are always relative to situations and there are always counterexamples in real-life situations. A sim-ple example is GOOD IS UP, which is considered a primary metaphor that is widespread, or perhaps potentially universal (see section 2.6, esp. Figure 2.7). In real-life situations, however, what is "up" can be very bad, for instance, when the inflation or unemployment rate is up. Another example is HAPPY IS UP, also considered a primary metaphor claimed to be grounded in the ex-periential correlation between emotion and body posture, but people may fall down on their knees, or backs, for joy, as often seen in sports, upon winning. Nevertheless, the existence of such obvious counterexamples do not invalidate respective conceptual metaphors, since a huge and growing body of exper-imental research has proved that they are psychologically real in individual minds in various languages and cultures (see, e.g., the reviews of psychological research on moral and affective metaphors in Chapters 3–5).

1.5 The methodology: Lexical and corpus-based approaches

As characterized by Lakoff (1993: 210–211), each conceptual metaphor is a fixed pattern of conceptual correspondences across conceptual domains. Such conceptual mappings are realized on two different levels of language use. At the lexical level, source-domain lexical items may or may not have a convention-ally lexicalized sense in the target domain. Even if they do not, the knowledge structures associated with them can still be activated and mapped by concep-tual metaphors onto the target domain as novel metaphorical expressions at the level of discourse. For example, in the song lyric, "We're driving in the fast lane on the freeway of love", the English lexical items *fast lane* and *freeway* do not have extended senses conventionally lexicalized in the target domain of LOVE. Nonetheless, as a result of the activation of the conceptual metaphor LOVE IS JOURNEY, the knowledge structures of driving in the source domain of JOURNEY are mapped onto the target domain for romantic love and relationship development, at the level of discourse, or the level of mental spaces, under the influence of contextual factors (Kövecses 2020). Thus, "fast lane" and "freeway" in the song lyric constitute novel instantiations of the conventional conceptual metaphor LOVE IS JOURNEY.

At this juncture, I would like to digress a little and discuss a technical issue about the formulation of conceptual metaphors. The conventional way of formulating the conceptual metaphor LOVE IS JOURNEY in the CMT literature is LOVE IS A JOURNEY, where "JOURNEY", encoded by an English countable noun, is preceded by an indefinite article "A" to denote singularity. By dropping the indefinite article on purpose, I am departing from the conventional way for the following reason. Here we are dealing with a conceptual metaphor, which connects one concept with another concept, or one conceptual domain with another conceptual domain, whereas the use of the indefinite article *a* or *an*, in contrast with the definite article *the* as well as the null article, is a syntactic feature and distinction in the English language following the phrase structure rule NP → Det N. Conceptual metaphors, which supposedly represent abstract conceptual mappings applicable in any language and are therefore language-independent, do not have to be subject to and constrained by English syntactic rules. In fact, there exists inconsistency anyhow in this regard in the CMT literature. For example, we see different versions of the same conceptual metaphor: THE MIND IS THE BODY, THE MIND IS A BODY, and MIND IS BODY. To me, the last one, MIND IS BODY, is preferable not only because it is simpler, with non-crucial or irrelevant syntactic details eliminated at the conceptual level, but also because, abstracted away from specific English grammatical restrictions, it best fits the purpose of conceptual mapping. Furthermore, there is a shorthand way of formulating conceptual metaphors in the CMT literature, where the English syntactic features are conventionally eliminated anyway: for instance, the MIND AS BODY metaphor, or the LOVE AS JOURNEY metaphor. Thus, in this book, I will use the "streamlined" forms of conceptual metaphors, for example, STATE IS LOCATION instead of STATES ARE LOCATIONS, CHANGE IS MOVEMENT/MOTION instead of CHANGES ARE MOVEMENTS/MOTIONS (unless the latter appear in direct quotes).

Additionally, I use two sets of terms interchangeably in this monograph when referring to the conceptual metaphors for morality from the three different subsystems. For example, when discussing the moral metaphors from the physical subsystem, I will be using "physical moral metaphors" and "moral-physical metaphors" interchangeably. In the former case, "physical", which represents the metaphoric source, modifies "moral metaphor", in which "moral" represents the target. In the latter, "moral-physical" is a compound in which, following the CMT convention, "moral" expresses the target concept and "physical" the source, on a par with the MORAL IS PHYSICAL or MORAL AS PHYSICAL metaphor. The same applies throughout the book.

For this study, I employ mixed methods applying both lexical and corpus-based approaches to the description and analysis of linguistic data for a comparative perspective on English and Chinese. Indeed, these two approaches, both being popular with cognitive linguists, are complementary to each other (see, e.g., Kövecses 2015b, 2020; Kövecses et al. 2019). According to Kövecses's (2020) multilevel view of extended CMT, these two methods primarily apply to different levels of metaphor. The lexical method targets metaphors at the domain and frame levels, which are the focus of this study, whereas the corpus-based method is utilized mainly to study metaphors at the level of mental spaces. The lexical approach, which is the principal method I adopt here, is the more traditional method for conceptual metaphor research. Kövecses (2015b, 2020) has discussed this approach at some length, making a distinction between *types* and *tokens* with respect to lexical items under study. Types are the lexical items that are lexicalized in, and conventionally related to, a target domain. Tokens, on the other hand, are actual occurrences of such lexical items as embedded in discourse. The researcher using the lexical method searches for various lexical items related to the target domains under investigation, including synonyms, antonyms, related words, idioms, collocations, and even definitions. The most likely sources for this approach are various kinds of dictionaries, monolingual and bilingual, and thesauri. Based on the assumption that a higher degree of linguistic conventionalization goes together with greater conceptual centrality, the lexical approach deals with conventionalized "types" of linguistic expressions as part of decontextualized language at the "supraindividual level" (i.e., the levels of domains and frames), as opposed to the "individual level" (i.e., the level of mental spaces), at which the focus is on particular "tokens" as part of contextualized linguistic usage by individual speakers in real-life discourse (Kövecses 2015b, 2020). In metaphor research, frequency of linguistic tokens is undoubtedly very significant in indexing the strength of underlying conceptual pattern (see, e.g., section 7.2); yet we cannot ignore the important fact that linguistic tokens do not carry the same weight in natural discourse and, as such, they should not be weighed solely according to their frequency either (see Gibbs 2015).

As Kövecses (2020: 89) points out, the merit of the lexical approach, if deployed sensibly and appropriately, lies in its strength to "uncover the most conventionalized metaphorical linguistic expressions related to a target domain (i.e., the types)" so that the researcher can "hypothesize the existence of systematic conceptual correspondences between two domains—the conceptual metaphors". The conceptual patterns so discovered and hypothesized can then be further studied for their psychological reality through experimental research on individual speakers' nonlinguistic behavior, or for their strength in linguistic manifestation via corpus-based quantifications of tokens used by individual speakers in actual discourses. In brief, "the lexical approach can reveal a considerable portion of the shared metaphorical conceptual system in a linguistic community, though not the metaphorical conceptual systems of individual speakers" (Kövecses 2020: 89).

By its very nature and design to work at the supraindividual level and on the metaphorical conceptual system shared by speakers of a linguistic community, the lexical method can, perhaps, make its best contributions at the cultural level, to the study of cultural cognition (e.g., D'Andrade 1989; Sharifian 2008, 2009).

My research on moral metaphors, therefore, was carried out at two levels, lexical and discursive, with the help of both dictionaries and linguistic corpora. My first step was to consult English and Chinese dictionaries and to find out if the key lexical items that can represent the source concepts of the hypothetical conceptual metaphors have extended lexicalized senses in the target domain of MORALITY, as collected in the dictionaries. If they do, it means that they are so conventionally used in the target domain that a fixed pattern of semantic extension has been established from their primary, original senses to their moral senses, as is guided and governed by the putative conceptual metaphors. This is polysemy in semantics. Polysemous words have multiple, related senses linked to a central, prototypical sense in a network of radial category (see, e.g., Lakoff 1987a). If the key lexical items do not have lexicalized moral senses collected in the dictionaries, the possibility still exists that they have potential moral senses that can be activated as more novel cases of metaphorical expressions at the level of discourse. Such activation is possible because these lexical items are linked to those that have lexicalized senses in the domain of MORALITY, by being the latter's synonyms, antonyms, etc., and, as such, being their "close neighbors" living in the same "vicinity". After all, dictionaries are compiled by lexicographers who have to make their own judgments and decisions on the selection and omission of senses of words, as well as of words themselves, in the dictionaries they compile. For that matter, dictionaries are highly selective as collections. While they have the function of guiding current use of words, they may also be, and often are, lagging behind lexical usage in the process of language change.

For my first step to check if source-domain lexical items have conventional senses in the target domain, I utilized both hard-copy and online dictionaries. The hard-copy English dictionaries are: (i) *Webster's new collegiate dictionary* (WNCD 1977), (ii) *The concise oxford dictionary of current English* (CODCE 1976), and (iii) *Longman dictionary of contemporary English* (LDCE 1978). The online English dictionaries are: (i) *Merriam-Webster*, (ii) *Oxford Lexico*, and (iii) *Longman*. When their specific information is not crucial, I will simply refer to them as *Webster, Oxford*, and *Longman* respectively. The online *Merriam-Webster* includes a thesaurus and additional definitions from the *English language learners dictionary*. Those were also consulted in the searches when needed.

On the Chinese side, I utilized the following three hard-copy dictionaries: (i) 汉语大词典 [*Grand dictionary of Chinese language*] (HYDCD 2000), (ii) 现代汉语词典 [*Contemporary Chinese dictionary* (7th ed.)] (XDHYCD 2016), and (iii) 新现代汉语词典 [*A new dictionary of modern Chinese language*] (XXDHYCD 1992). Two of the earlier editions of (ii), the 5th and 6th, were consulted whenever needed for a diachronic perspective. The online Chinese dictionaries are: (i) 汉语大辞典 [*Grand dictionary of Chinese language*] (HYDCD), and (ii) 在线汉语词典 [*Online Chinese dictionary*] (ZXHYCD). In addition, I also used two hard-copy Chinese-English bilingual dictionaries, chiefly for the purpose of English translation: (i) 现代汉语词典 [*Contemporary Chinese dictionary* (Chinese-English ed.)] (XDHYCD 2002), and (ii) 新时代汉英大词典 [*New age Chinese-English dictionary*] (XSD-HYDCD 2004). Throughout the book, the English translations of Chinese lexical, phrasal, and sentential examples are purposively literal, to retain the metaphorical structure and imagery of the Chinese originals. Where deemed needed or necessary, more strictly literal English translations are added in parentheses, like (lit. ...), immediately following more free translations. Focused key lexical items in the examples are bolded for easier grasping.

As mentioned above, the second step for my research was to conduct corpus-based searches for the key lexical items as they occur in real-life discourse. In doing so, I intended to see if the key words that have physical, visual, or spatial senses as their primary, central senses are used in metaphorically extended moral senses in actual discourses and, if yes, how such linguistic usages

Table 1.1 The capacities of the corpora at the time of research

Corpus	Capacity	Unit
COCA Contemporary American English	560,000,000+	words
CCL Contemporary Chinese	581,794,456	characters

instantiate the conceptual metaphors for morality that are hypothesized to function underlying the linguistic surface. For this research purpose, I explored the following two major English and Chinese language corpora for my searches in English and Chinese respectively: (i) Corpus of Contemporary American English (COCA; Brigham Young University), and (ii) Corpus of Center for Chinese Linguistics (CCL; Peking University).

The capacities of the two corpora at the time of research are listed in Table 1.1. Note that the capacity listed in the table is for "Contemporary Chinese" of CCL, which also contains 201,668,719 characters for "Classical Chinese", with a total capacity of 783,463,175 characters. The capacity for COCA is currently more than 1.0 billion words, with the last update in March 2020. Additionally, I used another major Chinese language corpus, the Corpus of Beijing Language and Culture University Corpus Center (BCC), mainly for the purpose of double checking.

The reference information on all the English and Chinese dictionaries, corpora, and other online databases or resources that I have used (i.e., FrameNet, MetaNet, Google Images, Baidu Images, and Wikipedia) is provided in full as a separate section behind the regular References section at the end of the book.

As discussed above, my chief method of research for this study is the lexical approach (Kövecses 2015b, 2020). Although I used the linguistic corpora for the search of linguistic evidence that shows how relevant lexical items are used metaphorically in real-life discourse, I did not attempt any quantifications. This is because, for one, I focused on "types" at the supraindividual levels of domains and frames, not "tokens" at the individual level of mental spaces (Kövecses 2020). Therefore, a qualitative study is a natural choice. Also, I was looking at English and Chinese from a comparative perspective, using two linguistic corpora in two different languages. Quantitative methods with which a corpus-based approach can perhaps work best nonetheless did not seem to be the best choice for my study. After all, my study aims at an overview, a survey, of the landscape for a possible moral metaphor system shared by English and Chinese. If the framework of such a system can be established, then future studies can fill in this system with more details, either qualitatively or quantitatively or both, on these two or any other languages.

This is a linguistic study of moral metaphors. My study examined what I see as a possible moral metaphor system comprising three subsystems, and how this system is manifested comparably in two languages with systematic patterns of linguistic expressions used in specific contexts. I targeted a total of 14 pairs of moral metaphors, with each pair formed by a positive version (e.g., MORAL IS LIGHT) and a negative version (e.g., IMMORAL IS DARK). In other words, it amounts to a total of 28 individual conceptual metaphors for morality. The 14 pairs of conceptual metaphors are divided into the three subsystems (5 + 4 + 5). While some of these moral metaphors have been covered by preceding studies in the literature, others have not. To my knowledge, they have not been examined as clusters of metaphorical mappings or as pairs of positive and negative versions of metaphors, especially in two different languages side by side, and from a single holistic and cross-linguistic perspective.

Nonetheless, my study cannot be exhaustive. I can merely claim to have studied conceptual metaphors for morality that I have found so far as belonging to this complex moral metaphor system. Far less exhaustive are the metaphorical expressions, in English or Chinese, that I have included in this book as linguistic instantiations of those metaphors. I can only hope that my study will serve as a solid foundation on which future studies can build.

One challenge of using linguistic corpora for data collection is that the key lexical items that belong to particular source domains are highly polysemous. They have multiple extended senses lexicalized in different but somewhat related target domains. Sometimes it is not easy to determine whether the extended sense under consideration is indeed in the moral domain. My strategy was to try to search for such extended moral senses of the lexical items in the proximity of explicit moral words. In the pairs of moral metaphors with positive and negative versions (e.g., MORAL IS LIGHT and IMMORAL IS DARK), both the source and the target concepts are encoded by adjectives, but they represent cross-domain mappings between concepts. Actual lexical items that instantiate them in language, however, can take on nominal, verbal, prepositional, as well as adjectival forms. For example, the word *light* can be an adjective, a noun, or a verb in the instantiation of the conceptual metaphor MORAL IS LIGHT depending on the specific linguistic context in which it occurs.

As discussed above in section 1.4, this study takes moral metaphors as forming a system with three subsystems, characterized and categorized by the kinds (physical, visual, or spatial) and levels (more schematic or more specific) of concepts, source and target, involved in the metaphorical mappings. After describing and analyzing the three subsystems separately in Chapters 3–5, I will take a decompositional approach to metaphor in Chapter 6, in order to attempt a "deep" analysis of the moral metaphor system. I call this approach "DAMCA", an acronym standing for "a decompositional approach to metaphorical-compound analysis". It will be introduced in more detail in Chapter 2 and, subsequently, in Chapter 6. As an analytical tool, its objectives are to go beneath the "skins" of conceptual metaphors and gain "insights" into the possible frames and structures of their source and target concepts and, furthermore, into the possible compositions and levels of mappings between them. In so doing, we can obtain better understandings of how metaphors are related with one another, horizontally and vertically, by sharing the same inheritance relations or common components within multifaceted and multilevel hierarchical structures linked in networks. This decompositional approach to metaphor analysis, which I hope to further develop in this monograph, is to be contributed to, and embedded in, a large theoretical and methodological framework that CMT has established during the past 40 years. This framework studies metaphors as forming systems and networks. I tried to adopt and, to some extent, develop this holistic perspective and systematic paradigm in my study of moral metaphors. In particular, my research was conducted in light of the limitations and weaknesses of CMT reviewed in section 1.1 so that I could avoid or overcome them as much as possible. The results of my research will be presented in the chapters that follow.

1.6 What follows in the book

Following this introductory chapter, Chapter 2 reviews CMT with a focus on its systematicity in metaphor research. Since its birth 40 years ago, CMT has grown tremendously as a systematic approach to metaphor in language and cognition. The trajectory of its growth in this respect is traced in the next chapter.

After that, the following three chapters, i.e., Chapters 3–5, present my descriptive and analytical studies of the three subsystems, physical, visual, and spatial, of the moral metaphor system in English and Chinese. Each of these three chapters starts with an initial analysis of the source concepts with respect to their relations with one another and a general source frame that applies to them all for their metaphorical mapping onto the target concepts within the subsystem. Each chapter also reviews relevant psychological research before moving on to linguistic studies in English and Chinese separately. There, examples of linguistic metaphors from the English and Chinese corpora are analyzed to show how they are used to instantiate the putative underlying conceptual metaphors in moral talks in specific contexts.

From anatomic and multimodal viewpoints, Chapter 6 analyzes the nature of the moral conceptual metaphors with DAMCA, addressing some issues concerning their target and source concepts. It is shown that moral metaphors can be analyzed as multilevel structures composed of primary and complex metaphors, metonymies, and literal propositions. This chapter also looks at the unity of the moral metaphor system with a focus on the three different sets of source concepts from the three subsystems. In addition, this chapter analyzes some examples of visual or multimodal manifestation of moral metaphors, showing how verbal and visual metaphors reinforce each other in instantiating conceptual metaphors in the moral metaphor system.

The last chapter, Chapter 7, puts the complete moral metaphor system in a holistic perspective, examining the moral metaphor system as a whole, constructing a general model for the analysis of both source and target frame structures of the conceptual metaphors in the moral metaphor system that I study. This model displays the core elements and relations in the source and target frames, with central and essential constants and variables specified, and the metaphorical mappings from the source to the target frame. This chapter also examines the relationship between bodily, cultural, and linguistic experience and analyzes how they interact with metaphorical conceptualization. In this regard, CMT emphasizes that the interaction between our bodily and cultural experience gives rise to conceptual metaphors in our conceptual system, which are in turn manifested in our language when we use it in communication. I will cite some linguistic evidence, both qualitative and quantitative, and multimodal evidence, showing the possible impact the other way around, namely, the impact of our linguistic experience on our conceptual system and on our cultural experience. In particular, two general issues will be discussed concerning the relations between language and thought, and between language and culture, emphasizing the impact of the former on the latter. The chapter wraps up with some closing remarks summarizing the findings and conclusions.

2

Conceptual metaphor theory

A systematic approach

2.1 The systematicity of metaphor relations and metaphor studies

In this chapter, I discuss one of the most salient characteristics of conceptual metaphor theory (CMT), that is, its view of metaphors as being networked at and between different levels of conception and expression in a systematic way. Thanks to this view, CMT is able to study metaphors in a systematic fashion that is uniquely characteristic of this approach. The CMT claim that metaphors are networked in systematic ways is a tenet that is hypothesized to be operational in different respects and at different levels. The systematicity in metaphorical mappings in language and thought can be summarized as including the following aspects:

(i) The systematicity of metaphors exists at, and between, two different levels, linguistic and conceptual, with linguistic metaphors (i.e., metaphorical expressions) systematically manifesting underlying conceptual metaphors (i.e., metaphorical concepts).

(ii) Different linguistic metaphors may be linked with one another systematically to form a network because they are governed by a single conceptual metaphor.

(iii) One linguistic metaphor may also simultaneously instantiate and be linked to different conceptual metaphors as a result of different conceptual metaphors participating in and contributing to the meaning making of that linguistic metaphor.

(iv) Conceptual metaphors have the structures (elements and relations) of its source-domain frame corresponding with and mapping onto those of its target-domain frame in a systematic manner; such correspondences and mappings between the source and target frames may be further extended into the subframes of the source and target domains.

The Moral Metaphor System. Ning Yu, Oxford University Press. © Ning Yu (2022).
DOI: 10.1093/oso/9780192866325.003.0002

(v) Conceptual metaphors are linked horizontally because they share the same source domain or the same target domain, or because they share the same source-domain concept (and its frame), or the same target-domain concept (and its frame).

(vi) Conceptual metaphors are linked vertically, forming inheritance and schematicity hierarchies, with subordinate metaphors at lower, more specific levels elaborating the aspects of, or inheriting the structures from, superordinate metaphors at higher, more schematic levels.

(vii) Conceptual metaphors are linked into networks because they are based on the same image schema, or on contrastive image schemas, in a systematic manner.

(viii) Conceptual metaphors can be more or less complex in their constructions; more complex metaphors can often, but not always, be decomposed into less complex or primary metaphors, or, conversely, primary metaphors can be combined into more complex metaphors, in addition to nonmetaphorical, or literal, components.

It is along these dimensions that conceptual and linguistic metaphors form networks systematically. The recognition of such networks of metaphors at and between linguistic and conceptual levels have led to CMT's highly systematic approach to the study of metaphors. In the remainder of this chapter, I will illustrate the abovementioned aspects of systematicity of metaphors, conceptual and linguistic, with examples along a vertical line of relationship in the networks of conceptual metaphors: LOVE IS JOURNEY, LIFE IS JOURNEY, and the Event Structure Metaphor (ESM). It is hoped that my illustration and discussion can provide a sense of how metaphors work as a complex system that calls for a systematic research approach from a holistic perspective.

2.2 Linguistic and conceptual metaphors

Traditionally, metaphor is viewed as a figure of speech and metaphors are studied as linguistic expressions for the special rhetorical effects that they produce in specific contexts. Thus, what metaphor research focuses on is usually such linguistic expressions as *My love is a red rose, My job is a jail, My surgeon is a butcher, My lawyer is a shark,* and the like, which are based largely on similarity or resemblance (see Grady 1999 for a discussion). Moreover, these metaphors are treated in such research as if they are isolated linguistic expressions, with little regard for how they relate to other metaphors in broader contexts. What makes CMT unique is the important distinction between *conceptual metaphors* or *metaphorical concepts* on the one hand, and *linguistic metaphors* or *metaphorical expressions* on the other (Lakoff 1993; Lakoff and Johnson 1980). Conceptual metaphors are those abstract notions, such as ARGUMENT IS WAR and LOVE IS JOURNEY, which reside in the conceptual system, while linguistic metaphors are actual linguistic expressions (i.e., words, phrases, sentences, etc.) that realize or instantiate conceptual metaphors in one way or another when people communicate thoughts using language, and perhaps along with other multimodal means. That is to say, metaphor, according to this theory, is primarily conceptual in nature. Metaphorical language is but a surface manifestation or realization of underlying metaphorical thought. Conceptual metaphors are systematic mappings across conceptual domains: one domain of experience, the source domain, is mapped onto another domain of experience, the target domain. In short, metaphors are mappings across conceptual domains which allow us to understand a relatively abstract or less structured subject matter in terms of a more concrete or more structured subject matter (Lakoff 1993).

It must be pointed out at this point that CMT works on the assumption that language reflects the conceptual system, which is, nevertheless, not directly observable. Therefore, cognitive linguists study language as a "window to the mind". They set out on linguistic descriptions and analyses which then lead them to make hypotheses concerning the content and structure of the conceptual system. As linguists, however, we should bear in mind that it is not always safe to infer how people think from the way they talk (see, e.g., Gibbs 2007, 2011). As Casasanto (2009b) argues, for instance, the results of experimental studies do not always support the validity of conceptual metaphors hypothesized to exist in the conceptual system on the basis of linguistic metaphors "seen" in the language. Nevertheless, "even when linguistic metaphors fail to predict the exact relationships revealed by behavioral tests", they "point to important links between the source and target domains" and, as such, serve "as a source of *hypotheses* about the structure of abstract concepts" for further linguistic and extra-linguistic studies (Casasanto 2009b: 143).

Forty years ago, it was the discovery of a phenomenon in language that led to the establishment of CMT as one of the main forces in the takeoff of cognitive linguistics. That is, it was found that linguistic expressions literally meaning *B* are often used conventionally to mean *A*. It was also found that *A* usually represents a more abstract concept whose referent is not perceptible to our five senses whereas *B* is usually a more concrete concept whose referent falls into the physical domains of perception and action. What does this mean? Lakoff and Johnson (1980, 1999) believe that this linguistic phenomenon reflects how the human mind works in coping with abstraction, which is a "higher" cognitive capacity characteristic of human beings. That is, humans think and talk about the abstract or less accessible (*A*) in terms of the concrete or more accessible (*B*) which we can perceive in the physical world or in our experience interacting with it. The basic formula of a conceptual metaphor is, therefore, A IS B, where *A* is conceptualized metaphorically in terms of *B*. It is hypothesized that our conceptual systems contain a great number of conceptual metaphors such that abstract concepts are partially structured by them (see, e.g., Gallese and Lakoff 2005). That is, human abstraction is partly achieved through metaphorical thinking, understanding, and reasoning, and abstraction at such a level is unique to human beings. As Johnson (1995: 159) argues, metaphor is definitional of human beings: "whatever else we are, we humans are metaphorizing animals".

It is worth noting at this point that in his most recent work putting forth the "extended CMT", Kövecses (2020: chapter 2) argues that the extent of the literal may be considerably smaller than commonly assumed, as much of what appears to be literal today, whether abstract or concrete, is actually figurative (i.e., metaphoric and metonymic) from a historical viewpoint. For instance, the English words, *rage* and *fury*, which are taken to express an abstract concept (ANGER) literally, go back to Latin where they mean "madness" (metaphor: ANGER IS INSANITY), and the word *anger* can be traced back to its Indo-European root meaning "tight, narrow, painfully constricted" (metonymy: EFFECT OF EMOTION FOR EMOTION).

According to CMT, the human mind is embodied. The embodiment is realized, largely, by means of metaphor in thought, mapping the body onto the mind, hence the overarching conceptual metaphor MIND IS BODY (e.g., Gibbs 1994, 2006; Ibarretxe-Antuñano 2002; Lakoff and Johnson 1999; Sweetser 1990; Yu 2003). To the extent that language reflects thought, human language is embodied as well. Metaphor is thus pervasive in language. Metaphorical expressions, especially those conventionalized in everyday usage, constitute the very fibers interwoven into the fabric of human language.

What is of particular interest to cognitive linguists is the fact that linguistic metaphors are tied together in a systematic way, to form linguistic patterns, which arise from and correspond to the underlying conceptual patterns, or conceptual metaphors, in the conceptual system. For instance, LOVE IS JOURNEY is a conceptual metaphor that has received extensive discussion in the literature (see, e.g., Aksan and Kantar 2008; Gibbs 2006; Lakoff 1986, 1993; Lakoff and Johnson 1999). This conceptual metaphor has motivated numerous metaphorical expressions that are highly conventionalized in everyday English, such as those listed in (1) (Lakoff and Johnson 1999: 64):

(1) LOVE IS JOURNEY
   a. The relationship isn't *going anywhere*.
   b. Look *how far we've come*.
   c. We can't *turn back* now.
   d. We may have to *go our separate ways*.
   e. We're *heading in different directions*.
   f. It's been *a long, bumpy road*.
   g. Our relationship has hit *a dead-end street*.
   h. We're at a *crossroads*.
   i. We're *spinning our wheels*.
   j. The marriage is *out of gas*.
   k. Our relationship is *off the track*.
   l. The marriage is *on the rocks*.
   m. We're trying to keep the relationship *afloat*.
   n. We may have to *bail out* of this relationship.

As is shown, the conventional metaphorical expressions are linked and governed by a conceptual metaphor, LOVE IS JOURNEY, in a systematic way. The italic portions of the sentences all pertain to the conceptual domain of JOURNEY, but the sentences are all concerning love relationships between people even though they are open to other interpretations too, given specific contexts.

While the linguistic metaphors in (1) are systematically linked to LOVE IS JOURNEY as a conceptual metaphor in a multiple-to-one relationship, it is also possible for a single linguistic metaphor to be linked to more than one conceptual metaphor, in a one-to-multiple relationship. For instance, (1c), *We can't turn back now*, simultaneously instantiates PROGRESS IS FORWARD MOTION and REGRESS IS BACKWARD MOTION, which are entailments of LOVE IS JOURNEY in this case. Furthermore, the linguistic metaphor also instantiates the TIME IS SPACE metaphor, with its more specific mappings on the metaphorical "orientation" of time: FUTURE IS AHEAD OF EGO and PAST IS BEHIND EGO (see Lakoff 1993; Lakoff and Johnson 1999; Yu 1998, 2012).

As Lakoff (1993) argues, the conceptual metaphor LOVE IS JOURNEY, as manifested in (1) above, reflects "a general principle" that is part of the conceptual system underlying English. Thus, the conventional metaphorical expressions are used not only for talking about love, but for reasoning about love as well. The metaphor here is thus a conceptual mapping from a source domain (JOURNEY) to a target domain (LOVE), with both ontological and epistemic correspondences entailed by the mapping. The ontological correspondences are those in which some elements of the source domain are linked with the corresponding elements in the target domain, whereas the epistemic correspondences are those in which, activated by the ontological correspondences, knowledge of the source domain is mapped onto knowledge of the target domain to form rich inference patterns as parts of our inferential knowledge about the target.

How conceptual metaphors work at ontological and epistemic levels will be further illustrated in the next section when I discuss frames and subframes of conceptual metaphors. In this section, I have discussed the distinction between linguistic and conceptual metaphors with the example of LOVE IS JOURNEY and its linguistic instantiations. The systematicity of words and phrases drawn from the JOURNEY domain to express love relationship as the target can be accounted for by the hypothetical existence of an underlying conceptual metaphor, LOVE IS JOURNEY, which governs the metaphorical linguistic usages at the surface of language.

2.3 Frames and subframes of conceptual metaphors

To make metaphor analysis more systematic, some CMT researchers have applied the construct of *frame*, borrowed from frame semantics, to the study of conceptual metaphors (see, e.g., Dancygier and Sweetser 2014; Kövecses 2013, 2017a, 2017b, 2020; Lakoff 2014; Sullivan 2013, 2016). According to frame semantics (e.g., Fillmore 1975, 2006), the meaning of words is understood largely by virtue of the frames which the words evoke (see also Ruppenhofer et al. 2016; FrameNet). A frame is a coherent region of our encyclopedic knowledge, where certain concepts are linked together because they are associated in our experience (Croft and Cruse 2004). More specifically, a frame is a conceptual structure that represents the elements (core and noncore) and the relations between them, which together constitute the frame, describing a particular type of situation, object, or event and the participants and props involved in it (Dancygier and Sweetser 2014; Sullivan 2013). To Lakoff (2014), the concept of frame is relevant to metaphor study in that domains of conceptual metaphors appear to be characterized by hierarchically structured frames, which are complex schemas and mental structures that organize knowledge (see also MetaNet).

In CMT, the constructs *domain* and *frame* used to be interchangeable at times, but there is a distinction between them nowadays (see, e.g., Dancygier and Sweetser 2014; Kövecses 2017a, 2020; Sullivan 2013). The term *domain* refers to the two concepts, source and target, connected by a metaphor; the source and target domains identify the level of schematicity at which a conceptual metaphor is labeled and formulated. The term *frame*, on the other hand, refers to the internal structure (elements and relations) of a domain, or of some aspect of a domain. When we are interested in the internal structure of a whole domain, the name of the domain and that of the frame are one and the same. But if, however, we are concerned with some specific aspects of a domain, then there is a set of frames that characterize those aspects of the domain. For example, the BODY domain can include a number of frames, such as the body's EXERCISING frame, INGESTION frame, NUTRITION frame, STRUCTURE frame, HEALTH frame, FORCE EXERTION frame, and so on, depending on the metaphor's target domain (e.g., SOCIETY IS BODY, MIND IS BODY) and mappings or entailments (e.g., ECONOMIC CONDITION IS PHYSICAL CONDITION, MENTAL FITNESS IS PHYSICAL FITNESS, IDEA IS FOOD) (see Sullivan 2013: chapter 2).

If we apply frame analysis to the LOVE IS JOURNEY metaphor, we can come up with the correspondences and mappings of elements and relations, as laid out in Figure 2.1, between the source and target frames. The elliptical dots in the frames suggest that there can be other possible noncore elements and relations omitted here. For instance, in the source frame there is a STARTING PLACE for the travelers' journey, which should be connected with the "BEGINNING OF LOVE RELATIONSHIP" for the lovers in the target frame. Thus, the two frames

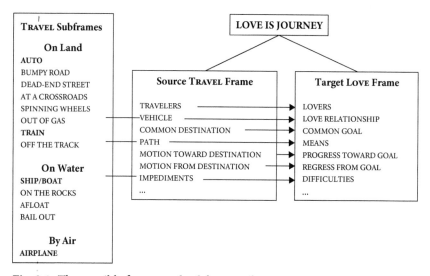

Fig. 2.1 The possible frames and subframes of LOVE IS JOURNEY

only present the more essential elements and relations, as manifested in the examples in (1). In the source, the travelers move in a vehicle along a particular path toward a destination, with possible impediments to their motion on the path; in the target, the lovers live on in a love relationship through particular means toward a life goal, with possible difficulties that they may encounter in their life experience. Thus, there are correspondences between elements and relations in both frames connected by metaphorical mappings, as indicated by the arrowed lines. For instance, TRAVELERS is mapped onto LOVERS, VEHICLE onto LOVE RELATIONSHIP (in the sense that it is this relationship that "holds" the lovers together and "carries" them on), and so on. In the target frame, MEANS refers to the actual life experience (consisting of events and actions) of the lovers who choose to live their life in a particular "way" leading to their life goal. Thus, the LOVE IS JOURNEY metaphor involves systematic mappings between the source and target frames. Figure 2.1 is just an example with some possible elements and relations furnished to the extent relevant to the linguistic metaphors in (1).

Such is what the LOVE IS JOURNEY metaphor involves in its mappings between the source and target frames. But that is not all. The source frame is also inclusive of its subframes, shown in Figure 2.1 as the three subcases inside the left-side box, again, merely to the extent relevant to the examples in (1), with the exception of the third "BY AIR" subcase. The subframe, with its additional elements and relations, inherits the structure of the generic frame to its right, but also invokes our additional knowledge about journey and travel on land, on water, or by air, as what is called metaphorical entailments. Thus, for instance, we know what the experience is like when driving on a bumpy road, what kind of potential damages will a bumpy road cause to our automobile, what kind of consequences we may have to face if we have a flat tire, and so on and so forth. Such additional knowledge is extensive and expansive, and can be activated as inference patterns to be mapped from the source onto the target. It constitutes metaphorical entailments stored as subframes of conceptual metaphors. Subframes inherit the structures of the higher-level frame but are substantiated and furnished with more details and specifics. They are activated when needed in specific contexts.

As represented by the three horizontal lines, only three elements in the JOURNEY frame are evoked for further subframe structures. These are VEHICLE, PATH, and IMPEDIMENTS. Travel path can be on land, on water, or by air. The last path, by air, is available as an alternative but not evoked in the examples in (1). Depending on which path is taken, the vehicle can be auto or train on land, ship or boat on water, or airplane by air. Impediments then will accord with the kind of vehicle on the kind of path taken. It is worth noting however that, though a core element, a vehicle is not a necessary element in the JOURNEY frame if the path is on land. People can still walk to some destination on foot. Indeed, a couple walking hand in hand, shoulder to shoulder, is a common image for LOVE IS JOURNEY. As long as the two are close to each other (i.e., INTIMACY IS CLOSENESS) moving in the same direction toward the same destination, they are "in love".

In sum, conceptual metaphors in our conceptual system form intricate systems. Lakoff and Johnson's (1980) methodology has demonstrated that studies of these systems can be accomplished by close examinations of linguistic metaphors instantiating putatively underlying conceptual metaphors. That is, one can gain an understanding of the nature of human concepts by systematically studying linguistic expressions. With a new definition of metaphor given, Lakoff and Johnson have also provided a new methodology that makes it possible to study metaphor in a systematic way. Although it is still under debate as to whether and to what extent this new research methodology can actually reveal underlying conceptual systems, there is no doubt that it has been the most productive and influential approach to date that makes metaphor analysis so systematic (see, e.g., Gibbs 2017).

2.4 Metaphor inheritance hierarchies

In the above it was shown that metaphorical expressions are systematically tied to a conceptual metaphor, with each of the former as a particular linguistic instantiation of the latter. It was also shown that a conceptual metaphor can activate the frames of the two conceptual domains with the structure (elements and relations) of the source frame systematically mapped onto that of the target frame. Besides, further structures with additional details can be mapped systematically through the activation of subframes in specific contexts. That is, each conceptual metaphor heads and governs a system of linguistic metaphors that reflect systematic frame structure mappings.

The systematicity of metaphor, however, exists in a larger scope than described above. Not only are linguistic metaphors systematically linked and governed by conceptual metaphors, but conceptual metaphors may themselves be systematically related to each other, vertically and horizontally, to form gigantic conceptual networks with hierarchical structures in our conceptual system. "Metaphorical mappings do not occur isolated from one another. They are sometimes organized in hierarchical structures, in which 'lower'

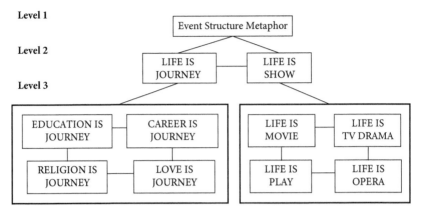

Fig. 2.2 An example of three-level inheritance hierarchy of conceptual metaphors

mappings in the hierarchy inherit the structures of the 'higher' mappings" (Lakoff 1993: 222). Lakoff calls this phenomenon "metaphor inheritance hierarchies" (Lakoff 1993; see also Dancygier and Sweetser 2014; Feyaerts 2000; Kövecses 2017a, 2020). Given in Figure 2.2 is an example of such a hierarchy including the LOVE IS JOURNEY metaphor on Level 3.[1]

Shown in the figure are three levels in this particular metaphor inheritance hierarchy. As a general principle, metaphors at the lower level inherit the structures (image schemas and basic frames) of the corresponding metaphors at the higher, superordinate level, but add to themselves some more specific details of their own. The idea is similar to the three levels of concepts in categorization: i.e., the superordinate level, the basic level, and subordinate level (e.g., Lakoff 1987a).[2] For example, since education, career, religion, and love are important aspects of life, the four conceptual metaphors in the left-wing box at Level 3 inherit the structure of the higher conceptual metaphor LIFE IS JOURNEY on Level 2, which is a more general metaphor superseding the four metaphors on Level 3 as its more specific target-subcase metaphors. These four "sister" metaphors are linked *horizontally* at the same level of the hierarchy,

---

[1] This example of inheritance hierarchy is modified and expanded from Lakoff's (1993: 222) list consisting the following metaphors: The ESM at Level 1, LIFE IS JOURNEY at Level 2, and LOVE IS JOURNEY and CAREER IS JOURNEY at Level 3. Specifically, I have "streamlined" the metaphor formulas as explained in Chapter 1, and added the following metaphors to the hierarchy: LIFE IS SHOW at Level 2, and six more metaphors at Level 3. I have also converted it into a diagram to provide a better "view" of the pyramidic nature and logical structure of metaphor inheritance hierarchies.

[2] Just to mention in passing that, in this monograph, I use *superordinate* and *subordinate* in a binary distinction in a hierarchy: any level is "superordinate" relative to the next level down, and any level is "subordinate" in relation to the next level up.

because they share the same source domain JOURNEY, adopted directly from their "parent" metaphor (LIFE IS JOURNEY) at Level 2, as well as because their target domains (EDUCATION, CAREER, RELIGION, and LOVE) are specific aspects or subcases (i.e., EDUCATIONAL LIFE, PROFESSIONAL LIFE, RELIGIOUS LIFE, and EMOTIONAL LIFE) of the LIFE domain. Also found at Level 2 is another life metaphor, LIFE IS SHOW (see Kövecses 2005; Yu 2017; Yu and Jia 2016), which is a sister metaphor to LIFE IS JOURNEY. For that matter, they are linked horizontally, too, by sharing a common target domain.

As mentioned above, the journey metaphors at Level 3 each add some specific details to themselves while inheriting the structure (image schemas and frames) from their higher, superordinate metaphor LIFE IS JOURNEY, as its target-domain subcases. As Lakoff (1993) points out, what is special about the LOVE IS JOURNEY metaphor is that there are two lovers, who are companionate travelers, and that the love relationship is a vehicle, while the rest of the mapping is a consequence of the LIFE IS JOURNEY metaphor. In a similar vein, what is special about the education and career metaphors is that successful education and career are often journeys upward since advances in education and career are often construed as motion upward (i.e., CHANGE IS MOTION, STATUS IS HEIGHT) (see, e.g., El-Sawad 2005; Inkson 2002, 2004; Reeder, Utley, and Cassel 2009; Saban 2006; Turner 1998). Similarly, what is special about the religion metaphor is that religious journeys are often conceptualized as spiritual in nature (i.e., journeys of or in the soul) and, for instance, as journeys guided by God toward heaven (see, e.g., Fuller 2000; Hargett 2006; Massengill 2008; Stewart 2005). While the four metaphors in the left wing on Level 3 share the same source domain JOURNEY, the actual frame structures mapped may differ considerably owing to different target domains, EDUCATION, CAREER, RELIGION, and LOVE. In the inheritance hierarchies of conceptual metaphors, subordinate subcases at a lower level are elaborations, with additional inputs, of the superordinate metaphor at the higher level (cf. Dancygier and Sweetser 2014; Kövecses 2017a, 2020). As such, metaphors at different levels are *vertically* linked in the inheritance hierarchies.

As the higher-level metaphor above LOVE IS JOURNEY, the LIFE IS JOURNEY metaphor has also received much attention in the literature (e.g., Forceville 2011; Lakoff 1993; Lakoff and Johnson 1999; Slingerland 2004; Winter 1995). For this metaphor, Lakoff and Johnson (1999) list the following mappings as represented by the arrow notation: TRAVELER → PERSON LIVING A LIFE; DESTINATIONS → LIFE GOALS; ITINERARY → LIFE PLAN. Lakoff (1993) cites the following English examples as its linguistic instantiations:

(2)   LIFE IS JOURNEY
    a.   He got *a head start* in life.
    b.   He's without *direction* in his life.
    c.   I'm *where* I want to be in life.
    d.   I'm *at a crossroads* in my life.
    e.   He'll *go places* in life.
    f.   He's never let anyone *get in his way.*
    g.   He's *gone through* a lot in life.

The conceptual metaphor LIFE IS JOURNEY can thus summarize and account for many English idiomatic expressions such as cited above. In fact, this metaphor also allows us to draw upon our large stock of commonplace knowledge about journeys and apply it to reasoning about life. For instance, Slingerland (2004: 12) shows that the LIFE AS JOURNEY metaphor "can have profound practical implications, influencing decision making and providing us with normative guidance".

As shown and mentioned above, LIFE IS JOURNEY and LIFE IS SHOW are sister metaphors at Level 2, sharing the same target domain. They are therefore linked horizontally at the same level in the hierarchy. We may say that these two metaphors have different "main meaning focuses" (Kövecses 2010, 2017b), with different source domains mapped onto the same target domain. The LIFE IS SHOW metaphor highlights social interactions, cooperative as well as competitive, and social "roles" people "play" in the "performance" of their social life-show. In contrast, the LIFE IS JOURNEY metaphor seems to focus more on people's personal experiences, growths, and advancements along their individual life-journey.

As exhibited in the three-level hierarchical structure in Figure 2.2, the two metaphors at Level 2, LIFE IS JOURNEY and LIFE IS SHOW, are sisters to each other. The LIFE IS SHOW metaphor also has "offspring", with four child or subordinate metaphors (LIFE IS MOVIE, LIFE IS TV DRAMA, LIFE IS PLAY, and LIFE IS OPERA) listed as examples, in the right-wing box at Level 3. They inherit the structure of their parent or superordinate metaphor at Level 2. Apparently, they are source-subcase metaphors of LIFE IS SHOW, in contrast with those in the left-wing box, which are all target-subcase metaphors of LIFE IS JOURNEY. As source-domain subcases, MOVIE, TV DRAMA, PLAY, and OPERA are all subcategories of SHOW, which is a generic, superordinate-level concept.

As analyzed here, the four third-level metaphors in the right wing are linked horizontally to each other, and they are linked vertically to LIFE IS SHOW as its child metaphors in the hierarchy. As such, they all inherit the image-schema and frame structure of their parent metaphor LIFE IS SHOW, while they each add more specific details to themselves, which make them different from one another. Such differences may exhibit interesting contrasts between cultures and languages. For example, Lakoff and Turner (1989) suggest that LIFE IS PLAY (i.e., theatrical play) is an extraordinarily productive basic metaphor for life in English (e.g., *That's not in the* **script**. *He blew his* **lines**.). This makes perfect sense in English-speaking culture, or Western culture in general, where play has been a major form of performing arts or "show", as represented and high-lighted by the Shakespearean tradition, through its history of civilization (Yu 2017). In contrast, however, the most salient subversion of the LIFE IS SHOW metaphor in Chinese culture is the LIFE IS OPERA metaphor, where "opera" is a shorthand term referring to Chinese opera, with Beijing (or Peking) opera as its prototype (Yu 2017; Yu and Jia 2016). I argued that LIFE IS OPERA "plays a central role in the Chinese conceptualization of events and phenomena in various domains of life, constituting a core component of the Chinese cultural model of life" (Yu 2017: 67). It is worth mentioning that the play metaphor is still applicable in Chinese to a lesser degree, but the Chinese or Beijing opera metaphor is unique to Chinese, with a highly culturally constructed frame of a folk type of performing arts. This is a good example showing that two languages and cultures can share one common superordinate metaphor but contrast with each other in employing different subordinate metaphors (see also Yu 1998: chapter 3).

Earlier, I showed in the example of inheritance hierarchy how the metaphors at Level 2 and Level 3 are related to one another systematically along both ver-tical and horizontal dimensions. First, at Level 2, the two metaphors, LIFE IS JOURNEY and LIFE IS SHOW, are linked with each other horizontally by sharing the same target domain while differing in the source domain. Second, these two metaphors are linked vertically to the metaphors at the lower level in two contrastive ways. The child metaphors under LIFE IS JOURNEY are its target subcases, whereas those under LIFE IS SHOW are its source subcases. These two ways reflect the two constructs discussed in Kövecses (2010), the *range* and *scope* of metaphors. The former refers to the possible target domains onto which a particular source domain can map. Conversely, the latter refers to the possible source domains that can map onto a particular target domain.

So far, I have only discussed how the metaphors at Level 2 and Level 3 are related with one another both vertically and horizontally. I have not, how-ever, touched upon the ESM, which is, among others, located at Level 1. This is because ESM is a metaphor system in its own, with two subsystems: the Location Event Structure Metaphor (LESM) and the Object Event Structure

Metaphor (OESM) (Lakoff 1993; Lakoff and Johnson 1999; see also Dancygier and Sweetser 2014; Kövecses 2010; Yu 1998). As such, it is quite complex and deserves a separate discussion. I will therefore focus on ESM in the next section.

2.5 Event Structure Metaphor: The location-object duality

As shown in Figure 2.2, the LIFE IS JOURNEY metaphor is but a Level-2 metaphor, on top of which at Level 1 is the ESM, which, as mentioned above, is actually a metaphor system with two dual subsystems. A central idea about metaphor inheritance hierarchies is that lower-level metaphors inherit the structures of higher-level metaphors. Then, what is the structure that the LIFE IS JOURNEY metaphor inherits from ESM?

Before I answer this question, I would like to mention in passing another pair of constructs, *primary metaphor* vs. *complex metaphor*, in the CMT literature (see, e.g., Grady 1997a, 1997b, 1999, 2005; Lakoff and Johnson 1999, 2003). The distinction between the two will be discussed in detail in the next section (2.6). In terms of inheritance hierarchies discussed in section 2.4, primary metaphors stay at a high level of schematicity whereas complex metaphors tend to stay at a lower level of schematicity. For example, the well-known linguistic metaphor *glass ceiling* (see, e.g., Dancygier and Sweetser 2014: 58–59) instantiates, among others, a complex metaphor PROMOTION IS UPWARD MOTION, which can be analyzed as a combination of three primary metaphors, CHANGE IS MOTION, STATUS IS HEIGHT, and SUCCESSFUL IS UP. That is, promotion is a successful change in social status. Further, that linguistic metaphor also instantiates two more primary metaphors, DIFFICULTY IS IMPEDIMENT (TO MOTION) and KNOWING IS SEEING. Here, the "glass ceiling" is an "invisible barrier" that keeps certain people from "moving up" in promotion.

Now, I go back to ESM and its relation to LIFE IS JOURNEY. As a complex metaphor, LIFE IS JOURNEY can be analyzed as being composed of two primary metaphors, PURPOSE IS DESTINATION and ACTION IS SELF-PROPELLED MOTION. This is exactly what LIFE IS JOURNEY inherits from the Level-1 ESM. It so happens that the two primary metaphors, PURPOSE IS DESTINATION and ACTION IS SELF-PROPELLED MOTION, are part of ESM, which is in effect a metaphor system in itself (see, e.g., Dancygier and Sweetser 2014: chapter 3; Kövecses 2010: chapter 11; Lakoff 1993; Lakoff and Johnson 1999: chapter 11; Yu 1998: chapter 5).

Table 2.1 Event Structure Metaphor with its location-object duality

Event Structure Metaphor	
Location Event Structure Metaphor	**Object Event Structure Metaphor**
STATE IS LOCATION	ATTRIBUTE (or STATE) IS OBJECT
CHANGE IS MOTION	CHANGE IS MOTION
CAUSE IS FORCE	CAUSE IS FORCE
PURPOSE IS DESTINATION (DESIRED LOCATION)	PURPOSE IS POSSESSION (DESIRED OBJECT)
ACTION IS SELF-PROPELLED MOTION	ACTION IS SELF-CONTROLLED ACQUISITION/LOSS
MEANS IS PATH	MEANS IS WAY
DIFFICULTY IS IMPEDIMENT TO MOTION	DIFFICULTY IS IMPEDIMENT TO ACQUISITION/LOSS

According to Lakoff (1993), ESM has events as its target domain and space as its source domain. The central claim about ESM is that various aspects of event structure, including such basic notions as state, change, action, cause, purpose, and means, are conceptualized via metaphor in terms of location, object, motion, and force. It is suggested that ESM has two subsystems: one based on locations, i.e., the LESM, and the other based on objects, i.e., the OESM. These two subsystems constitute a duality in the event structure construal, and each of them consists of a number of primary metaphors, as displayed in Table 2.1.[3]

Table 2.1, adapted and modified from Lakoff (1993), shows how the primary metaphors in LESM and OESM are consistent and coherent with one another to form unified subsystems. In OESM, the first metaphor is ATTRIBUTE IS OBJECT. It is worth noting that the target concept ATTRIBUTE (or, alternatively, PROPERTY) here and STATE in the corresponding LESM metaphor STATE IS LOCATION may actually refer to the same referent. It may simply be an alternative way of construing the same situation. For that reason, this metaphor is also formulated as STATE IS OBJECT. In LESM, STATE IS LOCATION and CHANGE IS MOTION, i.e., the entity (person or thing) that changes "moves" out of one location and into another location. In that case, location is the Ground

---

[3] It is worth noting here that the general TIME IS SPACE metaphor, which as a metaphor system has received much more attention than ESM in the literature, is also analyzed as being based on the location-object duality. It has two major subversions: the Moving Time Metaphor and the Moving Ego Metaphor. In the latter, time is conceptualized as a stationary sequence of locations over which the human ego moves; in the former, time is conceptualized as a moving sequence of objects that pass the stationary human ego one by one. See, e.g., Lakoff (1993), Lakoff and Johnson (1999: chapter 10), Yu (1998: chapter 4; 2012).

(or Landmark) which is fixed, and the changing entity is the Figure (or Trajector) which "moves" relative to the Ground. In OESM, ATTRIBUTE IS OBJECT and CHANGE IS MOTION, but in this case the changing entity does not "move"; instead, it is the attribute-object that "moves", either into, or away from, the possession, or the co-location, of the changing entity. Put it another way, in this case, the changing entity serves as the Ground that is stationary whereas the mobile attribute-object is the Figure which "moves" relative to the Ground.

As expounded above, ESM is truly a metaphor system with two subsystems that, to some extent, overlap and complement each other in the conceptualization of a situation or a relation between participants. In this regard, the two subsystems often show reversal in the Figure-Ground relationship (see Talmy 2000: vol. 1, chapter 5). In LESM, what is changing is the Figure that "moves" in relation to some "location" as the Ground. In OESM, conversely, what is changing is the Ground in relation to which some "object" as the Figure "moves". This conceptual and linguistic phenomenon is called "duality".

What "duality" means here is that metaphors come in location-object pairs (Lakoff 1993; see also Cienki 1998; Lakoff and Johnson 1999; Yu 1998). In the case of duality, the same abstract entity can be construed in alternative ways, namely "duals", as either a location or an object. For example, a person can either *have a serious depression* (DEPRESSION IS OBJECT) or *be in a serious depression* (DEPRESSION IS LOCATION), and this person can either *have a good relationship* (RELATIONSHIP IS OBJECT) or *be in a good relationship* (RELATIONSHIP IS LOCATION) with another person (Dancygier and Sweetser 2014: 49).

Another good example is the pair of English sentences involving *trouble*: *I'm in trouble* vs. *I have trouble* (Lakoff 1993: 225). This pair demonstrates two alternative ways of conceptualizing and expressing the same abstract concept TROUBLE and the same situation in which "trouble" is attributed to a person ("I") so that a relation (of location or possession) is established between the two elements, the trouble and the person. The first sentence is an instantiation of LESM, by which trouble is conceptualized as a location in which a person can be trapped, whereas the second sentence is an instantiation of OESM, by which trouble is conceptualized as an object that a person can receive and possess. It is worth stressing that ESM accounts for an extremely large amount of linguistic data in everyday language because its conceptual patterns are systematically manifested in linguistic patterns. For instance, the location-object duality with *trouble* can be extended in a parallel fashion as follows:

(3)   LESM   OESM

    a. I'm in *trouble.*   I have *trouble.*   (STATE)

    b. I will *get into* trouble   I will *get* trouble if I   (CHANGE)
        if I do this.   do this.

    c. Will I get into trouble   Will I get trouble *this*   (MEANS)
        this way?   *way?*

    d. I finally *got out of* the   I finally *got rid of* the   (PURPOSE)
        trouble.   trouble.

    e. *It kept* me *from*   *It kept* me *from*   (DIFFICULTY)
        getting out of the   getting rid of the
        trouble.   trouble.

    f. *He got* me into   *He gave* me trouble.   (CAUSE)
        trouble.

In these linguistic metaphors, the italic portions represent the target concepts contained in the parentheses to the right. For instance, in (3a) *trouble* represents a state that can be construed as either a location or an object; in (3b) both *get into* and *get* refer to change which is construed either as motion to an undesirable location or as possession of an undesirable object. In brief, as a metaphor system with its location-object duality, ESM consists of clusters of conceptual mappings and inferential entailments that are manifested in systematic linguistic patterns. As Lakoff (1993: 220) puts it, ESM "is a rich and complex metaphor whose parts interact in complex ways", and its system of mappings "generalizes over an extremely wide range of expressions for one or more aspects of event structure". Indeed, this is true not only in English, but in Chinese (Yu 1998) and Arabic (Aldokhayel 2008) as well.

Of course, when it is said that ESM manifests itself "in systematic linguistic patterns", systematicity is still a matter of degrees. In fact, there are always gaps of various extents in linguistic patterns in the manifestation of conceptual metaphors. The recognition of such gaps is one of the reasons leading to the invention of the theoretical construct of *primary metaphor* in contrast with *complex metaphor* (Grady 1997a, 1997b). According to the theory of primary metaphor, the linguistic manifestation of complex metaphors reflects more directly the primary metaphors they contain since it is primary metaphors that are more directly motivated by and derived from embodied experience. The reality is that this is a truly complicated issue resulting from the interaction between language, thought, and culture. It is an enormous task confronting cognitive linguists and scientists to describe and analyze how such interaction works.

In the above, I presented an overview of ESM, which is placed on Level 1 in Figure 2.2. The LIFE IS JOURNEY metaphor at Level 2 therefore inherits its structures, particularly the structures of two primary metaphors, PURPOSE IS DESTINATION and ACTION IS SELF-PROPELLED MOTION, in LESM. ESM is concerned with event structures. After all, life is full of events and a journey is itself an event.

In talking about networking of conceptual metaphors, Lakoff (1993: 224) suggested that the hierarchical organization is a very prominent feature of metaphor systems, and that "the metaphors higher up in the hierarchy tend to be more widespread than those mappings at lower levels". He proposed ESM as a "candidate for a metaphorical universal" (Lakoff 1993: 249). My study (Yu 1998) in Chinese and Aldokhayel's (2008) study in Arabic show that ESM is systematically manifested in Chinese and Arabic as well, thus lending some support to Lakoff's proposal from entirely different languages.

ESM, as discussed in this section, consists of primary metaphors, which stay high in inheritance hierarchies, in contrast with complex metaphors, which are lower in the hierarchies. Besides, it is possible for one complex metaphor to be composed of different primary metaphors and, in reverse, for one primary metaphors to be a component in different complex metaphors. Therefore, the distinction between primary and complex metaphors adds to the systematicity of CMT as an approach to metaphor analysis. In the next section, I focus on how these two kinds of metaphors are related to each other and contribute to the systematic organization of conceptual metaphors.

2.6 Primary and complex metaphors

CMT has been one of the most fruitful areas of research in cognitive linguistics. Despite its enormous success, CMT has also encountered considerable criticisms for its limitations both within and beyond cognitive linguistics (for discussions and evaluations of CMT see, e.g., Cameron and Low 2011; Gibbs 2009, 2011, 2014, 2017; Kertész and Rákosi 2009; Kövecses 2017b; Ritchie 2013; see also section 1.1). One limitation, as Gibbs (2011) points out, is that linguistic research favoring CMT suffers from a lack of details about the ways these analyses are conducted. Growing out of the CMT tradition for the purpose of improving and refining it is primary metaphor theory (PMT) (Grady 1997a, 1997b, 1999 2005; see also Lakoff and Johnson 1999, 2003), which distinguishes between two kinds of conceptual metaphors: *primary metaphor* and *complex metaphor*. As the contrast between these two constructs is crucial to my forthcoming decomposition analysis of moral metaphors in Chapter 6, I would like to go into more detail in this section on what they are and how they function.

In the CMT literature, metaphors like LIFE IS JOURNEY are considered complex metaphors in contrast with primary metaphors that may compose them (e.g., PURPOSE IS DESTINATION, ACTION IS MOTION). In short, as posited, complex metaphors are conceptual patterns that often can be decomposed into more basic metaphorical mappings called primary metaphors in combination with forms of commonplace knowledge in one's culture, such as cultural models, folk theories, or simply knowledge or beliefs that are widely accepted in a culture (Lakoff 2014; Lakoff and Johnson 1999). Primary metaphors, on the other hand, are based on direct correlations between two distinct dimensions of our recurring embodied experiences in specific scenarios known as primary scenes (Grady 1997a; Grady and Johnson 2002; Lakoff 2012). In other words, primary metaphors, with their simple mapping schemes, directly link two kinds of experience: sensorimotor experience (e.g., warmth, closeness) and subjective experience (e.g., affection, intimacy) that co-occur regularly in specific situations, giving rise to a mental association between two conceptual domains. Thus, for instance, when parents hold their children affectionately, the experiences of affection and warmth correlate, yielding the primary metaphor AFFECTION IS WARMTH. Also, people in an intimate relationship are often in close proximity with each other, thus giving rise to the primary metaphor INTIMACY IS CLOSENESS, grounded again in the recurrent experiential correlation. This kind of experiential correlation, typically characteristic of primary metaphors, is referred to in CMT as metonymic basis, metonymic motivation, or metonymic stage, of conceptual metaphors (see, e.g., Barcelona 2000b; Kövecses 2013; Radden 2000). This is because, in traditional terms, metonymy is based on the relationship of association or adjacency between the two elements involved. Thanks to their emergence from our embodied experience, primary metaphors tend to be widespread or potentially universal. In contrast, complex metaphors may be composed of primary metaphors in combination with common-sense knowledge and cultural beliefs. For that reason, they are less likely to be universal or widespread, and instead more likely to be culture-specific.

According to the more recent neural theory of metaphor, or neural theory of language in general, primary metaphors emerge from repeated simultaneous activations of the two brain regions because of real-world experience. Such experiential correlations lead to the connections of the two distinct neural areas via neural mapping circuits, as the source and target domains of primary metaphors (Lakoff 2008a, 2012, 2014). As Lakoff (2008a) discussed in detail, even the linguistic metaphor *My job is a jail*, which appears to be an isolated metaphorical expression, can be analyzed as having primary metaphors as its components, such as PURPOSE IS DESTINATION and ACTION IS MOTION, and hence ACHIEVING PURPOSE IS REACHING DESTINATION. Since a jail restricts one's freedom of motion to desired external destinations, the *jail*, and metaphorically the *job*, thus produces frustration and other negative emotions.

Let us now go back to the example of complex metaphor PURPOSEFUL LIFE IS JOURNEY. Lakoff and Johnson (1999) use it to illustrate how complex metaphors are constructed out of primary metaphors plus forms of cultural knowledge and beliefs. They suggest that this complex metaphor can be anatomized, or decomposed, into the following components (modified from Lakoff and Johnson 1999: 60–63):

(i) Cultural belief: PEOPLE ARE SUPPOSED TO HAVE PURPOSES IN LIFE, AND THEY ARE SUPPOSED TO ACT SO AS TO ACHIEVE THOSE PURPOSES
(ii) Primary metaphor 1: PURPOSE IS DESTINATION
(iii) Primary metaphor 2: ACTION IS MOTION

That is, the complex metaphor PURPOSEFUL LIFE IS JOURNEY builds from three components: a cultural belief and two primary metaphors. While the cultural belief is a literal proposition, the two elements it contains, the concepts PURPOSE and ACT (and its corresponding nominal form ACTION), are structured and defined metaphorically, via two primary metaphors. As mentioned before, primary metaphors are based on experiential correlations. That is, people often go to a destination to achieve a purpose, and therefore purposes are experientially correlated with destinations. Similarly, people often move through space when they take actions, and therefore actions and motions are often associated intimately in our embodied experience. Such tight experiential correlations give rise to the primary metaphors PURPOSE IS DESTINATION and ACTION IS (SELF-PROPELLED) MOTION.

According to Grady and Ascoli (2017) and Lakoff (2014), the two more recent and comprehensive discussions on the subject, primary metaphors are metaphorical mappings between "primitive" (Lakoff 2014) or "primary" (Grady and Ascoli 2017) source and target concepts. Lakoff (2014) is a neural account of primary metaphor. From this neural point of view, primary metaphors, based on regular correlations in real-world experience, use embodied primitive concepts and combine through neural binding to form complex metaphors. Thus, embodied primitive concepts and primary metaphors are building blocks for complex abstract thought, aided by the compositional properties of language.

Grady and Ascoli (2017) present a review and a preview of the development of PMT. In their review of the existing work on the nature of primary metaphors in CMT, Grady and Ascoli (2017: 29–37) outlined six characteristics of primary metaphors and their primary source and target concepts:

(i) Their source and target are equally *basic* concepts, "grounded in universal (rather than culturally determined) aspects of human experience"; though such basic concepts may still be subject to cultural variation, there should be "a shared element of experience across cultures that forms the basis for these concepts" (p. 29).

(ii) Their source concepts are *sensory* (e.g., heaviness, height, and brightness), in contrast to their target concepts as being nonsensory (e.g., difficulty, social dominance, and happiness).

(iii) The mappings between their source and target concepts are *unidirectional*, going from the sensory source (e.g., heaviness) to the nonsensory target (e.g., difficulty).

(iv) Primary metaphors are characterized by the *correlation* and *covariation* found between primary source and target concepts, e.g., the weight of an object correlates and covaries with the amount of effort needed to handle it.

(v) Primary metaphors are *widely distributed* across languages since they reflect universal aspects of human experience, cognition, or neural structure, or a combination of these.

(vi) Primary metaphors serve as bases for more complex metaphorical conceptualizations.

In the spirit of PMT as a decompositional account, I have been trying, over the last decade, to develop a decompositional approach to metaphorical-compound analysis (DAMCA), an approach potentially capable of analyzing metaphorical compounds with multilevel structures of complexity through decomposition (e.g., Yu 2008, 2009a, 2011a, 2011b). As an analytical tool, this approach is designed to conduct "deep analyses" of more complex cases of conceptual metaphors so as to reveal (a) their possible internal structure and composition comprising metaphoric and metonymic mappings at different levels of schematicity or specificity, as well as literal propositions, and (b) their underlying embodied and situated bases in terms of experiential and cultural motivations that reflect cognitive universality and cultural variation.

In my analysis, the process of decomposition is expressed in both formulaic and diagrammatic formats. In the formulaic format, five types of components may constitute a multilevel metaphorical compound: (a) complex metaphor (CM), (b) primary metaphor (PM), (c) metonymy (MY), (d) proposition (PR), and (e) pre-metaphor (P-M). The last one is newly added, referring to those "cognitive associations" based on experiential correlation, which have not yet reached the status of primary metaphors (Grady and Ascoli 2017). I will return to this construct in Chapter 6. In the diagrammatic format, lines with solid arrowheads represent metaphorical mappings, and lines with open arrowheads represent metonymic mappings. Depending on specific cases, lines with stealth arrowheads or without arrowheads at all represent literal, propositional relations, such as opposition, correlation, interrelation, subcategorization, or predication. The bold font type represents primary concepts, in contrast with the regular font type for more complex concepts. A smaller box within a larger box indicates that the former is a more specific subcase of the latter, which is more schematic or generic than the former.

In what follows, I will present four examples of my decomposition analysis, of which two are modified from previously published forms. To save space, I will only provide the diagrammatic versions, which are more self-evident and easier to understand. The first example is a complex metaphor PRESTIGE IS FACE in Chinese (see Yu 2008, 2013). The entities, relations, and mappings involved in this metaphorical compound are presented in Figure 2.3. As shown in the figure, this complex metaphor involves three primary metaphors: MORE IS BIG, AMOUNT IS SIZE, and FEELING IS OBJECT. Of these three, the first is on a par with MORE IS UP. The second one is related to the first, i.e., the amount of something abstract (e.g., emotional feeling) is construed as the size of a physical object: the more of the amount, the bigger of the size. The third one instantiates the object-dual, in contrast with the location-dual (e.g., FEELING IS LOCATION, so one can *get in* or *out of* a feeling), in ESM discussed in section 2.5. The location-dual and the object-dual, which form a pair known as duality, are two fundamental forms of "ontological metaphor" (Lakoff and Johnson 1980). They constitute the two subsystems (LESM and OESM) of the ESM system.

In this specific case, the feeling is prestige. Metaphorically, a prestigious person has "a big face"; therefore, there is a mapping between the feeling "prestige" and the body part "face". Note that FACE in this metaphorical compound refers to "social face" rather than the physical face. This concept serves both as the source for the target PRESTIGE and as the target for the source VALUABLE POS-SESSION, which is ultimately a physical OBJECT, thus forming a metaphoric chain. This is why one can "lose" and "save" face (as an object), in its social, instead of physical, sense of "face". In the target frame, PRESTIGE is a kind of DESIRABLE FEELING, which is a FEELING in general. Note again that the complex metaphor under analysis, which contains a metaphoric chain (where FACE is both source and target), is grounded in some fundamental bodily experience, in which one's physical face with its facial expression is associated with one's affective feeling (Yu 2001, 2008, 2020). This relationship of association is represented in Figure 2.3 as a metonymic mapping FACE FOR FEELING, which grounds the complex metaphor PRESTIGE IS FACE, along with the primary metaphor FEELING IS OBJECT through the intermediate complex metaphor DE-SIRABLE FEELING IS VALUABLE POSSESSION. In section 7.2.2, I will return to the discussion of "social face" (based on Yu 2020) as an example illustrating the impact of linguistic experience on metaphorical conceptualization.

My second example is the complex metaphor BEST IS HEAD, which is found in Chinese expressions for things of the best or super quality (Yu 2013). In this case, a body-part term for "head" is used as the source concept mapping onto the target BEST, a concept of subjective judgment. My analysis, as shown in Figure 2.4, is that this complex metaphor involves two frames: the source is the frame of spatial relations based on the structure of the human body or of a body-shaped object; the target is the frame of qualitative variation. In this one, however, the source concept itself also involves a metonymy, HEAD FOR HIGHEST. That is, HEAD, the highest part of the human body, is mapped

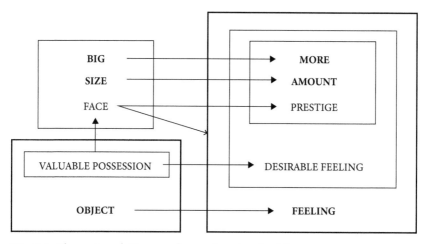

Fig. 2.3 Elements, relations, and mappings involved in PRESTIGE IS FACE

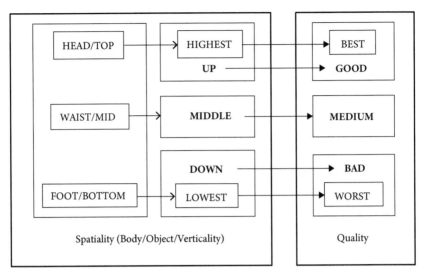

Fig. 2.4 The mappings for the BEST IS HEAD metaphor in a conceptual network

metonymically onto the spatial concept HIGHEST. According to this analysis, the concept of subjective judgment BEST, which is the superlative degree of GOOD, is conceptualized metaphorically in spatial terms, HIGHEST, based on the primary metaphor GOOD IS UP. In Chinese, however, HEAD, referring to the highest part of the body, often substitutes metonymically for HIGHEST in the spatial domain to mean the "best" in quality.

Note that my analysis holds the mapping relationship between HEAD and HIGHEST as that of metonymy because the human body or body-shaped object and the vertical spatial scale are seen as two frames located within the same conceptual domain SPATIALITY: while the head is the upmost part of the human body in the shape of a vertical axis, the highest is the upper limit of a vertical scale. Contrastively, FOOT maps onto BAD (e.g., 蹩脚 biéjiǎo (lit. sprang-foot) "inferior; shoddy (in quality)"). On the whole, the mappings do not seem to be systematic enough for the whole body to be a source domain for concepts of qualitative judgments and relations. It would be interesting to see what other languages do in this respect.

It is also worth noting that the BODY frame can alternate with that of VERTICAL OBJECT. This seems to be the case in English as well, where *top* and *bottom* (perhaps the former (e.g., *top students, top schools*) to a greater degree than the latter (e.g., *the bottom tier*)) can be used in the rating of quality. In Chinese, the word 顶 *dǐng* "top" is also used in a similar fashion: e.g., 顶尖 *dǐngjiān* (top-tip) "top; top-notch; tip-top"; 顶级 *dǐng-jí* (top-grade) "top-rate;

top-class". On the other hand, its antonym 底 *dǐ* "bottom" can mean "the low-est", e.g., 底价 *dǐjià* (bottom-price) "base price". After all, a body is a living object, and an object is also sometimes called a body. As shown in the figure, the primary metaphor for the downside is BAD IS DOWN, and the one in the middle is MEDIUM IS MIDDLE.

In Chinese, the body-part noun for "waist" is 腰 *yāo*, which is sometimes mapped onto the mid part of an object. For example, the mid part of a hill or mountain is called 山腰 *shānyāo* "halfway up the mountain (lit. mountain waist)", in contrast to 山头 *shāntóu* "top of a mountain (lit. mountain head)" and 山脚 *shānjiǎo* "foot of a mountain (lit. mountain foot)". More recently, 腰 *yāo* "waist" is also mapped onto classifications of more abstract nature. For instance, accounts on social media are classified into "head-part" (头部 *tóubù*), "waist-part" (腰部 *yāobù*), and "bottom-part" (底部 *dǐbù*) accounts according to their impact on the public (e.g., the number of their followers or reads of their posts). Also, corporate management is sometimes classified into three levels as the "head-part", "waist-part", or "leg-part" (腿部 *tuǐbù*) administrators.

Next, I want to show that DAMCA can be applied to the analysis of conceptual metaphors of a much more complex nature, those that are highly culture-specific and occasion-specific, as well as novel and dynamic. These metaphors occur at the "mental-space level" (Kövecses 2020). I will use two examples revised from my earlier work on multimodal metaphors in the China Central Television (CCTV) educational commercials about 2008 Beijing Olympics (Yu 2011a, 2011b). Both of the metaphors are also the central themes of the commercials conveyed through multimodal means throughout the duration of the commercials. The first of them is the following:

HOSTING THE BEIJING OLYMPICS IN LIFE IS PERFORMING BEIJING OPERA ON AN INTERNATIONAL STAGE.

In that commercial, 10 famous Beijing opera actors and actresses talk (metaphorically and metonymically) about the honor for, and pride of, Chinese people to host the 2008 Beijing Olympics. What the screen shows however is mostly them performing Beijing opera in various theatrical and natural settings. The commercial ends with a female martial role posing at the center of a huge stage after the curtains have been raised, looking over the panoramic view of a metropolitan area crowded with skyscrapers. At this moment, the verbal message appearing on the screen is: "Mount the stage of the world; perform (lit. sing) the opera of China" (登世界的台, 唱中国的戏), accompanied by a voice-over.

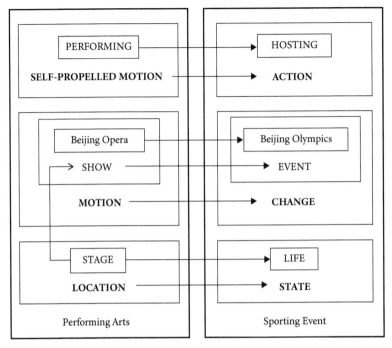

Fig. 2.5 Elements, relations, frames, and mappings involved in the Beijing Opera TV commercial

In Yu (2011a), I worked out a formulaic version. Here, I present a dia-grammatic version in complementarity. As can be seen in Figure 2.5, the above novel and dynamic metaphor actually rests on the conceptual founda-tion comprised of three primary metaphors that are part of the ESM system. Specifically, the three primary metaphors are (a) ACTION IS SELF-PROPELLED MOTION, (b) CHANGE IS MOTION, and (c) STATE IS LOCATION. All three belong to LESM, one of the two subsystems of ESM. Thus, parallel on both sides of the mappings, performing is a self-propelled motion whereas hosting is an action. While Beijing opera is a show which consists of a series of motions, Beijing Olympics is an event that comprise a series of changes. The show takes place on the stage, which is a location; the event happens within the totality of life, which can be construed in this case as a state, the static background against which a particular event unfolds. Depending on the way we construe it, life is also a dynamic process comprising a myriad of events and changes. In such a case, life itself is a titanic "show" (i.e., LIFE IS SHOW), which holds a metonymic relation with STAGE (LOCATION FOR ACTIVITY). Thus, LIFE IS STAGE can be decomposed as LIFE IS STAGE FOR SHOW, where the metonymic mapping is made explicit in the source frame.

My final example, revised from Yu (2011b), relates to an even more complex metaphor, which again serves as the central theme of a different CCTV Beijing Olympics commercial. The commercial's central metaphor is:

PEOPLES OF THE WORLD MAKING CONTRIBUTIONS TO THE BEIJING OLYMPICS ARE BIRDS FLYING FROM VARIOUS COUNTRIES TO BEIJING WITH TWIGS TO BUILD A BIRD'S NEST.

This commercial shows all varieties of birds, big and small, myriads of them, flying from various countries, each carrying a twig, to Beijing China, to build a bird's nest. Finally, the bird's nest built fades into the Bird's Nest Stadium, the national Olympics stadium of China, with a bilingual message in Chinese and English showing up on the screen: "One world, one dream" (同一个世界, 同一个梦想).

Again, a decomposition analysis in Figure 2.6 shows that this complex metaphor is composed of a variety of metonymic and metaphoric mappings and literal propositions. When a "deep analysis" of the metaphorical structure of the TV commercial was conducted level by level, and component by component, with DAMCA, it came down to a few primary metaphors, which serve as the conceptual "cornerstones" of the metaphorical compound. Most of these primary metaphors instantiate both LESM and OESM. Thus, for instance, all the birds flying to Beijing to build a bird's nest (i.e., ACTION IS SELF-PROPELLED MOTION) instantiates the two metaphorical entailments for achieving a purpose: (a) achieving a purpose is reaching a desired location (i.e., PURPOSE IS DESTINATION), which is Beijing, and (b) achieving a purpose is acquiring a desired object (i.e., PURPOSE IS POSSESSION), which is the bird's nest. The bird's nest that all the birds construct is of course an image metaphor for the Bird's Nest Stadium, which in turn is a metonymy for the Beijing Olympics as an event (VENUE FOR EVENT). Other mappings include a metonymic chain in which the landmarks of the countries stand for the countries (i.e., SALIENT FEATURE FOR ENTITY), and the countries stand for the whole world (PART FOR WHOLE). The ultimate themes here are "unity" and "harmony" of the "global village".

In summary, PMT provides a better account of the experiential basis for conceptual metaphors. According to this account, the grounding of the whole is the grounding of its parts (Lakoff and Johnson 1999). So, LIFE IS JOURNEY as a complex metaphor does not appear to have a direct experiential grounding of its own. But this complex metaphor is composed of two primary metaphors, PURPOSE IS DESTINATION and ACTION IS MOTION, which have their own

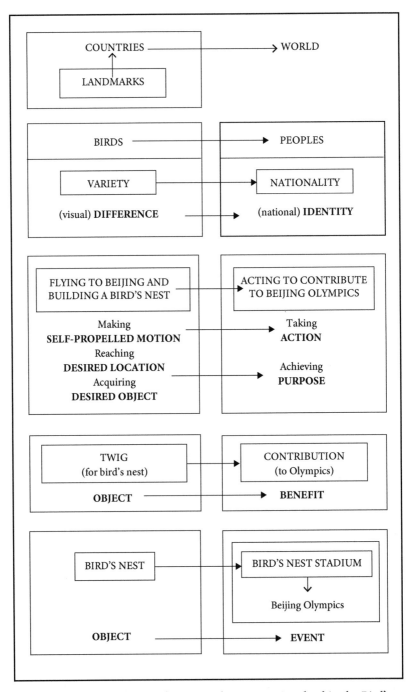

Fig. 2.6 Elements, relations, frames, and mappings involved in the Bird's Nest TV commercial

experiential grounding. "That grounding is perceived when the primary metaphors are combined into the larger complex metaphor" (Lakoff and Johnson 1999: 63; see also Dancygier and Sweetser 2014: chapter 3). Thus, the grounding of the complex metaphor LIFE IS JOURNEY as a whole is provided by the individual groundings of two primary metaphors as its parts.

As discussed in this section, one salient type of vertical relationship among metaphors is captured by the distinction between primary and complex metaphors: primary metaphors function at a high, schematic level, and complex metaphors at a lower, more specific level. Further, a complex metaphor may be composed of one or more primary metaphors in combination with encyclopedic, cultural knowledge. As exemplified above with four examples, the decompositional approach to metaphor analysis that I have developed builds on the distinction between primary and complex metaphors. In Chapter 6, I will utilize this analytical instrument to anatomize the moral metaphors to be discussed in the following three chapters, in order to get a better understanding of their nature and composition, as well as the components involved in their metaphorical mappings.

2.7 Metaphor networks: New developments in research on metaphor systems

In this penultimate section of the chapter, I discuss more recent developments of CMT that have taken place during the last few years. One such recent development is associated with the construction of the MetaNet as a metaphor cataloging repository (see David, Lakoff, and Stickles 2016; Dodge 2016; Dodge, Hong, and Stickles 2015; Lakoff 2016; Petruck 2016; Stickles et al. 2016).[4] The collective effort is aimed at formalizing CMT (see Dodge 2016; Stickles et al. 2016). As a novel way of performing metaphor analysis, this approach incorporates the concept of *cascades*, which further extends the notion of metaphor inheritance hierarchies (see section 2.4) in characterizing the networking nature of conceptual metaphors. According to David et al. (2016), the notion of cascades is grounded in the Neural Theory of Language (e.g., Lakoff 2008a). This theory holds that the production and comprehension of the sentence *He grasped the idea*, for instance, involves mental simulation using some of the same parts of the brain used in the action or perception of

---

[4] MetaNet is a computationally implemented and maintained collection of semantic frames and metaphoric mappings linked via inheritance relations, containing, as of 2016, over 700 metaphors and metaphoric entailments, organized in hierarchical inheritance networks, and more than 500 frames that act as the source and target domains of those metaphors (David et al. 2016).

physically grasping an object (Gallese and Lakoff 2005). Such embodied simulation allows us to reenact our bodily experiences, thus experiencing the source domains of action, perception, and emotion of bodily metaphors in order to build cross-domain mappings (Cuccio 2015; Gibbs 2006).

Dancygier and Sweetser (2014: 57) suggest that there are two primary characteristics of cascade relationships among metaphors: (i) a higher, more schematic structure is fully inherited by lower more elaborated subcases; and (ii) one specific metaphor can inherit fully the structures of multiple higher-level metaphors. Thus, metaphor cascades are "preexisting packages of hierarchically organized primary and general metaphors that occur together" (David et al. 2016: 214). David et al. (2016: 215) provide a definition of "cascade" as follows:

> A *cascade* is a hierarchically organized conceptual combination of image-schemas, frames, and metaphors that has been used often enough to become fixed as a single complex entity, though each of its parts continues to occur separately.

As in this definition, cascades pertain to different levels of cognitive mechanisms: image schemas, frames, and metaphors. Fundamentally, the notion of metaphoric cascade builds on the observation of frame semantics that "frames are bundles of coherent roles dynamically related to one another" (p. 215). As discussed in section 2.3, frames are schematized structures representing elements (or "roles") and their relations that constitute frames as coherent regions of our encyclopedic knowledge. As such, frames are structured, taxonomically related to one another, with varying degrees of generality and specificity (Stickles et al. 2016). The concept of frame is particularly relevant to CMT in that frames serve as structures of source and target domains of conceptual metaphors, specifying the correspondences between them for metaphorical mappings and entailments. That is, "metaphors are cross-domain mappings between frames"; so defined, metaphors are structured as well, "both in terms of the internal structure of individual metaphors and the structured relationships between metaphors" (Stickles et al. 2016: 171).

As for *image schema*, it is another important, basic concept that links conceptual and linguistic metaphors systematically into networks in CMT. As defined in cognitive linguistics, image schemas are schematic idealizations that capture recurring dynamic patterns in our embodied experience, pertaining to and abstracted from our sensorimotor interactions with the world around us (see, e.g., Gibbs and Colston 1995; Hampe 2005; Johnson 1987). As highly schematic gestalts, image schemas are fundamentally embodied, directly meaningful, and preconceptual structures that are utilized to structure abstract concepts and reason in a way that is more likely universal (e.g., Dodge and Lakoff 2005; Stickles et al. 2016). Again, what is especially relevant to CMT is that image schemas help us order and organize our abstract experiences via metaphorical extension and elaboration. For instance, the journey metaphors discussed in the preceding sections all involve the SOURCE-PATH-GOAL image schema, which, idealized from our recurring experience of moving from one point to another in space, originates in the source-domain frame but is metaphorically mapped onto the target to structure our understanding of and reasoning about our mental, emotional, and spiritual experiences with life, love, education, career, religion, and so on. In the metaphorical mapping, the presence of this image schema invokes a schematic source-domain frame structure involving the following elements as its core roles: trajector, source, path, and goal. Thus, for instance, our life experience is conceptualized metaphorically as motion along a path toward a destination.

For another example, as discussed in section 2.5 on ESM, our dual conceptualization of trouble, as exemplified by the pair of sentences *I'm in trouble* and *I have trouble*, is rooted in two common image schemas: CONTAINER and OBJECT. The CONTAINER image schema, including two- and three-dimensional locations, entails a schematic frame that involves the following elements as its core roles: interior, exterior, and boundary. Metaphorically, abstract states such as trouble are construed as spatially bounded locations in or out of which we stay or move. Similarly, the OBJECT image schema, derived from our routine bodily experience dealing with physical objects, triggers off a schematic frame including the following elements as its core roles: size, weight, solidity, and shape (see, e.g., Yu, Yu, and Lee 2017; Yu and Huang 2019). Thus, abstract attributes (properties or states) such as trouble are construed in metaphorical terms as solid matters that we can or cannot manipulate as we want. As a matter of fact, both CONTAINER and OBJECT image schemas play pivotal roles in ESM as a metaphor system with its LOCATION (CONTAINER) and OBJECT subsystems (LESM and OESM).

As argued by David et al. (2016: 216), a cascade theory of metaphor enables "fleshed-out analyses of metaphor hierarchical structure, including metaphoric entailments, frame-based knowledge, and image-schema structure". Here, cascade structure of metaphors is hierarchical because it is characterized by dependency and inheritance relations among them.

The activation of the lowest and most specific item should by default also activate each and every dependent and higher node in the hierarchy as a whole. Viewed as such, all the metaphoric entailments are established at a very high level in the cascade network and apply to every subcase at a lower level in the structure. Thus, novel linguistic metaphors fit into the existing system easily.

In their introduction to the innovative formalization of CMT and its implementation in the MetaNet, Stickles et al. (2016) provide a detailed description of how conceptual metaphors are related to one another, at and between different levels of generality and specificity, to form lattice-like networks based on the parallel networks of similar nature among the frames that define the internal structures of conceptual metaphors with regard to their source and target domains and the mapping relations between them. In other words, the metaphor-to-metaphor relations are determined by the frame-to-frame relations. In the network, the relationships among metaphors exist both vertically and horizontally on the basis of similar frame structures that characterize them. Horizontally, sister metaphors at the same level in the hierarchical network hold some sort of nonhierarchical relations between their frames (e.g., temporal, causal, or as variants of another frame) while sharing some common frame structure via bindings to the shared parent frame.

Vertically, the hierarchical nature of metaphors and frames is such that child metaphors inherit some of their frame structures from those of their more general parent metaphors and those of their parent's parent metaphors. Note that, within this hierarchical structure, child frames do not copy or duplicate the frame elements inherited from their parent frames; instead, they each only add more information specific to themselves while binding to the elements they commonly inherit from their parent frames. In such a way, inferential information originating in embodied conceptual primitives "trickles down" in the cascades of metaphors and is inherited throughout the network.

For example, Figure 2.1 in section 2.3 displays the frames (target and source) and subframes (i.e., child frames) of the metaphor LOVE IS JOURNEY, based on the linguistic data presented in (1). As child frames, the subframes do not have to duplicate the elements, as well as the relations between them, in the source parent frame; that conceptual information is inherited, i.e., activated, via bindings to the elements in the parent frame. Thus, each child frame only adds more information on the kind of path taken, the kind of vehicle involved, and possible impediments to motion thereof. In this particular case, the linguistic metaphors in (1) all evoke the source JOURNEY (or TRAVEL) frame in general, while possibly activating one of its specific subcases (child frames): namely, Travel on Land by Auto or by Train, and Travel on Water by Ship or Boat, etc.

In order to sort out various kinds of relations between metaphors in the network of hierarchical structure, Stickles et al. (2016) have identified 13 different types of frame relations that have been used to characterize frame-to-frame relations in the MetaNet. These relations are categorized into two groups: (i) structure-defining relations (No. 1–9), and (ii) nonhierarchical relations (No. 10–13), which are summarized in Table 2.2, adopted from Stickles et al. (2016: 186). The structure-defining relations are vertical, between a parent and a child frame. The child frame directly incorporates the semantic structure (elements and relations between them) of its parent frame while adding more semantic information to it. The corresponding elements within this hierarchical structure, between higher and lower frames, are connected via bindings. For example, the JOURNEY frame is the parent of the JOURNEY ON LAND and JOURNEY ON WATER frames, the latter being the former's child frames and subcases (see Figure 2.1).

In contrast, nonhierarchical relations are not structure-incorporating or hierarchically related to each other. Instead, they exist between sister frames with a common parent; their shared structure is through bindings to the shared parent frame, rather than as bindings between themselves. Such sister frames are related to each other as alternative variants of a shared parent. Referring back to Figure 2.1, we say that in the subframes, JOURNEY ON LAND and JOURNEY ON WATER are sister frames differentiated by the path of travel, and JOURNEY BY AUTO and JOURNEY BY TRAIN are sister frames, under JOURNEY ON LAND, distinguished by the means of transportation.

As Stickles et al. (2016) suggest, a major innovation in the formalization of CMT is the development of the metaphor network that is based on and parallel to the frame network. Therefore, conceptual metaphors are classified into two broad categories of relations as well, structure-defining and nonhierarchical, according to the relations between the frames that constitute their source and target domains. For instance, Figure 2.7 displays the relations between some of the basic and entailed metaphors in the LESM subsystem in combination with GOODNESS IS VERTICALITY (i.e., GOOD IS UP and BAD IS DOWN). In this figure, the bold font indicates primary metaphors whereas the remaining ones are their entailments formed through composition, or combination, of the primary metaphors. Of the primary metaphors, STATE IS LOCATION, CHANGE IS MOTION, and CAUSE IS FORCE on the left side are basic metaphorical mappings from LESM. They are combined with another primary metaphor, GOODNESS IS VERTICALITY, and the two of its subversions, to form other entailed complex metaphors. The lines with stealth arrowheads represent the relations between metaphors, with the solid lines denoting structure-defining

Table 2.2 Summary of frame relations

	No.	Frame relations	Description	Example
Structure-defining relations	1	*Is a subcase of*	Full incorporation of frame structure	Purposeful Action *is a subcase of* Action
	2	*Is a special case of*	No additional structure added	Boat *is a special case of* Seafaring Vehicle
	3	*Makes use of*	Partial incorporation of frame structure	Purposeful Action *makes use of* Desiring
	4	*Incorporates as role*	Frame fully included as an element	Eating *incorporates as a role* Food
	5	*Has affordance of*	Frame is an intrinsic property	Food *has affordance of* Eating
	6	*Is a process that makes use of*	Scene is incorporated into a perspectivized process	Experience Harm *is a process that makes use of* Harm to Living Entity
	7	*Profiles part of*	Foregrounds element of the frame	Curriculum *profiles part of* Education
	8	*Is a subscale of*	Profiles element of a scale	Light *is a subscale of* Luminosity
	9	*Is a subprocess of*	Profiles stage in a process	Diagnosis of Physical Affliction *is a subprocess of* Physical Affliction
Nonhierarchical relations	10	*Is in causal relation with*	Causal variants	Cause Motion Along a Path *is in causal relation with* Motion Along a Path
	11	*Precedes*	Temporal ordering between frames	Departing *precedes* Arriving
	12	*Mutually inhibits*	Frames are in semantic opposition to one another	Aids to Motion *mutually inhibits* Impediments to Motion
	13	*Is in scalar opposition to*	Opposite elements of a scale	Good *is in scalar opposition to* Bad

Source: Adopted from Stickles et al. (2016: 186); reproduced with kind permission from John Benjamins Publishing Company, Amsterdam/Philadelphia.

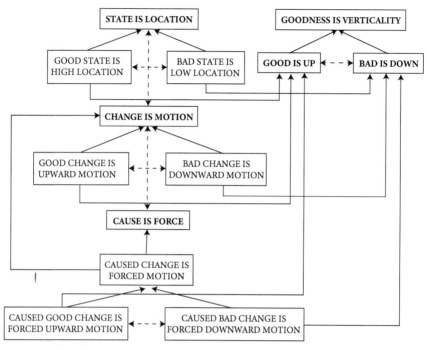

Fig. 2.7 The relations between some of the basic and entailed metaphors in LESM in combination with GOODNESS IS VERTICALITY

(i.e., hierarchical, inheriting) relations between parent and child metaphors, and dashed lines with arrows on both ends denoting sisterhood between metaphors.

In the spirit of Table 2.2, which is a summary of 13 different types of relations between metaphor frames in the MetaNet, I characterize the relations between metaphors in Figure 2.7 as follows (with the numbers given in the parentheses referring to the No. in Table 2.2). First of all, the primary metaphor on the right, GOODNESS IS VERTICALITY, has two child metaphors, which each focuses on one end region of the two scales, GOODNESS and VERTICALITY, which respectively constitute the target and source domain of the metaphor. Thus, these two child metaphors, GOOD IS UP and BAD IS DOWN, each represent "a sub-scale" (No. 8) of their parent's whole scale. At the same time, they are also sister metaphors "in scalar opposition" (No. 13) to each other, representing the opposite valence values of the two scales: one value-judgment scale as the target frame, and the other spatial-orientation scale as the source frame. When these three primary metaphors, with parent-child and sister relations, are "married" with other metaphors, they together "give birth to" other entailed complex metaphors, as is illustrated in Figure 2.7.

In Figure 2.7, the three primary metaphors aligned on the left side are sister metaphors, each being "a special case" (No. 2) of LESM. Now we look at them one by one and see how they combine with GOODNESS IS VERTICALITY and its two subversions to produce more entailed metaphors in the LESM subsystem. First, STATE IS LOCATION is the archetypal metaphor in LESM. When combined with GOODNESS IS VERTICALITY, it bears two child metaphors that simultaneously inherit from both primary metaphors at a higher level, but they do so in different relations. Both GOOD STATE IS HIGH LOCATION and BAD STATE IS LOW LOCATION are "subcases" (No. 1) of STATE IS LOCATION; at the same time, they "make use" (No. 3) of GOOD IS UP and BAD IS DOWN, respectively. As such, they are also "in scalar opposition" (No. 13) to each other as sister metaphors that are in nonhierarchical relations but inherit some shared structures from their common parents.

The next primary metaphor in LESM is CHANGE IS MOTION. As shown in Figure 2.7, it also has two child metaphors as a result of its composition with GOODNESS IS VERTICALITY. As child metaphors, they are again "subcases" (No. 1) of their parent metaphor CHANGE IS MOTION. However, since CHANGE and MOTION are both processes, GOOD CHANGE IS UPWARD MOTION and BAD CHANGE IS DOWNWARD MOTION are therefore "processes that make use" (No. 6) of GOOD IS UP and BAD IS DOWN separately. Finally, the third primary metaphor CAUSE IS FORCE in LESM has a child metaphor, CAUSED CHANGE IS FORCED MOTION, which it shares with CHANGE IS MOTION. In this case, CAUSED CHANGE IS FORCED MOTION is "a subcase" (No. 1) of CHANGE IS MOTION; it is simultaneously "a process that makes use" (No. 6) of CAUSE IS FORCE. As shown in Figure 2.7, CAUSED CHANGE IS FORCED MOTION is but an intermediate-level metaphor, which, when combined with GOOD IS UP and BAD IS DOWN, respectively, gives rise to two child metaphors of their own: CAUSED GOOD CHANGE IS FORCED UPWARD MOTION and CAUSED BAD CHANGE IS FORCED DOWNWARD MOTION. These two are sister metaphors that are "in scalar opposition" (No. 13) to each other.

It is in this way that metaphors are linked to one another, both vertically and horizontally, to form metaphor "cascades", or lattice-like networks of metaphors, which are interwoven together by both hierarchical and nonhierarchical relations among conceptual metaphors.

Lastly, contributing to the body of literature on systematic relationships among metaphors, Kövecses has just published his most recent book *Extended conceptual metaphor theory* (2020). The "extended CMT" is an extension from the "standard CMT" (Lakoff and Johnson 1980, 1999), including a multilevel view of metaphor as one of its important components. According to this view (Kövecses 2020: chapter 4), metaphors are organized at four different levels in schematicity hierarchies: image schemas, domains, frames, and mental spaces, ranging from the most schematic to the least schematic, or most specific, levels. At the top level, image schemas are highly schematic, directly meaningful gestalt structures that are preconceptual and analog in nature. At the level immediately below image schemas, domains are coherent areas of conceptualization which, unlike image schemas, are not analog or imagistic patterns of experience, but propositional in nature in a highly schematic fashion, and meaningful on the basis of relevant image schemas that structure them. At the next level down, frames are less schematic conceptual structures than domains and, involving more conceptually specific information, they elaborate particular aspects of a domain. At the lowest level, mental spaces are conceptual structures constructed as we think and talk for the purpose of local understanding and action. Structured by frames and elaborating on frames, mental spaces function in actual discourse in specific communicative situations where frame roles are filled by particular values under the influence of "contextual factors" (see Kövecses 2015a). While image schemas, frames, and domains work in long-term memory, mental spaces operate online in working memory, making frames as specific as required by the given discourse situation, expressing contextual meanings in particular chunks of discourse, and evoking the entire schematicity hierarchies above them. Readers are referred to Kövecses (2020: chapter 4) for specific examples of how metaphors are identified at four different levels of schematicity, ranging from the most to the least schematic level. The basic idea is that conceptual metaphors at different levels of schematicity license the use of linguistic metaphors at corresponding levels of schematicity.

With the differentiation of four different levels of hierarchical schematicity, Kövecses (2020) argues that metaphor research focusing on different levels of metaphorical patterns, conceptual and linguistic, aims at different research objectives with different research methods. Image schemas belong to what Kövecses (2010) calls the "subindividual" level, domains and frames to the "supraindividual" level, and mental spaces to the "individual" level. Linguistic research at the levels of image schemas, domains, and frames focuses on "types", i.e., lexicalized linguistic expressions with conceptual contents from decontextualized language. The research method applied is chiefly the lexical approach, among others. In contrast, linguistic research attending to the level of mental spaces deals with "tokens", i.e., linguistic expressions used by individual speakers in real communicative situations to meet their communicative needs and goals using fully contextualized language. In this case, linguistic research mainly conducts discourse analysis or utilizes the corpus-based approach, among others.

2.8 Summary

In this chapter, I have focused on one keyword that, in my view, best characterizes CMT as a theory of and approach to metaphor. That is *systematicity*. Up to this point it should have been clear about the fundamental distinction between the traditional theories of metaphor and CMT. The traditional approaches study metaphor as individual linguistic expressions or rhetorical devices: what artistic or aesthetic effects they have produced in a particular piece of discourse, which is primarily literary or poetic in nature. Just as Lakoff (1987b: vii–viii) points out, "traditional theories of metaphor assume that metaphors occur one by one, that each distinct metaphorical expression is individually created". In the CMT paradigm, on the other hand, "metaphor is not just a linguistic trope, but a complex conceptual systematic mapping network with linguistic manifestations" (David et al. 2016: 219). Viewed as such, metaphor is studied as systems of human conceptualization, operating deep in human thought and cognition and, at the same time, surfacing in everyday language in a systematic manner. On this view, metaphor in poetry or in literature at large is but a special case of metaphor in general, based on the same mechanisms (Gibbs 1994; Lakoff 1993; Lakoff and Turner 1989; Sweetser 1992; Turner 1987, 1991).

In short, CMT, especially its recent developments in theorization and formalization, studies networks of metaphors, with their various preconceptual and conceptual structures, such as image schemas, domains, frames, and cascades, at several different levels of generality or specificity. It analyzes individual metaphorical expressions as systematic linguistic instantiations of conceptual metaphors that are themselves linked with other metaphors in a systematic fashion, capturing broad generalizations across the board of our conceptual systems.

My goal is to take this holistic and systematic view of CMT for the study of moral metaphors in this book. In the three chapters to follow (Chapters 3–5), I study moral metaphors from the domains of bodily and physical experience as a system with three subsystems, physical, visual, and spatial. I will devote one chapter to each of the subsystems, comparing English and Chinese with regard to the conceptual metaphors in the subsystem and how they are instantiated in linguistic expressions, before I take up, in Chapters 6 and 7, an anatomic and holistic view of the three clusters of moral metaphors constituting the whole system.

3

Physical subsystem of moral metaphors

3.1 Moral-physical metaphors: Source concepts and frames

This chapter focuses on the first subsystem of moral metaphors, the physical subsystem, which revolves around a central metaphor MORALITY IS PHYSI-CALITY, where "physicality" is a shorthand term for physical being in general, organic or nonorganic, natural or artificial, and as such it can be any sort of physical entity, including human being. Physical entities have outer appearance and inner essence. Very often, external appearance reflects and affects internal essence, and therefore these two aspects of physical entities may be correlated or interrelated in our understanding and judgment of their being, well or ill. This subsystem consists of five conceptual metaphors in nominal form that each have positive and negative parametric versions in adjectival form, as listed in Table 3.1. The five pairs of source concepts are, roughly, BEAUTIFUL and UGLY, STRONG and WEAK, SOUND and ROTTEN, WHOLE and BROKEN, and HEALTHY and ILL. These source concepts map separately onto their corresponding target concepts MORAL and IMMORAL.

Table 3.1 The cluster of moral metaphors grounded in physical experiences

Conceptual metaphors	Positive versions	Negative versions
MORALITY IS BEAUTY	MORAL IS BEAUTIFUL	IMMORAL IS UGLY
MORALITY IS STRENGTH	MORAL IS STRONG	IMMORAL IS WEAK
MORALITY IS SOUNDNESS	MORAL IS SOUND	IMMORAL IS ROTTEN
MORALITY IS WHOLENESS	MORAL IS WHOLE	IMMORAL IS BROKEN
MORALITY IS HEALTH	MORAL IS HEALTHY	IMMORAL IS ILL

As in Table 3.1, the five bipolar source concepts of the moral metaphors, with their positive and negative parametric versions, lie in five dimensions of what constitutes physical wellbeing: beauty, strength, soundness, wholeness, and health. These five dimensions form a unified and coherent system of

The Moral Metaphor System. Ning Yu, Oxford University Press. © Ning Yu (2022).
DOI: 10.1093/oso/9780192866325.003.0003

wellbeing, applicable to both human being and other forms of physical being. The five categories are linked into a conceptual network as shown in Figure 3.1.

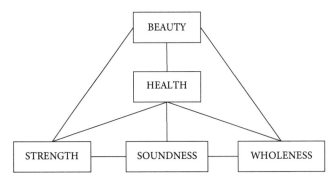

Fig. 3.1 A conceptual network for human and other physical wellbeing

The category of beauty is perhaps the most visible or conspicuous of all, consisting in such visual features as color and shape in simple spatial dimensions or more complex physical configurations. As such, beauty refers to "the quality or aggregate of qualities in a person or thing that gives pleasure to the senses or pleasurably exalts the mind or spirit" (*Webster*). While beauty vs. ugliness is the subject of aesthetics (Parret 2011; Suojanen 2016), people all have intuitions about what is beautiful and what is ugly in nature, in object, in art, or in humans, although whether or not beauty, in opposition to ugliness, is rooted in objectivity of aesthetic qualities may be a matter for debate (Suojanen 2016). The physical attractiveness stereotype, known as "What is beautiful is good", in social interaction is a research topic that has long attracted attention of researchers (e.g., Dion, Berscheid, and Walster 1972; Eagly et al. 1991; Lemay, Clark, and Greenberg 2010; Lorenzo, Biesanz, and Human 2010; Tsukiura and Cabeza 2011). Morality has been associated with beauty ever since the time of Plato; ideally, therefore, a moral person is both good and beautiful rather than simply good or simply beautiful (see, e.g., Martin 2008).

Strength is another dimension of physical attractiveness and wellbeing, with bipolar values being "strong" and "weak". Among human beings, strength is always perceived as a desired quality although it is generally attributed more to males just as beauty is generally more often attributed to females. As a matter of fact, physical strength is viewed by all as demonstrating both beauty and health, and that is the reason why it has become an aspect of culture for both men and women to engage in all sorts of physical exercise and workout, including yoga and bodybuilding (in Chinese, bodybuilding is called 健美 *jiànměi*, which literally means "healthy-beauty"). The moral meaning of engaging in physical fitness and wellness activities is that such activities are seen as a good in themselves, inherently linked to the pursuit of virtue and a moral life (Conrad 1994). That is, being physically fit and strong is seen as the bodily basis for one's moral capacity, with the body being "the site for moral action", and with a healthy life being equated to a good life (Conrad 1994: 385). A moral person has self-control, which refers to "the self's ability to alter its own states and responses, and hence it is both key to adaptive success and central to virtuous behavior, especially insofar as the latter requires conforming to socially desirable standards instead of pursuing selfish goals" (Baumeister and Exline 2000: 29). Therefore, self-control is one's "moral strength" and "moral muscle" (Baumeister and Exline 1999, 2000; see also Arcimavičienė 2007). That is also the reason why morally "strong" people are conceived of as being "upright" and "upstanding" (cf. section 5.3.2), those who have a strong body.

The remaining three categories of wellbeing, i.e., soundness, wholeness, and health, all revolve around the physical conditions of the being, be it as a human being or as any other form of physical being. They are somewhat synonymous to one another, or even mutually defining in some sense or another, but place emphasis on different aspects of physical conditions of the being. In English, for example, *sound* means "free from injury or disease" (*Webster*) or "in good condition; not damaged, injured, or diseased" (*Oxford*), while its negative or opposite *unsound* means "not healthy or whole" (*Webster*) or "not healthy or well" (*Oxford*). The adjective *whole* means "physically sound or healthy; free of wound or injury" (*Webster*) or "healthy; in an unbroken or undamaged state" (*Oxford*). The adjective *healthy* means "free from disease; showing physical, mental, or emotional wellbeing" (*Webster*) or "in a good physical or mental condition; not diseased" (*Oxford*). In contrast, its antonym *ill* means "not in good health; not normal or sound" (*Webster*) or "suffering from an illness or disease or feeling unwell" (*Oxford*). As defined precedingly, the three categories of wellbeing all pertain to physical health, which however is directly related to physical strength. A healthy person is physically strong whereas an ill or sick person is physically weak. Additionally, a human person, however beautiful when healthy, would lose his or her glowing beauty and look grossly ugly when suffering from and tortured by a hideous disease.

As the preceding paragraph suggests, HEALTH, which primarily refers to good physical conditions of a human being, is a central concept in the source domain of MORALITY IS PHYSICALITY. The cultural link between health and morality has long been established, with evidence present in both theological and secular writings (Cronin 1995). On the one hand, health is tied with a moral fiber, with health and wellness linked with a positive moral valence, and disease or illness linked with a negative moral valence. Thus, we witness the moralization of health issues. For instance, hygiene is expected to exalt moral character, dieting is viewed as a virtual battle between good and evil, and the pursuit of fitness and wellness is seen as a path of virtuous and moral action, and physically healthy life is considered morally good life (Conrad 1994). On the other hand, we also see the medicalization of moral issues. Thus, for instance, AIDS has become a symbol of spiritual pollution or moral decay (Palmer 1989). Such epidemics as TB and malignant diseases as cancer have become apt metaphors for social deviations and disorders, and illness or disease imageries are commonly used to express concerns for social problems such as corruption or injustice (Sontag 1978). Human society is regarded metaphorically as an organism so that morally evil influence can infect the "body" of society (Cronin 1995). That is the very reason why we can talk about a "healthy" or "ill" society.

Figure 3.2 presents a general source frame for the physical subsystem of moral metaphors. It is interpreted as follows. This source frame involves three core roles represented by the three inner circles which form a triangular structure. In this frame, there is a HUMAN PERCEIVER at the top, who perceives some physical entity with a salient property, hence, ENTITY PROPERTY as the stimulus and second role, which is something being perceived by the perceiver. The physical entity and its salient properties can include the perceiver's own

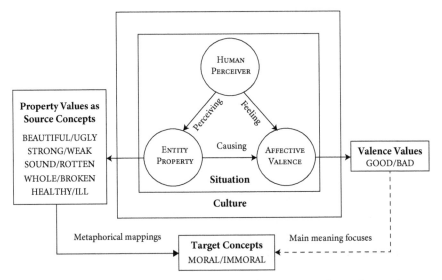

Fig. 3.2 A general source frame for the physical subsystem of moral metaphors

body and bodily states or conditions. As indicated by the arrow line pointing to the left, any of the physical adjectives in the box are possible values that can fill this role. While the HUMAN PERCEIVER sees the ENTITY PROPERTY (i.e., any of those values represented by the physical adjectives in the box to the left), this salient property being perceived causes the perceiver to feel an affective state with its valence, namely AFFECTIVE VALENCE as the third core role of the frame. This AFFECTIVE VALENCE evoked by the ENTITY PROPERTY in the HUMAN PERCEIVER can only be one of the two alternative and opposite values: either GOOD (positive) or BAD (negative), as is represented in the box to its right, depending on which salient ENTITY PROPERTY is being perceived, BEAUTIFUL or UGLY, STRONG or WEAK, HEALTHY or ILL, for instance. As a central component of all affective states, valence "is an intrinsically motivating nonconceptual representation of goodness or badness" (Carruthers 2018: 675). The value of the AFFECTIVE VALENCE, GOOD or BAD, underlies the moral valence, MORAL or IMMORAL, as the target concept that receives metaphorical mappings from the property values as source concepts. In Chapter 6, I will argue that moral valence is affective valence in general applied to the domain of MORALITY.

The value of the AFFECTIVE VALENCE, GOOD or BAD, serves as the metaphorical main meaning focus carried over by the metaphorical mapping to the target domain, as represented by the dashed line with a stealth arrowhead. According to Kövecses (2010: 137–138), the "main meaning focus" is the major theme, or meaning orientation, of a given source-target pairing of a metaphor, conventionally fixed, predetermined, and agreed upon within a speech community. In this particular case, the pairing is between the source concepts encoded by the physical adjectives and the target concepts represented by the moral adjectives *moral* and *immoral*. Its main meaning focus is that morality is good (or positive) whereas immorality is bad (or negative). As illustrated in Figure 3.2, however, such moral judgments in metaphorical terms are embodied, that is, rooted in our experiential correlations between certain perceptual stimuli and our affective responses to them. The general frame structure represented schematically in Figure 3.2, therefore, assumes an inseparable link between emotional affect and moral judgment. As has been argued, moral judgments involve brain areas related to emotion (Haidt and Kesebir 2010) and are based primarily on intuition rather than reason (Haidt 2001). After all, human cognition cannot be divorced from human emotion (Damasio 1994; see also Meier, Sellbom, and Wygant 2007; Zhai, Guo, and Lu 2018).

So analyzed, emotionality or affectivity is always involved in morality to a certain degree upon the perception of the stimulus. That is, affective states with intrinsic valence, positive or negative, in a moral situation influence people's moral judgments. Understood as such, moral judgments cannot be a cognitive function purely based on rational reason, but instead involving at least some affective function and emotional expression (e.g., Haidt 2001; Haidt et al. 1993; May 2014).

3.2 Psychological research on physical moral and affective metaphors

After I decided to study the moral metaphor system, I started to search for psychological research on morality in order to find out if results of experimental studies were consistent or inconsistent with the moral metaphors in the system. I realized that there existed a growing body of literature in this area of research. After I sorted out the literature as pertaining to physical, visual, or spatial subsystems of moral metaphors, I realized that there were not many experimental studies that can be categorized into the physical subsystem, and those that I actually found were mainly related to the first pair of moral metaphors in this subsystem, i.e., MORAL IS BEAUTIFUL and IMMORAL IS UGLY, whose source concepts represent the most obvious and intuitive physical traits in this subsystem. More psychological research, however, looks at the interrelationship between beauty and goodness, namely, the bidirectional stereotypes "What is beautiful is good" (e.g., Dion et al. 1972; Lemay et al. 2010) and "What is good is beautiful" (e.g., Gross and Crofton 1977; Little, Burt, and Perrett 2006).

Thus, for example, in consistence with the so-called "beautiful is good" stereotype, physically attractive people are assumed to possess more socially desirable personality traits than those who are less physically attractive (Dion et al. 1972). This is because people desire to form and maintain close social bonds with physically attractive people so that they attribute desirable interpersonal qualities to their attractive targets as part of the projection of their desires to bond with attractive people (Lemay et al. 2010). Studies showed that physically attractive applicants for employment received a higher rate of selection than those of lesser physical attractiveness (Shannon and Stark 2003). The physical beauty of a firm's executives could even help produce affect earnings with a positive impact on its revenues (Pfann et al. 2000). In political elections voters tended more often to cast their votes for physically attractive candidates rather than for unattractive candidates (Efran and Patterson 1974).

Conversely, the existence of the "good is beautiful" stereotype was also supported by experimental research. Therefore, information about people's personality and character could affect judgments of their beauty in a way that was consistent with "what is good is beautiful" (Gross and Crofton 1977). According to one study, if a personal trait is desired, then faces perceived to possess that trait are found more attractive than faces which do not possess that trait; in other words, what people desire about others in appearance reflect what they consider good, and they find attractive faces reflecting the desired traits (Little et al. 2006). Such a process was called "reading into faces" in one study, according to which information about personality changed the perception of facial features (Hassin and Trope 2000; see also Paunonen 2006).

As mentioned above, many studies confirmed the interrelationship between the judgment of people's inner character and the attractiveness of their outward appearance. That is, there exist mutual effects between moral judgment and aesthetic evaluation. One experimental study that linked a moral trait to physical attractiveness is Paunonen (2006), who found a substantial effect of the honesty manipulation on perceptions of people's physical attributes. The researcher designed an experiment involving undergraduate psychology students who served as judges to rate target persons' personality traits and physical attractiveness on nine-point rating scales. The judges first read the targets' personality profiles and immediately rated their personality traits. Then the judges were given photos of the targets and asked to rate them on their physical attractiveness. What is of special interest are the results that showed a relationship between honesty and physical attractiveness. Because the same targets were described as being either honest or dishonest, two groups of judges rated them very differently as being more or less attractive even though exactly the same target faces were rated by both groups. However, the same results were not found with the targets who were described as being either more or less intelligent, or as either independent or dependent. This is because, as Paunonen (2006) suggested, honesty-dishonesty is a stronger determinant of liking-disliking, compared with intelligence and independence. Emotional liking (vs. disliking) for the target was a possible mediator of any effects that the manipulated personality characteristics had on facial feature attributions.

It is clear that, of the three personality traits (i.e., intelligence, independence, and honesty), honesty, vs. dishonesty, carries the strongest moral sense. More recently, Wang et al. (2017) investigated the relationship between morality or, more specifically, honesty and beauty. The study, consisting of two experiments, was designed to test whether the presence of an attractive face would influence individuals' honesty. In two experiments, the researchers randomly divided 225 male college students into three groups, and assigned the three experimental groups to high, middle, and low attractiveness conditions. Participants were asked to predict the outcome of computerized coin-flips and to self-report the accuracy of their predictions. They would be rewarded based on their self-reported (rather than actual) accuracy. Their self-reports were made in the presence of a facial photo of a female (as recorder of participants' self-reports) who had been rated as high attractive, middle attractive, or low attractive by other volunteers. The results showed that the subjects tended to give more dishonest self-reports when in the presence of middle or low attractive facial images than in the presence of high attractive facial images. That is, in the high attractiveness condition, the participants' self-reported accuracy was significantly higher than the random level. These results showed that facial attractiveness can influence people's moral behavior.

This is because, as was suggested, beauty influences people's moral behavior through emotional priming. Priming positive moral emotions (e.g., proud, grateful, sympathetic) helps to encourage people's good behavior whereas priming negative moral emotions (e.g., guilty, ashamed, disgusted) is more likely to cause bad behavior (Janoff-Bulman, Sheikh, and Hepp 2009). Thus, for instance, social exclusion was associated with feelings of anger, which in turn was associated with anti-social behavior (Chow, Tiedens, and Govan 2008). Also, while it was argued that a moral person possesses self-control as "moral strength" or "moral muscle" (Baumeister and Exline 1999, 2000), re-search found that happy (vs. neutral or unhappy) people perform better on self-control tasks which are compatible with self-improvement (Fishbach and Labroo 2007). According to Wang et al. (2017), both "goodness is beauty" and "beauty is goodness" are mediated by positive emotions. When people perceive moral behaviors, or when they perceive beautiful stimuli (e.g., attractive faces), positive emotions will be primed and serve as inner mechanisms of the beliefs that "what is good is beautiful" and its reverse "what is beautiful is good".

It is suggested that processing both beautiful stimuli and morally good stimuli activates the medial orbitofrontal cortex (OFC), which is related to the emotion of pleasure (Wang et al. 2017). The neural evidence for such connections in the brain was found in the research by means of functional magnetic resonance imaging (fMRI). For example, Tsukiura and Cabeza (2011) hypothesized that the existence of the "beauty is good" stereotype suggested that the neural mechanisms for judging facial attractiveness and moral goodness overlap. To test this hypothesis by fMRI, they came up with three findings. First, activity in the medial OFC, known as a region associ-ated with processing positive emotions, increased as a function of perceived attractiveness and goodness, and this activity was significantly correlated be-tween two judgment tasks. Second, activity in the insular cortex, known as a region associated with processing negative emotions, increased as a function of negative attractiveness and goodness ratings, and was correlated between these ratings. Third, an opposing relationship was found between medial OFC and insular cortex during aesthetic and moral judgments, with activations in these two regions negatively correlated with each other between attractiveness and goodness ratings. Thus, the results of this study based on the fMRI data were consistent with the dual process hypothesis about the "beauty is good" stereotype that both brain regions were involved, possibly in opposition to each other, in the processing of positive and negative stimuli respectively.

Wang et al. (2015) also conducted an fMRI study on the question of whether moral beauty is different from facial beauty. Their experimental research led to the following findings: (i) moral aesthetic judgments and facial aesthetic judgments both involved the joint participation of perceptual, emotional, and cognitive components; (ii) facial beauty was associated with both physiological and social needs whereas moral beauty is associated with social needs only; and (iii) in addition to the overlapping regions activated during both types of aesthetic judgments (moral and facial), moral aesthetic judgments also recruited several cortical regions which served as the extra neural resources recruited for more advanced and comprehensive mental processing of moral aesthetic judgments.

For my purpose, however, the literature of psychological research discussed in this section provides empirical evidence for the link between beauty and morality, although this link is merely one of the several that we can observe in language, both English and Chinese, to which we turn below in the next two sections.

3.3 Physical moral metaphors in English

What Table 3.1 in section 3.1 lists are the main conceptual metaphors for morality in the physical subsystem. Since they are hypothetically conceptual in nature, they are not tied particularly to the English language in which they are cast. Table 3.2 provides the conventionally lexicalized moral senses of physical adjectives in three major English dictionaries: *Webster*, *Oxford*, and *Longman*. According to these dictionaries, some of the English words used in Table 3.1 to represent the source concepts have lexicalized moral senses whereas the others have not, as shown in Table 3.2.

As displayed in Table 3.2, only two English words, *rotten* and *ill*, have their moral senses listed in all three dictionaries. Another two, *beautiful* and *ugly*, have their moral senses listed in two of the three dictionaries: *Oxford* and *Longman* for *beautiful*, and *Webster* and *Oxford* for *ugly*. It is worth mentioning in passing that the closest moral senses listed in *Longman* of *beautiful* and *ill*

Table 3.2 Lexicalized moral senses of the physical words in the three English dictionaries

Dictionary	Webster	Oxford	Longman
Word	**Conventionally lexicalized moral senses**		
beautiful		Morally or intellectually impressive, charming, or satisfactory	Very good
ugly	Morally offensive or objectionable; repulsive	Morally repugnant	
strong	Having moral or intellectual power		
weak			
sound			
rotten	Morally corrupt; not morally good; not honest, kind, etc.	Morally, socially, or politically corrupt; very bad	Unkind or dishonest
whole			
broken			
healthy			
ill	Immoral; vicious; resulting from, accompanied by, or indicative of an evil or malevolent intention; attributing evil or an objectionable quality	Morally bad; hostile, unkind	Bad; harmful

are "very good" and "bad; harmful" respectively. As such, these meanings are not specific to morality, but they are listed in Table 3.2 only because they apparently include and supersede the moral senses of the words, namely "morally good" and "morally bad or harmful" as their subcases. In Table 3.2, *strong* has its moral sense listed only in *Webster* and the remaining words, *sound*, *whole*, *broken*, *weak*, and *healthy* have no moral senses listed in any of the three dictionaries. Nonetheless, the absence of their moral senses from the English dictionaries does not mean that they cannot be deployed to express moral meanings metaphorically, especially in real-life discourse. The following sections will show that the contrary is the case.

3.3.1 MORAL IS BEAUTIFUL and IMMORAL IS UGLY

The contrast between beauty and ugliness is a fundamental category in human experience, although its judgment or assessment may vary in degree across cultures, or even from individual to individual, and over time (Parret 2011;

Suojanen 2016). As a contrast in valence, its bipolar values primarily refer to our aesthetic reactions, positive or negative, to the physical appearances of external objects, scenes, or people. As shown in Table 3.1, in this pair of moral-physical metaphors, BEAUTIFUL maps onto MORAL, and UGLY onto IMMORAL. Let us first look at the examples from the Corpus of Contemporary American English (COCA) in (1).

(1) a. Various columnists defending the **moral beauty** of the established order ... condemned Brown as "a demagogue", an irresponsible hypocrite, "a spoiler", an enemy of meaningful political reform, "a false messiah", an opportunist ...

  b. She is anxious about the stain of mortal sin that may be creeping across her spiritual landscape at this very moment, darkening her capacity to love and causing a **moral ugliness** that can't be disguised or washed away.

The two key collocations in our focus here are *moral beauty* and *moral ugliness*. In (1a), "Brown" refers to Jerry Brown, an American politician who served as the 34th (1975–1983) and 39th (2011–2019) Governor of California. During his career, Brown also ran for the U.S. president three times, the last time being in 1992. That was, according to the preceding context of the example, when he was portrayed as "a wicked radical" by some eminent journalists who "keep watch of the nation's pulse and conscience". Example (1b) contain three immoral words, *stain*, *darken*, and *ugliness*, which are coherent and interact with one another to instantiate the conceptual metaphors for immorality: IMMORAL IS DIRTY, IMMORAL IS DARK, and IMMORAL IS UGLY. The first two moral metaphors will be discussed in the next chapter, Chapter 4. The examples in (2) provide further illustration of lexical instantiations of MORAL IS BEAUTIFUL and IMMORAL IS UGLY.

(2) a. Since one could not chop logic to arrive at Christian truth, since every formula turned out to be false, ideas like "trinity and atonement" had "their reality in and through the imaginative and **morally aesthetic** powers—truths of form and feeling, not of the logical understanding".

  b. David Girolmo plays Quasimodo, big-hearted but physically hideous servant of the cold-hearted and **morally hideous** archdeacon Frollo (Neil Friedman).

  c. Olive may be physically flawed, but she is **morally angelic**; Christal, in contrast, is physically attractive but at times **morally monstrous**.

These three examples involve four different adverb-adjective collocations: *morally aesthetic*, *morally hideous*, *morally angelic*, and *morally monstrous*. In (2a), *aesthetic* is used in the sense "of or relating to the beautiful". Example (2b) introduces the musical adaptation from Victor Hugo's novel *The Hunchback of Notre Dame* (the original French title *Notre-Dame de Paris*), in which Quasi-modo is the "big-hearted" but "physically hideous" bell-ringer in contrast with Frollo, the Archdeacon who is "cold-hearted" and "morally hideous". The last example, (2c), highlights the contrast between two fictional characters: one is "physically flawed" but "morally angelic" while the other is "physically attractive" but "morally monstrous". Here, the moral contrast in character is de-picted as the physical contrast in appearance between an angel and a monster. Other similar collocations found in the collection include *morally beautiful* and *morally ugly*.

3.3.2 MORAL IS STRONG and IMMORAL IS WEAK

This pair of moral-physical metaphors is complementary to the preceding one in that physical beauty and strength are two important aspects of physicality, appearance, and essence, which are the ideal and optimal combination of ex-ternal and internal conditions of anything physical. Things that are beautiful and strong are more likely to be attractive and appealing; on the other hand, if they look ugly and weak, they are certainly less attractive, and could even be repulsive or disgusting. Physical things can be strong or weak both mate-rially and structurally. Material and structural strengths and weaknesses are inherent properties that determine the physical wellbeing of things. In addi-tion, this pair of moral metaphors is coherent with the first pair, MORAL IS BEAUTIFUL and IMMORAL IS UGLY, as well. Something being beautiful is cer-tainly its "strong" point, not a "weak" point. On the other hand, if something is ugly, it is considered its "weakness" rather than "strength".

Note that STRENGTH as a concept extends far beyond moral metaphors. This is because strength and force go hand in hand in the construct of "force dy-namics" that plays a major role in the understanding of interaction between abstract entities construed as physical entities with "physical forces" of vari-ous "physical strengths" (Talmy 2000: vol. 1, chapter 7). Thus, for example, Kövecses (2000: 194–199) analyzed metaphorical conceptualizations of emo-tion, morality, and rational thought as three faculties of the human mind. These three aspects of the mind are related and unified by the notion of two interacting physical forces. Namely, the emotional self loses control over emotion as a stronger force, the moral self with a stronger force maintains control over the evil force, and the rational self exerts a strong force on "objects" of thought in an attempt to "manipulate" them. That is, the workings of the human mind are understood in terms of interaction between physical forces with different physical strengths.

In their primary senses, being strong means having physical power and being weak means lacking physical power. As shown in Table 3.2, of the three dictionaries I consulted, only *Webster* defines *strong* as "having moral and intellectual power" (WNCD 1977: 1154). However, both *strong* and *weak*, as well as some words that are semantically related to them, are utilized to realize the conceptual metaphors for morality: MORAL IS STRONG and IMMORAL IS WEAK. "Moral strength" derived metaphorically from physical strength "consists of both the strength to maintain an upright and balanced moral posture and also the strength to overcome evil forces" (Lakoff and Johnson 1999: 299) (see also sections 5.3.2 and 5.4.2). Look at the following examples from COCA.

(3)   a.   … the United States can't simultaneously proclaim "America first" and then claim any kind of **moral strength.**

b.   Saying loudly and repeatedly that American values are not going to be a cornerstone of American foreign policy strips you of any **moral power** whatsoever.

In these two examples, *moral strength* and *moral power* are the focal collocations. They refer to what one must possess to "stand up to" immoral or evil forces, and what one must build through "self-discipline and self-denial" (Lakoff and Johnson 1999: 300). Synonymous collocations found in the data collection also include *moral might* and *moral fortitude*. In reality, mental strength and physical strength can reinforce each other in interaction even though they are of categorical difference.

(4)   a.   His theory, shared by many, was that yellow fever was caused by immoral personal behavior or **moral weakness.**

b.   Prolonged exposure to moral distress that is unrelieved by acts of moral courage may result in **moral fatigue** and **moral residue.**

The examples in (4) contrast with those in (3) with their expressions of negative valence in scalar opposition to strength. In (4a), "moral weakness" is "in itself a form of immorality" because a morally weak person "is likely to fall, to give in to evil, to perform immoral acts, and thus to become part of the forces of evil" (Lakoff and Johnson 1999: 300). Lakoff and Johnson (1999) suggest that there are two forms of moral strength, depending on whether the evil to be faced is external or internal. Courage is the strength to stand up to external evils whereas willpower is the strength of will necessary to resist the temptations of immoral or evil desires. As in (4b), one's "moral strength" can turn into *moral fatigue* and *moral residue*. To a greater extent, people can also suffer *moral exhaustion* and *moral loss*, which are other collocations found in my data collection.

(5)   a.   ... Sallie was as mentally and **morally sturdy** as a racehorse, and that some things occurred for no demonstrable reason, no matter how Dr. Freud had viewed it.

      b.   This moral lack constitutes a key element in this possession literature, because it renders protagonists such as Rosemary **morally impotent.**

The examples in (5) contain adverb-adjective constructions: *morally sturdy* and *morally impotent*. These two are joined by the more common ones such as *morally strong* and *morally weak*. Another instance found in the data pool, *morally fragile*, is obviously linked also with another pair of moral metaphors, MORAL IS WHOLE and IMMORAL IS BROKEN, to be discussed in section 3.3.4. If something is fragile, it will be easily broken, damaged, or destroyed.

3.3.3   MORAL IS SOUND and IMMORAL IS ROTTEN

The source concepts for this pair of moral-physical metaphors are SOUND and ROTTEN. The English word *sound*, as an adjective, has two primary senses referring to physical beings: (i) free from injury or disease, i.e., exhibiting normal health; and (ii) free from flaw, defect, or decay (WNCD 1977: 1110). While both of these senses are relevant in a metaphorically moral sense, it is the second of these that is utilized in contrast to *rotten*. Whatever is materially and structurally strong is physically "sound"; in contrast, things that are weak are more likely to turn "rotten" under the impact of external force or as a result of internal cause. When something is "rotten", it is decayed, "marked by weakness or unsoundness" (WNCD 1977: 1007). In the following, let us look at some COCA examples that illustrate how MORAL IS SOUND and IMMORAL IS ROTTEN are instantiated lexically in English.

(6)　a.　Trust in leaders is sustained as long as they achieve and maintain "good governance", which consists of the creation of economic wealth and the maintenance of stability, order, and **moral soundness** in society.

　　　b.　We've been discussing for weeks now the whole issue of American values sparked in part by the debate that's going on about what some see as a **moral rot** in America, American values fraying at the edges.

　　　c.　Unfortunately, the rise of these films was just one of several new manifestations of **moral decay**.

In this group of examples, the first contains *moral soundness*, which represents one polarity of the moral dimension. Example (6a) contrasts with (6b) and (6c), which display the other polarity with *moral rot* and *moral decay*. Along the moral scale between the two end points, there are possible intermediate points, which are indicated by the three examples in (7).

(7)　a.　I think this again is a **moral deterioration** of the moral fiber in our country.

　　　b.　Look, the American people know this guy as a guy with a lot of **moral defects** and they also know he was a very good president.

　　　c.　In contrast, Arthur Schmidt's "The Internationalization of the Economic Crisis in Mexico and Central America" gives more weight to circumstances than to **moral flaws**.

The examples in this group present cases of deviation from "moral soundness". In (7a), *moral deterioration* refers to the process of becoming worse in morality. When the "moral fiber" (i.e., moral character or quality at the societal level) is deteriorating, it is no longer in its normal, good condition; it is instead marked by more and more *moral defects* (7b) and *moral flaws* (7c). The process of *moral deterioration* (7a), if not stopped, will result in utter "moral rot or decay" (cf. 6b and 6c).

　　The examples in (6) and (7) above are all characterized by a key expression in the form of an adjective-noun construction. The ones in (8) and (9) below contain, instead, the construction in which an adjective is modified by an adverb.

(8) a. This means we make use of every **morally sound** means to promote health for all.

   b. That's partly because the psychedelia springs from a common-sense-filled, well-informed, experience-tempered and **morally solid** soul.

   c. … it is thus unafraid to invoke faith and awe while standing **ethically firm** and socially decent.

The relevant collocations in this group of examples are *morally sound* (8a), *morally solid* (8b), and *ethically firm* (8c). As we know from our sensorimotor experience, when something hard or tough is in its normal "sound" condition, it should remain "solid" and "firm", with more resistance to the damage of external forces and possibility of internal deterioration. These linguistic expressions deploy the SOLIDITY dimension of the OBJECT image schema derived from our fundamental sensorimotor experience dealing with physical objects (see, e.g., Yu and Huang 2019). This is also the reason why the English adjective *sound* can mean "solid" and "firm", which are meanings associated with "sound", according to WNCD (1977: 1110).

(9) a. He wanted to be sure that his boss wasn't a "Jesse Helms radical" or an Alfonse D'Amato, the **ethically impaired** New Yorker who headed up the Senate Whitewater investigation while serving as a cochairman of the Dole for President campaign.

   b. One of the truths that the **morally defective** always fail to grasp is that, when we act on the basis of our fear and our hate, we are on a fast track to becoming what we fear and hate.

The two examples in (9) instantiate IMMORAL IS ROTTEN with more constructions of the "adverb + adjective" type. Other examples include *morally rotten* and *morally flawed*. When something is rotten, it is easier for it to fall apart. On the other hand, if it is sound, it is more likely to stay whole. This experience with the physical world leads to the next pair of moral-physical metaphors I will discuss.

3.3.4 MORAL IS WHOLE and IMMORAL IS BROKEN

This pair of moral-physical metaphors is related to and coherent with the preceding one in that, as mentioned above, when something is "sound" in material that makes it up or in structure in which its elements are held together, it is more likely to stay "whole". On the other hand, if something has gone "rotten", it is likely to fall into pieces, becoming "broken". Here "broken" is used in the sense of "damaged or altered by breaking or as if by breaking". If something is "broken", it is no longer "whole". As such, its meaning covers a range of possibilities, from something having one or more of its parts missing to the whole thing crumbling and falling apart. In fact, this pair of moral-physical metaphors is coherent with the first two pairs discussed above, too. If something is beautiful as a whole, it is no longer so when it is broken (the Venus de Milo perhaps being an exception). It is certainly an ugly scene to see when something beautiful is broken into fragments. Also, things that are strong or weak also determine if they can "stand as wholes" or will "break into pieces" under the impact of internal causes or external forces. If something is strong, it is less likely to deteriorate or disintegrate, whereas the opposite is true if it is weak.

In this section, let us look at the COCA examples that show how MORAL IS WHOLE and IMMORAL IS BROKEN are realized lexically in English discourses.

(10) a.   Here I mean an aesthetic integrity rather than a **moral integrity**, though the distinction should not signal too great a separation.

   b.   The **ethical wholeness** of actors in a capitalist marketplace is not a minor, supplementary matter.

The key collocations in the examples in (10) are positive in their moral senses. In (10a), *moral integrity* is a very common phrase in English used to describe one's moral character as being "high" and "strong". People who possess "moral integrity" are honest and trustworthy. Example (10b) emphasizes the importance of "ethical wholeness" to actors, without which their fame and wealth may be procured by immoral means. Another collocation that showed up in my collection is *moral unity*. "Moral unity" would be an ideal state for the human race. In reality, however, the human world is still marked by disunity and fragmentation among various ethnicities and nationalities where many practices are immoral from the point of view of the "whole" humankind.

(11) a.   From one bleak episode to another, we follow Henriette's social and **moral disintegration** as she moves from prostitution to crime, and from the brothel to the prison.

   b.   The **moral fallout** from the dual-anthropology model is that when Jesus' maleness is emphasized it leads to odd and disturbing questions.

In the two examples in (11), the key collocations suggest the loss of wholeness in one way or another. The process of losing one's moral wholeness is one of "moral disintegration" in which one's morality splits into smaller parts and pieces (11a). A "moral fallout" refers to a part that has fallen out of a "moral whole", from which the separation leads to immoral consequence (11b). Similar examples include *moral damage* and *moral destruction*. Moral wholeness is lost as a result of "moral damage" or "moral destruction". In the former case we have "moral wounds", and in the latter we have "moral perils".

(12) a. Where conservatives attribute our burgeoning underclass to **moral breakdown,** he blames capitalism.

   b. Similarly, **moral collapse** in business affects far more individuals than ever before.

The key collocations in (12) present further examples of "moral disintegration" (11a). Both *moral breakdown* (12a) and *moral collapse* (12b) suggest a sudden "crash" of morality, which has "fallen apart" and "split into fragments". When this happens, what is left over is nothing but "moral ruin".

(13) a. These executives have ravaged the roots of cultural traditions, professing not dismay, but dollar-driven self-satisfaction at the **moral mudslides** that inevitably follow such deliberate destruction of America's religious roots.

   b. The analysis then drills down on the importance of values; it looks at the factors that contribute to **moral meltdowns,** the leadership strategies that can help prevent them, and the opportunities for leaders to express their ethical commitments through pro bono service.

The two examples in (13) manifest the conceptual metaphor IMMORAL IS BROKEN, using words that express "moral disintegration" in more specific and evocative ways. Moral disintegration happens in a rapid and forceful manner in (13a), like "mudslides" rushing and surging down the mountains. In (13b) the key collocation is *moral meltdowns*, which suggests a complete loss of morality, like a huge block of ice disappearing under heat after turning into liquid. Other examples include *moral erosion* and *moral corrosion*, which refer to slow and gradual processes of wearing morality away bit by bit.

(14) a. If the point of the operation was to pass—as physically and **morally whole,** as naturally beautiful, as a member of another group—secrecy was essential.

   b. Bending rules and calling in favors to give one's kid a competitive edge is **morally corrosive.**

The last two examples contain the adverb-adjective constructions. Example (14a) is taken from an article about plastic surgery. Those who receive it to look different in a certain way want to keep it secret in order to remain "physically and morally whole". Similar examples found in my data pool include *morally intact, morally broken,* and *morally destroyed.* As we can see, the key adjectives (including past participles) in this set can be divided into two groups: those that mean "remaining complete" and those that mean "causing or being caused to become incomplete". That is, they instantiate either MORAL IS WHOLE or IMMORAL IS BROKEN. As is common sense, when something remains whole or when the parts are combined into a whole, it is stronger than if the thing is split into parts or the parts stay divided. That is, the strength and weakness of things are related to whether they are whole or divided.

3.3.5 MORAL IS HEALTHY and IMMORAL IS ILL

The last pair of moral-physical metaphors involves HEALTHY and ILL as their source concepts. This pair of metaphors is again conceptually tied with the preceding ones based on our embodied experience. When we are healthy, we are physically strong, sound, and whole. When we are ill or sick, we are physically weaker, have less physical strength, and are no longer in a physically sound or whole condition. That is, in our life experience, our health and strength as well as our illness and weakness are correlated.

In the following, we look at some linguistic examples for illustration.

(15) a. Catholic social teaching emphasizes that the **moral health** of a nation is gauged by the way it treats its most vulnerable members.

    b. Problem drinking, they believed, was the root of her unhappiness and **moral illness**, as well as the symptom of her unhappiness and **moral illness** ...

In the above examples, (15a) manifests the positive pole, and (15b) the negative pole, of the conceptual scale between HEALTHINESS and ILLNESS. Similar to (15a) are *moral fitness* and *moral wellbeing.* The former involves the nominal form of the adjective *fit.* According to *Longman* (1978: 416), *fit* means "in good health" and "strong in bodily condition". The two definitions also exhibit the inherent connection between good health and physical strength. In the latter, "wellbeing" is of course more general, and wider in scope, than "good health" as its component.

(16) a. I'm not much of a philosopher, but I deeply believe that only phys-
         ically and **morally healthy** people will be able to revive and restore
         Russia.

      b. There are untold incidents of betrayal committed by these weak,
         morally sick wretches who had sought and obtained government
         employment.

These two examples are again distinguished in relations to whether the key
collocations express the positive or negative pole of the moral-immoral opposition. Synonymous expressions include *morally fit*, *morally ill*, and *morally
unfit*. All these collocations invoke the very general HEALTH frame, characterizing general health conditions as being either good or bad. In the following
examples, the more specific health conditions are evoked to give a sense
of where or what has gone wrong with one's "moral health". They evoke
more specific subcases of the general DISEASE frame, mapping richer inferential knowledge about specific kinds of disease onto the target domain of
MORALITY.

(17) a. He is pandering to the pro-life view which Nixon calls "**morally
         shortsighted**".

      b. Anyone who challenges their control is deemed a sexist, a racist, a
         xenophobe, and **morally deformed.**

For instance, (17a) suggests that the moral agent is "defected" or "diseased"
with the eyes or vision, and cannot see far. Another example is *morally blind*,
which suggests that the moral agent cannot see at all. In either case, they are
"ill" with their moral outlook. Other than IMMORAL IS ILL, these examples also
instantiate a primary conceptual metaphor, namely KNOWING IS SEEING or
KNOWLEDGE IS VISION. If people are "shortsighted" or "blind" morally, they
cannot "see" (i.e., know or understand) things that go wrong morally. In (17b),
the moral agents are "deformed". With this moral "disease", their bodies, or
one or more parts of them, are out of the normal shape. These examples are of
course metaphorical, residing under the common roof of the general metaphor
MIND IS BODY if "mind" is used broadly and loosely to refer to one's entire inner
life in mentality, spirituality, and morality.

(18) a. Yet there is no outrage and no response. How did we become so
         morally benumbed?

      b. As a society, we suffer today from a peculiar form of **moral
         anesthesia.**

In (18a), "benumbed" is the past participle of the transitive verb *benumb*, which means "to make numb, especially by cold". When "morally benumbed", one has lost one's "moral sense" and is unable to feel any "moral pain" or "moral distress", as if one has received "moral anesthesia" (18b). In addition, I also found such collocations as *moral paralysis* and *ethically handicapped*, which suggest total or partial disfunction of one's moral conscience.

(19) a. One senses a **moral cancer** beneath the surface: the all-American spirit of the music, far from including all Americans, actually seems a form of exclusion for people and issues.

   b. Yes you are, mentally dead, spiritually dead, **morally dead**.

As in (19a), the kind of "moral disease" one suffers can be "moral cancer". The moral agent who has contracted serious "moral cancer" would likely be "morally dead" (19b).

(20) a. His sense of **moral immunity**—that he was mostly good in the big picture, so it was OK to take small transgressions—was his greatest liability.

   b. "Muscular Christianity", fashionable during the Victorian era, prescribed sports as a sort of **moral vaccine** against the tumult of rapid economic growth.

As a moral disease, immorality can be "a plague that, if left unchecked, can spread throughout society, infecting everyone" (Lakoff and Johnson 1999: 309). That is, moral diseases may be contagious, like an epidemic or pandemic that has burst out, and therefore it may be necessary for people to have "moral immunity" (20a), which they can acquire from getting "moral vaccine" (20b). Besides, those who have already contracted moral diseases need to be treated in a moral sense. If moral diseases are widespread in a society, then the whole society needs a treatment.

(21) a. Like the American, the pope saw the need for a **moral treatment** of the problem.

   b. Rwanda needs not only physical rehabilitation, but a "**moral rehabilitation**", the formation of a new society in which killing is no longer accepted with impunity ...

   c. Whether or not the returned soldiers were brainwashed or whether they experienced a form of **moral regeneration** remains an open question.

According to the preceding context of (21a), racism is the problem of which the pope saw the need for a "moral treatment". If people have had their moral senses damaged or lost, then the best treatment is for them to go through a "moral rehabilitation" (21b). Only in this way can they receive a possible "moral regeneration" (21c).

In this section, we have seen some linguistic examples from COCA that show how the physical subsystem of moral metaphors, with its five pairs of moral-physical metaphors summarized under MORALITY IS PHYSICALITY, is manifested in the English language, with clusters of linguistic expressions evoking particular frames and subframes within physical domains. At this point, we will switch to Chinese for an analysis of its possible Chinese counterpart.

3.4 Physical moral metaphors in Chinese

In comparison with its counterpart in English, the linguistic manifestation in Chinese for MORALITY IS PHYSICALITY is not so much lexicalized with its metaphorical extension, but is realized more in the discourse. Table 3.3 provides five pairs of antonymous physical words in Chinese that can be seen as typically represent the five pairs of source concepts in Table 3.1. The lexicalized moral senses are taken from three popular Chinese dictionaries: HYDCD (2000 + online), XDHYCD (2016, 7th ed.), and XXDHYCD (1992). It must be pointed out upfront that these words, especially some of them, are not real "equivalents" to the English words encoding the source concepts. It may very well be the case that one English word has several Chinese "counterparts", but all of them occupy conceptual spaces that fall in the close neighborhood of the conceptual lot occupied by that English word. In this case, only one Chinese near "counterpart" is chosen which may at best partially overlap with the English original. In a sense, Table 3.3 should merely be taken as a "spaceholder" for the time being. There are apparently quite a few empty cells in it, which means that lexicalized moral senses are not found with the words in the dictionaries consulted. However, a very salient characteristic of present-day Chinese is the dominant use of compounding as a major morphological process. Therefore, many definitions of semantic extensions of words are provided not at the level of monosyllabic, single-character words, but at a lower level of a large number of compound words that contain the former as a component. Compound words usually combine single-character words with other single-character words to form disyllabic, two-character words. This will be seen in the discussion of specific examples below.

Table 3.3 Lexicalized moral senses of the physical words in the three Chinese dictionaries

Dictionary	HYDCD	XDHYCD	XXDHYCD
Word	**Conventionally lexicalized moral senses**		
美 *měi* "beautiful"	善 good (vs. evil); 好 good (vs. bad)	好事 good deed	美好 good
丑 *chǒu* "ugly"	邪恶 evil; 指坏人、恶人 bad people, evil people	叫人厌恶或看不起的 disgusting or contemptuous; 不好的、不光彩的事物 bad, disgraceful thing	可恶 hateful, detestable; 污秽 dirty; 指事物不好 something bad; 令人厌恶的, 可耻的 disgusting, shameful
强 *qiáng* "strong"			
弱 *ruò* "weak"			
鲜 *xiān* "fresh"			
腐 *fǔ* "rotten"	腐烂 rotten; 腐朽 decadent; 腐败 decayed; 腐化 corrupt; 腐蚀 corrode or corrosion	腐烂 rotten; 变坏 turning bad	腐烂 rotten, corrupt
完 *wán* "whole"			
缺 *quē* "incomplete"			
康 *kāng* "healthy"			
病 *bìng* "(be) ill"			

Specifically, as shown in the table, HYDCD provides the moral sense of the Chinese word for "beautiful", 美 *měi*, as 善 *shàn* "good", which contrasts with 恶 *è* "evil" as a pair of bipolar opposition in moral valence. The other two dictionaries only give more general senses "good deed" and "good", which are less specific to morality, although "morally good" is certainly included as their more specific subcategories. In the table, the third pair of antonyms is 鲜 *xiān* "fresh" and 腐 *fǔ* "rotten", of which the second is a close equivalent of English *rotten*, but the first, translated into English as "fresh", has an obvious gap with English *sound* in meaning. The English word *sound* was chosen in Tables 3.1 and 3.2 in the sense "free from flaw, defect, or decay", and in particular "free from decay", thus in contrast with *rotten*. The Chinese word 鲜 *xiān*, however, is somewhat equivalent to English *fresh*, in the sense "not stale, sour, decayed", used especially for such food as fruits, vegetables, and meat. Alternatively, a more general word in Chinese as a near counterpart of English *sound* is just 好 *hǎo* "good", in the sense of "qualitatively or substantially good", in contrast with 坏 *huài* "bad", that is, "qualitatively or substantially bad".

As shown in Table 3.3, none of the three Chinese dictionaries lists any moral sense of the word 鲜 *xiān* "fresh". According to HYDCD, however, some compound words with 鲜 *xiān* "fresh" as one of their two morphological components do have a moral sense, as shown in (22).

(22)　a.　冰鲜 *bīngxiān* (ice-fresh) 比喻品行高洁 "(*fig.*) of moral character, noble and unsullied"

　　　b.　不鲜 *bùxiān* (not-fresh) 不善; 不美 "unkind; not beautiful"

　　　c.　行鲜 *xíngxiān* (behavior-fresh) 行为光明 "of behavior guileless, aboveboard"

These words are not commonly used at all, and that is the reason why they are not collected in the other two dictionaries that are compiled for daily use. The negative word in the third pair is 腐 *fǔ* "rotten", which is often used as one of the two elements forming a compound word that can mean "decadent", "decayed", "corrupt" (see the definitions under HYDCD in Table 3.3), etc., which are readily interpretable in a moral sense. But its definitions in either XDHYCD (2016) or XXDHYCD (1992) are limited to more central senses of something (organic) turning bad even though these are readily extendable into the moral domain when combined with another element to form compounds.

As shown in Table 3.3, none of the six words in the remaining three pairs (the 2nd, 4th, and 5th) of antonyms have morality-specific meanings listed in any of the three dictionaries. What needs to be stressed again is that not having their moral meanings listed in the dictionaries does not mean that they cannot be used to express moral meanings. On the contrary, their moral meanings are realized at the level of lexical compounding or in the fiber and fabric of discourse. In the following, we will see how these and other related words manifest the underlying conceptual metaphors for morality in real-life discourses.

3.4.1 MORAL IS BEAUTIFUL and IMMORAL IS UGLY

As reviewed in section 3.2, the literature on psychological research looks at the interrelationship between beauty and goodness, including moral goodness, namely, the bidirectional stereotypes "What is beautiful is good" (e.g., Dion et al. 1972; Lemay et al. 2010) and "What is good is beautiful" (e.g., Gross and Crofton 1977; Little et al. 2006). More specifically, experimental studies showed that subjects tend to behave following moral codes more in the presence of beautiful faces than in the presence of less attractive faces (Wang et al. 2017). In fact, the close interrelationship between beauty and morality was supported by neural evidence demonstrated with fMRI data (Tsukiura and Cabeza 2011; Wang et al. 2015). All this empirical research is relevant to the pair of moral-physical metaphors MORAL IS BEAUTIFUL and IMMORAL IS UGLY.

The Chinese examples in (23), taken from the Corpus of the Center for Chinese Linguistics (CCL), illustrate how the beautiful and ugly are brought into contrast with each other, representing metaphorically what is moral and what is immoral, respectively.

(23) a. 古今中外, 真善美和假恶丑不容混淆, 公众心中也有一条道德红线。

In ancient or modern times, in China or elsewhere, the true, the good, and the **beautiful** cannot be confounded with the false, the evil, and the **ugly**, and there is also a moral red line in the heart of the public.

  b. 应及时对这一是非之争加以引导, 使人们在美与丑的鲜明对比中树立正确的道德观念。

There should be timely guidance through this debate on what is right and what is wrong so that people can establish the right moral sense in the clear contrast between the **beautiful** and the **ugly**.

  c. 他确实很清醒, 这样才会不知不觉地审视起道德来,
左看右看, 才发现好与坏、善与恶、美与丑等等等等,
并不是那么非此即彼的......

He was fully aware that this way he would start examining morality without knowing it, and looking around he would realize that good and bad, benevolent and evil, **beautiful** and **ugly**, and so on, are not so much in an either-or relationship ...

In (23a), the general public, anytime and anywhere, have a "moral red line" in their heart that distinguishes between what is moral and what is immoral. As in (23b), it would be easier to develop a moral sense in the clear contrast between the moral and the immoral. Example (23c) suggests that the distinction between the moral and the immoral may not be as clear as expected. There could be gray areas in between.

(24)   a.   我们向未成年人提倡的是中华传统道德中的"**美德**"。
            What we advocate to minors is the "**beautiful virtue**" in the traditional Chinese ethics.

       b.   读者......并从中领悟出正义必将战胜邪恶, **美好**必将取代**丑陋**的道德信念。
            The reader ... would also derive from it the moral belief that justice must triumph over evil and the **beautiful** (lit. **beautiful-good**) must substitute for the **ugly** (lit. **ugly-ugly**).

       c.   文章揭露了......一起车祸中, 个别人道德沦丧、见死不救的**丑恶**行为。
            The article exposed ... the **ugly** (lit. **ugly-evil**) behavior of some individuals who, having lost their moral sense, would not rescue the dying in a traffic accident.

The examples in (24) show that the Chinese words for "beautiful" and "ugly" are also combined with other words to form compounds used in a moral sense. Thus, virtue is perceived as beautiful in traditional ethics, hence the compound 美德 *měidé* "beautiful virtue" (24a). As in (24b) and (24c), "beautiful" co-occur with "good" (美好 *měihǎo*), and "ugly" with another "ugly" word (丑陋 *chǒulòu*) and with "evil" (丑恶 *chǒu'è*) in compounds. In (24b) the word for "justice" is 正义 *zhèngyì*, which literally means "upright righteousness". In Chinese, 正义 *zhèngyì* "justice" contrasts with 邪恶 *xié'è* "evil". Although the latter does not carry a spatial sense anymore in modern Chinese, its first component 邪 *xié*, however, used to have the same meaning as another homophonous word 斜 *xié*, which has purely spatial meanings "tilted; slanting; oblique; askew" in modern Chinese, according to HYDCD. That is, justice and evil, if traced back in time, literally mean "upright righteousness" and "slanted evil", respectively, instantiating MORAL IS UPRIGHT and IMMORAL IS SLANTED in their separate ways (see also section 5.4.2).

(25)   a.   全总树标兵、表彰先进的目的正在于推进职业道德的建设、**美化**我们的社会环境。

The purpose of the National Labor Union setting up role models and commending advanced workers consisted in promoting the construction of professional ethics and **beautifying** our social environment.

   b.   色情的东西有损于人性,是真正好的两性关系的**丑化**。

Pornographic stuff does damage to human nature, making real, good sexual relations appear **ugly**.

The two examples in (25) show that the Chinese words for "beautiful" and "ugly" can undergo a morphological process which adds a derivational suffix 化 *huà* denoting a change. The process, in these two cases, changes the adjectives into causative verbs meaning "make X beautiful" (美化 *měihuà* "beautify") and "make X ugly" (丑化 *chǒuhuà* "smear; vilify", lit. ugli-fy) respectively. As in (25a), the purpose of "beautifying the social environment" is to moralize it. Pornography is immoral because it makes sexuality look "ugly" (25b).

3.4.2 MORAL IS STRONG and IMMORAL IS WEAK

In the discussion of how this pair of moral-physical metaphors is manifested in English, I already suggested that it is related to and coherent with the preceding and following pairs. In short, the strength and weakness of something depend on whether it is sound or rotten materially and structurally. Furthermore, its strength and weakness determine if it will remain whole or get broken with the impact of external forces or as a result of internal causes. Moreover, being beautiful is regarded as a strength and being ugly a weakness.

Let us now see some CCL examples of how the pair of moral-physical metaphors, MORAL IS STRONG and IMMORAL IS WEAK, is instantiated in natural discourses in Chinese.

(26)   a.   道德是**强大**的社会制约,是绝大多数人都能自觉遵守的行为规范。

Morality is a **strong** (lit. **strong-big**) social constraint, being norms of behavior with which the majority of people consciously comply.

b. 关键是......真正化作一种道德情感和道德观念,
    形成**强大**的道德力量, 从而用以去规范人们的行为。

    The key is ... to truly transform it into a kind of moral sentiment
    and moral conception, thus forming a **strong** (lit. **strong-big**)
    moral force, which will regulate the behavior of people.

c. 他们想用具有更**坚实**的道德基础的规范, 去取代他们认为
    在道义上受怀疑的那些规范。

    They wanted to use norms with an even more **solid** (lit. **sturdy-
    solid**) moral base to replace the norms which they believed were
    questionable in terms of morality and justice.

As all three examples in (26) show, morality is social norms applied to regulating people's social behavior. It is a "strong" (强大 *qiángdà*) social constraint by
which most people consciously obey (26a). This is because morality, with its
"strong moral force", plays a powerful social function in regulating human behavior (26b), and serves as a "solid" (坚实 *jiānshí*) moral foundation for such
regulation (26c). It is worth noting that, syntactically, the "strong" and "solid"
adjectives modify "social constraint", "moral force", and "moral foundation".
A question to ask is: Do they instantiate the conceptual metaphors MORAL
IS STRONG and IMMORAL IS WEAK? The answer is yes. In all these constructions, the "morality" and "moral" words represent the target concept whereas
"strong constraint", "strong force", and "solid foundation" represent the source
concepts (see Sullivan 2013 for discussions of how grammatical constructions
instantiate conceptual metaphors). In such cases, STRONG and SOLID only correlate and covary with MORAL, in contrast with WEAK that merely goes with
lack of morality or immorality.

While morality is a "strong" force regulating human behavior at a social
level, it is also a decisive factor in determining whether a human being has
a "strong" or "weak" moral character at an individual level, as illustrated by
the examples in (27) and (28).

(27) a. 毋忘"我"也包括建立**强大**的道德自我。

          Not forgetting "me" also includes building a **strong** (lit. **strong-
          big**) moral self.

      b. 她的艺术魅力源于她**坚强**的道德观......

          Her artistic charm originates in her **strong** (lit. **solid-strong**)
          moral conception ...

      c. 一位衷心地热爱自己的事业, 忘我地、全身心地投入到自己
          的工作中去的教师, 他的一言一 行, 便具有了**强大**的道德感
          召力。

A teacher who sincerely loves his/her own career, and who is self-lessly and whole-heartedly devoted to his/her work, naturally possesses a **strong** (lit. **strong-big**) moral appeal in whatever he/she says and does.

As in (27a), a moral person has a "strong" moral self. Importantly, one's "strong" moral conception that goes with one's "strong" moral self is the source of one's success in other aspects of one's career (27b). Example (27c) shows that a selfless and devoted moral person has a "strong" moral appeal that yields a strong impact on the people around. In all these examples, the moral agents are people of moral integrity. In other words, they are morally "whole". As already explained, the conceptual coherence based on physical experience is such that what can stand "whole" is "strong" whereas what has gone "broken" is "weak". That is to say, there is conceptual association between being "whole" and being "strong", and vice versa. If being moral is being "whole", being moral is being "strong" too. Such conceptual correlation or association is the grounding for MORAL IS STRONG and IMMORAL IS WEAK.

(28) a.   ……**脆弱**的道德堤防, 宛似烈日下的融冰, 顿时消逝无踪。
            … the **fragile** (lit. **fragile-weak**) moral dams, just like melting ice under the scorching sun, suddenly disappeared without a trace.

      b.   这一情况无疑将会为世人所知……而且会被认为是您的一个**懦弱**和不道德的行为。
            This will, beyond doubt, be widely known … and will be believed to be a **cowardly** (lit. **cowardly-weak**) and immoral act of yours.

In (28a), as can be seen, one's moral sense is said to be "dams" that help stop the flooding of immorality. However, if the "dams" are "fragile" and "weak", they are useless. In this case, the "weak" moral sense is said to be like "ice" under the "scorching sun", which would soon melt down and disappear without a trace (cf. 13b). As in (28b), an immoral act is at the same time "cowardly" and "weak". Again, it is conceptual association that is in play. That is, immoral acts are always associated conceptually with, for instance, "pettiness", "weakness", or "crookedness", as much as the reverse is true with moral acts, which are always associated conceptually with, say, a "great" person, a "strong" body, or an "upright" body posture. This is for the same reason why terrorism, which is extremely immoral and evil, is always said to be "cowardly" even if terrorists can be and often are suicidal. Being "cowardly", terrorists are "ill", not "healthy", "weak" rather than "strong".

The examples in (29) show that one's morality can be "strengthened" or "weakened", which will result in one becoming more or less moral as a person.

(29) a. 一年来, 该院......**强化**医务人员的职业道德和修养, 使医
疗作风有了较大改观。

In the past year, this hospital … has **strengthened** its medical
personnel's professional ethics and self-cultivation so that their
work style has improved considerably.

b. 北京大学开展了以提高学生道德修养水平和培养良好行为习惯
为目标的 "**加强**道德修养, 促进校园文明建设" 的活动。

Peking University administered the activities to "**strengthen**
(lit. **add-strength**) moral cultivation and spurs campus civility
construction" in order to achieve the goal of raising the level of
moral cultivation and fostering good behavioral habits among its
students.

c. 正人先正己, 成年人首先需要**增强**近年来有所**弱化**的道德感。

In order to straighten others, one must straighten oneself first;
adults should first **strengthen** (lit. **increase-strength**) their moral
sense that has been **weakened** in the past few years.

d. 社会责任感和道德感**淡化**, 社会理想、信念和自我牺牲
精神**弱化**......

The senses of social responsibility and morality have been
weakened (lit. **made-thin/diluted**), and social ideals and beliefs
as well as the spirit of self-sacrifice have been **weakened** …

In (29a–c), three different compound words with the meaning of "strengthen"
are used: 强化 *qiánghuà* (lit. make-strong), 加强 *jiāqiáng* (lit. add-strength),
and 增强 *zēngqiáng* (lit. increase-strength), all of them containing the word
for "strong". In (29c), 正人 *zhèngrén* (lit. straighten-people) and 正己 *zhèngjǐ*
(lit. straighten-self) are both used in a moral sense. That is, people have to
first "straighten themselves morally" before they should attempt to "straighten
others morally" (cf. MORAL IS UPRIGHT and IMMORAL IS SLANTED, and MORAL
IS STRAIGHT and IMMORAL IS CROOKED; see Chapter 5). Examples (29c) and
(29d) each contain a word that means "weaken": 弱化 *ruòhuà* (lit. make-weak)
and 淡化 *dànhuà* (lit. make-thin, light, or diluted). When people have a "weak",
"thin", or "diluted" sense of morality, they are more prone to behave immorally.
In (29d), "the spirit of self-sacrifice" is morally lofty, but if it is "weakened",
people who possess it become less selfless and more selfish.

   Now, let us turn to the next pair of moral metaphors: MORAL IS SOUND and
IMMORAL IS ROTTEN.

3.4.3 MORAL IS SOUND and IMMORAL IS ROTTEN

In this pair of moral metaphors, the two source concepts, SOUND and ROTTEN, describe the condition which some object or substance is in, namely its essence or quality. The former refers to its original "good" condition whereas the latter refers to its changed "bad" condition. The change in the internal state, however, may also, and often will, bring about a change in the appearance of the object or substance. Thus, something may look fresh, stale, decayed, and so on. Fresh-looking things are good, and stale- or decayed-looking things are bad. Also, things that are new and fresh and look "beautiful" can become "ugly" when they turn staled and decayed. Look at the examples in (30).

(30) a. 苏格拉底......提出了理性的、道德的人的思想, 对人的**本质**进行了规定。
          Socrates ... put forward the idea of rational and moral person, stipulating the **essence** (lit. **root/original-quality**) of the human being.

     b. ......不断增强政治上的坚定性和思想道德上的纯洁性, ...永保人民军队的**性质**、**本色**和作风。
          ... to continually strengthen the political resolution and ideological and moral purity ... so that the **quality**, the **character** (lit. **original-color**), and the style of the people's army will be preserved forever.

     c. 但是有的人没有经受住权力、金钱、美色的考验, **腐化变质**, 既断送了自己, 也损害了党和政府的形象。
          But some of them could not stand the tests of power, money, or beauty, and became **corrupted** (lit. **rotten**) and **degenerate** (lit. **changed-quality**), thus ending their career as well as damaging the image of the party and the government.

     d. ......抵制......**腐朽**思想的**侵蚀**和影响, 保证我们党永不**变色**。
          ... resist ... the **erosion** and influence of **rotten and decadent** (lit. **rotten and decayed**) ideas so that our party will never **change color** (i.e., **become morally corrupt**).

According to example (30a), Socrates stipulated human nature as including two crucial aspects: being rational and being moral. In other words, human beings should be rational and moral beings by nature, and rationality and morality are part and parcel of their "original quality". Examples (30b–d) are situated in the political discourse of contemporary China, where the anti-corruption campaign has been a major battle against corrupt elements in the party, the government, and the People's Liberation Army (PLA) for the past few years. In (30b), the compound 本色 *běnsè*, literally "original color", refers to the distinctive character of something. This "original color" matches the "original quality" (本质 *běnzhì* "essence; nature") of the thing (cf. 30a). If its "original quality" has changed, its "original color" should change accordingly. The change of color is an index to the change of quality. Examples (30c) and (30d), which contain the compounds 变质 *biànzhì* (lit. change-quality) and 变色 *biànsè* (lit. change-color) respectively, show that both the "original quality" and the "original color" will "change" as a result of moral degeneration of the moral agent, resulting from "corruption" (腐化 *fǔhuà*) as well as "erosion" (侵蚀 *qīnshí*) of "rotten and decayed" (腐朽 *fǔxiǔ*) ideas. Such ideas can "corrupt" and "erode" the moral character of a vulnerable moral agent. In (30c) the moral agent is those officials of the party and the government who failed the tests of power, money, and beauty as individuals. In (30b) and (30d) the moral agent is the "people's army" and the "party" as collectives.

As discussed above, the two sentences in (30c) and (30d) each contain a Chinese compound word with 腐 *fǔ* "rotten" as a morphological component, which is often used in connection with moral corruption and degeneration. In (30c), 腐化 *fǔhuà* "degenerate; corrupt; depraved" is a derived word consisting of the stem *fǔ* "rotten" and the causative suffix *huà*, thus having the literal meaning "to cause X to be rotten" (cf. 25a and 25b). In (30d), 腐朽 *fǔxiǔ* (lit. rotten-decayed) is a compound meaning "decadent; depraved; dissolute; degenerate; rotten". In fact, a few other Chinese compound words with similar meanings are used in such a moral sense. Those in (31) are more examples.

(31) a. 他思想蜕化, 道德堕落, 是一个极为典型的**腐败**分子。
He was ideologically and morally degenerate (lit. ideologically exuviated and morally fallen), being an extremely typical **corrupt** (lit. **rotten-spoiled**) element.

  b. 《红楼梦》中的色情描写, 多数是暴露封建贵族家庭荒淫**腐烂**的人伦关系。
The depictions of sex in *Dream of the Red Chamber* mostly expose the dissolute and **decadent** (lit. **rotten-rotten**) human relations in the feudal aristocratic family.

c. 社会风气**糜烂**, 对人心的**腐蚀**最大。

The social morals are **rotten** (lit. **rotten-rotten**), thus **corroding** (lit. **rotting** and **corroding**) the human hearts to the largest extent.

d. 既有作者对新道德的追求, 也有为**陈腐**的儒家道德的说教。

There is not only the author's pursuit of new ethics, but also his preaching for the **obsolete** (lit. **stale and rotten**) Confucian ethics.

e. 王代表说: "法制是最好的'**防腐剂**'"。

Representative Wang said, "Legal system is the best 'antiseptic'".

All these examples contain compound words that denote a change in state and quality from a "good" to a "bad" condition. In (31a) the moral agent has undergone "ideological exuviation and moral fall", and for that matter has become a "rotten and spoiled" (腐败 *fǔbài* "decadent; degenerate; corrupt") element. In (31b), *Dream of the Red Chamber* is one of the best known classic Chinese novels containing some sexual descriptions. The aim, however, is at exposing the "rotten and rotten" (腐烂 *fǔlàn* "decadent; corrupt") human relations in a big feudal aristocratic family. What (31c) suggests is that the morals have gone "rotten and rotten" (糜烂 *mílàn* "rotten; dissipated; debauched") at the societal level, which is doing the greatest damage to individuals' hearts (and minds) by "corroding" (腐蚀 *fǔshí* "corrupt; deprave") them. Example (31d) contains 陈腐 *chénfǔ* "stale; old and decayed; outworn; obsolete"), which literally means "stale and rotten". In all these examples, one key element is 腐 *fǔ* "rotten", referring to the change in quality or essence of some material that has gone bad and decayed. As part of the linguistic instantiation of the conceptual metaphor IMMORAL IS ROTTEN, the word 防腐剂 *fángfǔjì* "antiseptic; preservative", i.e., the chemical fluid for the purpose of preventing things from getting rotten, is also used metaphorically to mean "measures or means taken to prevent moral degeneration or corruption", as exemplified by (31e). Only a sound legal system can effectively prevent corruption from spreading in a society.

Note in (31a) that the use of the word 蜕化 *tuìhuà* "exuviate; (morally) degenerate" is related to the Chinese conceptualization of corrupt elements as "dangerous eggs" (危卵 *wēiluǎn*), "borers; moths; insects" (蛀虫 *zhùchóng*), "worms; vermin" (蠹虫 *dùchóng*), and "parasites" (寄生虫 *jìshēngchóng*), which, though very small in size, can do great damage to the material in which they stay and on which they feed. They cause things to become rotten and decayed. Given in (32) are some examples of this sort.

(32) a. ......他以权谋私, 中饱私囊, 是一个十恶不赦的国家**蛀虫**。

          ... he abused his power for personal gains, diverted public money to his private purse, and was therefore a national **borer** that was too wicked to be pardoned.

    b. 他从一个受领导、同事好评的党员干部**堕落**为一个社会的 **蠹虫**, 其自身私欲恶性膨胀, 无视党纪、国法, 是导致他犯罪 的主要原因。

          From a party member and an official commended by his leaders and colleagues, he **degenerated** (lit. **fall-fall**) into social **vermin**; it was his selfish desires expanding without limits and his disregard of the party disciplines and national laws that were the major causes leading to his crimes.

    c. 你的内心里有一丝细微的声音在说: "你是行尸走肉, 你是社会 的**寄生虫**, 你在世上白占一块空间。"

          You could hear a faint (lit. **thin and tiny**) voice speaking in your heart: "You're a walking corpse, you're a social **parasite**, and you're occupying a space in this world for no good".

The kinds of small insects or worms mentioned in these examples can do great harm to the things in or on which they live because they either eat into and do damage to them or they make them weak or sick in the case of human or animal bodies. For example, termites are one kind of 蛀虫 *zhùchóng* "borer; moth", and they are very destructive to trees and wood structures. In the examples in (32), people who are said metaphorically to be such small insects or worms are immoral because they do harm to the wellbeing of a society as a whole.

3.4.4 MORAL IS WHOLE and IMMORAL IS BROKEN

As already explained previously in the discussion of its English counterpart, this pair of conceptual metaphors for morality is closely related to the preceding three. Something that is sound in substance and structure is more likely to remain as a "whole" than the same thing if it is rotten. In the latter case, the thing that is rotten is easier to split into parts or pieces, i.e., "broken", because it is no longer strong, solid, or firm. Besides, what is beautiful as a "whole" can be very ugly if it is "broken" into pieces. Now look at the examples in (33).

(33) a. 有所不为才能保持道德人格的**完整**。
          One can maintain the **integrity** (lit. **wholeness and complete-ness**) of one's moral character only if one can restrict oneself from doing certain things.

      b. 单就作为社会的人来说, 我以为他的道德也几近**完满**。
          Just speaking of him as a social person, I believe his morality is almost **perfect** (lit. **whole and full**).

      c. 她执着地追求**完美**的道德风尚。
          She insists on seeking **flawless** (lit. **whole and beautiful**) moral practice.

      d. 她说修理花园界为了使它完好无损也意味着她修补道德的栅栏, 到它**完好**为止。
          She said that she repaired the garden fence to keep it intact, which also meant that she was mending the moral fence until it was **in good condition** (lit. **whole and good**).

      e. 传统经典以伦理纲常为核心, 强调道德人格的主体**完善**。
          Traditional classics center around moral principles and ethics, stressing the subject **perfection** (lit. **whole and good**) of the moral character.

The key element in all five examples is the Chinese word 完 *wán* "whole", which in all five cases is combined with another word to form a compound to characterize the moral integrity or perfection of some moral agent. As in (33a), people's moral "integrity" (完整 *wánzhěng*, lit. whole-complete) lies in restraining themselves from doing certain things that are considered immoral. Example (33b) is about a late Chinese mathematician, who the author believes was almost "perfect" (完满 *wánmǎn*, lit. whole-full) in his moral integrity. In example (33c), the moral agent aims at "flawless" (完美 *wánměi*, lit. whole-beautiful) moral practice in her attempt to reach moral perfection. The moral agent in (33d) regards her habitual act of repairing the garden fence as a symbolic way of pursuing moral perfection. To her, the garden fence being "in good condition" (完好 *wánhǎo*, lit. whole-good) means solid and firm moral boundaries that stop any moral transgressions. In (33e), which pertains to the Confucian classics on moral principles and ethics, moral integrity means that the moral subject of a human person should be maintained in "whole and good" (完善 *wánshàn*) condition, through self-cultivation. All five examples in (33) instantiate the positive parameter of the pair of moral metaphors, MORAL IS WHOLE. The examples provided below instantiate its negative version, IMMORAL IS BROKEN.

(34) a. 评论家撰文说这件事展示了国民素质和道德的**残缺**。
Critics wrote essays arguing that this incident exhibited the **incompleteness** of the national quality and morality.

b. 当人们终于发现那种政治本身是空洞的乃至罪恶的时候，道德也随之**瓦解**。
When people eventually discovered that that kind of politics was hollow and even evil, morality would **fall apart** with that discovery.

c. ……道德**崩溃**不是由于西方文化固有的弱点, 而是工业化的结果。
… moral **collapse** was not due to the inherent weakness of Western culture, but was a consequence of industrialization.

While the examples in (33) focus on the wholeness of morality as an object (hence the OBJECT image schema), which represents the positive valence of moral assessment, the examples in (34) evoke the imagery of incompleteness or disintegration of morality, i.e., the sense of morality as an object is either damaged or lost. Thus, (34a) suggests that morality is "incomplete" (残缺 *cánquē*, lit. fragmentary with parts missing) at the national level, seen through a particular incident. Example (34b) again suggests a moral issue at a social level as people find morality "falling apart" (瓦解 *wǎjiě*) as a result of politics being "hollow" and "evil". In (34c), moral "collapse" (崩溃 *bēngkuì*) in the West is attributed to industrialization rather than culture.

(35) a. 道德! 一个声音在大喊。我都要去死了,道德也不复存在了。……赵钢心中的天平在这无声的对话中倾斜了, **坍塌**了。
Morality! A voice was screaming. I'm going to die, and morality won't exist anymore. … The scales in Zhao Gang's heart tilted, and then **collapsed**, in this voiceless dialogue (i.e., monologue).

b. 如果忽视了道德修养, 同样会出现道德**滑坡**的问题。
If moral cultivation is neglected, there will emerge the problem of a moral **landslide**.

Compared with those in (34), the two examples in (35) set their metaphorical mappings at a more specific level of frames. In (35a), the moral sense of an individual is the "scales" (天平 *tiānpíng*, lit. heaven-level), a weighing instrument and a common symbol for moral balance and legal justice (cf. MORAL IS

LEVEL and IMMORAL IS UNLEVEL; see section 5.4.3). Unfortunately, this instrument of moral "scales" in the individual's heart "tilted" and "collapsed", which means, metaphorically, that the person has lost his moral balance and then his moral sense. In this case, that the moral scales "tilted" instantiates IMMORAL IS SLANTED (see section 5.4.2), and that the moral scales "collapsed" instantiates IMMORAL IS BROKEN. In (35b), the use of the word 滑坡 *huápō* "landslide" evokes the image of morality being a mountain with steep sides. In the relevant frame of encyclopedic knowledge, mountains like this may undergo landslides caused by external forces such as continuous heavy rains and earthquakes. As a result, the parts of the mountain that are sliding will be "collapsing" (i.e., IMMORAL IS BROKEN) and "falling down" (cf. MORAL IS HIGH and IMMORAL IS LOW; see section 5.4.1).

(36) a. 文学批评承担着思想改造、道德**建设**的重任......
          Literary criticism shoulders the heavy responsibility of ideological remold and moral **construction** ...

      b. 这是道德受到严重损害、而且缺少道德**重建**能力的一个重要原因。
          This is an important reason why morality has been seriously damaged, yet ability is lacking to **reconstruct** it.

As we have seen in (34) and (35), with the metaphorical mapping, morality, at an individual or a societal level, is conceptualized as an object, small or huge in size, which could "fall apart" or "collapse". In (35b), for instance, morality at the societal level could be a "mountain" in danger of landslides. The examples in (36) show that morality could also be a large artificial object, like a building of enormous size, which could be "constructed" (建设 *jiànshè*), and "reconstructed" (重建 *chóngjiàn*) if it is damaged. The conceptual contrasts deployed for source concepts are HIGH VS. LOW, WHOLE VS. BROKEN, and additionally STRONG VS. WEAK, and SOUND VS. ROTTEN.

3.4.5 MORAL IS HEALTHY and IMMORAL IS ILL

The last pair of moral metaphors is again closely related to and coherent with the preceding ones in an obvious way. Health is correlated with strength and illness with weakness. Also, healthy people are physically sound and whole. Being broken is associated with bodily injuries and wounds, and being rotten is linked to physiological diseases and sicknesses, with which people are no longer healthy. It is common-sense knowledge that illnesses harm people's health and weaken their physical (as well as mental) wellbeing. In the metaphorical conceptualization of morality, a moral person is a "healthy" person whereas an immoral person is an "ill" or "sick" one. This metaphorical conceptualization is also extended to society via the conceptual metaphor SOCIETY IS PERSON.

Please look at the following examples:

(37) a. 世界卫生组织最近给健康下了一个新定义: 除了躯体健康, 心理健康和社会适应良好外, 还要加上道德**健康**。

The World Health Organization recently put forth a new definition of "health": What should be added to physical health, mental health, and good social adaptivity is moral **health.**

b. 青年志愿者行动......有利于引导青年树立良好风尚, 抵制各种**不健康**道德观念的侵蚀。

Young volunteers' action ... helped lead youth to foster good social ethics and resist the corrosion of **unhealthy** moral conception.

c. 在一个社会中, 如果言论自由竟发展成撒谎自由, 这就说明这个社会的道德观出了**毛病**。

If, in a society, freedom of speech evolves into freedom of lie, it means this society is **diseased** with its moral conception.

d. 对物质财富的挥霍态度, 这是最可怕的**道德病**, 别的许多**道德病**也由之而生。

The most dreadful **moral disease** is the extravagant attitude toward material wealth, from which many other **moral diseases** spring up.

e. 文学目睹了社会生活中随着现代工业和商业文明到来的种种**弊病**和负面现象, 特别是社会道德秩序的滑坡现象......

Literature witnessed various kinds of social **ills** and negative phenomena that came along with the arrival of modern industry and business culture, especially the phenomenon of landslides in social and moral orders ...

According to (37a), the World Health Organization (WHO) extended the definition of "health" to the realm of morality, which can be seen as an instance of metaphorical extension. Thus, immoral conception is "not healthy" (不健康 *bù jiànkāng*) (37b) or "diseased" (毛病 *máobìng*) (37c), and one of the most dreadful "moral diseases" (道德病 *dàodé bìng*) is the extravagant consumption of material wealth (37d). It is suggested that various kinds of social "ills" (弊病 *bìbìng*), such as "landslides in social and moral orders" (cf. 35b), came with industrialization and commercialization (37e).

In the examples in (38) the mappings from disease to morality are made at a more specific level in frame structure, with reference to particular kinds of diseases, especially fatal diseases.

(38) a. 如果听任这种**瘟疫**传布, 将诱使许多意志不坚定的人道德败坏, 精神堕落。

If this kind of **plague** is allowed to spread, it will lure many people without strong will into moral corruption and spiritual degeneration.

b. 如今, 偷窃行为犹如**癌细胞**一般在我们的社会**肌体**上扩散、蔓延, 已成为百姓生活中的一大祸害……

Today, stealing is just like **cancer cells** that are proliferating and spreading in our social **body** (lit. **muscular body**), having become a major disaster in the life of ordinary people …

c. 色情服务、卖淫嫖娼这类行为, 自古以来, 就被视为是有伤风化、道德败坏的行为, 被视为社会的 "**顽症**" 和 "**毒瘤**"。

Ever since ancient times, pornography and prostitution have been seen as behaviors of moral corruption and degeneration, and as "**persistent diseases**" and "**malignant tumors**" in our society.

d. 对于这种奴性之劣, 人格之贱已**深入骨髓**的文人, 我们就不浪费笔墨了。

We will not waste our words commenting on those men of letters who have base servility and inferior personality **deep in their bone marrows.**

In (38a), "plague" (瘟疫 *wēnyì*), which is known to be highly contagious and spread very fast, actually refers to "cultural garbage", which pollutes the moral environment of a society. In (38b), the immoral conduct of stealing is said to be "cancer cells" (癌细胞 *áixìbāo*) that are "proliferating and spreading". We know too well that people in such critical conditions are doomed to die soon, but the knowledge about the source domain, with the CANCER DISEASE frames, is mapped onto the society as a "muscular body" (肌体 *jītǐ*). In (38c), pornography and prostitution are said to be "persistent diseases" (顽症 *wánzhèng*) and "malignant tumors" (毒瘤 *dúliú*) that fatally threaten the wellbeing of a society. As in (38d), we know when diseases like cancer spread "deep into bone marrows", they are fatal and hard to treat. All these examples show that moral diseases can be very dangerous to a society and should be treated and contained before they spread.

(39) a. 本书最为典型, 说明 "美国家庭生活" 中不断加速发展
的道德**病态**问题。

This book is most typical, illustrating the fast-evolving problems
of moral **morbid state** in "American family life".

  b. 不言而喻, ...道德意志是可以**锻炼**的。

It goes without saying that ... moral will can be **trained** (lit.
forge-smelted).

  c. 领导干部要......增强拒腐防变的 "**免疫力**" 。

Leaders and officials should ... increase their "**immunity**" against
corruption and degeneration.

As the examples in (39) show, moral problems constitute a "morbid state"
(病态 *bìngtài*) where people with moral issues are "sickly looking" (39a). As
much as one's physical wellbeing can be strengthened through "physical training" (锻炼 *duànliàn*) and workout, one's moral strength can be increased
through "moral exercise" in a similar way (39b). This, of course, must be mental rather than physical "training". The purpose of such "training" is to increase
one's "immunity" (免疫力 *miǎnyìlì*) against moral corruption or degeneration
(39c).

It is reported that the anti-corruption campaign that has been going on in
China in the past years to "raise the moral level" (提高道德水平 *tígāo dàodé
shuǐpíng*) of the party members has a thematic slogan attributed to Xi Jinping,
the Party General Secretary. That is: 照镜子、正衣冠、洗洗澡、治治病,
which, by literal translation, means "Look in the mirror, straighten the dress
and hat, take a bath, and treat illnesses". The slogan, which calls for "self-
examination and rectification" in a moral sense (and in a legal sense as well
in more serious cases), is of course based on some moral metaphors that have
been discussed in this chapter and will be discussed in the two chapters that
follow (i.e., MORAL IS LIGHT and IMMORAL IS DARK, MORAL IS CLEAN and IM-
MORAL IS DIRTY, MORAL IS STRAIGHT and IMMORAL IS CROOKED; MORAL IS
HEALTHY and IMMORAL IS ILL). In response, the Commission for Discipline Inspection of the Central Committee conducts "inspection tours" (巡视 *xúnshì*)
to uncover moral corruption (and legal crimes) and corrupt officials. As an
instantiation of MORAL IS HEALTHY and IMMORAL IS ILL, such tours are also
called "physical check-ups" (体检 *tǐjiǎn*) conducted to "diagnose" moral and
legal diseases of the party.

(40) a. 拜金主义这个怪物, 浑身弥漫着**传染性极强的细菌和病毒**,
倘若我们不采取有效的**大剂量的抗菌药物**予以扼杀,
势必会……把人的道德、情操、信念、理想统统**腐蚀掉**。
The monster of Mammonism (lit. money-worship-ism) is permeated **with extremely contagious bacteria and viruses**; if we do
not kill them with **high doses of antibiotics**, they will certainly …
rot human morals, sentiments, beliefs, and ideals in their entirety.

b. 哲学批判是防止社会腐败和制度恶化的重要武器, 哲学批判
是文化的**消毒剂**和**防腐剂**。
Philosophical criticism is an important weapon to prevent social corruption and institutional deterioration, and it is the
disinfectant for and **antiseptic** of culture.

c. 党委成员……发现不好的苗头及时提醒、教育,加固思想上、
道德上的防线。用他们的话说,这样做叫 "打**预防针**"。
After the party committee members … saw symptoms of a bad
development, they would send out reminders for educational purpose, thus consolidating the ideological and moral defense line. In
their words, this was to "give **vaccine shots**".

d. 儒家管理哲学……成为拯救社会道德危机的 "救世**药方**"。
The Confucian philosophy of management … became the "world-
saving **prescription**" to rescue the society from moral crises.

e. 中国的婚姻与家庭, 是否要付同样的代价在长出巨型
毒瘤大出血后再动**大手术**?
Should Chinese marriages and families pay the same price as a
major surgery only after the growing of a huge **malignant tumor**
has caused a **massive hemorrhage**?

The examples in (40) are further linguistic examples that instantiate the conceptual metaphors MORAL IS HEALTHY and IMMORAL IS ILL. The structures
(elements and relations) in the DISEASE frame have been enriched considerably through elaborations on various kinds and aspects of diseases, their
symptoms and treatments. Thus, the common practice of money worship is
a social "monster" that carries and spreads extremely contagious "bacteria"
(细菌 *xìjūn*) and "viruses" (病毒 *bìngdú*) that would cause "moral diseases"
and put the social "body" in jeopardy (40a). To kill bacteria and viruses and to
prevent things from getting rotten it is common to use "disinfectant" (消毒剂

xiāodújì) and "antiseptic" (防腐剂 *fángfǔjì*) as means of prevention and treatment (40b). In medicine, a very common measure taken to prevent contagious diseases from spreading is to provide "vaccine shots" (预防针 *yùfángzhēn*). The same measure can be taken for "moral diseases" as well (40c). Diseases are often treated with "prescriptions" (药方 *yàofāng*) of medication, and this is also the case for the treatment of social and moral crises (40d). Not every disease, however, can be treated with a prescription. In (40e), for instance, the treatment of a huge malignant tumor calls for a major "surgery" (手术 *shǒushù*). In its social and moral sense, "surgical treatment" usually implies some kind of "social operation" that would cause "social pain" in the "social body".

As we have seen, the source concepts involved in this section form a coherent network that includes a number of elements in the HEALTH domain. Diseases could be epidemic, cancer, tumor, or something that penetrates into bone marrows. A body that is strong through physical training or possesses immunity is more resistant to illness like these. Diseases are often caused by contagious bacteria and viruses, which need to be treated with prescriptions or antibiotics, or prevented by vaccine shots, disinfectant, or antiseptic. Cancer and tumors, however, are often treated with surgery.

3.5 Summary

In summary, the moral-physical metaphor subsystem, as discussed in this chapter, with the source domain centering on the wellbeing of physical entities, human beings included, with respect to their outer looks and inner states. The five dimensions of properties of physical being have bipolar values with scalar opposition to each other: BEAUTIFUL and UGLY, STRONG and WEAK, SOUND and ROTTEN, WHOLE and BROKEN, and HEALTHY and ILL. They serve as source concepts mapped onto their respective target concepts, MORAL and IMMORAL, in corresponding positive and negative parametric versions of moral metaphors. It is argued that these MORAL and IMMORAL metaphors build on the contrast between the good and bad feelings about physical wellbeing and illbeing in embodied human experience.

As we have seen, both English and Chinese resort to the moral-physical metaphors in their natural discourses, even though most of the physical words encoding the source concepts do not have lexicalized moral senses listed in the major English and Chinese dictionaries. This commonality arises from a fundamental understanding of morality based on human experience with bodies and objects, especially with regard to their appearance and essence. Such human experience could be positive or negative, good or bad, depending on specific configurations of the components that constitute the appearance or essence. What is especially relevant to my study is the fact that human morality is conceptualized in terms of metaphor arising from our embodied experience. First, fundamentally, MIND IS BODY, where MIND includes morality as one of the cognitive aspects of the human subject, and BODY includes bodily states and conditions felt internally and bodily experience in the interaction with external objects. Second, and more specifically, morality, which is abstract in nature, is construed metaphorically as some sort of physical being with a particular physical shape, structure, and substance, i.e., the general conceptual metaphor MORALITY IS PHYSICALITY. This physical being can look "beautiful" or "ugly", "strong" or "weak", "whole" or "broken"; it can also be "sound" or "rotten", "healthy" or "ill". It is these conceptual oppositions that serve as source concepts mapped onto their respective target concepts MORAL and IMMORAL. Third, this metaphorical understanding is further mapped from the individual to the societal level via the metaphor SOCIETY IS BODY or SOCIETY IS PERSON. By this metaphor, a society is conceptualized as a human person with an organic body, and medical conditions afflicting the human body can intrude into a society as well.

In this chapter, we have seen some good examples of how metaphorical mappings can be established at different levels of schematicity or specificity in both English and Chinese. For example, the conceptual opposition between MORAL and IMMORAL can be achieved on the generic contrast between BEAU-TIFUL and UGLY, which, though pointing to a direction for moral imagination, does not lead to direct access to specific images in metaphorical mapping. Concrete images, however, can be forged when the contrast goes down to a more specific level, say, between ANGELIC and MONSTROUS (see 2c). At this level, a more elaborate frame structure is triggered, evoking rich images based on our knowledge about how angels and monsters look and act. It is worth noting that cultural differences can certainly emerge from the same cognitive process, because the concrete images invoked in different cultures can be very different, arising, for instance, from different cultural traditions of mythology in this case. This is also what Kövecses (2017a, 2020) calls the level of "mental space", which is under the direct influence of contextual factors. Another example of a similar kind is that IMMORALITY can be construed as DISINTE-GRATION or DESTRUCTION at a generic level, but the mappings can be enriched a great deal at a more specific level when the source frames are elaborated by more specific source concepts such as RUIN, EROSION, CORROSION, MUDSLIDE,

LANDSLIDE, COLLAPSE, and MELTDOWN (see sections 3.3.4 and 3.4.4), which represent common natural phenomena in the physical world.

This chapter has also presented examples showing how the source concepts are coherent with one another in clusters under one parent source concept or among sister source concepts within the subsystem. In the latter case, for instance, morality is supposed to be "strong" so that it can resist the impact of immoral or illegal forces. That is why we talk about "moral foundation", which can endure the weight of the building built upon it, about "moral bank", which can help prevent waters from flowing over the river bed in a potential flood, and about "moral fence", which can help stop other people from transgressing the property enclosed. Things however strong, can become "rotten" if they are not maintained or repaired over time. Foundations can crack in land shift for whatever causes, banks can be eroded by flowing water or termites, and fences can decay in mold or rust. That is to say, "strong" things can be "broken" if "rotten". In the former case, we have seen in both English and Chinese the source-domain concept of ILLNESS or DISEASE (for IMMORAL IS ILL) is extensively elaborated and enriched with a wide variety of frames. For instance, the frames for contagious diseases or epidemics comprise such elements and relations as bacterium, virus, the preventative measures like using disinfectant and taking vaccine for immunity, and the treatment with antibiotics or strong doses of drugs. The frames for more serious diseases contain such elements and relations as cancer, cancer cells proliferating, malignant tumor, massive hemorrhage, major surgery, and numbing the body or its parts with anesthesia. The frames for impairments with mind, body, or body parts include shortsightedness or blindness in eye vision, paralysis of the body, or handicaps of body parts, and rehabilitation as treatment in physical therapy. In short, our rich knowledge about disease makes it an ideal source domain for the elaboration of source frames mapped onto morality.

I just want to mention in passing that the Chinese examples discussed in this chapter involve some compounds composed of two physical concepts. I have seen the following combinations of source concepts in compound words: STRONG-BIG, SOLID-STRONG, SOLID-FIRM, WHOLE-COMPLETE, COMPLETE-FULL, COMPLETE-BEAUTIFUL, FRAGILE-WEAK, etc. Of these, the first is a combination of a physical and a spatial concept, from two different subsystems. In the two chapters that follow, we will see more examples of this kind, i.e., a Chinese compound word composed of two components from two different subsystems.

Now, let us turn to the second subsystem of moral metaphors, the visual subsystem.

4

Visual subsystem of moral metaphors

4.1 Moral-visual metaphors: Source concepts and frames

For the present chapter, I focus on the visual subsystem of moral metaphors, which is summarized by a general metaphor MORALITY IS VISUALITY, as identifying and labeling the two conceptual domains involved. Again, when I say that this subsystem is "visual", the term is used in a broad sense to mean that the visual aspect is a salient dimension of the sensorimotor experience under consideration. In other words, this subsystem comprises a cluster of moral metaphors grounded especially in aspects of our visual experience, specifically in terms of brightness, clarity, cleanness, and purity. Each of these dimensions forms a scale in our visual experience which has two parametric poles characterized by opposite values. The concepts that represent these opposing values serve as the source concepts mapped onto their respective target concepts MORAL and IMMORAL, the pair of positive and negative valence values in the domain of MORALITY. Morality is itself one dimension of social cognition that forms a scale with bipolar values in opposition to each other: MORALITY and IMMORALITY, the former also being the default value representing the whole dimension or scale. Table 4.1 lists the cluster of moral metaphors along with their positive and negative parametric versions, to be studied in this chapter.

Table 4.1 The cluster of moral metaphors grounded in visual experiences

Conceptual metaphors	Positive versions	Negative versions
MORALITY IS BRIGHTNESS	MORAL IS LIGHT	IMMORAL IS DARK
MORALITY IS CLARITY	MORAL IS CLEAR	IMMORAL IS MURKY
MORALITY IS CLEANNESS	MORAL IS CLEAN	IMMORAL IS DIRTY
MORALITY IS PURITY	MORAL IS PURE	IMMORAL IS IMPURE

In Table 4.1, the conceptual metaphors in the left column can be seen as the source subcases of the general metaphor, MORALITY IS VISUALITY, in that they all possess visual source concepts. They identify the general mappings between the source and target frames with scalar structure (i.e., MORALITY and one

The Moral Metaphor System. Ning Yu, Oxford University Press. © Ning Yu (2022).
DOI: 10.1093/oso/9780192866325.003.0004

dimension of VISUALITY, such as BRIGHTNESS or CLARITY), and they are expressed in nominal forms. The general mappings they express, however, entail subversions of metaphors that take the form of positive and negative parametric versions (respectively, in the central and right column), profiling the two end regions of the target and source scales (see Nos. 7 and 8 frame relations in Table 2.2). These parametric versions are expressed in adjectival forms. Thus, for instance, MORAL IS LIGHT and IMMORAL IS DARK are entailed metaphors of MORALITY IS BRIGHTNESS, profiling the bipolar ends of the MORALITY and BRIGHTNESS (or LUMINOSITY) scales. They are also sister metaphors, with their target and source frames in scalar opposition to each other (see No. 13 of Table 2.2), representing the two end subscales of the MORALITY and BRIGHTNESS scales (see No. 8 of Table 2.2).

That is, as shown in Table 4.1, the visual subsystem of moral metaphors contains four pairs of MORAL and IMMORAL metaphors whose source concepts represent some contrastive categories in our visual experience: LIGHT and DARK in brightness, CLEAR and MURKY in clarity, CLEAN and DIRTY in cleanness, and PURE and IMPURE in purity. As will be seen below, the source concepts for MORAL and IMMORAL as target concepts are actually related to and coherent with one another in our visual experiences, and the metaphorical mappings between them have emerged from our everyday perceptual experiences in our physical surroundings.

Apparently, the source concepts are closely linked in our visual experience. To illustrate the experiential coherence among, as well as the scalar opposition between, the visual categories, Figure 4.1 shows how the source concepts cluster together in a conceptual network with its elements relating to and contrasting with one another. The lines with arrows on both ends indicate bipolar contrastive relations, and those without arrows represent experiential links that can be correlative, associative, or implicative in

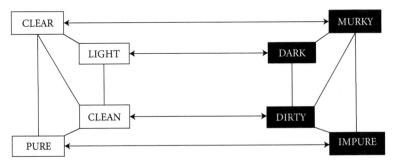

Fig. 4.1 The network of source concepts for the cluster of moral-visual metaphors
Source: Adapted from Yu (2015a: 165).

relation. Thus, for instance, LIGHT contrasts with DARK as bipolarities in scalar opposition to each other, so does CLEAN with DIRTY. On the right side, DARK, DIRTY, MURKY, and IMPURE correlate and associate with one another; the only two categories that do not necessarily come together in our visual experience are DARK and IMPURE. What is dark may not be impure, and vice versa. DARK and DIRTY hold associative relations with MURKY and IMPURE. The relations among the elements on the left side of the network mirror the ones on the right.

As illustrated in Figure 4.1, the source concepts of the moral metaphors in the visual subsystem are linked into a network that looks symmetric on both sides. Each of these source concepts evokes a particular source frame in the visual domain that is mapped onto the corresponding target frame of the moral-visual metaphor. Because the source concepts are linked in a network as illustrated in the figure, the source frames evoked by these source concepts also form a network of frame-to-frame relations upon which the network of moral metaphors in the visual subsystem is based (cf. Stickles et al. 2016; see also relevant discussions in section 2.7 above). To account for why and how the cluster of moral metaphors in Table 4.1 form a coherent subsystem, I would like again to construct a general source frame, a schematic representation of all the crucial elements and relations involved in the visual subsystem of moral metaphors, as in Figure 4.2. When this general frame is applied to each of the individual cases, some of the elements and relations are brought to the fore whereas the remaining ones concede to the background.

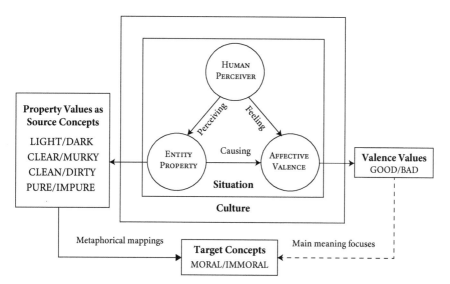

Fig. 4.2 A general source frame for the visual subsystem of moral metaphors

This source frame is interpreted in a similar fashion as Figure 3.2 for the physical subsystem except that, since this is the visual subsystem, "Perceiving" here refers particularly to visual experience through seeing. In this frame, that is, the HUMAN PERCEIVER sees some entity with a salient property, hence, ENTITY PROPERTY as the stimulus and second role, which is something being seen by the perceiver. The entity can be any one of the three forms of physical substance, or states of physical matter, solid, liquid, or gas (e.g., in the case of air pollution like smog, haze, etc.), but it is its salient visual property as the stimulus that is in focus here. As indicated by the arrow line pointing to the left, any of the visual adjectives in the box are possible values that can fill this role. As is obvious, these visual adjectives represent the source concepts for the visual moral metaphors in Figure 4.1. While the HUMAN PERCEIVER sees the ENTITY PROPERTY (i.e., any of those values represented by the visual adjectives in the box to the left), this salient property being seen causes the perceiver to feel an affective state with its valence, namely AFFECTIVE VALENCE as the third core role of the frame. This AFFECTIVE VALENCE evoked by the ENTITY PROPERTY in the HUMAN PERCEIVER can only be one of the two alternative and opposite values: either GOOD (positive) or BAD (negative), as is represented in the box to its right, depending on which salient ENTITY PROPERTY is being seen, LIGHT or DARK, CLEAN or DIRTY, for instance.

As explained in the preceding paragraph, the general source frame involves again three core roles—HUMAN PERCEIVER, ENTITY PROPERTY, and AFFECTIVE VALENCE—related to one another in a triangular way: i.e., a human person perceives a salient property of something and this property causes the person to feel a valenced affective state. This trilateral relationship displays a sort of experiential correlation, namely, the person is seeing something (e.g., LIGHT or DARK) when, at the same time, feeling something (e.g., GOOD or BAD). Note again that such experiential correlation is metonymic in nature (see section 2.6), with two dimensions of experience connected in the same source-domain frame, but it motivates primary metaphors (e.g., GOOD IS LIGHT and BAD IS DARK). I will come back to this issue in Chapters 6 and 7 when I discuss the nature of moral metaphors.

What should be stressed is that the kind of experiential correlation indicated in Figure 4.2, as well as in Figure 3.2, is relative to situational and cultural contexts, which are the two background elements in the frame. As can be seen, Situation is the square that encompasses the three core elements and Culture is the largest square that contains Situation. The influences of situation and culture are forces of contextual factors that cannot be ignored at the frame level because the perceiver's affective state upon seeing the salient entity property may hinge upon them.[1] For instance, as diurnal animals, human beings generally prefer lightness while not sleeping but darkness when sleeping, and some people may even have to put on an eye mask to sleep in light. Nevertheless, Situation and Culture are not "roles" in the frame; instead, they are the "props" that constitute the "settings" of the scene, in contrast with the "roles" as "participants" in the scene.

Lastly, as shown in Figure 4.2, the target concepts are MORAL and IMMORAL, which receive metaphorical mappings from their respective source concepts: LIGHT, CLEAR, CLEAN, and PURE for MORAL; DARK, MURKY, DIRTY, and IMPURE for IMMORAL. As mentioned before, these adjectival concepts serve as possible values that each can fill the role of ENTITY PROPERTY. In my notation system, as noted previously, any metaphorical mappings are represented by lines with solid arrowheads, in distinction from the stealth arrowheads that represent relations between frame elements and their extensions to their values.

Now, the question to ask is why those source concepts encoded by the corresponding lexical items can mean what they mean metaphorically. The general source frame that I proposed in Figure 4.2 answers that question. The metaphorical mappings are based on our emotional reactions, or affective responses, to the visual stimuli in specific situational and cultural contexts. In many such contexts we have salient and recurring experiential correlations between perception and emotion. That is part of the grounding for our embodied cognition. In this case, our perceptual experience in seeing the salient visual property of something evokes a strong affect in us that is either positive or negative in valence. Our immediate emotional response would be, for instance, "I feel good about it" or "I feel bad about it". And, therefore, GOOD or BAD serves as the value that fills the role of AFFECTIVE VALENCE. At the same time, they also serve as the main meaning focus of the moral metaphors under consideration, as indicated by the dashed line with its arrowhead pointing to the metaphorical target concepts.

In the above, I laid out the moral metaphors in the visual subsystem as in Table 4.1. I argued that these moral-visual metaphors are linked in a conceptual network because their source concepts form a coherent network with relations of opposition, correlation, association, or implication, as shown in Figure 4.1. That is the reason why the moral-visual metaphors form what I

---

[1] In Kövecses's (2020) terms, contextual factors exert their influences on frames (and domains and image schemas) through mental spaces where the frame roles are filled with specific values by individual speakers. See his figure 5.2 displaying "The influence of context on schematicity hierarchies" (Kövecses 2020: 105).

call the visual subsystem of moral metaphors (cf. Dodge 2016; Stickles et al. 2016). I also constructed a general source frame, a schematic representation of the elements and relations, which accounts for the embodied motivation for the moral metaphors of this cluster. The motivation lies in the relationship between affectivity and morality.

4.2 Psychological research on visual moral and affective metaphors

Since its inception 40 years ago, conceptual metaphor theory (CMT) has gained a much more solid empirical grounding from interdisciplinary and multidisciplinary research with corpus-based methods (e.g., Deignan 2005; Stefanowitsch and Gries 2006), experimental psycholinguistic studies (e.g., Gibbs 2013a; Gibbs, Gould, and Andric 2006; Wilson and Gibbs 2007), multimodal analyses (e.g., Cienki and Müller 2008; Forceville and Urios-Aparisi 2009), and discoveries about the neural basis of metaphor (e.g., Feldman 2006; Lakoff 2008a, 2014). An immense amount of support, however, has come from psychology, with experimental research, a good portion of which is on moral valence (moral vs. immoral) in particular and affective valence (positive vs. negative) in general.

In the past two decades or so, researchers in psychology, especially social psychology, have conducted various experimental studies, of which the findings have shown that moral metaphors (target: MORAL VS. IMMORAL), and affective metaphors (target: POSITIVE VS. NEGATIVE) more generally, are psychologically real, thus lending support to the validity of CMT with strong empirical evidence. Such research has been carried out along different visual dimensions, for instance, along the dimension of brightness with bipolar values of lightness and darkness (e.g., Banerjee, Chatterjee, and Sinha 2012; Chiou and Cheng 2013; Harms and Spain 2015; Hill and Lapsley 2009; Lakens et al. 2013; Meier, Robinson, et al. 2007; Persich, Bair, et al. 2018; Zhong, Bohns, and Gino's 2010), and along the dimension of cleanness or purity with bipolar values of cleanness and dirtiness or purity and impurity (e.g., Huang et al. 2016; Lee and Schwarz 2010; Schaefer et al. 2015; Schnall, Benton, and Harvey 2008; Sheikh, Botindari, and White 2013; Zhong and Liljenquist 2006; Zhong, Strejcek, and Sivanathan 2010; see also Lee and Schwarz 2011; Schnall 2011; Tobia 2015; Zhong and House 2014). In the following discussion, I will just briefly introduce some examples of these experimental studies in the literature.

Along the brightness dimension, the bipolar source concepts for moral metaphors are LIGHT and DARK. Moral metaphors, and affective metaphors (positive vs. negative) more generally, link LIGHT to MORAL or POSITIVE, and DARK to IMMORAL or NEGATIVE: namely MORAL/POSITIVE IS LIGHT and IMMORAL/NEGATIVE IS DARK (e.g., Lakens et al. 2013; Meier, Robinson, and Clore 2004; Zhang et al. 2016). For instance, with a series of studies, Chiou and Cheng (2013) found that experiencing brightness increases the salience of moral considerations and the likelihood of engaging in ethical behavior. Thus, for instance, participants in a well-lit room acted less selfishly and were more likely to return undeserved money than were those in a moderately or a dimly lit room, and their monetary donations were positively associated with environment lighting. In a similar vein, Zhong, Bohns, and Gino (2010) examined the relation between the level of darkness in the environment and moral transgression. They found that darkness, induced by room dimness or wearing sunglasses, increased dishonesty and self-interested behaviors. These findings suggest that the level of lightness or darkness can influence people's moral behavior.

In their studies exploring whether recalling moral or immoral behaviors can influence people's perception of brightness, Banerjee et al. (2012) asked participants to recall any ethical or unethical behavior in the past and then to judge the brightness of the room. They found significant difference in perception of the room's brightness between the two conditions. That is, the participants in the immoral condition judged the room to be darker than did participants in the moral condition. Furthermore, those in the immoral condition exhibited a greater preference for such light-producing objects as lamps, candles, and flashlights (cf. Zhong and Liljenquist 2006). Their findings show that recalling moral or immoral behavior changes the perception of brightness. While Zhong, Bohns, and Gino's (2010) studies point to the influence of perception of brightness on moral behavior, Banerjee et al.'s (2012) studies appear to point to the influence in a different direction, i.e., the reflection on moral behavior can change perception of brightness (cf. Brandt, IJzerman, and Blanken 2014, which did not replicate the results of Banerjee et al. 2012).[2]

In a series of four studies, Meier, Robinson, Crawford, and Ahlvers (2007) asked participants to evaluate the meaning of words as being positive

---

[2] The influence going both ways between domains is a case of bidirectionality observed and raised by some psychologists (e.g., IJzerman and Semin 2010; Lee and Schwarz 2012; Schneider et al. 2011; Zhong and Leonardelli 2008) as evidence for doubts about CMT, which states that metaphorical mappings are unidirectional, from source to target. Responses from CMT can be found in Grady and Ascoli (2017), Lakoff (2014), and Yu et al. (2016).

(e.g., *love*) or negative (e.g., *rude*) and, following that, to make a perceptual judgment on the level of brightness of a square on the computer screen. It was found that after evaluating positive words participants consistently judged the square as being lighter than after evaluating negative words. The results were therefore consistent with the prevailing affective metaphors that link lightness to positive affect and darkness to negative affect: that is, POSITIVE IS LIGHT and NEGATIVE IS DARK. Their research therefore supports the CMT claim that metaphor structures representation itself instead of just linguistic utterances, and proves that affective metaphors can influence perceptual judgments in a metaphor-congruent way. Lakens et al. (2013), in contrast, investigated how the brightness of affective pictures was related to the affective evaluation of these pictures. They conducted a series of five studies and came to the following findings. Positive pictures are brighter than negative pictures in two affective picture databases; pictures selected for positive conditions of experiments turned out to be brighter on average than those selected for negative conditions. Brighter versions of neutral pictures were evaluated more positively than darker versions of the same pictures. Participants categorized positive words more quickly than negative words after a bright picture prime, and vice versa for negative pictures. Their findings therefore suggested that brightness differences influence the evaluation of affective pictures and that the valence of pictures is in part determined by their brightness or "brightness bias": i.e., brighter pictures are evaluated more positively while darker pictures are evaluated more negatively (cf. Lakens, Semin, and Foroni 2012). These findings are also congruent with those of the studies of conceptual metaphors (e.g., GOOD IS LIGHT and BAD/EVIL IS DARK) as manifested multimodally in movies (e.g., Forceville and Reckens 2013; Ortiz 2011; Winter 2014).

Along the cleanness dimension, which is closely related to the purity dimension, the bipolar source concepts for moral metaphors are CLEAN and DIRTY, and the moral metaphors are MORAL IS CLEAN and IMMORAL IS DIRTY (parallel to MORAL IS PURE and IMMORAL IS IMPURE). Zhong and Liljenquist (2006) investigated the psychological association between "bodily purity" (clean vs. dirty) and "moral purity" (moral vs. immoral) in three studies. In study 1, participants were asked to recall an ethical or unethical deed from the past and then to engage in a word completion task consisting of six word fragments, of which three could be completed as cleansing-related words (*wash*, *shower*, *soap*) or as cleansing-unrelated words (*wish*, *shaker*, *step*). It turned out that participants who recalled an unethical deed generated more cleansing-related words than those who recalled an ethical deed, suggesting that unethical behavior enhances the accessibility of cleansing-related concepts. In study 2, participants were asked to hand-copy a short story written in the first person describing either an ethical or unethical act. They were then asked to rate the desirability of various products. The result is that copying the unethical story increased the desirability of cleansing products as compared to copying the ethical story. In study 3, participants having recalled an ethical or unethical deed were offered a free gift and given a choice between an antiseptic wipe and a pencil. As a result, those who recalled an unethical deed were more likely to take the antiseptic wipe than those who recalled an ethical deed. These findings, as the researchers claimed, showed that a threat to one's moral purity stimulates a need for physical cleansing.

Following Zhong and Liljenquist (2006), a good number of other studies have been carried out along this line of research on the psychological association between physical purity and moral purity (see Lee and Shwarz 2011). For example, while Zhong and Liljenquist (2006) found that, after recalling a moral transgression from their past, participants were more likely to think of cleansing-related words and to show a desire to engage in cleansing behavior, Schnall, Benton, and Harvey (2008) reported their investigation of the reverse relationship, i.e., the feeling of cleanliness reduced the severity of participants' moral judgments on moral transgressions. The researchers concluded that their findings supported the idea that moral judgment can be influenced by physical purity, rather than deliberate reasoning, because physical purity has a strong connection to moral purity (cf. Helzer and Pizarro 2011; Johnson, Cheung, and Donnellan 2014).

Lee and Schwarz (2010) tested if participants prefer to clean the body part involved in a perceived moral transgression. They induced participants to perform an immoral act (conveying a malevolent lie) or a moral one (conveying a benevolent message) with their mouths (by using voice mail) or their hands (by using email). The researchers found that participants evaluated mouthwash more positively after lying in a voice mail than after lying in an email, but evaluated hand sanitizer more positively after lying in an email than after lying in a voice mail. In contrast, the same was not found with the participants who had performed a moral act. These findings indicate that the embodiment of moral purity is specific to the motor modality involved in a moral transgression, such that participants wanted to clean their "dirty" body part more than other body parts. Adopting Lee and Schwarz's (2010) experimental design, Schaefer et al. (2015) conducted neurophysiological research employing functional magnetic resonance imaging (fMRI) approaches. They found similar results, i.e., mouthwash products were particularly desirable after lying in a voice mail and hand wash products were particularly desirable after writing a lie, thus demonstrating that the moral-purity metaphor is specific to the sensorimotor modality involved in earlier immoral behavior. Further, their fMRI results for this interaction showed activation in sensorimotor cortices during the evaluation phase that was organized with respect to preceding lying in a voice mail (mouth area) or in a written note (hand area). These results, as they concluded, provide evidence for a central role of the sensorimotor cortices for embodied metaphors.

In general, the studies discussed above have established the links between some contrastive visual categories (in brightness, cleanness, or purity) on the one hand and affective and moral valences on the other, which are by and large congruent with the moral-visual metaphors in Table 4.1. Although psychological researchers do not necessarily agree with each other on some of the details in the interpretation of their findings, their research nonetheless has largely confirmed the embodied nature and metaphorical character of moral cognition in particular, and social cognition in general (see, e.g., Landau 2017; Landau et al. 2010; Landau et al. 2014; Meier and Robinson 2005).

Having reviewed some psychological research on the embodied nature of moral metaphors and moral cognition, I now move on to the focus of this chapter: the linguistic manifestation of moral-visual metaphors in English and Chinese (respectively, in the next two sections).

4.3 Visual moral metaphors in English

This section looks at the cluster of moral-visual metaphors in English. As characterized by Lakoff (1993: 210–211), each conceptual metaphor is a fixed pattern of conceptual correspondences across conceptual domains. Such conceptual mappings are realized on two different levels of language use. At the lexical level, source-domain lexical items may or may not have a conventionally lexicalized sense in the target domain. Even if they do not, the knowledge structures associated with them can still be mapped by conceptual metaphors onto the target domain as inference patterns at the level of discourse.

Although there is a substantial body of literature on moral metaphors in English, relatively few such studies fall into the field of linguistics and none of them have looked at the same cluster of metaphors as a coherent visual subsystem of the moral metaphor system. Thus, for instance, cognitive-semantic studies of morality have chiefly focused on the systematic manifestation in English of the moral accounting metaphor, family model metaphor, moral strength metaphor, moral purity or dirtiness metaphor (e.g., Johnson 1993; Lakoff 1996, 2006a: chapter 4; 2006b: chapter 4; Lakoff and Johnson 1999: chapter 14; Lizardo 2012; McAdams et al. 2008; Spencer 2013; Taub 1990).

Table 4.2 Lexicalized moral senses of the visual words in the three English dictionaries

Dictionary	Webster	Oxford	Longman
Word	**Conventionally lexicalized moral senses**		
light			
dark	Arising from or showing evil traits or desires; evil or wicked	Suggestive of or arising from evil; sinister	Evil or threatening
clear	Free from guile or guilt; innocent; free from feelings of guilt or blame	(of a person's conscience) free of guilt	Free from guilt or blame; untroubled; e.g. *a clear conscience* = the knowledge that you have done the right thing and should not feel guilty
murky	Involving dishonest or illegal activities that are not clearly known	Obscure or morally questionable	Involving dishonest or illegal activities that are kept secret; shady
clean	Free from moral corruption or sinister connections of any kind; free from offensive treatment of sexual subjects and from the use of obscenity	Morally uncontaminated; pure; innocent; not sexually offensive or obscene	Morally or sexually pure; honorable; free from guilt; fair or legal; not offensive or about sex
dirty	Morally unclean or corrupt; dishonorable; indecent; vulgar; base; unsportsmanlike; ill-gotten; not fair or honest	(Of an activity) dishonest, dishonorable; concerned with sex in lewd or obscene way; sordid, mean, despicable; ill-gotten	Relating to sex in a way that is considered immoral or unpleasant; (of someone or something) bad, dishonest, or immoral
pure	Free from moral fault or guilt; marked by chastity; morally good; free from sexual or evil thoughts	Wholesome and untainted by immorality, especially that of a sexual nature; not corrupt; morally undefiled, guiltless, sincere; sexually undefiled, chaste	Morally good; free from evil; without any sexual experience or evil thoughts
impure	Lewd, unchaste; sexual in a way that is considered morally wrong	Morally wrong, esp. in sexual matters; unchaste	Morally bad; of bad sexual habits

Table 4.2 provides the conventionally lexicalized moral senses of visual adjectives in *Webster, Oxford,* and *Longman*. These English words are the ones that typically encode the source concepts of the moral-visual metaphors. As shown in this table, the moral senses of the English adjectives are listed in all three dictionaries with only one exception: namely, *light* has no moral sense listed in any of the three dictionaries. In contrast, its antonym *dark* has its lexicalized moral senses listed in all three dictionaries. Again, having no conventional moral sense listed under *light* in the dictionaries does not mean that there is no conceptual correspondence between LIGHT and MORAL. Its moral senses can be activated by being the antonym of *dark*, whose moral senses such as "evil" are more entrenched in the target domain. The difference between *light* and *dark* in this respect echoes the so-called "immoral bias" observed in psychological research (Hill and Lapsley 2009; see also Lakens et al. 2012). That is, people may be more likely to use metaphors when discussing immoral rather than moral individuals. Positive moral traits appear to be represented only along those perceptual dimensions specifically invoked in the metaphorical expressions we use in everyday life. This provided evidence for a close link between our language use and our representations of the world. As we will see below, the activation of the moral senses of *light* can take place at the level of language use in actual discourse, mapping the inference patterns of the source onto the target domain.

At the level of language use, as I have found, all of the English words listed in Table 4.2 have their moral senses realized, to varying degrees and with various emphases, in real-life discourses, instantiating the cross-domain mappings of the conceptual metaphors in Table 4.1, as illustrated by the examples from the Corpus of Contemporary American English (COCA). In what follows, I discuss the COCA examples instantiating the moral-visual metaphors in pairs in Table 4.1.

4.3.1 MORAL IS LIGHT and IMMORAL IS DARK

The first pair of moral-visual metaphors consists of MORAL IS LIGHT and IMMORAL IS DARK in the category of brightness. Experimental studies have led to findings in a metaphor-consistent direction: i.e., lightness or brightness is associated with morality or positivity whereas darkness is associated with immorality or negativity (see, e.g., Banerjee et al. 2012; Harms and Spain 2015; Hill and Lapsley 2009; Meier et al. 2004; Meier, Robinson, et al. 2007;

Persich, Bair, et al. 2018; Persich, Steinemann, et al. 2018). Such metaphorical conceptualizations likely build on basic human experiential correlations linking lightness to certainty and safety and darkness to uncertainty and vulnerability. They are also reinforced through linguistic and multimodal expression (Forceville and Renckens 2013; Winter 2014; Winter and Matlock 2017). Even though *light* does not have lexicalized moral senses listed in any of the three major dictionaries as shown in Table 4.2, such senses are realized in the discursive level, as illustrated by the following COCA examples.

(1) a. The narrative is of the alcoholic as shirker, with the intended meaning conveyed through the binary opposition of **light** and shade that signal the drinker's moral failure.

  b. He has given you the **light** of conscience to guide your moral decisions, to love good and avoid evil.

Example in (1a) contains nominal *light*. The sentence is from an essay analyzing anti-alcohol posters in Poland after the Second World War. In a particular poster under analysis, the intended moral message is brought out by the contrast between "light and shade", with the alcoholic shirking into moral failure. Example (1b) involves another instance of nominal *light*. One's moral conscience is a light source that guides one's moral decisions on what is good and what is evil.

(2) a. Decorated in honors for bravery, Serling, a man of high moral integrity, withdraws into a **dark** world of alcoholism when he is forced to keep quiet and speak untruthfully, going against his anxious desire to tell the truth about the disaster.

  b. ... when we start to be the judges of human worth, or forget principles of equality even in the name of scientific or technological advancement, we start down a **dark** path toward moral and social chaos.

The next two examples in (2) involve *dark* used as an adjective. Example (2a) offers another example on alcoholism, revolving around the metaphor ALCO-HOLISM IS DARK WORLD (cf. 1a). Such a world is "dark" because alcoholism leads to a type of "moral failure" that crushes "moral integrity". Example (2b) warns against the impulse to act as "the judges of human worth" because those who do it are following "a dark path" leading to moral as well as social chaos (i.e., LIFE IS JOURNEY).

(3) a. ... there's two forces within all of us. There's the good side, the **light** side, the side that's giving and caring and loving, and there's—the **dark** side, the negative side, the opponent.

   b. These lessons are also communicated through aspects of our popular culture in which there are very clear distinctions between the forces of **light** and **dark**, the moral and the wicked.

   c. Exploring the spiritual and moral **light** and **dark** sides of musical experience and appreciation.

The examples in (3) contain both *light* and *dark* in opposition to each other, representing the distinction between the moral and the immoral. That is, the "light side" is the moral side whereas the "dark side" is the immoral side (3a). As is often the case, popular culture is very dynamic, engaging forces that can be either "light" or "dark" in a moral contrast (3b). Example (3c) is the title of a research article published in an academic journal. As this title shows, "light and dark sides" can be spiritual as well as moral because, as mentioned above, lightness is associated with positivity and darkness with negativity more generally. Such associations may be determined by the human nature as diurnal creatures (Adams and Osgood 1973; Lakens et al. 2012; Meier, Robinson, et al. 2007; Persich, Bair, et al. 2018).

4.3.2 Moral is clear and immoral is murky

The next pair of conceptual metaphors for morality is MORAL IS CLEAR and IMMORAL IS MURKY. The pair of source concepts is coherent with the preceding and following ones in that what is clear is often light or clean, and what is murky is often dark or dirty. Also, as visual properties, that which is clear allows people to see through and beyond as what is murky does not. The contrast between "clear" and "murky" is therefore that between transparency and opacity, of which the former is generally considered morally positive and the latter negative (e.g., Menéndez-Viso 2009). Besides, clarity is also metaphoric of moral vision, especially in self-examination, like the reflective function of a mirror (e.g., Stokes 2007). The examples in (4) instantiate the MORAL AS CLEAR metaphor.

(4) a. You're a good man with a clean heart, not perfectly clean but **clear** (yes, a **clear** heart), and you had good intentions ...

   b. In addition, students will need to act as people of moral character, good judgment, and **clear** conscience.

In (4a), the person ("you") had a "clear" as well as "clean" heart because this person had ethically good rather than bad intentions. As in (4b), "conscience" refers to a person's moral sense of right and wrong, viewed as acting as a guide to one's behavior, and "clear conscience", an idiomatic expression, refers to one's knowledge or belief that one has done nothing bad or wrong.

(5)   a.   He's drawn into the **murky** underworld of this secret killing cult
            and he has to decide if good is going to triumph over evil.

       b.   And the death of Littlefinger certainly signals a symbolic shift
            the show is experiencing, from the sneaky backroom politics and
            morally **murky** alliances of the first few seasons to the much more
            standard fantasy clash between forces of good and evil.

The two examples in (5) contains *murky*, an antonym of *clear* (along with *muddy*, *turbid*, etc.). Thus, the underworld is "murky" as the venue for illegal and immoral activities (5a). In (5b), "Littlefinger" is a fictional character originally created by American author George R. R. Martin. In this example, the alliances, which are special relationships of bond among members or parties, are "morally murky" if they are formed for dubious and questionable mutual benefits.

4.3.3 MORAL IS CLEAN and IMMORAL IS DIRTY

Now we turn to the third pair of moral-visual metaphors, MORAL IS CLEAN and IMMORAL IS DIRTY. In moral reasoning, moral propriety and impropriety are often metaphorically conceptualized on the basis of clean-dirty dichotomy, where "clean" describes a condition in which an entity or setting is in "ordered arrangement" whereas "dirty" refers to the subversion of that ideal arrangement with "matter out of place" (Lizardo 2012; see also Ignatow 2009; Klaassen 1998; Sherman, Haidt, and Clore 2012). Psychological research has demonstrated the embodied connection between physical cleanliness and moral judgment (see, e.g., Huang et al. 2016; Lee and Schwarz 2010, 2011; Sheikh et al. 2013; Tobia 2014), and between emotional disgust resulting from physical dirtiness and moral disgust (e.g., Haidt et al. 1997; Royzman and Kurzban 2011; Rozin, Haidt, and Fincher 2009; Rozin et al. 1999; Schnall 2011; Schnall, Benton, and Harvey 2008; Schnall, Haidt, et al. 2008; Sherman et al. 2012; Tobia 2014).

In the following we look at some linguistic instantiations of MORAL IS CLEAN and IMMORAL IS DIRTY in (6) and (7), respectively. The examples in (6) from COCA all involve the moral sense of *clean*.

(6)   a.   There were great detectives as well, ethically and morally **clean** and fueled, in part, by a desire to take down Mackey and **clean up** the squad.

      b.   This money was laundered **clean** in the process but with dubious moral and economic effects on Romania.

In (6a), *clean* is used both as an adjective and as a verb in its moral sense. After "cleaning up", there is no more "moral dirt" inside the squad. In (6b), *clean* qualifies money, which was originally "dirty", but was "laundered clean". The process of money laundering is deemed to be illegal as well as immoral.

(7)   a.   The lyrics are sexually explicit and laced with a hard bass beat. If this musical genre could be defined, it would fall under **dirty** rap— it's like the **dirty** blues our grandparents listened to.

      b.   Can there be anything more gross and obscene, more nonaesthetic and repulsive, than a woman who writes lascivious, **dirty**, sadistic, and morally corrupt stories?

      c.   ... effectiveness may sometimes demand "**dirty** hands" not moral purity.

In (7a) the kinds of rap and blues are said to be "dirty" because they are "sexually explicit"; in (7b) the stories written by the woman are "dirty" because they are "morally corrupt". Example (7c) pertains to the "effectiveness" of politicians. It is suggested that a moral politician sometimes has to get his or her hands "dirty" to be effective and has to be willing to acknowledge and accept responsibility for morally problematic choices.

The adjectives *clean* and *dirty* are often used together, too, in examples that manifest the pair of conceptual metaphors for morality, such as those in (8).

(8)   a.   Every generation has its **dirty** and **clean** versions of popular music.

      b.   ... these female sex workers indicate that they operate with a finely grained moral system of respectability ... Many of them still conform to the gender ideals of Puerto Rican society by cultivating intimacy and trust with male clients, by prioritizing their identity and duties as mothers, or simply by maintaining distinctions between **clean** and **dirty** sex or **clean** and **dirty** clients.

Popular music is a salient part of popular culture, which can be vibrated by both "light" and "dark" forces. As such, it produces perhaps the most dynamic forces of popular culture, and has its own "clean" and "dirty" versions with each generation that inhabits popular culture (8a). Example (8b) is interesting in that "sex workers", who are perceived as altogether "dirty" in many cultures, act according to a "moral system" in the said society, where morality and immorality are distinguished at the level of "clean" vs. "dirty" sex or "clean" vs. "dirty" clients. This example shows that moral conception is relative to cultural contexts, and to the metaphors people live by.

4.3.4 MORAL IS PURE and IMMORAL IS IMPURE

The last pair of conceptual metaphors for morality in the visual subsystem is MORAL IS PURE and IMMORAL IS IMPURE, which is closely related to the preceding pair, MORAL IS CLEAN and IMMORAL IS DIRTY. This pair, especially the positive version, is a common one that has received much attention in the study of moral cognition (e.g., Denke et al. 2016; Ignatow 2009; Lee and Schwarz 2010; Schaefer et al. 2015; Schnall, Benton, and Harvey 2008; Sherman and Clore 2009; Zhong, Strejcek, and Sivanathan 2010). What is pure is free from pollution or contamination. In contrast, being impure is being soiled, tainted, blemished, and stained (Lakoff and Johnson 1999). The examples in (9), which contain the adjective *pure*, instantiate MORAL IS PURE.

(9) a. Those who are outraged are **pure**. Moral **purity** is the new prerequisite for outrage, it seems ...

b. Or you could say that the standard of normal public behavior is being maintained very high—in other words, that we're expecting really very **pure** moral behavior from our public officials.

Example (9a), taken from an article titled "Outrage!" in the magazine *Vanity Fair*, is cast in a sarcastic tone as the author is commenting on the widespread outrage in American public discourse, in which, ironically, those outraged appear to be "morally pure". Example (9b) is from a comment on Israeli politics on Cable News Network (CNN). According to the commentator, the standard of normal public behavior is too high and therefore public officials are expected to have "really very pure moral behavior".

(10)   a. In an ideal world where its interests were completely secure, the United States perhaps could dispense with morally **impure** agents.

     b. Then there are the interviews with jocks on both sides of the issue: the **pure** Carl Lewis, the **impure** Ben Johnson ...

The two examples in (10) contain *impure* as the antonym of *pure*. Example (10a) is taken from an article in *World Affairs* about the U.S. intelligence in the post-Cold War era. One view is that in a world of real threats it is acceptable to use morally "impure" agents as long as the likely benefits outweigh the potential moral and political costs of association with them. In (10b), the contrast between the "purity" of Carl Lewis and "impurity" of Ben Johnson lies in the "clean" and "stained" records in doping of the two athletes.

As shown in (1) and (3), even though the English word *light* has no lexicalized sense in the domain of MORALITY according to the three English dictionaries (see Table 4.2), its moral sense can still be activated at the level of discourse. This activation is initiated presumably in response to the underlying force of the metaphor MORAL IS LIGHT, in contrast to IMMORAL IS DARK, in our conceptual system. This phenomenon is consistent with some psychological research findings about a general negativity bias to give greater weight to negative entities (Rozin and Royzmann 2001; see also Hill and Lapsley 2009; Lakens et al. 2012). Also, it is worth noting that *clear*, which primarily means "transparent" in a visual sense, is often used to mean "free from misinterpretation or doubt" in a mental sense, triggered by the conceptual metaphor KNOWING IS SEEING or KNOWLEDGE IS VISION. Its moral sense is usually limited to the collocations *clear heart* and *clear conscience* in English. Its three possible antonyms, *murky*, *muddy*, and *turbid*, are chiefly used in a mental rather than moral sense too, but *muddy* does have a lexicalized moral sense, "morally impure", listed in WNCD (1977).

The next section will switch to Chinese so as to provide a comparative perspective on the study.

4.4 Visual moral metaphors in Chinese

This section examines the Chinese lexical items that are counterparts or near counterparts of those English words studied in the preceding section. Table 4.3 lists lexicalized moral senses of some words, which express the source concepts in Table 4.1, in the three Chinese dictionaries: HYDCD (2000 + on-line), XDHYCD (2016, 7th ed.), and XXDHYCD (1992). The listed words are meant to be the best examples because there are other words that encode the same or similar concepts in Chinese. Provided in the parentheses are literal translations, followed by more natural translations. I used XSD-HYDCD (2004), an authoritative Chinese-English dictionary, for the English translations wherever possible.

Table 4.3 lists four pairs of antonyms. All eight words are primarily visual adjectives with metaphorically extended moral senses, although the metaphorical meaning extensions are not necessarily listed as conventionally lexicalized senses in all three dictionaries owing to their different sizes and purposes. Specifically, only six of the eight visual words have their moral senses listed in all three dictionaries (with HYDCD including both the paper and online versions). Three of the eight have such moral senses listed in two dictionaries. The last item, 不纯 *bùchún* "impure", is disyllabic, literally meaning "not pure" (negative + adjective). As such, none of the dictionaries I consulted lists it as a single lexical item, except the online HYDCD, which lists it as a compound word with extended moral senses (see Table 4.3). Another online dictionary, ZXHYCD, also lists it as a single lexical item, with the following example from classic Chinese that clearly illustrates its use in a moral sense: 德不纯, 民乃失常 "If morality is *impure*, people would be abnormal". Another monosyllabic word in Chinese that can express a similar moral meaning is 杂 *zá* when it means "mixed", i.e., "impure". For example, the idiom 私心杂念 *sīxīn zániàn* (lit. selfish-heart impure-thought) means "selfish ideas and personal considerations"; the expression 心头的杂质 *xīntóu de zázhì* (lit. in-heart mixed-substance) means "impure thoughts in one's heart"). Both expressions refer to the "heart" as the locus of one's moral sense (see Yu 2009a: section 4.3.3).

It is no surprise that HYDCD (including the online version) is the one that provides the moral senses of all eight words in the table. This is by far the most comprehensive one among the three Chinese dictionaries consulted. It is worth noting that, if the moral senses of a particular visual word are not provided by the other two dictionaries, it does not mean that such moral senses do not exist at all. This will become clear as we turn to CCL examples from real-life discourses which instantiate the cluster of conceptual metaphors in Table 4.1.

Table 4.3 Lexicalized moral senses of the visual words in the three Chinese dictionaries

Dictionary	HYDCD	XDHYCD	XXDHYCD
Word		Conventionally lexicalized moral senses	
明 *míng* "light"	心地光明 (heart-bright) pure-hearted	光明 (light-bright) honest; open-hearted; guileless; aboveboard	心地光明 (heart-bright) pure-hearted;
暗 *àn* "dark"	黑暗 (black-dark) dark; corrupt; evil; reactionary	黑暗 (black-dark) dark; corrupt; evil; reactionary	良好 (fine-good) good
清 *qīng* "clear"	公正 (fair-upright) fair; just; impartial; 廉洁 (honest-clean) honest and clean; 纯洁 (pure-clean) pure and honest; 高洁 (high-clean) noble and unsullied; 高尚 (high-esteem) noble; lofty	公正 (fair-upright) fair; just; impartial; 廉洁 (honest-clean) honest and clean; 纯洁 (pure-clean) pure and honest	清高 (clear-high) morally superior; 清白 (clear-white) pure; clean; immaculate; 清正 (clear-upright) honest and upright
浊 *zhuó* "murky"	贪鄙 (corrupt-low) impudently greedy; avaricious and despicable; 卑污 (low-dirty) despicable in character; evil-minded; 卑劣 (low-inferior) base; mean; despicable		品行坏 (conduct-bad) bad in moral conduct; of loose morals; 卑劣 (low-inferior) base; mean; despicable

Continued

Table 4.3 Continued

Dictionary	HYDCD	XDHYCD	XXDHYCD
Word		Conventionally lexicalized moral senses	
洁jié "clean"	洁白 (clean-white) pure and innocent; 清白不污 (clear-white not-dirty) immaculate and clean; 操行清白 (behavior clear-white) of immaculate behavior; 品德高尚 (moral-character high-esteem) of noble moral character	清白 (clear-white) pure; clean; immaculate; 纯洁 (pure-clean) pure and honest; with a spotless reputation; 廉洁 (honest-clean) honest and clean	操行清白 (behavior clear-white) of immaculate behavior; 品德高尚 (moral-character high-esteem) of noble moral character
污wū "dirty"	卑鄙 (low-low) base; mean; contemptible; despicable; 卑下 (low-down) base; lowly; 淫乱 (lewd-messy) loose in sexual relations; 腐败 (rotten-decayed) decadent; corrupt	不廉洁 (not honest-clean) dishonest and unclean	污秽 (dirty-dirty) filthy; 卑污 (low-dirty) despicable in character; evil-minded; 腐败 (rotten-decayed) decadent; corrupt
纯chún "pure"	美 (beautiful) good; 善 (good) good (vs. evil); 淳厚 (honest-thick) simple and honest	单纯 (simple-pure) pure and simple	美 (beautiful) good; 善 (good) good (vs. evil); 纯正 (pure-upright) pure and upright
不纯bùchún "impure"	不纯正 (not pure-upright) impure; 不纯净 (not pure-clean) impure		

4.4.1 MORAL IS LIGHT and IMMORAL IS DARK

It has been argued from the cognitive-linguistic point of view that LIGHT and DARK are biologically rooted image schemas which are often metaphorically elaborated and mapped onto GOOD and BAD, and GOOD IS LIGHT and BAD IS DARK, as a pair of conceptual metaphors, are richly manifested not only in language, but in visual art as well (Forceville and Renckens 2013; Winter 2014; Winter and Matlock 2017). It is due to the experiential correlation between LIGHT and GOOD and between DARK and BAD that experimental studies show that people automatically assume bright objects are good whereas dark objects are bad, and that positive evaluations primed light perceptual judgments while negative evaluations primed dark perceptual judgments (see, e.g., Meier et al. 2004; Meier, Robinson, et al. 2007).

In Chinese, the contrast between LIGHT and DARK is encoded by a pair of antonyms, 明 *míng* "light; bright" and 暗 *àn* "dark; dim", among others. The connection between LIGHT and MORAL is found in one of the ancient Confucian classics, *The Great Learning* (大学 *dàxué*), where it is said that the purpose of great learning is 明明德 *míng míngdé* (lit. to brighten or lighten the bright or light virtue), i.e., "to promote high moral character". The moral sense of *míng* "light; bright" and *àn* "dark; dim" as a pair of antonyms is also illustrated by the saying: 明人不做暗事 *míngrén bù zuò ànshì*, which, literally "A light or bright person does not do dark things", means "An honest person will never do anything underhand (lit. anything dark)". In this saying, a "light or bright person" is morally good whereas "dark things" are morally bad. Furthermore, the two antonyms can each combine with other words to form compounds or idioms. For instance, 光明 *guāngmíng* "light; bright; aboveboard" and 黑暗 *hēi'àn* "dark; corrupt; evil" both have their metaphorically extended moral senses, often used in contrast with each other as illustrated by the two examples in (11).

(11) a. 越在**黑暗**中越做**光明**的事, 这就是道德教育。
      The more one is in the **dark**, the more one does **bright** things, and that is ethical education.

   b. **光明**与**黑暗**不能并存, 正义与邪恶不能兼容。
      Light and **darkness** cannot coexist, and justice and evil are not compatible with each other.

As in (11a), the goal of ethical education is to teach people to do "light" things in a "dark" environment. In (11b), the parallel structure between the two co-ordinate clauses reinforces, syntactically, the conceptual mappings between LIGHT and JUSTICE on the one hand, and DARK and EVIL one the other. "Light" and "dark" forces, whether in the moral or legal domain, always clash with each other in a zero-sum fashion. The examples in (12) also instantiate the conceptual metaphor MORAL IS LIGHT.

(12)   a. 在经济活动中, 他们身上体现着**廉明**, 也体现着合理的利润追求。

In economic activities, they demonstrate themselves as being **honest and light** (i.e., **honest and clean**) while seeking reasonable profits.

   b. 古人的道德**光辉**照亮了我......

The ancient's moral **brilliance illuminated** me ...

   c. 冯契教授一生高风**亮节**、崇德敬业......

Throughout his life, Professor Feng Qi displayed high moral character and **bright moral integrity** (lit. high wind and **bright joint**), esteemed virtue and dedicated himself to his work ...

Example (12a) is about some business people who stick to their moral principles by striking a balance between being morally honest and "light" and making reasonable profits in economic activities. In (12b), 光辉 *guānghuī* is used as a noun meaning "brilliance" or "radiance". In this case, the first-person narrator is reading about an ancient politician, literary scholar, and poet, Wen Tianxiang (1236–1283), of the Song dynasty, and is feeling very much "enlightened" by his moral vision and behavior. In the third example, (12c), the idiom 高风亮节 *gāofēng liàngjié*, which literally means "high wind and bright joint", is a common and typical term depicting someone's "high moral character and bright moral integrity". What is worthy of attention is the two adjectives meaning "high" and "bright" are utilized to describe someone's "moral character" and "moral integrity", respectively, thus instantiating the conceptual metaphor MORAL IS LIGHT (as well as MORAL IS HIGH to be discussed in Chapter 5). The three examples in (13), in contrast, instantiate IMMORAL IS DARK.

(13) a. 该电影揭露了学术界中不讲道德、追逐名利的**阴暗现象**。

The film exposed the **gloomy and dark** (or **seamy**) phenomena of paying no attention to morality and of hankering after fame and gain in the academic circles.

b. 你爸就让一个坏女人勾引走了......那女人更是条**阴险**毒辣的笑面蛇!

Your dad was seduced (away) by a bad woman … That woman was even a **sinister** (lit. **gloomy and dangerous**) and vicious smiling-faced snake!

c. 他看透了口头道德的虚伪和官僚们**阴阳**两面的真相。

He has seen through the hypocrisy of morality in words only and the true looks of the bureaucrats with their **seamy** and **sunny** sides.

The three examples in this group all contain the key element 阴 *yīn*, which contrasts with its opposite 阳 *yáng*. This pair of words refers primarily to the *Yin* and *Yang* principles in ancient Chinese philosophy, according to which *Yin* and *Yang* respectively represent the feminine or negative, and the masculine or positive, forces in nature. The two natural forces interact with each other, opposing but complementary to each other, constituting the law of unity of opposites in Chinese cosmology (see, e.g., Yu 1998). In the Chinese language, this pair of words can also refer to the moon vs. the sun as well as the lunar vs. the solar calendars. In terms of weather, 阴 *yīn* means "overcast; cloudy; gloomy"; it is when the sun (阳 *yáng*) is covered behind the overcast clouds and the day looks gloomy.

Example (13a) concerns the social phenomena that look "gloomy and dark" (阴暗 *yīnàn*), like a gloomy and dark day. It means that the academic circles under discussion are corrupt with ethical problems. In (13b) the relevant compound word 阴险 *yīnxiǎn*, literally "gloomy and dangerous", means "sinister". The woman, who seduced the addressee's father into running away with her, was a "smiling-faced snake", according to the speaker. Such a "snake" appears to be good-natured, but is indeed immoral and dangerous, and will inflict enormous harm to other people. In (13c), 阴 *yīn* and 阳 *yáng* are used together as antonyms in a moral context. Those bureaucrats are hypocritical in that they are double-faced: their "sunny" (阳 *yáng*) side looks moral, but their "seamy" (阴 *yīn*) side is really immoral.

4.4.2 MORAL IS CLEAR and IMMORAL IS MURKY

As a pair of concepts, CLEAR and MURKY refer to the degrees of transparency which is possible only in light and impossible in the dark. When associated with things that are transparent, such as water or glass, they mean "clean" and "dirty", respectively. In Chinese, the concepts of CLEAR and MURKY are mainly encoded by a pair of antonyms: 清 *qīng* "clear" and 浊 *zhuó* "murky", both of which originally describe liquids that are clear or murky in a visual sense. That both words originally describe liquids as being clear or murky is indicated by the semantic radical on the left side of the two characters that represent them. That radical is called "three-drop water" radical. The Chinese characters that have it as their semantic component usually denote something related to liquids. In northern China, there are two rivers called the Jing (泾 *jīng*) and the Wei (渭 *wèi*). Again, both characters that encode the names of the two rivers have the "three-drop water" radical on their left side. These two rivers eventually merge into one. It is said that the Jing river has clear water whereas the Wei river has murky water such that there is a sharp contrast in water colors at the place of their merging. In Chinese, the idiom 泾渭不分 *Jīng-Wèi bùfēn* (lit. make no distinction between the Jing and Wei rivers) means figuratively "fail to distinguish between the good and the bad". This figurative meaning contains two links in semantic extension: one metonymic and the other metaphoric. That is, (i) the names of the rivers metonymically stand for the clear and murky waters of the rivers, and (ii) the colors of the waters, "clear" and "murky", are mapped metaphorically onto "good" and "bad", respectively. Hence, they instantiate the pair of conceptual metaphors (MORALLY) GOOD IS CLEAR and (MORALLY) BAD IS MURKY. The two words under consideration, 清 *qīng* "clear" and 浊 *zhuó* "murky", also each combine with other words to form compounds with a metaphorical moral sense. The three examples in (14) instantiate MORAL IS CLEAR.

(14)   a. 评议对提倡**清廉**高洁的道德风尚起到一定的作用。
        Appraisals produced an effect on the promotion of the **honest and upright** (lit. **clear and honest**), and noble-and-unsullied (lit. high-clean) social ethics.

        b. 如果可能的话, 让他涤尽心灵上的邪恶, 成为道德上**清白**的人。
        If possible, let him wash away the evil in his heart, and become a morally **clean** (lit. **clear and white**) person.

        c. 此人为官**清正**, 作事廉明……
        This person is an **honest and upright** (lit. **clear and upright**) official who acts in a clean and honest (lit. honest and light) way …

In (14a), the compound 清廉 *qīnglián* (lit. clear-honest) is used to describe someone who is morally "honest and upright" or "fair and square". Literally, however, it means "clear and honest". In (14b), the compound word 清白 *qīngbái* (lit. clear-white) means "pure; clean; immaculate" in a moral sense. An evil, immoral person is "dirty" in the heart. Only when the heart is "washed clear and white" can this person become moral again. In (14c), the compound word 清正 *qīngzhèng* (lit. clear and upright) means "honest and upright" in a moral sense. As is obvious, the compound in (14c) also instantiate MORAL IS UPRIGHT (to be discussed in Chapter 5), in addition to MORAL IS CLEAR.

The next three examples in (15) involve 浊 *zhuó* "murky", the opposite of 清 *qīng* "clear". The words that contain it are lexical instantiations of IMMORAL IS MURKY.

(15) a. 腐败分子把许多正直善良的人的心灵世界也搅得越来越阴暗**混浊**。

Corrupt elements stir the mental world of many honest and good people, causing it to be darker and **murkier** (lit. **muddy and murky**).

b. 他们所倡导的是孔孟的仁义道德, 而真心去鼓励的是**污浊**与无耻。

What they promoted was virtue and morality of Confucius and Mencius, but what they really encouraged was **filthiness and murkiness**, and shamelessness.

c. 一些低级庸俗的 "通俗文学" 在抢占文化市场, **浊化**了社会风气, 也对严肃文学形成强劲的冲击波。

Some "popular literature" of low and vulgar tastes is racing to occupy the cultural market, **making** the social morals **murky**, and setting off pounding waves onto serious literature.

In (15a) and (15b), both 混浊 *hùnzhuó* (lit. muddy-murky) and 污浊 *wūzhuó* (lit. filthy-murky) involve *zhuó* "murky" and have the meaning of immorality in contrast with the compounds in (14) containing *qīng* "clear". As in (15a), the hearts and minds (or "mental world") of honest and good people originally contain "clear water", which is however so stirred up by the corrupt people that it is losing its "clarity" and becoming "muddier and murkier". That is, the mood of society is getting worse and worse in moral terms. As in (15b), "filthiness and murkiness" are the opposites of "virtue and morality". In other words, "they", the people who promoted Confucian virtues and morals, are hypocrites according to the writer. In example (15c), the word 浊化 *zhuóhuà* consists of two morphemes: the root *zhuó* "murky" + the causative suffix *huà*, literally meaning "murki-fy". In this case, some "popular literature", considered "low and vulgar" in taste, is being blamed for the social morals becoming "murkier".

In Chinese, when 清 *qīng* "clear" and 浊 *zhuó* "murky", the two antonyms, are combined into a compound, 清浊 *qīngzhuó* (lit. clear-murky), its meaning is either "pure and impure" or "good and evil", commonly used in the domain of MORALITY. Thus, for instance, the idiomatic expression 清浊同流 *qīngzhuó tóngliú*, literally "clear and murky waters flow together", means "the good and the evil are mixed". Three examples are given in (16).

(16)   a. 而这**清浊**之分则内在其心净与不净, 外在其言行举止淡与不淡之间......

And this distinction between **clearness and murkiness** (i.e., **good and evil**) lies internally in one's heart being clean or unclean, and externally in one's manner of talking and acting being calm or uncalm ...

   b. 无论中画西画, 看画要辨**清浊**......画品的**清浊**, 是作者人品**清浊**的直接反映......

Regarding paintings, whether Chinese or Western, we must tell if they are **morally good or bad** (lit. **clear or murky**) ... Whether paintings are **morally good or bad** (lit. **clear or murky**) is a direct reflection of their artists' moral qualities being **good or bad** (lit. **clear or murky**) ...

   c. 他是管干部**清浊**的, 群众早就知道并且议论纷纷的事, 他竟"没想到", 别的不敢说, 至少他应属失职吧!

He is the one in charge of overseeing officials' **ethics** (lit. **clearness and murkiness**); when the mass has long known something and has been talking a great deal about it, he would have "never thought about it"; it must at least be his negligence of duty if nothing else.

Example (16a) is concerned with one's moral quality, which, whether good or bad, is determined, internally, by whether this person has a "clean or unclean" heart, and is displayed, externally, in whether this person has a "calm or un-calm" way of talking and acting. Example (16b) concerns the moral quality of fine arts. As is argued, the moral quality of a painting is a direct reflection of the moral quality of its producer. As shown in the following context of the example, if a painting is "murky" in moral quality, then the painting looks vulgar, filthy, and seductive. If, on the other hand, the painting is "clear" in moral quality, it is then full of nobility and purity. In (16c), the person's job is to oversee the officials' ethical conducts, regarding whether they are "clear" (i.e., morally clean) or "murky" (i.e., corrupt) while exercising their power as governmental officials.

4.4.3 MORAL IS CLEAN and IMMORAL IS DIRTY

The clean-dirty contrast is a major source-domain distinction for moral-visual metaphors (see, e.g., Johnson 1993; Lakoff and Johnson 1999; Lee and Schwarz 2010; Lizardo 2012; Sherman and Clore 2009). Such metaphors are grounded in our embodied experience of physical cleanliness. For instance, experimental studies show that people tend to physically cleanse their "dirty" body parts believed to have been involved in immoral acts or in contact with morally tainted people or objects, and that moral judgments are sensitive to and affected by physical cleanliness manipulations (e.g., Haidt 2001; Lee and Schwarz 2010; Schnall, Benton, and Harvey 2008; Zhong and Liljenquist 2006). In a cognitive-linguistic study that attempts an image-schematic characterization of dirt and cleanliness metaphors applied to moral reasoning and moral cognition, DIRT is conceptualized as a substance in a "container" where it does not normally belong, whereas CLEAN is conceptualized as that substance being kept free from the "container" (Lizardo 2012).

In Chinese, numerous words encoding the concepts CLEAN and DIRTY are involved in the expression of ethical good and evil. The examples are 净 *jìng* "clean" and 洁 *jié* "clean; pure; clear" in contrast with 污 *wū* "dirty; filthy; foul" (see 15b) and 脏 *zāng* "dirty; filthy; unclean". Again, these words can combine with others to form compounds. Look at the following three examples containing 净 *jìng* "clean":

(17) a. 领导自身不**干净**, 怕"拔出萝卜带出泥", 反腐败必然走过场......
      If the leaders themselves are not **clean**, and they are afraid that "the turnips being pulled out will bring mud out with them", then the corruption crackdown must be reduced to mere formality ...

   b. 他们为当代人灵魂的丰富、精神的提升、道德的**净化**做出贡献。
      They made contributions to the enrichment of souls, the elevation of spirits, and the **cleansing** of morals of the people of this generation.

   c. 总之是: "诸恶莫作, 众善奉行, **自净**其意, 是诸佛教"。
      In sum, it should be: "Abandon all the evil deeds, pursue all the good practices, **(self-)cleanse** one's own thoughts, and those are Buddhist teachings".

As shown in (17a), if the leaders themselves are not morally clean, the corruption crackdown will merely be a show with no real results. This is because the leaders are afraid that the crackdown will eventually hurt themselves when, as the old proverbial saying goes, their ethical violations (the "mud") is exposed ("brought out") as a "side effect" of the anti-corruption campaign (on the "turnips being pulled out"). In (17b), the key word 净化 *jìnghuà* (lit. clean-ify or clean-ize) "cleanse; purify" is an antonym of 浊化 *zhuóhuà* (lit. murki-fy) "make murky" in (15c), formed with the same causative suffix and morphological process.

The examples in (18) contain the other common "clean" word in Chinese, 洁 *jié* "clean; pure; clear", used in the moral domain.

(18) a. 你要恪守新闻工作者职业道德准则，**廉洁**自律。

You should hold onto the professional moral codes for journalists, and be **honest and clean** and self-disciplined.

b. 有最**洁白**的良心, 跟全没有良心或有最漆黑的良心, 效果是相等的。

It is of equal effect if one has a most **clean-and-white** conscience (i.e. is morally good) and if one has no conscience at all (i.e. is conscienceless) or has a pitch-black conscience (i.e. is immoral or evil).

c. 一个人得经过艰巨的道德斗争, 才能使自己**洁净**。

One has to go through a rough moral struggle before one can make oneself **clean** (lit. **clean-clean**).

d. 从道德上要求人们**洁身自好**、以义相交。

It requires in morality that people **refuse to be contaminated by evil influence** (lit. **cleanse** their own body and restrain themselves from bad temptations), build social relationships on the basis of righteousness.

With this group of examples, the relevant compounds are 廉洁 *liánjié* (lit. honest-clean) "incorruptible" in (18a), 洁白 *jiébái* (lit. clean-white) "pure white" in (18b), and 洁净 *jiéjìng* (lit. clean-clean) "clean", which is a compound with the two "clean" words combined in one. In (18a) journalists have to be "clean" to adhere to the ethical principles of their profession. In (18b) one's conscience can be "clean and white" or "pitch black" (i.e., extremely dirty) in its moral contrast. Example (18c) shows that for any person, making oneself "clean" means "a rough moral struggle". Example (18d) contains a common four-character idiom about making effort to cultivate one's own moral character. In this idiom, 洁 *jié* "clean" is used as a verb meaning "cleanse".

The examples provided below all involve "dirty" words as lexical instantiations of the conceptual metaphor IMMORAL IS DIRTY. The first group contains 污 *wū* "dirty; filthy; foul", in combination with another word in compound words.

(19) a. 面对社会**污秽**, 保持自己洁净的肌肤。

Faced with social **dirt and filth**, we should maintain our clean skin.

b. 服装行业中假冒伪劣产品却像一股**污浊**暗流泛滥成灾。

In garment industry, fake name brands and imitation products are flooding into a disaster with a **dirty and murky** undercurrent (lit. dark current).

c. 我要主动积极改造, 用自己的汗水洗刷心灵深处的**污垢**。

I want to reform myself initiatively and actively, washing off with my own sweat the **dirt and filth** in the depths of my heart and soul.

d. 对我国社会主义思想道德会有影响, 甚至造成较严重的精神**污染**。

It will affect the socialist ideology and morality of our country, and will even cause rather serious spiritual **pollution** (lit. **dirty-dye**).

e. 越来越多的兴奋剂丑闻也许会**玷污**奥运会纯洁的形象。

More and more doping scandals perhaps will **smear** (lit. **stain-dirty**) the pure and clean image of Olympics.

When we are in a social environment that is "dirty and filthy" (污秽 *wūhuì*), the best we can do is to keep our skin "clean" so that we can be "immune" to evil influence (19a). In (19b), garment industry is said to be flooding with counterfeits, which is an immoral and unethical social problem, and the flood as a disaster is therefore "dirty and murky" (污浊 *wūzhuó*; cf. (15) and (16) above). As in (19c), people with moral problems have "dirt and filth" (污垢 *wūgòu*) in the depths of their hearts and souls, which however can be "washed off with their own sweat". As in (19d), ideological and moral issues may lead to serious spiritual "pollution" (污染 *wūrǎn*), which will result in widespread damage. In (19e), 玷污 *diànwū* "stain; sully; tarnish" is a verb literally meaning "to stain X so that X will look dirty". This is what will happen to Olympics if more and more doping scandals are detected. The examples in (20) display more "dirty" words in a moral sense.

(20) a. 作者竟是一个毕生钻在最无耻、最卑鄙**龌龊**的泥沼和最**污秽**的泥浆里的家伙!

Unexpectedly, the author is a guy who has for the whole life crouched in the most shameless, basest and **dirtiest** mire and the **foulest** (lit. **dirtiest and filthiest**) mud!

b. 一个人如果在道德情操方面是**肮脏**的, 那么他就是一个卑鄙讨厌的人。

If a person is **filthy and dirty** in morality and sentiment, then he is a base and disgusting person.

c. 不是每个人都能给予应有的理解, 甚至招来劈头盖脸泼下的一盆**脏水**, 更有目光短浅的长舌妇们的**污秽**诽谤、人格**污辱**。

Not everyone could give you due understanding; instead, some would pour a basin of **dirty water** right onto your head and face; what's more, there would be those short-sighted, long-tongued women's **foul** (lit. **dirty and filthy**) slanders, and personal **insults** (lit. **dirty-insults**).

In (20a) there are two "dirty" words: 龌龊 *wòchuò* "dirty" and 污秽 *wūhuì* (lit. dirty-filthy) "foul" (cf. 19a). The guy who has crouched in the "dirtiest mire" and "foulest mud" for his whole life must be one of the most immoral persons one can imagine. In (20b) 肮脏 *āngzāng* (lit. filthy-dirty) "dirty" is another common "dirty" word, and a person's ethics and sentiment are "filthy and dirty" if this person is problematic morally. In (20c), "to pour dirty water on someone" means "to smear or slander someone" in a moral sense. As shown in this example, the Chinese word for "insult", 污辱 *wūrǔ*, is another compound that contains 污 *wū* "dirty", literally meaning "dirty insult", i.e., to humiliate someone in a "dirty" way.

Obviously, the source concepts CLEAN and DIRTY are related to those discussed previously in a coherent way. For instance, water clear in light is perceived as clean whereas murky water is associated with contamination or pollution that is essentially dirty. In a similar vein, CLEAN and DIRTY are related with PURE and IMPURE, to which we now turn.

4.4.4 MORAL IS PURE and IMMORAL IS IMPURE

The concept of PURE or IMPURE is not necessarily a visual one, but instead refers to a state of being mixed or unmixed in material, substance, quality, character, etc. Whether something is pure or impure, however, is often noticeable visually. Therefore, both color and light can be pure or impure, and what is clear or clean is seen as pure and what is murky or dirty is considered impure. In our moral cognition, physical purity serves as the experiential grounding for moral purity, and moral impurity is a result of moral taint, contamination, or pollution (e.g., Daniel 2010; Howe 2006; Johnson 1993; Lakoff and Johnson 1999; Landau et al. 2010; Lee and Schwarz 2010; Lizardo 2012; Schnall, Benton, and Harvey 2008; Sherman and Clore 2009; Zhong and Liljenquist 2006).

The pair of concepts PURE and IMPURE is represented by 纯 *chún* "pure" and its negative form 不纯 *bùchún* "impure" or 杂 *zá* "mixed" in Chinese, as illustrated by the examples in (21).

(21)   a.   作家在道德上应该是**纯洁**的人。
          Writers should be morally **pure and clean** people.

      b.   **纯净**的心灵才能出**纯净**的文字。
          Only **pure and clean** hearts and souls can produce **pure and clean** language.

      c.   奴隶社会的道德已从原始社会 "**纯朴**道德的顶峰" 跌落了下来。
          The ethics of slave society had already fallen off "the peak of the **pure and simple** ethics" of primitive society.

      d.   尽管他口不择言, 但心地却**纯良**无比。
          Although he does not pay much attention to what he says (lit. his mouth does not choose or select words), his heart is incomparably **pure and good**.

In the four examples in (21), *chún* "pure" combine with other components to form compounds that are primarily used in a moral sense. It is important that writers be morally "pure and clean" (纯洁 *chúnjié*) (21a) because only "pure and clean" (纯净 *chúnjìng*) hearts and souls can produce "pure and clean" language (21b). It is suggested in (21c) that people are generally "pure and simple" (纯朴 *chúnpǔ*) staying on the "moral peak" in a primitive society, but morality "falls" from that height in a slave society. As in (21d), what the person says can be hurtful to other people, but he is by nature an exceptionally "pure and good" (纯良 *chúnliáng*) person.

(22)   a.   近年来出现了道德滑坡、党风**不纯**、世风恶化。
          What happened in recent years are: moral landslide, **impure** party ethics, and deteriorating social ethics.

      b.   为片面追求轰动效应、上座率、收视率而迎合观众**不纯洁**、不健康的消费口味。
          In order to stir up a sensational effect and raise box-office and TV audience ratings by all means, they made a special effort to cater to the **impure** (lit. **impure and unclean**), unhealthy tastes and interests of the audience.

      c.   然后, 充满了非道德性, 就是文化**混杂**以后的那种不知所属带来的没有约束感的气氛。
          Then, it was filled with immorality, i.e., the sort of atmosphere in which people don't feel restrained, without a sense of belonging, because their culture is all **mixed up**.

The first two sentences in (22) are examples in which the negative form 不纯 *bùchún* (not-pure) "impure" is used. When the party ethics is "impure", there is a "moral landslide" in social ethics (22a). Example (22b) is concerned with the immoral practices in the entertainment business. Higher ratings are sought after, at the cost of moral purity and moral health. Example (22c) involves a different word for impurity, 混杂 *hùnzá* "mix; mingle; confound". According to the author of the essay from which the example is taken, the city of Shanghai is "filled with immorality" because its culture is all "mixed up", contaminated by bad influence from other cultures. Such mixture makes their culture "impure", and therefore is immoral according to the author. That is, IMMORAL IS IMPURE. It is worth noting in passing that whether something being "impure" is viewed as good or bad depends at least to some extent on the perspective of the viewer (see further discussion in section 6.3).

In sum, this section has illustrated the linguistic manifestation in Chinese of the moral metaphors whose source concepts mainly cluster in the domain of visual experience. A prominent feature is that the source concepts are usually lexicalized as compound words, of which many consist of two elements that instantiate two different source concepts such as "pure and clean" or "dirty and murky".

4.5 Summary

The linguistic studies above have led to the qualitative findings summarized in Table 4.4. That is, the source concepts of the moral-visual metaphors in Table 4.1 are encoded by the corresponding lexical items in two languages. As we can see in Table 4.4, all of those lexical items except English *light* have lexicalized moral senses, which are listed in at least one of the three dictionaries in their respective language. Furthermore, all of those lexical items, without exception, have extended moral senses established in actual discourse. This means that the cluster of conceptual metaphors in the visual subsystem in Table 4.1 is applicable, in its entirety, in both English and Chinese. It should be pointed out again that these findings are qualitative, disregarding the varying degrees to which the conceptual metaphors are manifested in each language. For instance, as mentioned above, the pair MORAL IS CLEAR and IMMORAL IS MURKY is apparently manifested more marginally in English, where CLEAR and MURKY seem to play a more central role in the metaphorical conceptualization of mental comprehension (i.e., KNOWING IS SEEING and KNOWLEDGE IS VISION). Studies that quantify differences in linguistic manifestation of the conceptual metaphors in each language as well as between the two languages are yet to be conducted.

Table 4.4 Lexicalized and extended moral senses of the English and Chinese visual words

Language		English		Chinese		
Source concepts	Lexical items	Lexicalized moral senses	Extended moral senses	Lexical items	Lexicalized moral senses	Extended moral senses
LIGHT	*light*		X	明 *míng*	X	X
DARK	*dark*	X	X	暗 *àn*	X	X
CLEAR	*clear*	X	X	清 *qīng*	X	X
MURKY	*murky*	X	X	浊 *zhuó*	X	X
CLEAN	*clean*	X	X	洁 *jié*	X	X
DIRTY	*dirty*	X	X	污 *wū*	X	X
PURE	*pure*	X	X	纯 *chún*	X	X
IMPURE	*impure*	X	X	不纯 *bùchún*	X	X

Regardless of whatever differences there might be in linguistic manifestation, English and Chinese appear to exhibit a high degree of similarity, at the conceptual level, with respect to the applicability of the cluster of moral-visual metaphors in Table 4.1. The question is why this is the case. The answer lies at least partially in the theoretical construct of embodiment in cognitive science (see, e.g., Gibbs 2006). That is, our moral cognition arises partly through metaphor from our embodied experience in the physical world. The four pairs of moral-visual metaphors, I suggest, are grounded in two image schemas, which, as preconceptual gestalt structures that are directly meaningful, are based on two contrastive visual categories in our fundamentally embodied human experience: LIGHT-DARK and CLEAN-DIRTY. These two image schemas can be represented visually as (a) and (b) in Figure 4.3. In case (a), the contrast between light and dark is represented to the maximal degree in two contrastive colors. Case (b) displays the contrast between a clean place and another one contaminated with dirty stains. The other two pairs of moral-visual metaphors, MORAL IS CLEAR and IMMORAL IS MURKY, MORAL IS PURE and IMMORAL IS IMPURE, can be claimed as being grounded in these two image schemas, too, which are apparently shared by English and Chinese.

(a)   (b)

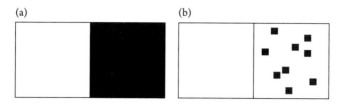

Fig. 4.3 The LIGHT-DARK and CLEAN-DIRTY image schemas

Of course, embodiment is always situated in a specific sociocultural context, and the interaction between bodily experience and cultural interpretation of such experience determines the selection of metaphors (see, e.g., Gibbs 1999; Kövecses 2005, 2015a; Yu 2008, 2015b). Thus, for instance, we cannot predict whether CLEAR and MURKY will serve as source concepts for moral metaphors in a particular language and culture. We can, however, hypothesize that if they do, CLEAR would map onto MORAL, and MURKY onto IMMORAL based on our embodied as well as cultural experience that causes us to feel positive or negative about aspects of our physical surroundings. In moral imagination, similar cultural interpretation of certain related and contrastive categories in our visual experience as positive or negative contributes to the commonality between English and Chinese in the cluster of visual moral metaphors under study. Given that English and Chinese are unrelated languages in terms of language families, one of Indo-European origin and the other Sino-Tibetan, the results of the study lend support to the hypothesis for the candidacy of at least some of the moral metaphors in the cluster being widespread or even universal. Further research is needed to falsify or support this hypothesis.

More specifically, we may say that, with respect to moral-visual metaphors, English and Chinese share the common contrastive valences at the image-schematic level in our fundamental visual experience: LIGHT-DARK, CLEAN-DIRTY, TRANSPARENT-OPAQUE, MIXED-UNMIXED. Based on these fundamental commonalities, English and Chinese share the moral-visual metaphors in Table 4.1 as well. In addition, English and Chinese may be common or different when it comes down to the level of specific frames deployed for metaphorical mappings. For example, a commonly used frame is the CLEAN-ING frame, which may have various subcases at a particular schematic level, such as those given below:

CLEANING: AGENT removes DIRT from x (with Y).
WASHING: AGENT removes DIRT from x with WATER.
SWEEPING: AGENT removes DIRT from x with BROOM.

VACUUMING: AGENT removes DIRT from x with VACUUM CLEANER.

MOPPING: AGENT removes DIRT from x with MOP.

DUSTING: AGENT removes DIRT from x with DUSTER.

In the above examples, the roles of AGENT and DIRT are constants, to be filled with various values, whereas X and Y are variables, to be substituted depending on specific situations. For instance, X could be "clothing", "floor", "carpet", "desktop", etc. Y refers to a chief instrument used in cleaning, such as "water", "broom", "vacuum", etc., but it could simply be "hand" as our most deployable instrument. In any of the subframes of CLEANING, further instruments can be added according to our encyclopedic knowledge. For instance, the Chinese compound word 扫黄 sǎohuáng (lit. sweep-yellow), in the "verb + object" construction, is often used metaphorically in a moral or legal context. It refers to the "movement" mobilized "to eliminate pornography and prostitution". It is worth noting here that, while the color yellow is negative in this case, linked with pornography and prostitution, in general the color yellow is perceived as positive in Chinese culture. For example, yellow is the main color of Chinese feudal emperors' imperial robes. The national flag of the People's Republic of China is red with five five-pointed stars that are yellow. Thus, Chinese athletes on the national teams often wear red and yellow uniforms when representing China in international sporting events. Therefore, it is of vital importance not to make simplistic or sweeping generalizations regarding cultural meanings of color or any other concepts. Culturally constructed meanings are also relative to the situations in which they are interpreted. For this very reason, I chose to encompass the three core roles (i.e., HUMAN PERCEIVER, ENTITY PROPERTY, and AFFECTIVE VALENCE) with a "Situation" frame enclosed within the "Culture" frame in the design and construction of the general source frames for the three subsystems of moral metaphor system under study (see Figures 3.2, 4.2, and 5.4).

While the compound 扫黄 sǎohuáng (lit. sweep-yellow) is a lexical instantiation of a moral or legal metaphor mapping a higher level of frame structure, the CLEANING frame, the specific use of the "sweep" word evokes one of its subcases, the SWEEPING subframe, with the instrument (Y) of a broom. A wide variety of options at different levels of schematicity or specificity for the deployment of frame structures opens up the possibility for cross-linguistic and cross-cultural variations under the influence of contextual factors (cf. Kövecses' 2020 multilevel view of metaphor, and 2015a contextual factors of metaphor). In the Chinese compound word above, pornography and prostitution's being "yellow" is specific to Chinese. Whether the same SWEEPING frame is evoked in a similar moral or legal situation is also questionable in English.

At the linguistic level, there are both similarities and differences in the linguistic expressions of both languages. To me, however, the most salient linguistic difference between English and Chinese lies in the nature of Chinese morphology. That is, in contemporary Chinese, a large number of Chinese words are disyllabic, consisting of two Chinese characters. As found in the Chinese examples discussed in section 4.4, very often the compound words encode two distinct source concepts, either both from the visual subsystem or one from the visual and one from another subsystem (cf. Chapter 3). For example, such Chinse compounds were found to represent the following combinations of two source concepts: DIRTY-MURKY, PURE-CLEAN, HIGH-CLEAN, CLEAR-UPRIGHT, PURE-UPRIGHT, etc. This means two-on-one mappings in Chinese. In English, on the other hand, it is usually one-on-one mapping.

Having presented my study on the visual subsystem of the moral metaphor system, I next turn to the spatial subsystem in Chapter 5.

5

Spatial subsystem of moral metaphors

5.1 Moral-spatial metaphors: Source concepts and frames

This chapter aims to examine the spatial subsystem of moral metaphors in English and Chinese. In this subsystem, the source concepts of moral metaphors come from the domain of SPATIALITY. The spatial conceptualization is acceptably central to human cognition, not only because "spatial understanding is perhaps the first great intellectual task facing the child, a task which human mobility makes mandatory", but also because, after all, "spatial thinking invades our conceptualizations of many other domains as diverse as time, social structures and mathematics" (Levinson 1996: 179). In his introduction to the *Cognitive Linguistics* special issue on "Spatial Language and Cognition", Sinha (1995: 7) points out:

> As we learn more both about the biological foundations of human spatial perception and cognition, and about the truly astonishing variation between languages in the way they express and schematize spatial meaning, we cannot fail to be struck by the thought that the spatial domain is a particularly rich one for empirical investigation both of possible linguistic and cognitive universals, and of possible cross-linguistic and cross-cultural cognitive differences.

Humans often depend on their ability to recruit spatial concepts and schemas for nonspatial, abstract tasks because abstract cognition is built on the indispensable foundation of spatial cognition and the spatial domain is an appropriate and appealing platform for higher cognitive processes (Casasanto 2010; Gattis 2001, 2002; Tversky 2011, 2015). This is also why cognitive scientists in general and cognitive linguists in particular have long treated spatial language and conceptualization as central topics in the study of abstract thought and embodied cognition (e.g., Casasanto and Bottini 2014; Cienki 1998; Dirven and Taylor 1988; Gibbs 1994, 2006; Heine 1997; King 1988; Lakoff and Johnson 1980, 1999; Sinha and Thorseng 1995; Yu 1998). Both cognitive semantics and cognitive grammar, the two branches of cognitive

The Moral Metaphor System. Ning Yu, Oxford University Press. © Ning Yu (2022).
DOI: 10.1093/oso/9780192866325.003.0005

linguistics, "rest upon an essentially visuo-spatial conception of meaning and conceptualization, in which symbolic structures are derived from embodied constraints upon human perception and agency in a spatial field" (Sinha 1995: 7).

In our spatial conceptualization, spatial metaphors help us understand and reason about abstract domains through mental representation or configuration of spatial structures that lay out their elements and relations in terms of spatial orientations, dimensions, and arrays. Space is relational, and therefore benefits relational reasoning about abstract structures and concepts on the basis of spatial relations and configurations. Because of its central role in human cognition, studies of spatial metaphor are found in various disciplines or areas of research or application. For instance, spatial metaphors are studied as cognitive tools utilized in the organization of information and knowledge (Howell, Love, and Turner 2005; Van Acker and Uyttenhove 2012), in the writing of hypertext for databases (Bromme and Stahl 1999), and as grounding diagrams and graphs showing abstract relations and organizations for the purpose of visualizing abstract thoughts (Gattis 2002; Gillan 1995; Tversky 2011, 2015). Also, they are studied in philosophical texts for interpreting philosophers' thoughts and constructs (Bradshaw 2011; Gow 2001), in feminist and ethnical discourse for challenging existing knowledge and power structures, applying spatial configurations of gender, and understanding particular ethnical experience (Price-Chalita and Saresma 1994; Leeman 1995; Shands 1999), in the consideration and evaluation of individual and social responses to health issues and epidemical and natural disasters (Austin 2013; Bourk and Holland 2014; Craddock 1995), and in youth research for the understanding of youth transition and belonging (Cuervo and Wyn 2014). Further, spatial metaphors are studied in the narration of experience of listening to music (Peltola and Saresma 2014), in the conceptualization of the mind (Reed 2003) and time (Graf 2011; Moore 2017; Sinha and Bernárdez 2015; Stites and Özçalişkan 2013), in the description of auditory events (Wolter et al. 2015), in thinking and talking about other people and perceived wellbeing (Gozli et al. 2018; Lomas 2019), in literary and dramatic works for various thematic significations, identity formations, and constructive functions (Brown 2006; Burgard 1987; Davies 2004; Halloran-Bessy 2009; Hyatt 1984; MacKay 1986), and as part of the development of metaphorical competence in first and second language acquisition (Jin 2011; Shayan et al. 2014).

Following the line of research on the metaphorical character of moral cognition, my primary goal for this chapter is to outline the linguistic patterns in English and Chinese that supposedly manifest and, in turn, reinforce the underlying spatial subsystem of moral metaphors. In this metaphor subsystem, spatial concepts are utilized as source concepts mapped onto MORAL and IMMORAL as their target concepts. In the literature of cognitive science, spatial concepts have been shown to play crucial roles in abstract thought and reason, and it is argued that abstract cognition builds on spatial cognition (e.g., Casasanto 2010; Gattis 2001; Tversky 2011). It is therefore not surprising that spatial concepts play a major role in moral cognition. According to conceptual metaphor theory (CMT), that role is played via metaphor.

In Chapters 3 and 4, I looked at the physical and visual subsystems of moral metaphors in English and Chinese. For this chapter, I investigate the metaphor subsystem for morality based on spatial conceptualization of moral constructs in English and Chinese. This subsystem can be summarized by a central metaphor: MORALITY IS SPATIALITY, with which moral concepts MORAL and IMMORAL are reasoned and talked about via spatial concepts. In this section, I first lay out the major spatial concepts engaged in this moral metaphor subsystem as source concepts, presenting a schematic configuration of how these spatial concepts are related to each other in pairs of valence mapped onto their respective target concepts MORAL and IMMORAL. In section 5.2, I review some literature in psychological research on moral and affective metaphors with spatial concepts as their source concepts. Again, this is a linguistic study. I, therefore, outline the linguistic patterns that manifest the putative metaphorical mappings at the conceptual level in English and Chinese, respectively in sections 5.3 and 5.4. I then take a deeper look at the linguistic evidence in section 5.5.

Table 5.1 The cluster of moral metaphors grounded in spatial experiences

Conceptual metaphors	Positive versions	Negative versions
MORALITY IS HEIGHT	MORAL IS HIGH	IMMORAL IS LOW
MORALITY IS UPRIGHTNESS	MORAL IS UPRIGHT	IMMORAL IS SLANTED
MORALITY IS LEVELNESS	MORAL IS LEVEL	IMMORAL IS UNLEVEL
MORALITY IS STRAIGHTNESS	MORAL IS STRAIGHT	IMMORAL IS CROOKED
MORALITY IS SIZE	MORAL IS BIG	IMMORAL IS SMALL

In Table 5.1, five moral-spatial metaphors are listed along with their positive and negative parametric versions as their entailed child metaphors. It is worth stressing that these moral-spatial metaphors, their source concepts representing five fundamental dimensions of space, are major ones involved in the spatial subsystem. There may be others that need further research. Similar to the visual subsystem, the spatial subsystem is again organized in a three-level hierarchical structure. At the top is the general metaphor MORALITY IS SPATIALITY, identifying and labeling the two domains in the mapping. At the middle level, the five metaphors have their source-domain concepts indicating five dimensions of spatiality. At the lowest level, the five pairs of metaphors each profile the parametric end regions of the five spatial dimensions.

Schematically, the configuration of spatial concepts, both orientational and dimensional ones, can be illustrated as in Figure 5.1(a) and (b) (Yu 2016: 111). The figure shows the image schemas of the spatial concepts involved and how they are related to one another in a system. Image schemas are schematic abstractions of recurring dynamic patterns of our perceptual interactions and motor programs that give coherence and structures to our experience while emerging from our bodily experience and constantly operating in our perceptual interaction, bodily movement through space, and physical manipulation of objects (Johnson 1987).

In Figure 5.1(a), one vertical line (ab) and one horizontal line (cd) cross each other at point (g) forming a perpendicular relation between them. A third slanting line (ef) also runs through point (g). The vertical line is divided by the horizontal line into the upper and lower halves. Its upper half (ag) is mapped onto morally positive valence, i.e., MORAL IS HIGH, in contrast with its lower half (gb), which is inherently negative, i.e., IMMORAL IS LOW. Also, there is a contrast in valence between line (ag) and line (eg): the former is positive because it is upright, hence MORAL IS UPRIGHT, whereas the latter, which is slanted or tilted, is negative in valence, namely IMMORAL IS SLANTED (or IMMORAL IS TILTED).

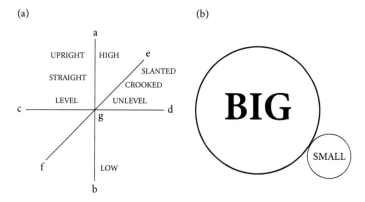

Fig. 5.1 Schematic configurations of spatial concepts for moral metaphors
Source: Yu (2016: 111).

As for the horizontal line (cd), it is also mapped positively onto morality because it is level, i.e., MORAL IS LEVEL in contrast with the unlevel line (ef) or (cge), which is negative, i.e., IMMORAL IS UNLEVEL. Note that "LEVEL" here refers to a horizontal line "that is straight and has both ends at the same height". According to this criterion, line (ef) is not level because it is inclined to one side, forming a slope down toward the left. Line (cge) is not level, either, because it is not straight, with a bend at point (g), and its two ends are not at the same height.

In fact, any single line that is bent into a crook, for instance, line (age) or (dge), is mapped negatively onto immorality, i.e., IMMORAL IS CROOKED, in contrast in valence with a straight line, i.e., MORAL IS STRAIGHT. Note that "STRAIGHT" here has to meet two relevant criteria: (i) not bent, and (ii) level or upright. With criterion (i), a straight line is simply the shortest distance between any two points disregarding its orientation in the environment. Criterion (ii), however, is dependent on the spatial context in which a straight line is situated. In Figure 5.1(a), lines (ag) and (cd) are straight because these two are upright and level, respectively. In contrast, line (ef) is not straight because it is neither upright nor level. Line (gb) is not straight either since it is "downright", not upright. Finally, Figure 5.1(b) merely displays one valence contrast in size mapped onto MORALITY and IMMORALITY: MORAL IS BIG and IMMORAL IS SMALL.

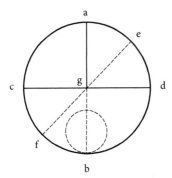

Fig. 5.2 Combined schematic configuration of spatial concepts for moral metaphors
Source: Adapted from Yu (2016: 120).

The spatial source concepts, both orientational and dimensional ones, can be unified into a single schematic configuration as in Figure 5.2 (adapted from Yu 2016: 120). The figure is meant to illustrate the image schemas of the spatial concepts involved. I would suggest that the five moral-spatial metaphors with their ten versions in positivity and negativity are based on four common image schemas: (i) UP-DOWN, (ii) BALANCE, (iii) PATH, and (iv) OBJECT. The UP-DOWN schema consists of a vertical axis with an imaginary division between UP and DOWN. The vertical axis is in general not symmetric in valence with its UP and

DOWN halves: the upper representing the positive, and the lower the negative.[1] This schema is responsible for the understanding of HIGH and LOW (including THICK and THIN). The BALANCE schema, as I suggested before (Yu 1998: 174), may have two possible variants as illustrated in Figure 5.3, where the dotted lines indicate off-balance shifts. Thus, Figure 5.3(a) stands for UPRIGHT vs. SLANTED, and Figure 5.3(b) for LEVEL vs. UNLEVEL. Version (b) can be seen as an image schema for the scales as a weighing instrument, which is a common symbol for legal justice and moral fairness.

(a)   (b)

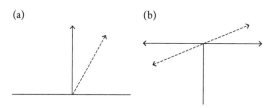

Fig. 5.3 Two versions of BALANCE and
OFF-BALANCE schemas
Source: Yu (1998: 174).

The third image schema involved in moral imagination, PATH, is simply a straight line by default in contrast with a crooked line, a line that is bent or twisted. The schematic contrast between STRAIGHT and CROOKED has long been noticed by cognitive linguists as mapping metaphorically onto the moral contrast between GOOD and EVIL (Cienki 1998; Jäkel 2002). Finally, our schematic understanding of OBJECT is that it occupies space with its physical existence of various sizes.[2] In Figure 5.1(b), I used circles, a prototypical shape conventionally utilized for the CONTAINER schema, to represent the size of OBJECT.

The four image schemas play a central role in our spatial conceptualization of morality. In summary, Figure 5.2 unifies these image schemas into one diagram, where the dashed lines represent IMMORALITY, as is opposed to

---

[1] As far as the human body is concerned, the UP-DOWN, as well as FRONT-BACK, asymmetry is obvious while the LEFT-RIGHT asymmetry is far less so. In terms of function, however, the LEFT-RIGHT asymmetry is clear in people's right vs. left-handedness. See Casasanto (2014) for the distinction between left- and right-handers in terms of bodily relativity and spatial mapping of valence. In the political domain of modern Chinese, it seems, the left-right distinction is a little complex, varying according to the political context of the time. Thus, "left" can mean "revolutionary" vs. "right" for "reactionary". During the Cultural Revolution (1966–1976), the "Gang of Four", generally perceived as "leftists", ended up being labeled "ultra-leftists", "counterrevolutionaries", and "leftists in form but rightists in essence". In older strata of Chinese, however, "left" indeed represents the negative (HYDCD 2000: 509), and "right" the positive valence (HYDCD 2000: 793), in the moral domain.

[2] For studies of primary metaphors based on the OBJECT image schema, see Yu, Yu, and Lee (2017) and Yu and Huang (2019).

MORALITY represented by solid lines. As seen in this figure, there is correlation between height and size: the longer the vertical axis (diameter), the larger the size of the circle. Such coherence finds a good example of linguistic instantiation in a Chinese compound word 高大 *gāo-dà* (lit. high/tall-big), meaning in particular: (i) (of physical body) tall and big; (ii) (of moral character) lofty and noble. As is displayed, this figure is designed to show how the source concepts of the moral-spatial metaphors fit together schematically and coherently in a conceptual network.

In Figure 5.4, I present a general source frame for the spatial subsystem of moral metaphors. As can be seen, this one is again very similar to Figures 3.2 and 4.2 presented for the moral-physical and moral-visual metaphors in Chapters 3 and 4, only with a different set of source concepts that are primarily spatial in character. In this case, what is perceived spatially is not just through the sense of sight, although vision is still the central sense through which it is known. Additionally, it may possibly be known through other senses or the whole body in motion or action. The blind can still sense spatial reality without actually seeing it.

As in Figure 5.4, what HUMAN PERCEIVER perceives in this source frame is some salient spatial property of an entity. The entity is abstracted away from its original physical form, as something one-dimensional (a line), two-dimensional (a plane), or three-dimensional (an object). The perception of the ENTITY PROPERTY in a particular situation as being HIGH or LOW, UPRIGHT or

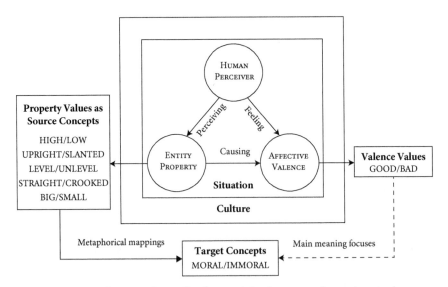

Fig. 5.4 A general source frame for the spatial subsystem of moral metaphors

SLANTED, LEVEL or UNLEVEL, STRAIGHT or CROOKED, or BIG or SMALL, should cause the HUMAN PERCEIVER to feel the AFFECTIVE VALENCE as being either GOOD or BAD (i.e., POSITIVE or NEGATIVE). That is, the affective valence (GOOD or BAD) is at the heart of the moral valence (MORAL or IMMORAL). Again, morality cannot be separated from emotionality or affectivity. After all, morality is an affectively-laden concept (Lakoff 2008b: chapter 4; Meier, Robinson, et al. 2007; see also Zhai et al. 2018).

5.2 Psychological research on spatial moral and affective metaphors

There is a large, and still growing, body of literature in psychology that presents experimental studies on affective and moral metaphors involving spatial concepts as their sources. It is fair to say, I think, that most, if not all, such studies are inspired or motivated by CMT even though some of them have actually questioned or challenged some of the fundamental tenets of CMT with their empirical findings. Of those findings some, for some reason, are contradictory to each other or have failed to be replicated. As a metaphor theory that originates from cognitive linguistics, CMT absolutely needs such questions and challenges, as well as supports and endorsements, from psychology for its development.

The first pair of source concepts for affective-spatial and moral-spatial metaphors is HIGH vs. LOW (or, more schematically, UP vs. DOWN) on the HEIGHT or VERTICALITY dimension structured along a vertical axis (see Figure 5.2). In fact, the vast majority of experimental studies on moral and affective metaphors concentrate on the mappings between MORAL or POSITIVE and HIGH or UP and between IMMORAL or NEGATIVE and LOW or DOWN. For example, in their studies of the vertical representation of morality, Meier, Sellbom, and Wygant (2007) conducted two experiments to determine the extent to which verticality is used to represent moral concepts. For their first experiment, they selected five words with a moral meaning (*caring, charity, nurture, truthful,* and *trustworthy*) and five words with an immoral meaning (*adultery, corrupt, dishonest, evil,* and *molest*), and asked the participants to perform quick and accurate categorizations. They found that participants were faster at categorizing the moral words when they were paired with the asterisks that appeared up and the immoral words when they were paired with asterisks that appeared down rather than when these pairings were reversed. In the second experiment, participants were asked to categorize words as having a moral or immoral meaning as the words randomly appeared near the top or bottom of a screen, and then to complete a self-reported psychopathy scale selection to detect their psychopathy level. It was found that participants low in psychopathy (i.e., more concerned with morality) were faster to categorize the moral words when presented near the top, but they were faster to categorize the immoral words when presented near the bottom. Both experiments suggest that people have implicit associations between morality and vertical space (i.e., MORAL IS HIGH and IMMORAL IS LOW) and that this effect might be specific to individuals low in psychopathy (i.e., those who care more about morality). The experimenters' findings, therefore, support the CMT view that abstract-knowledge representation is aided by conceptual metaphors (see also Li and Cao 2017; Lu, Jia and Zhai 2017; Xie et al. 2015; Zhai and Lu 2018).

In an attempt to replicate and extend the results of Meier, Sellbom, and Wygant (2007), Hill and Lapsley (2009) report two studies that focused solely on moral personality traits and evaluate whether they are represented metaphorically along two relevant metaphor dimensions: verticality and brightness (see also section 4.2). In Study 1, which investigated the interaction between moral personality and vertical position, participants were asked to categorize moral or immoral trait words appearing on the upper or lower computer screen. The study found that, while the moral/low and moral/high conditions did not differ significantly, participants categorized immoral trait words more quickly when these traits were presented in the lower visual field. The results showed that the moral personality is represented metaphorically along the vertical dimension, but this may only be true for the immoral personality, suggesting an adaptive attentional bias toward immoral traits. The researchers' speculation for the reason why people may be more likely to use metaphor to discuss immoral rather than moral individuals is that people may be more likely to discuss immoral people than moral people. This immoral bias in moral valence consists with the more general negativity bias in affective valence discussed by Rozin and Royzmann (2001) as well as the asymmetry between the good and bad contrast discussed by Lakens et al. (2012). As Hill and Lapsley (2009) suggested, their findings were both similar to and different from those of Meier, Sellbom, and Wygant (2007). One of the possible reasons, according to Hill and Lapsley (2009), is that they focused solely on moral personality traits whereas Meier, Sellbom, and Wygant (2007) dealt with moral concepts in general. Another interesting direction that Hill and Lapsley (2009) suggested for future research was the close link between language use and metaphorical representation of moral personality traits. That is, we only represent moral traits along those perceptual dimensions specifically invoked in the metaphors we use in language.

As a metaphorical extension to the relationship between verticality and morality, a different strand of psychological research on morality explores the relationship between moral "elevation", an emotion characterized by a sense of feeling morally "uplifted", and moral behavior (Schnall, Roper, and Fessler 2010; Schnall and Roper 2012) and clinical depression (Erickson and Abelson 2012). Apart from the probe into the connection between moral valence and vertical position, as well as that between power conception and vertical dimension (e.g., Giessner and Schubert 2007; Lakens, Semin, and Foroni 2011; Schubert 2005), psychological research is also overwhelmingly concerned with the association between affective valence and vertical space, i.e., POSITIVE IS UP and NEGATIVE IS DOWN (see Crawford 2009; Meier and Robinson 2005 for reviews). For instance, in a series of three experimental studies, Meier and Robinson (2004) found that (i) positive words were judged faster when in the up position whereas negative words were judged faster when in the down position; (ii) evaluations of positive words activated higher visual space whereas evaluations of negative words activated lower visual space; and (iii) while evaluations activate areas of visual space, spatial positions do not activate evaluations. Their findings suggested that affect is associated with vertical position in a metaphor-congruent way, and that such associations are unidirectional, for instance, GOOD activates UP, but UP does not activate GOOD. These findings, therefore, provided evidence that "affect is grounded in sensorimotor perception" (Meier and Robinson 2004: 247).

In their research on the spatial representation of affect, Crawford et al. (2006) examined how the association between valence and verticality influences memory for the locations of affectively valenced stimuli. The results of the three experimental studies indicated that participants' memories of location were influenced by stimulus valence, such that positive items are biased upward relative to negative items. Their findings suggested that spatial metaphors provide a way to recruit spatial cognition in order to reason about affective experience, thus reflecting the metaphorical mediation of affect. The studies of Crawford et al. (2006) differ from those of Meier and Robinson (2004) in that participants performed nonlinguistic tasks involving nonlinguistic stimuli.

Casasanto and Dijkstra (2010) investigated the relationship between motor action and emotional memory. In Experiment 1, they had participants retell autobiographical memories with either positive or negative valence while moving marbles either upward or downward. It was found that participants retrieved memories faster when the direction of movement was congruent with the valence of the memory: i.e., they retrieved positive memories faster when moving marbles upward and retrieved negative memories faster when moving marbles downward. In Experiment 2, participants were instructed to move marbles up or down. When they moved marbles up, they retrieved more positive memories; when they moved marbles down, they retrieved more negative memories. These results suggest that positive or negative life experiences are implicitly associated with upward or downward motion, which is "consistent with theories of metaphorical mental representation" (Casasanto and Dijkstra 2010: 179).

One issue lying in the psychological research on the relationship between vertical position and word meaning is that of polarity benefits—i.e., basic asymmetries in the way people process dimensions such as verticality, morality, affective valence—in contrast with metaphor congruency effects (Lakens 2011, 2012; Lynott and Coventry 2014). According to polarity benefits, in the processing of words (and concepts) expressing dimensions with bipolarities (e.g., *up* vs. *down*, *moral* vs. *immoral*, *powerful* vs. *powerless*, and *positive* vs. *negative*), plus polar words (e.g., *up*, *moral*, *powerful*, and *positive*) are categorized faster than minus polar words (i.e., *down*, *immoral*, *powerless*, and *negative*). Furthermore, the "polarity correspondence principle" predicts that stimuli where polarities correspond (e.g., positive words presented up and negative words presented down) provide an additional processing benefit compared with stimuli where polarities do not correspond (e.g., negative words presented up and positive words presented down) (Lakens 2012: 726). For example, in Figure 5.5, the image of an art clip displays the bipolar concepts of the MORALITY dimension: MORAL and IMMORAL. The design both exhibits metaphor congruency effects (i.e., MORAL IS UP and IMMORAL IS DOWN) and follows the polarity correspondence principle (i.e., plus words are placed above the minus words). From a linguistic perspective, what is of interest is why MORALITY, which has nothing to do with space, should be represented metaphorically in terms of VERTICALITY in the first place, and how such spatial representation of MORALITY manifests itself in language.

Fig. 5.5 An art clip instantiating MORAL IS UP and IMMORAL IS DOWN

Experimental studies have also been conducted along the horizontal axis, but are largely limited to the spatial representation of valence, i.e., GOOD (or POSITIVE) IS RIGHT and BAD (or NEGATIVE) IS LEFT (see, e.g., Casasanto 2009a, 2014; de la Fuente et al. 2015). Chen et al. (2018), however, conducted a cross-cultural study of horizontal spatial metaphor for morality in the majority Han Chinese and Hui ethnic minority in China. In two experiments, they found that Han participants exhibited no horizontal spatial metaphors for moral-ity at all. On the other hand, one of the two experiments showed that Hui participants categorized words with moral meaning faster when the spatial primes were on the right in contrast to the left; they evaluated words with im-moral meaning faster when the spatial primes were on the left in opposition to the right. According to the researchers, these results may be attributable to a difference in culture: i.e., Hui is a "right-superior and left-inferior" culture whereas there is "no stable horizontal positions for superiority and inferiority" in Han culture (Chen et al. 2018: 6). After all, left and right are body-centered directions dependent on the changing perspectives of mobile individuals, in contrast with verticality, which is absolutely grounded in the common, physical experience of gravity (Crawford et al. 2006).

As mentioned above, psychological research on spatial representation of morality focuses on the spatial dimension of verticality, i.e., high or low posi-tion or up and down orientation. One more recent study conducted by Pacilli et al. (2018), however, focused on straightness as a spatial concept associated with morality. Their Study 1 was designed to assess the relative strength of the implicit association between straight figures and morality-related words. It was found that participants strongly associated the concept of straight-ness with the concept of morality, the two of them being inherently linked. Study 2 further revealed that the results of Study 1 were not attributable to the general association between straight figures and positivity. Although the implicit association between straightness and positivity is correlated with the implicit association between straightness and morality, the latter remained significant beyond any effect of positivity. In Study 3, participants showed a stronger preference for straight figures after they recalled moral deeds than after they recalled immoral deeds. Study 4 showed that participants who re-called sociable (vs. unsociable) deeds did not exhibit any significant preference for straight figures, thus confirming that the stronger preference for straight figures found in Study 3 was particularly associated with morality. Through these experimental studies, therefore, Pacilli et al. (2018: 670) were able to re-veal "the crucial role of the spatial metaphor of straightness in the morality domain".

The last spatial metaphor listed in Table 5.1 is MORALITY IS SIZE. Size is a central spatial concept. While, to my knowledge, no psychological experiments have specifically worked on the association between size and morality, such experiments have been carried out on the association between size and power (Schubert, Waldzus, and Giessner 2009), size and aesthetic preference (Silvera, Josephs, and Giesler 2002), and size and affect (Meier, Robinson, and Caven 2008). Of these abstract categories, affect is closely related to morality. In their examination of affective metaphors (i.e., POSITIVE IS BIG and NEGATIVE IS SMALL) in Study 1, Meier et al. (2008) had participants evaluate positive and negative words presented in either larger or smaller font sizes. It was found that evaluation interacted with manipulation of font sizes in such a way that positive words were evaluated more quickly when presented in a large font size, whereas negative words were evaluated more quickly when presented in a small font size. Study 2, which aimed to test the automatic nature of the relations between evaluations and stimulus sizes, extended Study 1 by adding a response deadline procedure to its design. It was found that positive words were evaluated more accurately in a larger font size whereas negative words were evaluated more accurately in a smaller font size. Study 3 aimed to examine font size effects on evaluative judgments using neutral target words. The results showed that participants rated neutral words presented in a larger font size as more positive than neutral words presented in a smaller font size. These results are, as the researchers concluded, consistent with the metaphor-representation perspective.

As reviewed in this section, results of psychological research on the relationship between morality and spatiality are not entirely consistent, and they are sometimes contradictory. It is totally understandable that differences in findings may emerge from subtle differences in experimental designs or methodologies. There are also questions on whether particular effects observed in experiments stem from metaphorical representation or experiential association (see, e.g., Crawford 2009). In Crawford (2009), for instance, metaphoric representation and association were treated as alternative accounts of findings and issues in asymmetry and directionality between domains. Can they reconcile with each other for theoretic and pragmatic purposes? This question is further confounded with questions on the definition of metaphorical representation, the interaction between conceptual and linguistic representations of metaphors, and the relationship between language and thought in general. More specifically, for instance, is polysemy a purely linguistic phenomenon or guided by conceptual representation and driven by experiential association or correlation? Further, should conceptual metaphors, which are claimed to entail unidirectionality in mapping, rule out bidirectional activation of do-mains at the experiential level? More clearly, is bidirectional activation be-tween domains of experience, tested at the level of conceptual metaphor or the level of experiential association or correlation that grounds conceptual metaphor? All these issues remain to be addressed more carefully and compre-hensively (see also discussions in, e.g., Dong, Huang, and Zhong 2015; Grady and Ascoli 2017; Lakoff 2014; Lee and Schwarz 2012; Schneider et al. 2011; Yu et al. 2016; Zhong and Leonardelli 2008).

At this point, however, I just want to emphasize that, as reviewed above, experimental studies in psychology on spatial representation of morality have concentrated on the relationship between morality and verticality (see, e.g., Crawford 2009; Meier and Robinson 2005), with one exception that deals with the relationship between morality and straightness (Pacilli et al. 2018). There are, however, other moral-spatial metaphors in language that have not been studied by psychological research. In the next two sections, I will look at them as manifested linguistically in English and Chinese, respectively.

5.3 Spatial moral metaphors in English

I now turn to English for this study and examine its moral-spatial metaphor subsystem. I want to see if the five pairs of conceptual metaphors in Table 5.1 are applicable in English. It is known from previous studies in the literature that some of them are common moral metaphors in English, but what about the others? I look at them as forming a moral-spatial metaphor subsystem with its parts related to one another in a conceptual network as illustrated in Figure 5.2. I lay out the linguistic data collected from the Corpus of Con-temporary American English (COCA), with which we hope to show that the five pairs of conceptual metaphors are indeed manifested in the English language.

The English linguistic data in this section are partly adopted from Yu, Wang, and He (2016). That study presented and discussed the linguistic data collected from COCA, which appear to be instantiating the five pairs of conceptual metaphors in Table 5.1. But before discussing the COCA linguistic data, I first take a look at the lexicalization of moral senses of some English spatial words. Table 5.2 provides the conventionally lexicalized moral senses of the spatial adjectives in three major English dictionaries: *Webster*, *Oxford*, and *Longman*. As can be seen, only *unlevel* does not have lexicalized moral sense listed in either of the three dictionaries, and additionally, *small* does not have a moral sense listed in *Longman*, but it means "mean; petty" in *Webster*, and "morally mean, ungenerous, petty, paltry" in *Oxford*.

Table 5.2 Lexicalized moral senses of the spatial words in the three English dictionaries

Dictionary	Webster	Oxford	Longman
Word	**Conventionally lexicalized moral senses**		
High	Exalted or elevated in character; noble; morally good	Morally or culturally superior	Showing goodness
Low	Morally reprehensible; base; vulgar; morally bad	Unscrupulous or dishonest	Not respectable or good
Upright	Marked by strong moral rectitude; always behaving in an honest way; having high moral standards	Strictly honorable or honest	Always behaving in an honest way
Tilted	Changed so that a particular result or occurrence is more likely, a particular group is favored, etc.	Changed or caused to change in favor of one person or thing as opposed to another	Changed so that people start to prefer one person, belief, or action to others
Level	Reasonable; balanced; equal in advantage, progression, and standing	Even, equable, uniform, well-balanced in quality, judgment, etc.	Equal in position or standard
Unlevel			
Straight	Exhibiting honesty and fairness; behaving in a way that is socially correct and acceptable	Not evasive; honest; upright; candid	Honest; truthful
Crooked	Dishonest; done to trick or deceive someone	Dishonest; illegal; not straightforward	Dishonest
Big	Magnanimous; generous or kind	Generous	Generous
Small	Mean; petty	Morally mean, ungenerous, petty, paltry	

5.3.1 MORAL IS HIGH and IMMORAL IS LOW

Spatial metaphors in terms of vertical dimensions are very salient in understanding morality. Furthermore, the vertical dimension of space is commonly used to describe valence states more broadly, such as happiness, power, status, and health (Crawford 2009). Besides, verticality as a spatial dimension is coherent with brightness as a visual dimension in that the upward direction is the direction of light source whereas the downward direction is the direction of darkness (Tolaas 1991). In the case of spatial representation of morality, spatial height is mapped onto "moral height". "Moral height", however, can invoke two differing images. In the first one, an entity, be it an agent or anything associated with it (as below), is evaluated in terms of its "moral position" being either "high" or "low". If it takes a "high" location, the entity is or appears to be moral; in contrast, an entity that takes a "low" position is or seems immoral. In the second image, an entity itself is measured in terms of its "moral stature". It can "rise to a great height" with a "high stature" in contrast to an entity that "stays low" with a "low stature", or "falls low" to a "low posture". There is strong asymmetry with vertical space in the physical world, created and defined by gravity, which makes it more difficult to go up than to go down. This fundamental physical law finds its way, via metaphorical extension, into our understanding of morality: it takes much more effort to be moral than to be immoral. In real-life discourses, the pair of moral metaphors, MORAL IS HIGH and IMMORAL IS LOW, can be instantiated by varied linguistic expressions. Those in (1) are two examples:

(1) a. Wilson, earlier in his column, unctuously proclaims that he and
         The Chronicle "take no **moral high ground** here" (on the issue
         of publishing tobacco ads). It is clear to this reader that he and his
         newspaper do not take the **moral low ground**, either—or, for that
         matter any moral ground whatsoever.
     b. I need to mention another mark of Molly's mind: in her anger, she
         sits in judgment on Mort. It is as though she **looks down** from a
         moral height on his blameworthiness.

"Moral high ground" refers to the stance of being or "looking" morally right, whereas "moral low ground" is its opposite and suggests being morally wrong (1a). The disparity in morality is expressed in terms of different vertical positions. Thus, "claiming the moral high ground" for herself, Molly would "look down" upon Mort from "a moral height" (1b). Another expression found in the data are *moral high road*, referring to a morally superior approach toward things. So, if people take the moral high road, they do things in a way that is supposed to be morally right. Besides, the English expression *ride the moral high horse* is also used to refer to people who believe that they are morally superior to others. When they are asked to "get off their moral high horse", it means that they should stop behaving in a morally superior manner. Still another expression in the data is *high-flown moral code*. Moral codes are "high-flown", and for that matter it takes more strength and energy to "live up" to them.

In English, some other words or idioms have an original sense of spatial highness, but are often used in a moral sense, like *lofty, sublime, aboveboard, on the up and up*. Given in (2) are two examples.

(2)   a.   The regime's unfulfilled plans for fair redistribution of wealth and care of the disinherited have severely undermined its **lofty** moral claims.

      b.   Rather than believing that Jesus was a supernatural being, liberal Christians see him as a **sublime** moral teacher whose example they seek to follow through a lifetime of service—often directed primarily at the poor.

The word *lofty*, which means "rising to a great height" in a spatial sense (e.g., *lofty mountains*), also means "noble" in a moral sense (2a). "Lofty moral claims" can mean either "claims made on a moral high ground" or "claims that reach a great moral height". The word *sublime* means "to or in a high position" in its spatial sense, but it is extended to a moral sense "of outstanding moral worth" (2b). There is no doubt that the words like *lofty* and *sublime* express a positive valence that is not limited to morality. The relevant point here is that, when they are used in a moral sense, they instantiate MORAL IS HIGH.

The antonym of *high* is *low*, which, in its moral sense, means "violating standards of morality or decency". This word often instantiates IMMORAL IS LOW.

(3)   a.   ... there's only two ways to run for reelection in America. There's the **high road** and the **low road.**

      b.   Politics is such a **dirty low down** business now, I give up hope on it.

Example (3a) is about politicians running for reelection in American politics. There are only two approaches characterized as either "high" or "low" for a positive or negative campaign. From its following context left out here, we can see that candidates would talk about their own accomplishments during their tenure on the "high road", but be bent on attacking their opponents on the "low road" simply because they have no achievement to talk about. Example (3b) is another instance on "moral politics" (Lakoff 1996). In this case, politics has become "dirty" and "low down" in their "immoral" senses (see also Arcimavičienė 2007). This example simultaneously instantiates two moral metaphors: IMMORAL IS DIRTY (see section 4.3.3) and IMMORAL IS LOW. In English, a synonym of *low* is *base*, which originally means "low in place or position", but also means "devoid of honor or morality" in its moral sense. Another collocation found in the data is *moral baseline*. That is, whatever goes below it is in the space of immorality.

As seen above, the difference between morality and immorality is that between two locations, or two entities, with different heights, along a vertical dimension in space. It follows that the change of a moral agent, either positive or negative, would be its vertical motion between a "high" and a "low" plane, as shown below.

(4)   a.   Unanimity would be hard, but it would be the only way to ensure that this Commission could **rise above** partisanship, **above** the rotten state of our politics.

   b.   ... the bibliomaniac appears as a decadent, not only for having **fallen into** a state of physical and moral decay ...

The two examples in (4) show that positive and negative change in moral state is, respectively, "rise" and "fall" in vertical space. Here "rise" can refer to an entity either moving up to a higher location, or growing or standing up to a greater height. On the other hand, "fall" can also refer to an entity either dropping freely from a higher location (e.g., *The clock fell off the shelf.*) or going down from the upstanding position (e.g., *He fell to the ground.*). Given the direction of gravity, it would always take much more energy and strength to "rise" than to "fall". Moral change as vertical motion, upward and downward, is also represented by some other collocations, where the head element, though a noun, comes from a verb through derivation or conversion: e.g., *moral lift, moral uplift, moral upbringing, moral elevation, moral sink, moral lapse, moral debasement, moral decline, moral breakdown, moral collapse.*

5.3.2 MORAL IS UPRIGHT and IMMORAL IS SLANTED

This pair of moral-spatial metaphors is different from the preceding one in that it refers to the "moral posture" of an entity whereas the preceding one mainly refers to the "moral position" or "moral stature" of an entity. Nevertheless, the two of them appear to be coherent with each other, especially on the positive side. An "upright" entity reaches the greatest "moral height" possible. In contrast, an entity "slanted" to one side fails to reach the same "moral highness" or to keep its "moral balance", and is in danger of a "moral fall". For this pair of metaphors, the prototypical lexical items involved are *upright* and *upstanding*, with lexicalized moral senses such as "honest", "fair", and "responsible". Others acquire their moral meaning in contexts by being related to them as their synonyms or antonyms, distributed around them in close proximity.

(5) a. Narrators described themselves and their immigrant parents as essentially **morally upright**, selfless, hard-working, thrifty, and responsible people.

   b. Mrs. Dole got her biggest applause from the audience when she described her husband as **morally upstanding** and patriotic.

   c. I'm innocent, **straight up**. I was framed.

It can be presumed that the moral senses of these expressions derived from our fundamental embodied experience: the upright, upstanding, and straight-up posture of the human body is associated with strength, self-control, and balance, which are important aspects of morality in moral metaphors.

(6) a. And the BBC is under fire from British and Israeli governments for allegedly **slanted** news coverage.

   b. But it used to be that the liberal press just **tilted** coverage ignoring stories that reflected positively on conservatives and Republicans and hyping stories that help Democrats and liberals.

   c. Told in Heller's brawny and jagged prose, Stegner navigates his own **askew** moral compass and what it means to create as well as destroy.

The examples in (6) instantiate IMMORAL IS SLANTED. Both (6a) and (6b) comment on media coverage that is perceived as being biased, partial, or unfair. When something is "slanted" or "tilted", it has lost its "balance" and is prone to "fall". In (6c) the person's "moral compass" is "askew"; being so his moral principles are distorted and not right.

5.3.3 MORAL IS LEVEL and IMMORAL IS UNLEVEL

This pair of moral-spatial metaphors is related to the preceding one in that "level" and "upright" are mutually defining for a prototype of perpendicular relationship. In this case, the target of the moral metaphors is a state con- ceptualized as a "location", that is, STATE IS LOCATION in the Location Event Structure Metaphor (LESM; see section 2.5). When it is a "moral-level" lo- cation, it is equal and fair to all the people in that location. Conversely, an "immoral-unlevel" location is unequal or unfair to the people therein. The main English lexical items that instantiate MORAL IS LEVEL are *level* and *even*, which both mean "unvarying in height" in their spatial sense but are also used in a moral sense meaning "equal" or "fair".

(7)   a.   The core is the American people do not think the system is fair or
           on the level.

      b.   The school head in a free education system should not only super-
           vise the teachers, but also see to the **even and fair** distribution of
           books, pencils, chairs and other materials ...

If something is "on the level" (7a) or on an "even" surface (7b), it should be fair to all involved. The English word *evenhanded* has the moral meaning of "fair" and "impartial" as well. Another word *square*, which denotes a prototyp- ical shape on a two-dimensional plane, can be seen as relevant to both vertical (upright) and horizontal (level) metaphors. The shape of "square", which has four "equal" sides and four "right" angles, represents the concepts of being "fair" and "just".

(8)   a.   ... no, it's not about a **level playing field**, it's now about **a field
           that's gotten tilted** and they really stood up for the big financial
           institutions when the big financial institutions are just hammering
           middle class American families.

      b.   For example, electrical energy has **leveled** much of what was
           formerly a decidedly **unlevel playing field** for women.

As illustrated in (8), the moral-level and immoral-unlevel metaphors are often realized in the context of sports, where the field on which games like football are played should be, ideally, level. A playing field tilted to one side is not fair to both sides in the game (8a). "Fair play" will not be achieved unless the field is "leveled" (8b).

5.3.4 MORAL IS STRAIGHT and IMMORAL IS CROOKED

This pair of metaphors is also closely related to the preceding two, and STRAIGHT here can be either vertical (cf. UPRIGHT) or horizontal (cf. LEVEL) in orientation. In this case, "straight" or "crooked" can refer to either the "moral posture" of an entity or the "moral path" along which the entity moves (e.g., Basson 2011; Pacilli et al. 2018).

(9)   a.   We have before us a commander-in-chief who remembers the Boy Scout Oath—to do his best, "to help other people at all times", to keep himself "physically strong, mentally awake, and **morally straight**".

     b.   "It's helped me **straighten out** my life a bit", he said. "Boxing has kept me **on the straight and steady path**. If it wasn't for boxing I'd probably be in jail now, or worse".

We can assume that "morally straight" (9a) is oriented parallel to the vertical posture of the body that is "physically strong". This example contrasts with (9b), which evokes schematically horizontal "straight" lines (see also Cienki 1998; Jäkel 2002; Pacilli et al. 2018). Another idiomatic English expression in my data collection, *on the straight and narrow*, refers to a way of proper conduct and moral integrity. Admittedly, an honest and morally acceptable way of living is by no means an easy life path. In fact, it is the opposite. A real-life example would be the police asking possible drunk drivers to walk a "straight and narrow" line as an "embodied" test. It is worth noting that, according to *Oxford*, "straight" in this idiom is a misinterpretation of "strait" in its original biblical source. We could hypothesize that this happened as a result of the pulling force of the relevant moral-straight metaphor. For whatever reason, the misinterpretation having taken place, the linguistic expression now reinforces the conceptual metaphor underlying it.

The examples in (10) instantiate IMMORAL IS CROOKED.

(10)   a.   "We've just been led down a **crooked path**", he remarked.

     b.   Many people claim they aren't turned on by politics, that all politicians are **crooks**.

     c.   What a **twisted way** to justify corporate greed!

"A crooked path" (10a) is not a moral path of life (see also Cienki 1998; Jäkel 2002). This example instantiates both LIFE IS JOURNEY and IMMORAL IS CROOKED. Example (10b) involves a nominal use of *crook*, referring to politicians as being immoral. Also involving nominal *crook*, the English idiom *by hook or by crook* means "by fair means or foul", i.e., to accomplish a goal by all means regardless of whether they are moral or immoral. We can imagine that "a twisted way" is even worse, as found in (10c).

(11) a. … the Conservative government **bent** the rules to allow him to acquire the Times and Sunday Times.

  b. Have we now **stooped so low** as to throwing blame at people who try to help?

In (11a), an agent could "bend" something so that it is no longer "morally straight". Rules "bent" to meet the interests of individuals or groups are not fair to the general public. In (11b), the agents have "stooped" their own bodies so much that they are no longer "morally upright". For them to become moral again, they must "reform" themselves by "straightening themselves up". Apparently, these examples are grounded in our embodied experience.

5.3.5 MORAL IS BIG and IMMORAL IS SMALL

The last pair of moral-spatial metaphors is the one concerning size, with large size representing positive valence in contrast with small size for negative valence. Again, size as a source domain in space is mapped onto a range of abstract target domains, morality being merely one of them (see, e.g., Crawford 2009; Meier et al. 2008; Schubert et al. 2009; Silvera et al. 2002). It refers to the size of a moral entity. As already noted, size is generally coherent with height.

(12) a. He was a very, very charitable man and with a really **big** heart.

  b. He's just a—truly **a great human being**. And I think we should all use him as an example, and the world would just be a much nicer place if there was a lot more David Harpers around.

In (12a) "he" is a charitable man, and because of that he can be called a man with "a big heart", which refers to his moral character. The word *big* here means "magnanimous" or "generous" in a moral sense. In (12b), David Harper is called "a great human being" because, as we learned from the context of this example, he donated one of his kidneys to a 5-year-old child to save her life. The word *great*, which primarily means "notably large in size", also has a moral sense of "markedly superior in character or quality" or "noble". In the data pool, *great* and *moral* go together in collocations. Thus, for instance, a moral person is one with a "great moral character" who has a "great moral purpose" and acts with a "great moral force".

In contrast with the examples in (12), those in (13) involve three "small" words: *small, petty,* and *little*. The people or things they describe are immoral in nature.

(13) a. "I'm being **petty and small-hearted**, aren't I?" she asks, completely insincere.

   b. What they do with that, if their **sick little mind** decides to go out and shoot somebody—what are you going to do about it?

   c. Smith has fairly presented the **small human being** who nonetheless lived a **grand life** and achieved **great things**; and she has delivered a grand understanding and a resonant appreciation for the paradox and the incandescence that was William S. Paley.

Example (13a) involves both *petty* and *small*. While *small* means "morally mean, ungenerous, petty, paltry", *petty* also has a moral sense of "showing or having a mean narrow-minded attitude". Other than *petty and small*, *petty* occurs in a number of other collocations that have moral implications: e.g., *petty and selfish, petty and mean, petty and corrupt, petty and jealous, petty and unfair, petty and narrow-minded*. In the corpus, other collocations were found involving *small* in its "immoral" sense such as *small minds, small act of hypocrisy*, and *small acts of terrorism*. It is worth noting that there are entirely different readings of the collocation "small act(s)". For the "immoral" reading discussed here, e.g., any "act of terrorism" per se cannot be "small", but instead the person who conducts the act is "small" in the sense of "immoral" or "evil". Apart from this "immoral" reading there is also a "modest" reading, e.g., *a small act of kindness*, where "small" refers to the act itself being "unimportant" or "inconsequential" (i.e., IMPORTANT IS BIG and UNIMPORTANT IS SMALL; SIGNIFICANT IS BIG and INSIGNIFICANT IS SMALL).

In (13b), there is a collocation *sick little mind*, in which *little* means "mean, paltry, contemptible". Besides, *little* was found in other collocations with an "immoral" sense: e.g., *evil little thing, dirty little secrets, evil little people, evil little beast, evil little cockroach*. Finally, (13c) is about William S. Paley (1901–1990), the chief executive who built the Columbia Broadcasting System (CBS) into one of the foremost media networks in the U.S. (Wikipedia). As highlighted in bold in (13c), he was characterized as "the *small* human being who nonetheless lived a *grand* life and achieved *great* things". Such characterization is indeed a "paradox" as suggested in the example, but makes good sense because Paley is known both as "a notorious ladies' man" and as a magnanimous philanthropist during his life (Wikipedia). That is, there was at the same time a "small" side and a "grand" and "great" side to his moral character.

5.4 Spatial moral metaphors in Chinese

Spatial concepts and schemas have long been engaged in moral thinking and reasoning in Chinese thought, and this has left behind abundant traces in the Chinese language. In *The Analects of Confucius*, for example, Confucius (551–479 BC) said, "七十而从心所欲, 不逾矩", meaning "At seventy, I can follow my heart's desire, without transgressing what is right", where "transgressing what is right" is literally "crossing over the square". That is, there is a metaphorical mapping from "square", a shape in space, onto the "moral (and legal) boundaries within which one is supposed to stay socially". According to HYDCD (2000: 1970), 矩 *jŭ* "square" has the following three relevant senses, extended from the concrete to the abstract: (i) the tool with which the shape of square is drawn (the primary meaning); (ii) the shape of square drawn with it (a metonymic extension); (iii) moral standard, established norm, rule, law, etc. (a metaphoric extension). In the Chinese language today, the compound word 规矩 *guīju* has its two components separately refer to "compasses" and "square" as tools, and "circle" and "square" as shapes, means: (i) rule, established practice, or custom; (ii) well behaved, well disciplined, or honest. In other words, the tools of compasses and square, and shapes of circle and square are metaphorically mapped onto "rules" which regulate human behavior with "moral boundaries", and onto "morally good behavior" following socially established norms and standards. Such metaphorical senses of "circle" and "square" are also highlighted in the old saying attributed to Mencius (ca. 372–289 BC), the best known Confucian after Confucius himself, when he said, "不以规矩, 不能成方圆" (lit. Squares and circles cannot be drawn without the compasses and square), meaning "Nothing can be accomplished without norms or standards". Social norms and standards are established according to the moral values and principles of a society. The metaphorical meaning, however, is grounded in the prototypical shapes of circle and square.[3] In fact, the shapes of circle and square carry special significance in Chinese civilization, where ancient Chinese thought conceptualizes the heaven as being round and the earth as being square (天圆地方 *tiānyuán dìfāng*). As prototypical shapes, circle and square are indeed good spatial symbols for unity and regularity: A circle has equal distance (radius) from its center

---

[3] The metaphorical meanings of such shapes as circle and square are referred to as "form symbolism" or "symbolic forms" (see, e.g., Kennedy et al. 2003; Liu 1997). Thus, for instance, circle and square may have such contrastive metaphorical meanings as "warm" and "cold", "soft" and "hard", and "weak" and "strong" in various languages and cultures. It is suggested that such meanings are not based on clichés of particular languages. See section 5.4.2.

to any point on its circular boundary; a square has all its four corners at equal degree (90 degrees right angle) and all its four sides at equal length. They are therefore shapes of balance and equality, which are concepts important to an ideal harmonious society, with fair legal systems and sound moral standards.

As the historical examples above show, moral-spatial metaphors have existed in Chinese thought and language for a long time, and can be traced back to the times of Confucius and Mencius and much further. How do they fare today? This section investigates spatial metaphors as manifested in Chinese moral talk. Language plays an important role in mediating the adaption of spatial schemas to abstract thought (Gattis 2001). In this section, I will analyze the linguistic evidence from Chinese that may manifest the underlying conceptual metaphors for morality. While this is a linguistic study, my hope is that the linguistic patterns delineated through systematic analysis of linguistic data may serve as a basis for inferences about possible conceptual structures in our conceptual systems. Further, my larger goal is to show how our language and thought are embodied as part of embodied cognition in general.

5.4.1 MORAL IS HIGH and IMMORAL IS LOW

In this subsection, I focus on two pairs of conceptual contrasts involving six lexical items that encode HIGH and LOW on a vertical axis of which the two spatial values representing two valence poles in morality: MORAL and IMMORAL. Their spatial and moral senses are given in Table 5.3. The first pair comprises four spatial words: one "high" and three "low" words; the second comprises two: one "thick" and one "thin" word. The second pair is placed in this category because it also refers to relative points on a vertical dimension as being "high" or "low". Thickness and thinness on a horizontal axis as diameter, for instance, are encoded by a different pair of spatial words (粗 *cū* "thick" and 细 *xì* "thin") in Chinese.

In Chinese, 高 *gāo* "high" and 低 *dī* "low" form a common pair of antonyms in the spatial domain, and 卑 *bēi* "low" is usually found in the moral and social domains. 下 *xià* "down" is generally used in contrast with 上 *shàng* "up", but can also be used in contrast with 高 *gāo* "high". For instance, it can replace 低 *dī* "low" in the compound 高低 *gāo-dī* (high-low), hence 高下 *gāo-xià* (high-down), in the sense "relative superiority or inferiority". For illustration of the words in Table 5.3, first look at the examples in (14) which instantiate MORAL IS HIGH.

Table 5.3 Words encoding HIGH and LOW in the moral-spatial metaphors

Source concepts	HIGH	LOW
Lexical items	高 *gāo*: 1. (spatial) high; tall 2. (moral) noble; lofty; noble character; noble people	低 *dī*: 1. (spatial) low 2. (moral) bad; vile; odious; corrupt 卑 *bēi*: 1. (spatial) low; low-lying 2. (moral) of low character; inferior in quality 下 *xià*: 1. (spatial) below; under; underneath; down 2. (moral) lowly; base
	厚 *hòu*: 1. (spatial) thick (vertically) 2. (moral) kind; magnanimous	薄 *bó* (or *báo*): 1. (spatial) thin (vertically); slight; small 2. (moral) unkind; ungenerous; mean; frivolous; coldly

(14) a. 拾金不昧是一种**高尚**的道德行为。
     Returning money found is a kind of **lofty** (lit. **high-esteem**) moral behavior.

   b. 我以为一种优秀的、**高贵**的道德品质, 并非中国所独有的, 而是人类共同追求的理想。
     I think an excellent and **noble** (lit. **high-valuable**) moral character is not uniquely possessed by the Chinese, but an ideal that all humans seek in common.

   c. 文学应该以**崇高**的道德精神、道德理想, 烛照新的人生之路。
     Literature should illuminate a new life path with its **sublime** (lit. **lofty-high**) moral spirits and moral ideals.

   d. ......评议在客观上对提倡清廉**高洁**的道德风尚起到一定的作用。
     ... appraisals produced in reality an effect on the promotion of the honest and upright (lit. clear-honest), and **noble and unsullied** (lit. **high-clean**) social ethics.

All the examples in (14) contain a compound with 高 *gāo* "high" as one morphological component which, along with other moral-related elements, represents the positive moral valence. They offer a comment on, respectively, some moral behavior (14a), a noble moral character (14b), the moral function of literature (14c), and the evaluations of candidates for local and central government offices in ancient China (14d). Example (14a) praises the "good deed" that is advocated through ethical education started in early childhood in China. That is, one should try to return the money or valuables that others have lost, as expressed by a Chinese idiom that literally means "one should not hide or conceal the gold one picks up" (拾金不昧 *shíjīn bùmèi* "not pocket the money one picks up"). Example (14d) contains the compound word 高洁 *gāo-jié* which literally means "high and clean". The two elements of the compound are from two different subsystems of moral metaphors: spatial and visual (cf. section 4.4.3). That is, this compound simultaneously instantiates two moral metaphors: MORAL IS HIGH and MORAL IS CLEAN. The examples in (14) contrast with the following examples in (15) where 低 *dī* "low" and 下 *xià* "down" are involved, thus instantiating IMMORAL IS LOW.

(15) a. 道德的要义在于有所不为而不是无所不为; 这样, 才能使自己脱离开**低级**趣味……

    The essence of morality lies in refraining oneself from doing all, instead of letting oneself do all; only this way can one divorce oneself from **bad** (lit. **low-grade**) tastes …

  b. 文学失去了强有力的道德, 正在变成一种枯躁乏味的**低劣**便宜的购货券。

    Literature has lost its strong moral force, and is becoming a kind of coupon that is boring and uninteresting, **inferior** (lit. **low-bad**) and cheap.

  c. 这种商业道德**低下**、不正当竞争的做法, 为国际经贸界同行所不齿。

    This kind of practice, which reflects **lowly** (lit. **low-down**) business ethics and improper competition, is held in contempt by people in international economics and trade.

All three examples in (15) contain one (in 15a and 15b) or two (in 15c) "low" words as morphemes of the compounds. As in (15a), a morally bad person has "low-grade" (低级 *dījí*) tastes. As in (15b), once literature has lost its moral force, it will become "low and bad" (低劣 *dīliè*) coupon of little value. In (15c), immoral business practices are "low and down" (低下 *dīxià*) in terms of professional ethics. In the following examples, another "low" word, 卑 *bēi* "low", as well as 下 *xià* "down", is involved.

(16) a. 但也出现了一些平庸之作, 甚至出现了一些颓废消极、
卑琐低俗、淫秽色情的精神垃圾。

However, there appeared some mediocre works, too, and even
some moral garbage that was decadent and negative, **mean**
(lit. **low-petty**) and **vulgar** (lit. **low-vulgar**), and obscene and
pornographic.

b. 一些人还骂他"道德沦丧", "**卑鄙无耻**"。

Some even scolded him for being "morally degenerate" and "**base**
(lit. **low-mean**) and brazen".

c. 别讲了, 别讲您那些**卑鄙**、**下流**的笑话了, 您这个道德败坏
的、**下流**的色鬼!

Stop it. Stop telling those of your **base** (lit. **low-mean**) and **low**
(lit. **low-flow**) jokes. You're such a morally degenerate and **low** (lit.
low-flow) lecher!

d. 先进的科学发明掌握在道德高尚的人手中就成为幸福的源泉,
而一旦为道德**卑下**的人所控制, 它就会变成罪恶的帮凶。

If an advanced scientific invention is mastered in the hands of
morally **lofty** (lit. **high-esteem**) people, it will become the source
of wellbeing; once it is controlled in the hands of morally **base** (lit.
low-down) people, it will serve as a cat's paw for evil.

Example (16a) is from a newspaper article that addresses some moral problems in China's contemporary literature and art since the end of the Cultural
Revolution (1966–1976) and the beginning of the reform and opening-up. According to the author, all the problems have arisen from the wrong ideological
tendency "to shy away from loftiness and highness and to go lower than real
life" (躲避崇高, 低于生活 *duǒbì chónggāo dīyú shēnghuó*). Here, the spatial
meanings of "loftiness", "highness", and "lower" all have an intrinsic moral implication (cf. the examples in (14) and (15)). As in (16d), whether scientific
inventions will make contributions or damages to the wellbeing of humankind
depends on if they are utilized by morally good or bad people.

The commonality among the examples in (15) and (16) is that the spatial
concept LOW is instantiated linguistically and is mapped onto IMMORAL as the
target concept. In consistency with this conceptual mapping is the fact that
the verbs expressing changes from morality to immorality do so by mapping
"downward motions" onto such changes (see discussions of LESM in, e.g.,
Lakoff 1993; Lakoff and Johnson 1999: chapter 11; Yu 1998: chapter 5). In
Chinese, for instance, there are following compounds referring to the "fall"
of people in morality: 堕落 *duò-luò* (fall-fall) "degenerate", 沉沦 *chén-lún*

(sink-sink) "sink into (sin, vice, degeneration, etc.)", and 沦落 *lún-luò* (sink-fall) "decline; degenerate". That is, the moral agent is originally morally "high", but ends up being morally "low", and the moral change is spatial motion (i.e., CHANGE IS MOTION in LESM). Since these are changes from moral to immoral states, the movement is therefore from a high location to a low position (cf. Figures 2.7 and 6.8).

The examples in (17) illustrate the contrast between the "thick" and "thin" words in their moral senses.

(17)   a.   诚, 即在对待利润上要诚实**厚道**, 讲求互利互惠。
            Sincerity means that one must be honest and **magnanimous** (lit. in a **thick way**) in making profits, stressing reciprocity and mutual benefit.

       b.   他一贯以身作则, **宽厚**待人, 关心人民的疾苦......
            He always set personal examples, treated others with **generosity and kindness** (lit. **broadness and thickness**), and was concerned with people's hardship ...

       c.   髯黑大将本是举止谨慎、行为检点的**忠厚**之人, 从无**轻薄**行径。
            General Ranhei was a **sincere and kindhearted** (lit. **loyal and thick**) man of careful manner and discreet conduct, and had never committed any **frivolous** (lit. **light-thin**) act at all.

       d.   其实, 徽州人或许并不比历史上出现过的商人更加**刻薄**或吝啬。
            In effect, Huizhou businessmen were not really **meaner** (lit. more **cutting-thin**) or stingier than other businessmen in history.

The four examples involve three instances of 厚 *hòu* "thick" (17a–c) and two instances of 薄 *bó* "thin" (17c and 17d) as elements of compounds. Example (17a) is about moral practices in business, where business people deal with each other in a mutually beneficial "thick way" (厚道 *hòudao* "honest and kind; magnanimous"). Examples (17b) and (17c) concern the moral character of individual people. If a person treats other people in a "broad and thick" manner (宽厚 *kuānhòu*), then this person is "generous and kindhearted" by nature (17b). In (17c), General Ranhei is a fictional character who is depicted as being "loyal and thick" (忠厚 *zhōnghòu* "sincere and kindhearted; honest and tolerant"). People of such morally "thick" character would not act flirtatiously, i.e., in a "light and thin" (轻薄 *qīngbó* "frivolous; flirtatious") manner to women. From our bodily experience interacting with physical objects in the physical world, we know that what is thick is heavier than what is thin given the same kind of material, and vice versa. Furthermore, a physical object that is heavier, i.e., "carrying more weight", is more stable and therefore more reliable than the one that is lighter. This aspect of common sense in physics is mapped metaphorically onto the abstract traits of human personality and moral character in Chinese culture, and the metaphorical mapping in this particular conceptual space finds its reflection in the Chinese language (see Yu 1998: 64–65). Example (17d) is a comment on the moral characteristic or stereotype of the business people in a region. Huizhou is in southern Anhui Province, historically known for its successful business people in the Ming and Qing dynasties. According to the stereotype, however, Huizhou business people are "cutting-thin" (刻薄 *kèbó* "mean; unkind") and stingy. People who are "thin" are believed to be morally inferior in contrast to those who are "thick".

At this point, however, it must be pointed out that, while the concept THICK is positive in its moral sense in Chinese, in contrast with THIN, which is generally perceived as negative in the moral domain. It does not mean that this opposition can be generalized into any other situation. If someone is said to have "thick face skin" in Chinese, for instance, it is definitely negative (e.g., 厚脸皮 *hòuliǎnpí* (lit. thick face skin) "cheeky; brazen; thick-skinned", 厚颜无耻 *hòuyán wúchǐ* (lit. thick face and shameless) "shameless; past shame; brazen as brass").

5.4.2 MORAL IS UPRIGHT and IMMORAL IS SLANTED

For this pair of moral-spatial metaphors, I focus on three Chinese words encoding UPRIGHT or SLANTED, whose primary spatial senses are extended into the moral domain, as shown in Table 5.4. The word prototypically encoding UPRIGHT in Chinese is 正 *zhèng*, whose metaphorical moral senses derive from the original spatial and bodily senses. For instance, "stand to

Table 5.4 Words encoding UPRIGHT and SLANTED in the moral-spatial metaphors

Source concepts	UPRIGHT	SLANTED
Lexical items	正 *zhèng*: 1. (spatial) upright; perpendicular; straight; straighten 2. (moral) upright; impartial; honest; correct; right; proper	歪 *wāi*: 1. (spatial) askew; tilted; inclined; slanting 2. (moral) improper; unethical; evil 偏 *piān*: 1. (spatial) inclined or leaning to one side; slanting; diverging 2. (moral) partial; prejudiced; biased

attention" or "attention" as an imperative is 立正 *lìzhèng* in Chinese, literally meaning "stand upright", namely, with one's body straight up. We could hypothesize that the upright body posture is the embodied basis for abstract understanding and reasoning in our moral cognition (see the discussion of visual or multimodal images in section 6.6).

As shown in Table 5.4, 正 *zhèng* "upright" can also be used as a verb meaning "straighten", i.e., "cause to be upright or straight". According to Confucianism, it is important to cultivate oneself or one's moral character. The Chinese compound for moral cultivation is 修身 *xiū-shēn* (cultivate-body) or 正身 *zhèng-shēn* (straighten-body). In its literal sense, one's moral character is embodied, manifested in one's posture, manner, and behavior with one's body. People with a good moral character have an "upright and straight body". In *The Great Learning* (大学 *dàxué*), a Confucian classic, it is said that "Those who want to cultivate one's body should first straighten one's heart" (欲修其身者, 先正其心). This is because, in traditional Chinese culture, the heart, taken as the central faculty of cognition, is the locus of one's moral character (Yu 2009a: 62–81). A strong moral character lies in "an upright and straight heart". A "slanted or crooked heart" must be "straightened" (正心 *zhèngxīn*) before one can "straighten one's body" to be a morally good person. The following sentential examples contain a compound involving 正 *zhèng* "upright" as one of the components.

(18) a. 遵守纪律和职业道德, 诚信廉明, 公道**正派**, 甘于奉献。
        One must abide by disciplines and professional ethics, be honest and clean (lit. light), impartial and **upright** (lit. **keeping an upright bearing**), and be willing to dedicate oneself.

      b. 当前医务工作者要努力树立**正气**, 切实加强职业道德。
        At present, medical workers should try to foster **a moral spirit** (lit. erect **an upright air**), strengthening their professional ethics in earnest.

      c. 他**廉正**朴实, 平易谦和, 胸怀坦荡, 光明磊落, 不思荣利。
        He is **honest and upright**, simple and plain, amiable and modest, openhearted and aboveboard, and not caring for fame or wealth.

      d. 忠者, 心地**中正**也, 忠于职, 忠于国, 忠于民, 忠于所办之事。
        The meaning of 忠 *zhōng* is that one has a heart that is **fair, just, and impartial** (lit. **middle and upright**), being dedicated to your job, loyal to your country, faithful to your people, devoted to what you do.

      e. 中国传统政治规范要求为官者清廉**方正**......
        The traditional political norms in China require that officials be clean (lit. clear) and honest, and **square and upright** ...

As the key words show in these examples, being morally good in a broad sense is keeping an "upright bearing" (正派 *zhèngpài*) in (18a), erecting an "upright air" (正气 *zhèngqì*) in (18b), being "honest and upright" (廉正 *liánzhèng*) in (18c), being "middle and upright" (中正 *zhōngzhèng*) in (18d), and being "square and upright" (方正 *fāngzhèng*) in (18e). The concept of 气 *qì* "air" in (18b) is an important one in traditional Chinese culture originally referring to a gaseous force functioning in the human body as the micro world as well as in the universe as the macro world (Yu 1998, 2009a). "Moral spirit", conceptualized as "upright air", is seen as such a force that keeps individuals and society as a whole "upright".

Example (18d) explains what is meant by the Chinese word 忠 *zhōng*, which is accepted as a central virtue in Chinese culture, and translated in XSDHYDCD (2004) as "loyal; staunch; faithful; devoted". As the explanation goes, it means, primarily, that one should have a "middle and upright" (中正 *zhōngzhèng*) heart, as testified also by the Chinese character 忠 *zhōng* that represents the concept, comprised of two parts: "middle" or "central" on top of "heart". With a "middle heart", one is impartial and faithful in thought and behavior. The Chinese character for "middle" 中 *zhōng* looks like a rectangular box with a vertical, "upright" line going through its middle. As such, it looks perfectly symmetric, thus embodying the abstract ideas it can encode: "balanced", "unbiased", and "impartial".

Example (18e) involves the word for "square", as well as "upright", in the compound. As discussed earlier, the image of square, which supersedes "upright", can be regarded as a symbol for moral fairness, with its four "right" angles and four "equal" sides as well as its "balanced" shape. That is perhaps the reason why English also has the idiomatic expression *fair and square*, meaning "in an honest and fair manner". It is the ethical manner required of government officials so that they do not abuse their power for personal gains.

Recently, I noted an interesting example in a newly released Chinese TV drama series, which contains the dialogue between two characters as follows: 甲: 你就是一个四方脑袋! 乙: 四方脑袋怎么了? 我正直。 A literal English translation is the following: "A: You're such a square head! B: What's wrong with a square head? I'm upright and straight". What *A* means is that *B* is not tactful and lacks flexibility in his way of thinking and speaking. What *B* means in his response is: So what? That's because I'm honest and straightforward. In Chinese, if someone is said to be 圆滑 *yuánhuá* (lit. round and slippery), it is usually derogatory, meaning this person is too slick and sly, and thus unreliable or dishonest. (See also footnote 3 in this chapter for a discussion of circle and square as "form symbolism" or "symbolic forms".)

(19) a. 我们的干部群众就可以有**清正**廉洁的道德品质和昂扬向上的精神状态。

Our officials and masses can then have **clear and upright**, and honest and **clean** moral qualities, as well as elated and upwardly-oriented mental states.

b. 这种高度的道德**纯正**从爱情这样的自私情感中无法得到完全满足。

Such high moral **purity and uprightness** cannot find its total satisfaction in the selfish sentiment of romantic love.

In the two examples in (19), the key compound words are composed of two elements drawn from two different subsystems of moral metaphors, one visual and one spatial. In (19a) the relevant compound is 清正 *qīngzhèng* "honest and upright", literally meaning "clear and upright". The relevant compound in (19b) is 纯正 *chúnzhèng*, which means "pure and upright". Both of the visual adjectives were discussed in Chapter 4 on the visual subsystem. In other words, the two compounds instantiate separately MORAL IS CLEAR and MORAL IS PURE, in addition to MORAL IS UPRIGHT.

In Table 5.4, the two words often used in contrast with *zhèng* "upright; straight" are 歪 *wāi* "tilted (to one side); askew" and 偏 *piān* "inclined or leaning (to one side)". They cover different conceptual spaces in the moral domain: the former ranging from "improper" to "evil"; the latter focusing on "partiality; bias; prejudice". The character of the former is comprised of two parts, one on top of the other. The upper part is 不 *bù* "not" and the lower part is 正 *zhèng* "upright". At face value, the word means "not upright", both spatially and morally. The contrast in a moral sense between 正 *zhèng* "upright" and 歪 *wāi* "tilted" can be found in a proverbial saying based on a building metaphor: 上梁不正下梁歪 (lit. If the upper beam is not straight, the lower ones will go aslant), meaning "If those above (e.g., higher in official ranking) behave immorally, those below will follow suit". Look at the following examples:

(20) a. ......要对经营者、商贩进行职业道德教育, "君子爱财, 取之有道", 靠**歪门邪道**长久不了。

... it's necessary to educate retailers and peddlers on work ethics: "A gentleman loves money but gets it through a (moral) way"; it won't last if he gets it through a **crooked path** (lit. **tilted-door evil-way**).

b. 文化衰落了, 道德败坏了, **歪风邪气**也盛行起来。

Culture declined, morality deteriorated, and **harmful trends and sinister practices** (lit. **tilted-wind evil-air**) became flourishing.

Here, (20a) also instantiates the LIFE IS JOURNEY metaphor, involving both "door" (or "gate") and "way". The idiom "tilted door and evil way" refers to an immoral means to an end, instantiating the metaphor MEANS IS PATH, which is again one of the mappings in the LESM subsystem. In (20b) the idiom "tilted wind and evil air" refers to unethical trends or practices at a social level (cf. 18b).

It is worth noting that both idioms in (20a) and (20b) contain 邪 *xié* "evil", which, also used in contrast with 正 *zhèng* "upright; straight" in its moral senses, does not seem to have a primary spatial sense in present-day Chinese. However, it at least did have a spatial sense, as can be found in the obsolete usage of 邪径 *xiéjìng* (lit. evil-path) and 邪路 *xiélù* (lit. evil-road). Both compounds mean "an evil path" in a moral sense today, but are defined in HYDCD (2000: 459) as having a primary spatial sense "a shorter path than the main road". This is a good example of how something that appears to be abstract and literal in synchrony is actually concrete and figurative in diachrony (Kövecses 2020: chapter 2).

In contrast with 邪 *xié* "evil", another word 斜 *xié*, pronounced exactly the same, is utilized primarily as a spatial word meaning "oblique; slanting; tilted; askew". Even this word can be used metaphorically in a moral sense, as in the proverbial saying 身正不怕影子斜 (lit. If one's body is upright, one should not be afraid that its shadow is askew), i.e., "If one is morally upright, one should not be afraid of false accusations". Note that the image of one's "shadow being askew" manifests two possible conceptual metaphors for immorality: IMMORAL IS SLANTED and IMMORAL IS DARK (see section 4.4.2).

As already mentioned, 偏 *piān*, which has the primary spatial meaning "inclined or leaning to one side", means "partial; prejudiced" in a moral sense. That is, when people are partial, biased, or prejudiced, they are inclined to one side, thus resulting in the loss of balance (cf. Figure 5.3). The mental, moral balance is conceptualized as physical balance with the MIND IS BODY metaphor. In Chinese, a person who is mentally partial or biased has an "inclined heart" (偏心 *piānxīn*). Again, one's heart is seen as the locus of one's moral character. The word 良心 *liángxīn* (lit. good-heart) means "conscience", and a conscienceless person is one who has "totally lost the good heart" (丧尽良心 *sàngjìn liángxīn*). Four sentential examples follow.

(21)　a.　"我"终于超越了世俗的、也是那些自视**高贵**、完美的绅士淑女的道德**偏见**。

　　　　"I" eventually transcended the moral **prejudice** (lit. **inclined or leaning [to one side] view**) of those worldly gentlemen and gentlewomen who considered themselves as noble (lit. high and valuable) and perfect.

b.   道德是关于善和恶、公正和**偏私**、诚实和虚伪等问题的观念，以及与之相适应的依靠社会舆论和人们的信念来实现的社会行为规范的总和。

Morality is concerned with the conception of good and evil, fairness (lit. fairness and uprightness) and **partiality** (lit. **being inclined and selfish**), honesty and hypocrisy, and so on, and the totality of related norms in social behavior realized on the basis of public opinion and human belief.

c.   这次出现的误判、漏判绝大部分不属于职业道德问题，并非有意**偏袒**一方，而是有些裁判经验不足。

This time around, most of the referees' errors in penalty calls or missed calls were not issues of professional ethics; they were not intentionally **partial to** (lit. **inclined and biased to**) one side, but some of them did not have adequate experience.

d.   ......他们和你们，同有一位主在天上，他并不**偏待**人。

... they and you, have a common Lord in the heaven, and He does not **treat** people **partially** (lit. **treat** people **in an inclined way**).

In (21a), "prejudice" is literally "inclined view" (偏见 *piānjiàn*), a view that is leaning to one side. As such, the person cannot "see" anything "straight". Example (21b) contains a definition of morality, in which the moral contrast between "fairness" and "partiality" seems to emerge from the spatial contrast between being "upright" for fairness and justness (公正 *gōngzhèng*) and being "inclined" for selfish purposes (偏私 *piānsī*). That is, once people have lost their "upright" posture, they will be leaning to their personal gains. Example (21c) is concerned with refereeing in sports. The referees made mistakes in calling the games not because they lacked professional ethics, being "inclined and biased" (偏袒 *piāntǎn*) to one side, but because they lacked professional experience. That is the reason why they have made some wrong calls, and missed others, by error. In (21d), what is said is that the Lord is fair to everyone. In this example, "to treat (people) partially" is literally "to treat (people) in an inclined way" (偏待 *piāndài*). As discussed above, the examples in (20) and (21) instantiate the moral metaphor IMMORAL IS SLANTED.

5.4.3 MORAL IS LEVEL and IMMORAL IS UNLEVEL

The Chinese adjective that represents LEVEL is 平 *píng* "level", with a basic spatial sense referring to a horizontal line that is straight with both ends at the same height, or to a horizontal plane with a flat surface and all its sides at the same height. The opposite of 平 *píng* "level" is its negative form 不平 *bùpíng* "unlevel", referring to the line or plane (i) being not straight or even, or (ii) having a slope toward one side. The latter case, i.e., when the straight line or even plane has a slope toward one side, can also be described by another aforementioned spatial word 斜 *xié* "oblique; slanting; tilted; askew". The moral senses of 平 *píng* "level" and 不平 *bùpíng* "unlevel" are found in Table 5.5.

In their moral senses, the pair of words means "fair; just" or "unfair; unjust" accordingly. That is, if a line or plane is "level", it means equality, equity, or justice to all. Conversely, if the line or plane is "not level", it means inequality, inequity, or injustice, which is a state in favor of some but against others. The Chinese saying 一碗水端平 (lit. hold a bowl of water level) refers to a moral situation where it is necessary to be fair and just, and therefore "to treat all people evenhandedly or impartially". In Chinese, 不平 *bùpíng* (lit. not-level) is often used as a noun meaning "injustice; unfairness; wrong", as illustrated in the old saying 路见不平, 拔刀相助 (lit. As one sees something unlevel on the road, one would unsheathe the knife to help), i.e., one would "stand out boldly to redress a social injustice". The following sentences show how the concepts LEVEL and UNLEVEL are used in moral contexts.

(22) a. 只有实现了**公平、平等**, 才能最大限度地消除种种社会问题。
     Only when **equity** (lit. **being fair and level**) and **equality** (lit. **being level and equal**) are realized can various social problems be eliminated to the greatest degree.

Table 5.5 Words encoding LEVEL and UNLEVEL in the moral-spatial metaphors

Source concepts	LEVEL	UNLEVEL
Lexical items	平 *píng*: 1. (spatial) level; flat; smooth; make even or level 2. (moral) equal; just; fair; impartial	不平 *bù-píng*: 1. (spatial) not level; not flat; not smooth 2. (moral) unfair; unjust; injustice; unfairness; wrong

b. 经营者在市场交易中, 应当遵循自愿、**平等**、**公平**、诚实信
用的原则, 遵守公认的商业道德。

Businessmen should follow the principles of voluntariness,
equality (lit. **level and equal**), **equity** (lit. **fair and level**), and
honesty and credibility in their market transactions, abiding by
the accepted business ethics.

c. **平心**而论, 以实力讲, 中国队要打入十六强实在很不容易。

Speaking **fairly** (lit. **with a level heart**), it is really not easy for
Team China to advance to the top sixteen with its strength.

d. 她亲自撰写文章, 着力宣扬妇女解放, 男女**平权**, 反对缠足、
买卖婚姻、男尊女卑。

She personally wrote essays to advocate earnestly women's liberation and **equal right** (lit. **level right**) for men and women,
and to fight against foot binding, mercenary marriage, and male
superiority (and female inferiority).

As shown in (22a), the Chinese compound words for "equity" and "equality",
two of the most critical elements for public wellbeing in a society, both contain 平 *píng* as a morphological component, which has a primary spatial sense
meaning "level" or "flat". On the societal level, only when all members of a society "play on a level field" can social problems be eliminated to the greatest
degree (cf. examples in (7) and (8) in section 5.3.3). This is especially true in
fair trade and business transactions (22b), because "equality" (平等 *píngdng*
(lit. level and equal)) and "equity" (公平 *gōngpíng* (lit. fair and level)) are essential in business ethics and practices. Example (22c), concerned with sports,
begins with the idiomatic expression 平心而论 *píngxīn érlùn* "speaking fairly;
in all fairness; to be fair", which literally means "to speak with a level heart". In
this expression, the compound word 平心 *píngxīn* (lit. level heart) is defined as
"(to do things) with a fair and level intent (lit. heart) and a fair and upright attitude". By face value, this compound simply means "(with a) level heart". That
is, when one's heart is "level", not inclined or leaning to any direction, one does
things in a fair and impartial manner. Note that the "level heart" is in contrast
and coherence with the "upright heart" (正心 *zhèngxīn*) discussed above in
section 5.4.2. Spatially, the former evokes a horizontal image, and the latter
vertical image. Functionally, however, both "level heart" and "upright heart"
evoke the image of "balance" (see (a) and (b) in Figure 5.3), which is crucial
to the wellbeing of a human or a society. Example (22d), which is about fight-
ing the feudal customs and ethics in the early twentieth century of China, the

key word is 平权 *píngquán* (lit. level rights) "equal right". That is, the rights for men and women should be "level" at the same spatial height, rather than "higher" rights for men and "lower" rights for women.

(23) a. 这是社会基本制度导致的**不公平**, 需要用正义原则来调整。
        This is **inequity** (lit. **being unfair and unlevel**) arising from the
        basic social system, and it needs to be adjusted with the principle
        of justice (lit. upright righteousness).

     b. 这种**不平等**的选举资格直到1948年才废除。
        This kind of **unequal** (lit. **unlevel and unequal**) qualification for
        the right to vote was not abolished until 1948.

     c. 按照这种论调, 发展中国家以低廉的劳动力价格扩展贸易,
        对于发达国家或发展中国家的劳工来说, 是"不道德"、"**不
        公平**"、"**不平等**"的。
        According to this (incorrect) view, if developing countries expand
        trade with low labor costs, it is "immoral", "**unfair** (lit. **not fair
        or level**)", and "**unequal** (lit. **not level or equal**)" to developed
        countries or laborers in developing countries.

The three examples in (23) display the negative forms of the compounds in (22a) and (22b). In (23a) the nominal compound for "inequality" (不公平 *bùgōngpíng*) refers to the state of "being unfair and unlevel". Example (23b) refers to the "unequal" (不平等 *bùpíngdng*) voting rights with which some people, for having more wealth or more power, can cast more than one vote in the elections. This unequal voting system was abolished in 1948, replaced by the equal one of "one person one vote". Example (23c) contains both key words found separately in (23a) and (23b). It is argued that fairness and justness can be relative to circumstances, especially at the international level, where the "players" are different nations, some "developing" and others "developed". The examples in (22) and (23) illustrate the linguistic instantiation of the underlying conceptual metaphors for morality: MORAL IS LEVEL and IMMORAL IS UNLEVEL.

5.4.4 MORAL IS STRAIGHT and IMMORAL IS CROOKED

In this subsection, I again focus on three Chinese spatial words that encode the source concepts STRAIGHT and CROOKED, as listed in Table 5.6.

The moral opposition represented by 直 *zhí* "straight" and 曲 *qū* "crooked" is well illustrated by the saying 宁在直中取, 不向曲中求 (lit. [I] would rather get from the straight than seek from the crooked) "I would rather

Table 5.6 Words encoding STRAIGHT and CROOKED in the moral-spatial metaphors

Source concepts	STRAIGHT	CROOKED
Lexical items	直 *zhí*: 1. (spatial) straight; vertical; upright; perpendicular; straighten 2. (moral) just; upright	曲 *qū*: 1. (spatial) bent; crooked; bend; crook 2. (moral) wrong; false; unjustifiable 勾 *gōu*: 1. (spatial) bent (in the shape of a tick or hook); crooked 2. (moral) collude with; gang up with; entice; seduce

get what I want by honest means than by crooked means". That is, STRAIGHT is mapped onto HONEST and CROOKED onto DISHONEST. The conceptual metaphor MORAL IS STRAIGHT is instantiated by the following examples in (24).

(24)   a. 他一生追求真理, **直道而行**, 学识渊博, 勤勉清正。

During his life time, he pursued truths, **acted impartially** (lit. **went along a straight path**), acquired profound knowledge, and was hardworking, and honest and upright (lit. clear and upright).

   b. 叶公告诉孔子, 说自己乡里有一位**直身而行**的人……

Ye Gong told Confucius that in his village there was a person who **was upright in behavior** (lit. **went forward with a straight body**) …

   c. **直人**, **直脾气**, 一生**耿直**, 一代文豪秉笔**直书**, 书写人间忠奸善恶。

An **upright** (lit. **straight**) person, with a **straightforward** (lit. **straight**) temperament (i.e., being candid and outspoken), one who was **honest and frank** (lit. **bright and straight**) throughout his life, a great writer of his generation who wrote in a **straightforward** (lit. **straight**) manner, writing about the loyal and the treacherous, and the good and the evil, in the human world.

Example (24a) summarizes the aspects of a person's virtuous life. Among them is that he, literally, "went along a straight path" (直道而行 *zhídào érxíng*) for his life. The Chinese idiom is translated as "act impartially" in XSDHYDCD (2004:1991). A "straight path" is perhaps a common metaphorical image for a moral way of life cross-linguistically (see, e.g., Basson 2011; Cienki 1998;

Pacilli et al. 2018). In this example, the compound 清正 *qīngzhèng* (lit. clear and upright) "honest and upright" is also used to describe the moral character of the person (cf. 19a). Example (24b) is another idiomatic expression that is very similar in meaning to that of (24a). In this expression, however, it is not a "straight path" along which a moral agent moves, but the moral agent itself moves along with a "straight body". Example (24c) is a characterization of a late, well-known playwright of China. He is said to be, first of all, a "straight person" (直人 *zhírén*), i.e., a morally upright person or a person of moral integrity. This example also involves three more instances of "straight": the person has a "straight" disposition, a "straight" life, and writes in a "straight" manner about the seamy and sunny sides of the human world. In all these cases in (24a–c), what is "straight" is moral, namely MORAL IS STRAIGHT.

(25) a. 小说中, 作者又热情颂扬了善良和**直诚**的品格。
          In the novel, the writer enthusiastically lauded the good, kind, **straight and sincere** qualities.

  b. 忠实**廉直**者, 括而言之, 曰"诚"而已。
      The people who are faithful and trustworthy, and **honest and upright** (lit. **honest and straight**) are, in a word, "sincere".

  c. 这正是一个**正直**学者的品格, 也是他成功的道德基础。
      This is exactly the quality of an **upright** (lit. **upright and straight**) scholar, and also the moral basis for his success.

  d. 这些精神特点正好与他们急公好义、耿介**刚直**、不苟合于污浊世态的道德风貌相补充。
      These mental characteristics complement their moral outlook with which they are zealous for fairness and righteousness, honest and straightforward, **upright and outspoken** (lit. **firm and straight**), refusing to yield to filthy (lit. dirty and murky) ways of the world.

The set of examples in (25) provides more linguistic instantiations of MORAL IS STRAIGHT. In (25a), the moral qualities of being "straight and sincere" (直诚 *zhíchéng*), among others, are praised in the novel. In (25b), a sincere person must be "honest and straight" (廉直 *liánzhí*), as well as faithful and trustworthy. As in (25c), one's moral character is good and strong if it is "upright and straight" (正直 *zhèngzhí*). In (25d), which refers to a good moral character, the two elements of the compound separately characterize the "material" and "shape" of that moral character as "firm and straight" (刚直 *gāngzhí*). With such a moral character, people can keep themselves "clean and clear" in a moral environment that is "dirty and murky".

(26)　a.　这是对人性和道德的**歪曲**。

This is a **distortion** (lit. case of **tilting and crooking**) of human nature and morality.

　　b.　法官多**偏曲**, 不能主持正义, 腐败行为时时发生。

Judges were mostly **unfair** (lit. **slanted and crooked**), and would not uphold justice, and therefore corruption happened quite often.

　　c.　从而, 大家看到的种种医生们见死不救认钱不认人等等医德 败坏医风荡然无存的**扭曲**行为就不奇怪。

Therefore, it should not be surprising for us to see all the **twisted and crooked** behaviors among many medical doctors, who would refuse to treat dying patients until money is paid, which shows that medical morals are corrupted and medical ethics totally lost.

　　d.　道德上的是非**曲直**, 除在一些极端的场合以外, 是一种很难 识别的标准。

The criteria for judging moral goodness and badness or **right and wrong** (lit. **crookedness and straightness**), unless under extreme circumstances, are often not so clear-cut.

The examples in (26) contrast with those in (25) with their involvement of the antonym of 直 *zhí* "straight", 曲 *qū* "crooked; bent", as one of the elements of the relevant compounds used in moral contexts. In (26a), the key compound is 歪曲 *wāiqū* "distort; distortion", which literally means "tilting and crooking" (cf. (20)). In (26b), the unethical judges' unfairness is expressed in spatial terms as being "inclined and crooked" (偏曲 *piānqū*). In other words, such judges are "inclined and bent to one direction" in their biased and partial legal practices (cf. (21)). Example (26c) concerns the immoral and unethical practices in the medical system after hospitals were turned into profit-making organizations. In such a medical system, medical staffs' behaviors were morally "twisted and crooked" (扭曲 *niǔqū*). The compound in (26d) comprises *qū* "crooked" and *zhí* "straight" as a pair of antonyms, extended into the moral domain meaning "right and wrong" (曲直 *qūzhí*).

In Table 5.6 the second word in contrast with 直 *zhí* "straight" is 勾 *gōu*. According to HYDCD (2000: 310), it has a primary spatial sense 弯曲 *wānqū* (lit. bent and crooked) "winding; zigzag; crooked". Particularly, it refers to the shape of a line being bent into a tick or hook. Thus, when utilized as a verb, it means "get with a hook". For my purpose in this study, 勾 *gōu* is often used in the moral domain to mean "collude with; gang up with; entice; seduce", evoking the image of "hook up" or "be hooked up with". Given in (27) are four examples.

(27) a. 小说......有力地揭露和批判了官厅中腐败的人际关系和官商**勾结**所犯下的无耻罪行。

The novel ... forcefully exposes and criticizes the corrupt human relations and the disgraceful crimes committed in **collusion** (lit. **hook and knot**) between governmental officials and businessmen.

b. 一个大商人, 和刘黑七这样的强盗有**勾连**, 事情传出去, 我达盛昌名声何在?

A prominent businessman **gangs up** (lit. **hook and connect**) with a bandit such as Liu Heiqi; when this is disclosed, what kind of reputation will my Dashengchang Business get?

c. 老板娘见人就想去**勾搭**, 人人都可以把她**勾搭**上, 可是偷人并不是杀人。

The proprietress wanted to **carry on an affair** (lit. **hook and partner**) with any man she saw, and every man could **carry on an affair** (lit. **hook and partner**) with her, but, after all, seducing (lit. stealing) people is not killing people.

d. ......她故态复萌, 竟至**勾引**一个17岁的学生, 被家长发现, 写信向校长投诉, 说她"道德败坏......"

... she slipped back into her old ways, and even **seduced** (lit. **hook and lead**) a seventeen-year-old student, whose parents would discover it and write to the principal complaining about her "moral degeneration ..."

In (27a), the immoral relations between governmental officials, who have power, and business people, who have money, are "hooked up into knots" (勾结 *gōujié*) for dirty deals. This is a common kind of corruption. In (27b), the prominent businessman believes that the reputation of his business will be ruined if he is "hooked and connected" (勾连 *gōulián*) with a bandit. Example (27c) is about a lewd, unchaste woman, the proprietress who, according to the narrator, wanted to "hook and partner" (勾搭 *gōuda*) with any man in sight. In Chinese, the compound 偷人 *tōurén*, which literally means "steal people", idiomatically refers to someone, especially a woman, committing adultery. In (27d), the Chinese compound for "seduce" is literally "hook and lead" (勾引 *gōuyǐn*). That is, in seduction, someone is "hooked and led" into a sexual relationship that is not considered moral. In sum, the three spatial words discussed in this subsection evoke an image-schematic contrast between STRAIGHT and CROOKED, mapped onto MORALITY and IMMORALITY, respectively.

5.4.5 MORAL IS BIG and IMMORAL IS SMALL

This last subsection focuses on three spatial words used in a moral sense to encode BIG and SMALL: 大 *dà* "big", 小 *xiǎo* "small", and 微 *wēi* "tiny". The first two are the most common antonyms representing the contrast in size in Chinese whereas the third one is somewhat synonymous to the second. Their spatial and moral senses are listed in Table 5.7. The examples in (28) show how the words are used in real-life discourses instantiating the moral metaphors.

(28)   a.   勿以善小而不为, 要积小善成**大德**......
           One should not step away from doing good because it appears small in amount; instead, one should accumulate small goodness until it becomes **big virtue** ...

       b.   然而我想说, 更**伟大**的道德力量存在于这样的信仰当中......
           However, what I want to say is that even **greater** (lit. **greater and bigger**) moral force exists in such a belief ...

       c.   妹妹, 是乔家祖上有德, 修来了你这样**大仁大义大贤大德**的媳妇!
           Sister, it is because the Qiao family's ancestors accumulated a lot of virtue that they obtained a daughter-in-law like you, of **great kindness and great righteousness**, and of **great benevolence and great virtue**!

Table 5.7 Words encoding BIG and SMALL in the moral-spatial metaphors

Source concepts	BIG	SMALL
Lexical items	大 *dà*: 1. (spatial) big; large; great 2. (moral) good; noble	小 *xiǎo*: 1. (spatial) small; little; tiny; minor 2. (moral) bad; evil; base; mean; contemptible, despicable 微 *wēi*: 1. (spatial) minute; tiny 2. (moral) lowly; base

Example (28a) talks about charities. It seems that *dà* "big" in this case refers to a "big amount" of virtue, but that is only its surface meaning in this context. 大德 *dàdé* (big-virtue), according to HYDCD (2000: 747), also has its intrinsic senses as a compound meaning "lofty moral character" and "person of noble moral conduct or high moral integrity". In (28b), the compound 伟大 *wěidà* (lit. great and big) "great" is deployed to modify "moral force". Although the head noun here is "force" and it appears that "great" ultimately modifies "force", the point is that the "force" cannot be modified by "great" if it is immoral or evil. That is, only "moral force" can be "great", and "great moral force" instantiates MORAL IS BIG. Of course, *wěidà* "great" as a modifier is not limited to morality, but when it is applied to morality, it encodes MORAL rather than IMMORAL. In ancient Chinese thought, there is a moral contrast between what is literally a "big man" (大人 *dàrén*) and a "small man" (小人 *xiǎorén*). A "big man" would seek "righteousness" (义 *yì*) and do what is right whereas a "small man" would seek "personal gains" (利 *lì*) and do what is profitable. In (28c), the daughter-in-law of the Qiao family is perceived as an utterly virtuous person of perfect moral integrity, a person of "great kindness and great righteousness" (大仁大义 *dàrén dàyì*) and "great benevolence and great virtue" (大贤大德 *dàxián dàdé*). The traditional Chinese way of thinking and speaking would attribute people's favorable situations to their ancestors' accumulation of virtue.

(29) a. 领导干部要**光明正大**, 表里如一, 做到对上与对下一致, 人前与人后一致; 当官以前与当官以后一致; 言论与行动一致。
   The officials should be **open and aboveboard** (lit. **bright-light upright-big**), think and act in one and the same way, and remain consistent to their superiors and subordinates, in front of and behind other people, before and after taking office, and between their words and deeds.

   b. 这是因为甲所具备的帮助同学、乐于助人、**大公无私**的品德符合社会的道德准则和规范……; 相反, 学生乙自私自利、撒谎等品德不符合社会道德准则和规范……
   This is because student A possesses such moral traits as assisting his fellow students, being happy to help others, and being **impartial and selfless** (lit. **big-fair no-self**), which accord with the social moral codes and norms …; in contrast, student B has such moral traits as being selfish, telling lies, and so on, which are not in line with the social moral codes and norms …

The examples in (29) contain two four-character idioms that are commonly used in the moral domain. Example (29a) involves the idiom 光明正大 *guāngmíng zhèngdà* (lit. bright-light upright-big) "open and aboveboard", which is a moral quality to be found supposedly in governmental officials as part of their professional ethics. Example (29b) contains 大公无私 *dàgōng wúsī* (lit. big-fair no-self) "perfectly impartial and selfless; just and fair". The examples below in (30) contain the words for "small", which contrast with the word for "big" in that they are deployed to form compounds describing the negative aspects of moral character and behavior.

(30) a. 中篇小说, 通过两家地主的纠纷, 刻划旧社会中的所谓三村名士拜上踩下、吝啬**小器**、见利忘义的精神状态。

Centering around the disputes between two landlords' families, the novelette depicts the mentality of the so-called renowned villagers who toadied to the people above and stamped on the people below, were stingy and **mean** (lit. **small-utensil**), and would forget righteousness at the sight of personal gains.

b. 不要吝惜自己的精力和东西, 以免在别人眼里成为**小气鬼**。

One should not be mean over one's energy or possession, or one would be a **miser** (lit. **small-air devil**) in the eyes of other people.

c. 他说:"人格伟大的艺术家产生伟大的艺术; 人格**渺小**的艺术家产生**渺小**的艺术; ......一言以蔽之, 艺术与道德的关系便是如此"。

He said, "An artist of great (lit. great-big) moral character produces great art; an artist of **petty** (lit. **petty and small**) moral character produces **petty** (lit. **petty and small**) art; ... In short, the relationship between art and morality is just that".

d. 人们常从某人的言谈举止来判定其人格的高尚与**卑微**。

Very often people judge a person's moral character as being noble (lit. high-esteem) or **base** (lit. **low-tiny**) according to his or her speech and bearing.

As shown in (30a) and (30b), those who are mean and stingy are either a "small utensil" (小器 *xiǎoqì*) or a "small-air devil" (小气鬼 *xiǎoqìguǐ*). In (30c) the relevant compound is 渺小 *miǎoxiǎo* (lit. petty and small) "petty". It is said that artists' moral character, "great" or "petty", are directly related to their artistic products which will be consequentially "great" or "petty". In (30d) the compound expressing the source SMALL is 卑微 *bēiwēi* (lit. low-tiny) "base", i.e., one's moral character can be "high" and "great" or "low" and "tiny". Such moral distinction is assumedly revealed in how one speaks and acts. As discussed above, the examples in (28)–(30) contribute to the linguistic manifestation of moral-spatial metaphors MORAL IS BIG and IMMORAL IS SMALL, with "big" and "small" words involved in compound words that are utilized in the moral domain.

5.5 Summary

As presented in the preceding sections, the examination of moral-spatial metaphors in English and Chinese shows that the five pairs of spatial metaphors for morality are manifested in both languages, just like the physical and visual subsystems. The five pairs of spatial concepts are mapped onto MORAL and IMMORAL as their target concepts. However, MORAL and IMMORAL have aspects, and the source concepts can be mapped onto different aspects of them as well as the more general moral senses such as right and wrong, good and bad or evil. In the visual subsystem discussed in Chapter 4, for instance, CLEAR and MURKY can be mapped onto TRANSPARENT and OPAQUE with a focus on whether social fairness and justness are attempted and achieved. Also, PURE and IMPURE can map onto CHASTE and UNCHASTE, characterizing individual attitudes toward and practices in sexual life. This phenomenon of source concepts mapping onto more specific aspects of morality exists in the spatial subsystem, as shown in Table 5.8.

In Table 5.8, the mappings between the five pairs of spatial concepts and various aspects of MORAL and IMMORAL as their targets are listed. These mappings appear to exist in both English and Chinese, thanks again to embodied cognition (e.g., Gibbs 2006). It has been suggested that the metaphorical mappings derive from and elaborate on the few image schemas illustrated in Figures 5.1 and 5.2. Those image schemas are largely relational in space: hence, UP-DOWN in verticality, UPRIGHT-SLANTED and LEVEL-UNLEVEL in balance (see the two versions of the BALANCE schemas in Figure 5.3), STRAIGHT-UNSTRAIGHT in line (the STRAIGHT schema), and BIG-SMALL in size (the OBJECT schema). Apparently, these image schemas can be characterized as fundamental categories of embodied human experience, including the structure and stance of our own body (e.g., the up-down contrast in structure and the balanced-unbalanced contrast in stance) and its operation in our physical environment (e.g., our movement from point A to point B along a path, level or unlevel, straight or un-straight, and our manipulation of objects of various sizes). Such basic

Table 5.8 Mappings from spatial concepts onto aspects of MORAL and IMMORAL

SPATIAL		MORAL	SPATIAL		IMMORAL
HIGH	→	LOFTY; NOBLE; GOOD	LOW	→	BASE; MEAN; EVIL
UPRIGHT	→	RIGHT; HONEST; IMPARTIAL	SLANTED	→	WRONG; DISHONEST; PARTIAL
LEVEL	→	FAIR; JUST; IMPARTIAL	UNLEVEL	→	UNFAIR; UNJUST; PARTIAL
STRAIGHT	→	RIGHT; HONEST	CROOKED	→	WRONG; DISHONEST
BIG	→	LOFTY; NOBLE; GOOD; GENEROUS	SMALL	→	BASE; EVIL; MEAN

categories of bodily experience should be shared by all humans, regardless of which cultures they are from. That is the reason why my study, based on systematic analyses of linguistic evidence from both English and Chinese, is largely consistent with many experimental studies in social psychology that found a strong link between sensorimotor experience and subjective experience in social cognition in general and in moral cognition in particular. Findings of linguistic and psychological studies support the views of embodied simulation and embodied cognition (e.g., Cuccio 2015; Gibbs 2006; Zwaan 2008, 2009, 2014).

Figure 5.2 also provides a geometric hint at an answer to the question why moral cultivation and ethical education are needed at both individual and societal levels. Morality exists in the upper axis and in the bigger circle, and it always takes more and costs more to get higher and bigger given the direction of the earth gravity. Also, straight, upright and level lines are lines of precision. Drawing them right usually requires some help in instrument. There is only a single way for a line to be straight between two points, but a crooked line can take an infinite number of ways. An upright line and a level line exist only at 90 and 180 degrees, respectively, but a tilted or slanted line can exist at any angles off them. If geometry is a science that emerges from embodied human experience, these simple geometric facts perhaps also provide a hint as to why we need spatial metaphors for morality in the first place.

At the linguistic level, however, there are both similarities and differences. For instance, Chinese has a close equivalent (i.e., 道德高地 *dàodé gāodì* "moral high ground") to *moral high ground*, a common English expression (frequency = 526, plus 69 for *high moral ground*, in COCA), but does not seem to have counterparts for *moral high road* or *moral high horse*. While the spatial concept LEVEL is an entrenched metaphorical source concept for FAIR, which is conventionally instantiated in Chinese, there does not seem to be any conventional expressions close to *level/unlevel playing field(s)*, which is commonly used in American English (frequency = 1008/34 in COCA). Also, *moral compass(es)* (see 6c) is a common English expression (frequency = 799 in COCA). On the other hand, the Chinese counterpart for *compass* (i.e., 指南[针] *zhǐnán[zhēn]*) is also used metaphorically for something that has a "guiding" function, but no close counterpart for *moral compass* can be found in the Corpus of Center for Chinese Linguistics (CCL) or the Corpus of Beijing Language and Culture University Corpus Center (BCC). In brief, linguistic instantiations of conceptual metaphors can differ remarkably in different languages due to the influence of a set of "contextual factors" (Kövecses 2015a).

English and Chinese may differ in how a shared conceptual metaphor is manifested at different levels of schematicity (or specificity). For example, as discussed above, the conceptual metaphor MORAL IS LEVEL (vs. IMMORAL IS UNLEVEL) is instantiated in both languages, but predominantly at different levels of schematicity. In Chinese, the linguistic instantiation is realized at a highly schematic level, the level of image schema (see version (b), the horizontal version, of the BALANCE schema in Figure 5.3). At this schematic level of the BALANCE frame structure, the core role is a horizontal line with its both ends being at the same height (or, if it is a plane, with all points being at the same height). That is what "level" means. In Chinese, MORAL IS LEVEL is chiefly manifested schematically in compounding: for instance, "level-equal" (平等 *píngděng*) means "equal" or "equality"; "fair-level" (公平 *gōngpíng*) means "equitable" or "equity"; "level-right" (平权 *píngquán*) means "equal right"; "level-straight" (平直 *píngzhí*) means "upright" or "honest"; "honest-level" (廉平 *liánpíng*) means "honest and fair"; "broad-level" (宽平 *kuānpíng*) means "tolerant and fair"; "upright-level" (正平 *zhèngpíng*) means "just and fair". These compounds still bear some image content, but the imagery they invoke are extremely skeletal, at the level of image schema like the one provided by Figure 5.3(b).

In contrast, it seems that in English MORAL IS LEVEL is largely instantiated at a fairly specific level, with its source concept set in the BALL GAME frame, where "ball game" refers specially to football or soccer, in which two teams play against each other on a rectangular field. The game is fair to both sides only if the field on which they play is "level" rather than "tilted". With such a fairly specific and enriched source frame structure, the English examples that instantiate the conceptual metaphors MORAL IS LEVEL and IMMORAL IS UNLEVEL are actually variants of a single idiomatic expression, *level playing field*, as is illustrated by the examples in (8). Thus, the source BALL GAME frame is able to activate our rich knowledge about football or soccer games in the understanding of such social concepts as fairness, justness, equity, and equality.

Note that MORAL IS LEVEL can also be instantiated at a more specific level of frame in Chinese, and an example cited in section 5.4.3 is "to hold a bowl of water level" (一碗水端平), meaning "to handle things fairly and impartially". That is, the linguistic instantiation of MORAL IS LEVEL is realized at both a schematic and a specific level in Chinese. In English, however, it happens mainly at a specific level, converging on a few variants of a single idiomatic expression. Yu and Huang (2019) discussed a reversed case in which English has a primary metaphor DIFFICULTY IS SOLIDITY manifested both at a schematic level based on the schematic OBJECT frame (e.g., **hard** questions, **hard** choices, **hard** decisions, **tough** situations, **tough** calls, **tough** issues) and at a specific level based on the specific DRY FRUIT frame (e.g., *a **hard nut** to crack*, **tough nuts** *to crack*). On the other hand, DIFFICULTY IS SOLIDITY is manifested chiefly at a specific level based on the MEAT BONE frame (e.g., 啃这块**硬骨头** (lit. gnaw on this piece of **hard bone**), meaning "take on this **difficult task**"). In Chinese, when a "task" is said to be "hard" (硬任务 (lit. hard task)), for instance, it means "non-negotiable, non-alterable task that has definite requirements on time, amount, quality, etc.", namely an "exacting task", a "task that must be carried out to the letter" (p. 122). This is how linguistic manifestation of a conceptual metaphor can vary across languages.

Finally, another difference between English and Chinese in the linguistic manifestation of moral-spatial metaphors reinforces what I observed in Chapter 4 about two source concepts mapping onto one target in Chinese compound words whereas in English we usually see one-on-one mappings between the source and target concepts. In this chapter, the relevant compounds containing two concepts, either two separate spatial ones or one from spatial and one from another category, include the following ones mapped onto either MORAL or IMMORAL: UPRIGHT-BIG, MIDDLE-UPRIGHT, BROAD-THICK, SQUARE-UPRIGHT, UPRIGHT-STRAIGHT, MINUTE-SMALL, LOW-PETTY, LOW-TINY, LOW-DOWN, TILTED-CROOKED, SLANTED-CROOKED, TWISTED-CROOKED,

FIRM-STRAIGHT, HIGH-CLEAN, CLEAR-UPRIGHT, PURE-UPRIGHT, LIGHT-THIN ("light" in weight). Again, this salient feature of modern Chinese is ascribed to compounding as a major morphological process.

Echoing the caveat made in section 1.4 at this juncture, it is worth stressing that, while spatial concepts such as STRAIGHT may be conceptually associated with morality in cross-linguistic and cross-cultural contexts (see, e.g., sections 5.3.4 and 5.4.4), such metaphorical conceptual links should always be interpreted with caution. For example, the studies of "form symbolism" or "symbolic forms" show that the shape of square, with its four straight lines, is associated with "hard", "cold", "dead", and so forth, in contrast with that of circle, with its curved line associated with "soft", "warm", "alive", and so on (Kennedy et al. 2003; Liu 1997). That is, it is never true that what is spatially straight, for instance, is invariably regarded as good or positive in real-life situations. For instance, curved or even twisted lines, edges, or surfaces are commonly seen in architectural and other artistic designs as common means to aesthetic ends. In Chinese culture, the so-called "zigzag bridge" (九曲桥 jiŭqūqiáo (lit. nine-turn bridge)) is just a classical and common example in traditional garden architecture. Another real-life example is that the world's longest bridges across sea bays are purposefully designed to follow curved rather than straight paths. Such purposive designs are, for one thing, out of safety concerns because straight paths, in such situations, are more boring than curved paths and tend to make drivers feel tired or sleepy. Again, it is exactly out of such situational considerations that when I designed Figures 3.2, 4.2, and 5.4, the three general source frames for the three moral metaphor subsystems, I added, within "Culture", the "Situation" frame that encompasses the three core roles and relations of these source frames.

In this chapter, I have presented my study of the spatial subsystem of moral metaphors. Up to this point, I have wrapped up the separate discussions of the three subsystems of moral metaphors, physical, visual, and spatial, in English and Chinese. In Chapter 6, I will take up anatomic and multimodal perspectives on the moral metaphor system as a whole, discussing some issues concerning this metaphor system.

6

Moral metaphors in anatomy and multimodality

In the preceding three chapters (Chapters 3–5), I laid out English and Chinese data in support of the claim that English and Chinese share a somewhat similar moral metaphor system consisting of three subsystems of physicality, visuality, and spatiality. That is, both English and Chinese speakers employ this metaphor system when reasoning and talking about morality even though their linguistic expressions furnishing this moral metaphor system may be similar or different. My description and analysis of the moral metaphor system should have covered some major moral metaphors utilized in both languages. This moral metaphor system is grounded in the bodily and physical domain broadly defined (see section 1.1). Based on the existing literature and personal research, this moral metaphor system is composed of three clusters of conceptual metaphors and instantiated by a wide range of linguistic metaphors. Other conceptual metaphors for morality that have not been covered in the preceding chapters can be added into the framework of this system, via accumulative research, to make it more comprehensive and substantive. The two further research questions are:

   (i) What are those conceptual metaphors for morality?
   (ii) What are the languages and cultures in which these conceptual metaphors for morality are manifested?

I am hopeful to see subsequent research carried out not only in English and Chinese, but also in many other world languages.

Having presented my study of the three subsystems in English and Chinese, I take up in this chapter a holistic perspective on the moral metaphor system as a whole, examining its components and relations in anatomy and multimodality.

The Moral Metaphor System. Ning Yu, Oxford University Press. © Ning Yu (2022).
DOI: 10.1093/oso/9780192866325.003.0006

6.1 Moral metaphors: Primary or complex?

In perspective, the three subsystems of moral metaphors contain the source concepts in clusters that can be differentiated as visual, spatial, and physical. In the physical subsystem, the source concepts refer to the physical wellbeing of physical entities, including human beings, with respect to their external appearance and internal essence. In comparison, the source concepts in the visual subsystem seem to relate to the factors of physical surroundings that can affect the wellbeing of the physical entities in a positive or negative way. The source concepts in the spatial subsystem, by nature, are those related to the spatial relations and structures of the physical entities from an external perspective. Those spatial relations or structures may reflect or affect the physical wellbeing of physical entities under consideration.

In this section, I discuss some issues involved in relation to conceptual metaphor theory (CMT) and primary metaphor theory (PMT). One central question I ask is whether the conceptual metaphors for morality, which I have studied in this book, are primary or complex metaphors. In attempting to answer this question, the exploration leads to further questions, to some of which I may not yet have definite answers. My hope, however, is that my exploration will contribute to the development of CMT and PMT in general and not just to the understanding of the moral metaphor system as it stands.

In the following, I will first review some relevant literature, and then present my own thoughts on the issue raised above. As Lakoff (2008b: chapter 4) points out, morality is fundamentally about wellbeing. From a neural point of view, our feelings of wellbeing and illbeing correlate with the activation of positive and negative emotions in our brains, which are "wired" to produce experiences of wellbeing and illbeing. Such experiences are linked to some sites in the forebrain, the prefrontal cortex, which embody our ability to make moral judgments and carry out moral reasoning, both conscious and unconscious. "The mechanisms for moral judgments in the brain are bound to the mechanisms for positive emotions (wellbeing) and negative emotions (illbeing): joy and satisfaction versus anger, fear, anxiety, and disgust" (Lakoff 2008b: 94). In my studies of English and Chinese presented in the preceding three chapters, one's perception of some stimuli, namely some salient entity properties of physical, visual, or spatial nature, as experienced in correlation with one's feeling of wellbeing or illbeing, leads to either positive or negative emotions. The positivity or negativity of the emotional reaction to the perception of the entity's salient property serves as the main meaning focus of the conceptual metaphors in the moral metaphor system. This moral metaphor system can be divided into three subsystems, as physical, visual, and spatial, depending on the source concepts mapped onto MORALITY and IMMORALITY as the target concepts.

The founding of PMT marked the beginning of a newer phase of CMT in development (see Grady 1997a, 1997b, 1999, 2005; Lakoff and Johnson 1999, 2003; see also section 2.6). According to the neural theory of metaphor (Lakoff 2008a, 2008b, 2012, 2014), metaphorical mappings have a lot to do with the structure of the human brain. So-called primary metaphors arise spontaneously and naturally, usually during childhood, from recurring experiential correlations, i.e., when two different kinds of experiences regularly occur together and activate two different brain areas at the same time in the primary scenes (Grady 1997a; Grady and Johnson 2002; Lakoff 2012). The two different parts of the brain, one characterizing sensorimotor experiences and the other subjective experiences, are linked to form neural circuits, or neural mappings, which physically constitute primary metaphors. Primary metaphors can then be combined via a neural binding mechanism to form more complex metaphors, conceptual or linguistic. This way, primary metaphors serve as bases and building blocks for more complex metaphorical thought and cognition. Many complex and culture-specific metaphors are based on and informed by primary metaphors, which "are often the starting points for richer, more vivid, specific, and idiosyncratic conceptualizations" (Grady and Ascoli 2017: 37).

Ever since its establishment as a newer development of CMT, PMT has also met some skepticisms and criticisms both inside and outside the circle of cognitive linguistics (see, e.g., Casasanto 2008; Zinken, Hellsten, and Nerlich 2008; see also Hampe 2017: 7–10 for a review). As a cognitive linguist who studies how linguistic data and patterns are related to conceptual patterns, I personally believe that the distinction between primary and complex metaphors is useful for deep and broad semantic analysis of metaphorical language and thought. Such analysis, if conducted properly, should enable us to get to the bottom and see the foundational stones upon which the giant buildings above the ground are constructed. As discussed in Chapter 2, and especially in section 2.6, PMT-informed analytical approaches can, hopefully and ideally, serve as useful tools for understanding how conceptual metaphors are connected systematically into hierarchical networks with vertical, diagonal, and horizontal links. Furthermore, because PMT aims to investigate conceptual patterns at a very schematic level and probe into conceptual categorizations and generalizations above and beyond more specific levels, PMT-guided research may lead to findings about fundamental, and sometimes subtle, commonalities and differences in cognition and communication between languages and cultures. These are what I targeted when I embarked on this book project.

In the next few sections of this chapter, I will take a decompositional approach (e.g., Grady 1997b) to analyzing the moral metaphor system studied in the preceding three chapters. With this approach, as I suggested before, I hope to be able to distinguish what is metaphorical from what is literal, and what is metaphoric from what is metonymic (very often indicating the experiential basis of metaphor), and to show how a metaphorical compound is constructed from combinations (or neural bindings if in terms of a neural theory) of simpler complex metaphors and primary metaphors, metonymies that motivate metaphors, as well as literal propositions as cultural schemas or frames (see, e.g., Yu 2011a, 2011b; Yu et al. 2017; Yu and Huang 2019). That said, however, I still do not think that PMT is already mature and sophisticated enough for handling what it is supposed to handle yet. There needs to be continued effort to sharpen it so that it can be turned into a useful tool and precise instrument for deeper and broader analyses of metaphorical thought and language. In the following, I will attempt to move toward that goal.

With this goal in mind, let us now go back to moral metaphors. As Lakoff (2008b) suggested, our experiences of wellbeing and illbeing correlate regularly with many other kinds of experiences, and with positive and negative feelings. Such experiential correlations provide experiential motivations for the moral metaphors discussed in the preceding chapters, which all take the form of MORALITY IS X, where X stands for one of those "other kinds of experiences" that correlate regularly with our experiences of wellbeing or illbeing, as well as with our positive or negative affect. In *The political mind* (2008b), Lakoff suggested that MORALITY IS X is a primary metaphor. For instance, MORALITY IS PURITY and IMMORALITY IS ROTTENNESS, MORALITY IS LIGHT and IMMORALITY IS DARKNESS, are two pairs of such primary metaphors for morality. Further, in the spirit of "moral politics" (Lakoff 1996), Lakoff argued in some detail that A GOVERNING INSTITUTION IS A FAMILY is a primary metaphor (Lakoff 2008b: 85–87). As he defined it, an institution is "a structured, publicly recognized social group that persists over time" whereas governing is "setting expectations and giving directives, and making sure they are carried out by positive and negative means" (p. 85). As he suggested, most people gained their first experience with governance in the setting of their family, where they were governed by their parents. Thus, their early experiences of governance and family life co-occur, and such co-occurrence gives rise to an extremely important primary metaphor: A GOVERNING INSTITUTION IS A

FAMILY, which includes mappings between the governing institution and the family, a governing individual and a parent, and governed citizens and family members.

Intuitively, the metaphor GOVERNING INSTITUTION IS FAMILY is quite different from those which are widely accepted as primary metaphors in the literature, such as IMPORTANCE IS SIZE and IMPORTANCE IS WEIGHT (e.g., Yu et al. 2017), DIFFICULTY IS WEIGHT and DIFFICULTY IS SOLIDITY (e.g., Yu and Huang 2019). Apparently, the source and target concepts involved in these primary metaphors are very different from those in GOVERNING INSTITUTION IS FAMILY. It seems that a legitimate question we can ask about this metaphor is: How is it more "primary" than, for instance, LIFE IS JOURNEY, which is generally agreed upon as a complex metaphor? For example, in terms of elements and relations in the target and source frames, for the LIFE IS JOURNEY metaphor, the LIFE frame can involve people in life, preconditions of life, actions taken in life, progress made in life, life experiences, life goals, difficulties in life, etc.; the JOURNEY frame can involve travelers, motions in space, distance covered on the journey, journey paths, journey destinations, impediments to motion, etc. On the other hand, for the GOVERNING INSTITUTION IS FAMILY metaphor, the GOVERNING INSTITUTION frame involves institution structure, people who govern, people who are governed, authority needed for some people to govern others, rules formulated for governance, means taken to implement governance, etc.; the FAMILY frame involves family structure, parents, children, parents having authority over children, children subject to the care of parents, family rules, ways family rules are implemented, etc. As listed here, it is hard to see that the latter concepts (i.e., GOVERNING INSTITUTION and FAMILY) are simpler or more primary than the former ones (i.e., LIFE and JOURNEY).

After all, what are the characteristic features of primary metaphors in contrast with complex metaphors? As found in the literature, primary metaphors are metaphorical mappings between "primitive" (Lakoff 2014) or "primary" (Grady and Ascoli 2017) source and target concepts (see also section 2.6). That is, both the source and target concepts of a primary metaphor have to be primitive or primary concepts (the latter is the one I adopt). In other words, as Grady and Ascoli (2017: 29) put it, the source and the target concepts must be equally "basic", as "associations between fundamental concepts" defined as "concepts that are grounded in universal (rather than culturally determined) aspects of human experience". In fact, basicness of concepts involved as source and target is the first of six characteristic traits of primary metaphor (Grady and Ascoli 2017; see also section 2.6).

At this juncture, however, I would like to point out that there is no clear dividing line that separates "basic" concepts from "nonbasic" concepts. Instead, basic and nonbasic concepts form a continuum on which concepts lying at and toward one end are clearly basic and those lying at and toward the other end are clearly nonbasic whereas those in between staying in a "gray" area. In other words, concepts are different only in degree in terms of their basicness. They are distinguished by scalar differences along a continuum that is gradient in nature. This view of concepts arises directly from the prototype theory in categorization. According to that theory, categories do not have clear boundaries between them, nor do members of a category have equal status defined by necessary and sufficient conditions. Instead, categories have fuzzy boundaries, merging into each other, and those members lying at and around the center of categories serve as their "prototypes", or "best examples", in contrast with those nonprototypical or peripheral members located closer to the boundaries. The theory of prototypes is especially relevant to the distinction between primary and complex concepts to be discussed below.

6.2 The target concepts of moral metaphors

In light of the above discussion, I would like now to further develop my earlier argument about moral metaphors (Yu 2015a, 2016), according to which the moral metaphors under study in Chapters 3, 4 and 5, in the nominal form of MORALITY IS X and IMMORALITY IS Y, as well as their adjectival form MORAL IS X and IMMORAL IS Y, do not qualify as primary metaphors. Instead, they are all complex metaphors. The central point of this argument is that, in these moral metaphors, the target concepts, MORAL and IMMORAL (and their nominal counterparts, too), are not primary, but more complex ones containing a primary concept as a component. As part of this argument, I suggest that MORAL and IMMORAL be considered middle-level concepts in a three-level hierarchical structure as rendered below:

Level 1:   GOOD and BAD
Level 2:   MORAL and IMMORAL ...
Level 3:   HONEST and DISHONEST, CHASTE and UNCHASTE, UNSELFISH and
           SELFISH, GENEROUS and UNGENEROUS, IMPARTIAL and PARTIAL,
           UNBIASED and BIASED, FAIR and UNFAIR, EQUAL and UNEQUAL ...

As listed on the three different levels, the concepts on Level 1, GOOD and BAD, are the most generic or schematic, distinguishing at the affective level between two fundamental and contrastive valence values, one positive and the other negative. Listed on Level 2, MORAL and IMMORAL are the two concepts that are the focus of my study. As concepts at a lower level, MORAL and IM-MORAL are more specific than GOOD and BAD, but they inherit the contrastive structure and valence values of the latter, applying them in the more specific domain of MORALITY. The elliptical dots behind the pair indicate that there are other sister pairs of concepts on this level, for example, LEGAL and ILLEGAL in the domain of LEGALITY, and RATIONAL and IRRATIONAL in the domain of RATIONALITY, which both inherit the contrastive structure and valence values of their parent pair, GOOD and BAD, at social and individual levels of human society. At the next level down, Level 3, those listed are pairs of even more specific concepts in the moral domain. As such, they inherit the contrastive structure and valence values of MORAL and IMMORAL and, through them, those of GOOD and BAD. Again, the elliptical dots at the end of the list indicate that more pairs of contrastive concepts may be added on this level.

At this point, I would like to suggest, for the purpose of my argument, that there exist two different types of relationship between the concepts listed above at three hierarchical levels. It is the category-subcategory relationship between Level 1 and Level 2, and the part-whole relationship between Level 2 and Level 3. To put it differently, category and subcategory hold the "type-of" relationship whereas part and whole hold the "part-of" relationship, even though these two kinds of hierarchical relationship are not always mutually ex-clusive (see Ungerer and Schmid 2013: 88–91). Let me cite a concrete example to show the difference between the two: a sports car is a type of car, and a rock-ing chair is a type of chair (i.e., a taxonomic relationship); in contrast, a car wheel is a part of a car, and a chair leg is a part of a chair (i.e., a meronymic or partonomic relationship). That is to say, in this respect, I categorize abstract concepts in parallel with the categorization of concrete concepts.

Now let us return to the three-level conceptual hierarchy above. As sug-gested precedingly, at the top level, GOOD and BAD constitute the most funda-mental distinction in valence judgment with two opposing values, one positive and the other negative. Below them at the second level, MORAL and IMMORAL are their subcategories in the domain of MORALITY, meaning "morally good" and "morally bad", respectively. In other words, MORAL and IMMORAL are more specific valence values applied to the domain of MORALITY, namely for moral judgment. This kind of judgment is made on the basis of whether particular behavior or conduct is good or bad for the wellbeing of the public or major-ity. The conceptual frame of MORALITY and IMMORALITY (adapted from the FrameNet) contains the following core elements and relations: Evaluee, Social

Behavior, and Evaluator (usually implicit). That is, the evaluee is evaluated as being moral or immoral by the evaluator with respect to the evaluee's partic-ular social behavior. In such a context, when the evaluee's behavior is "social" (vs. private or individual), it will then have moral implications in that such behavior may affect other people in a positive or negative way.

Note that "Social Behavior" in the moral frame above is a neutral element that has no positive or negative implications in itself. How does the behavior of the evaluee affect the wellbeing of other people such that this person can be judged as moral or immoral? To answer this question, we have to zoom in on the evluee's social behavior. This is when the concepts on Level 3 come into play for the moral judgment in a more specific way. Thus, at the third level, all the concepts represent specific aspects (i.e., parts) of MORAL and IMMORAL. They, each in its own way, substantiate and constitute the totality of what is judged as being moral or immoral. In other words, what is consid-ered more generally as moral or immoral manifests itself more specifically in one or another of these aspects as constituent parts of being moral or immoral as a whole. For instance, HONEST, which means "free from fraud or decep-tion" or "truthful or sincere", is a particular aspect of corresponding MORAL as a whole whereas the same kind of relationship characterizes DISHONEST and IMMORAL. This kind of part-whole relationship is somewhat different from the type-of relationship that characterizes the one between GOOD and MORAL, for instance. At Level 1, GOOD and BAD are generic and schematic concepts that are applicable widely. At Level 2, MORAL and IMMORAL inherit the structures and values of GOOD and BAD and apply them to the scope of morality (i.e., "morally good" and "morally bad") manifested at both individual and societal levels. At Level 3, in contrast, concepts like HONEST and DISHONEST are sim-ply constituent parts that compose MORAL and IMMORAL as wholes in the same domain of MORALITY.

Having defined the three-level hierarchical structure of the target concepts of moral metaphors, I will first take as an example one pair of moral metaphors from the visual subsystem discussed in Chapter 4. My goal here is to argue that the moral metaphors discussed in the preceding chapters are not primary metaphors because their target concepts are not primary concepts. Specifi-cally, let us first look at MORAL IS LIGHT and IMMORAL IS DARK. This pair of conceptual metaphors, which I claim to be two complex metaphors, can be taken apart, with a decomposition analysis. I called such an analysis DAMCA (see, e.g., Yu 2008, 2009a, 2011a, 2011b; see also section 2.6).

In brief, DAMCA attempts to display the major elements, relations, and frames involved in the mappings of complex metaphors, in order to be more specific about the "what", "why", and "how" of more complex metaphorical compounds: (i) What elements are involved in mappings from source to target? (ii) Why are these elements chosen in the context (i.e., the motivational factors)? (iii) How are the mappings related to one another and embedded within larger frames to form levels of inheritance and schematicity hierarchies? It is hoped that DAMCA is a more rigorous instrument for deeper analysis.

DAMCA has two alternative and complementary formats: the formulaic and the diagrammatic. In the formulaic format, as already mentioned in section 2.6, the following acronyms are used in the parentheses on the right: CM = complex metaphor, PM = primary metaphor, MY = metonymy, and PR = proposition. To this list, I here add one more acronym, P-M = pre-metaphor, which is needed in the following analyses (see Grady and Ascoli 2017).

Provided in (1) and (2) below is the formulaic version of the decomposition analysis of MORAL IS LIGHT and IMMORAL IS DARK. As is shown, this pair of moral-visual metaphors is a pair of complex metaphors, and as such can be analyzed as each being composed of three components, namely two literal propositions and one primary metaphor.

(1) MORAL IS LIGHT   (CM)
    a. MORAL IS GOOD FOR PUBLIC WELLBEING   (PR)
    b. LIGHT IS GOOD   (PR)
    c. GOOD IS LIGHT   (PM)

(2) IMMORAL IS DARK   (CM)
    a. IMMORAL IS BAD FOR PUBLIC WELLBEING   (PR)
    b. DARK IS BAD   (PR)
    c. BAD IS DARK   (PM)

The formulaic version of the decomposition analysis in (1) and (2) is interpreted as follows. In the two accounts above, (1a) and (2a) are literal propositions that represent the major contents of the target concepts MORAL and IMMORAL, providing what they mean intrinsically with contrastive valence between GOOD and BAD. Note that (1a) and (2a) contain two key notions. The first is GOOD in (1a) and BAD in (2a), which constitute the fundamental contrast in valence judgment between MORAL and IMMORAL, at a more basic, affective level. The affective valence values GOOD and BAD are inevitably correlated with our positive and negative emotions respectively when we make

moral judgments. As shown in Figures 3.2, 4.2, and 5.4, GOOD and BAD as valence values also serve as the main meaning focus of metaphorical mapping
from the source to the target frame. This accounts for the aptness of all the
moral metaphors which are shared between English and Chinese. In the target
frame, MORAL and IMMORAL inherit the structures of GOOD and BAD as their
superordinate-level concepts, the latter overlapping the main meaning focuses
of metaphorical mappings from the source domain. I will return to this point
in Chapter 7 when I discuss the mappings between the source and the target
of moral metaphors from a holistic perspective.

The second key notion is PUBLIC WELLBEING in both (1a) and (2a), which
represents the scope in which the conceptual contrast exists between GOOD
and BAD. In other words, people are "moral" only when they behave in ways
good for the public wellbeing, instead of behaving in ways good merely for
their self-wellbeing. In contrast, people are "immoral" if they do things good
just for their own wellbeing but bad for the wellbeing of others. The second
propositions in (1b) and (2b) account for why LIGHT and DARK are chosen as
source concepts for their corresponding targets MORAL and IMMORAL, based
on our experiential correlation in everyday life. That is, depending on normal
contextual factor of situation in our daily life, we correlate light with a positive feeling, hence LIGHT IS GOOD, and darkness with a negative feeling, hence
DARK IS BAD. The tight experiential correlation between LIGHT and GOOD and
between DARK and BAD in particular primary scenes, therefore, grounds the
primary metaphors GOOD IS LIGHT in (1c) and BAD IS DARK in (2c).

What is of interest in the metaphorical analysis under discussion is that, in
this case, the valence values GOOD in (1a) and BAD in (2a), which are superordinate concepts of MORAL and IMMORAL, are conceptualized metaphorically
in terms of LIGHT and DARK, respectively, as rendered in (1c) and (2c). This is
because, in our everyday experience, light, especially sunlight, is usually correlated with our physical and mental wellbeing and embraced with positive
emotions such as happiness (hence, the primary metaphor HAPPY IS LIGHT
or HAPPY IS BRIGHT). Conversely, darkness is often associated with negative
emotions such as sadness (hence, the primary metaphor SAD IS DARK), which
is linked with mental and physical illbeing. In this way, the valence values in
the literal propositions (1a) and (2a) rely on a pair of primary metaphors,
GOOD IS LIGHT in (1c) and BAD IS DARK in (2c), for their construal. Therefore, the conceptualization of MORAL and IMMORAL rests on a combination
of what is literal (the propositions) and what is metaphorical (the primary
metaphors). That is, if MORAL IS GOOD (a literal proposition) and if GOOD
IS LIGHT (a primary metaphor), then MORAL IS LIGHT (a complex metaphor);

contrastively, if IMMORAL IS BAD (a literal proposition) and if BAD IS DARK (a primary metaphor), then IMMORAL IS DARK (a complex metaphor). It is in this sense that MORALITY is not all metaphorical, but its understanding and reasoning are achieved with metaphors (see Lakoff and Johnson 1999: 325–326).

As analyzed above, the primary metaphors GOOD IS LIGHT in (1c) and BAD IS DARK in (2c) are, by definition, based on our experiential correlations, as is illustrated in Figure 4.2. They are derived from our fundamental embodied experience in which LIGHT and DARK (sensorimotor experience) are correlated respectively with GOOD and BAD (subjective judgment) in our everyday experience. As a pair of primary metaphors based on such experiential correlations, GOOD IS LIGHT and BAD IS DARK entail, and are grounded by, their nonmetaphorical reversals, LIGHT IS GOOD in (1b) and DARK IS BAD in (2b), which represent the valence judgments we make on lightness and darkness based on our everyday embodied experience in the physical world (see, again, Figure 4.2).

Analyzed in such a way, MORAL IS LIGHT and IMMORAL IS DARK are complex metaphors because they comprise a primary metaphor (1c and 2c) and two literal propositions (1a and 1b; 2a and 2b). Thus, in these two metaphors, while LIGHT and DARK, the source concepts, qualify as primary concepts, the target concepts MORAL and IMMORAL, onto which they map, do not. They are not primary concepts and their understanding depends on the primary concepts GOOD and BAD respectively in combination with another crucial notion PUBLIC WELLBEING. Only when both source and target are primary concepts can they constitute a primary metaphor (Grady and Ascoli 2017; see also section 2.6).

Provided in (1) and (2) is the formulaic format of DAMCA. The formulaic version also has its twin version, the diagrammatic format. To refresh what was provided in section 2.6, the following are the conventional notations utilized in this format. That is, lines with solid arrowheads represent metaphorical mappings, and lines with open arrowheads represent metonymic mappings. Depending on specific cases, lines with stealth arrowheads or without arrowheads at all represent literal, propositional relations, such as opposition, correlation, interrelation, subcategorization, or predication. The bold font type represents primary concepts (found in primary metaphors or pre-metaphors), in contrast with the regular font type for more complex concepts. A smaller box within a larger box indicates that the former is a more specific subcase of the latter, which is more schematic or generic than the former.

The decomposition analysis presented in (1) and (2) can be illustrated diagrammatically as in Figure 6.1(a) and (b). Note that in this particular case,

MORAL and IMMORAL are defined in terms of GOOD and BAD, respectively. As such, the former are special subcases of the latter, adding more details to the latter. This relationship is represented in Figure 6.1 as one concept being framed within the other. Thus, MORAL is "a kind of good", hence "morally good"; similarly, IMMORAL is "a kind of bad", hence "morally bad".

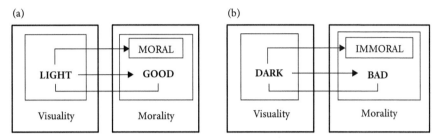

Fig. 6.1 A decomposition analysis of MORAL IS LIGHT and IMMORAL IS DARK

Analyzed in this way, LIGHT and DARK as primary source concepts map directly onto GOOD and BAD as primary target concepts, represented by the straight lines with solid arrowheads, thus forming a pair of primary metaphors in opposition to each other. In contrast, the metaphorical mappings from LIGHT and DARK to MORAL and IMMORAL are indirect, via GOOD and BAD, which are "behind" MORAL and IMMORAL, containing them as their subcategories. The indirect mappings from LIGHT and DARK to MORAL and IMMORAL are represented by the nonstraight, right-angled lines with solid arrowheads. In addition, as in Figure 6.1(a), there is a line without any arrowhead linking LIGHT and GOOD. This line indicates the correlational relationship between these two dimensions in our everyday experience. With this experiential correlation, LIGHT (sensorimotor experience) is associated with GOOD (subjective experience). Such perception-valence association forms the experiential basis for a potential primary metaphor, but it is by itself still not a primary metaphor yet. It can be what Grady and Ascoli (2017: 33) refer to as a "pre-metaphor". The actual primary metaphor arises from the mediation of culture and reinforcement in language. Figure 6.1(b) is interpreted in the same manner.

In light of the above decomposition analysis, which treats MORAL and IMMORAL as concepts more complex than primary concepts GOOD and BAD, we can hypothesize, for instance, that children would acquire GOOD IS LIGHT and BAD IS DARK before MORAL IS LIGHT and IMMORAL IS DARK, and that the latter would be acquired only when they develop the conception that morality is good for the public wellbeing. In short, GOOD and BAD are basic and primary (or primitive) concepts whereas MORAL and IMMORAL are more complex ones that are subcategories subordinate to GOOD and BAD. Moreover, GOOD IS LIGHT and BAD IS DARK, as primary metaphors, may appear in other more complex metaphors as well, as core metaphorical components participating in metaphorical composition and comprehension of more complex target concepts.

To illustrate how GOOD IS LIGHT and BAD IS DARK, as primary metaphors, can play their pivotal roles in more complex metaphorical mappings, I here take another pair of conceptual metaphors as examples: OPTIMISTIC IS LIGHT (e.g., **bright**, **shining**, or **gilded** *prospects for the future*) and PESSIMISTIC IS DARK (e.g., *a **dim**, **dark**, or **gloomy** view of human nature*). A decomposition analysis of these metaphors can be proposed as in (3) and (4).

(3) OPTIMISTIC IS LIGHT   (CM)
    a. OPTIMISTIC IS EXPECTING GOOD THINGS TO HAPPEN   (PR)
    b. OPTIMISTIC IS GOOD   (PR)
    c. GOOD IS LIGHT   (PM)

(4) PESSIMISTIC IS DARK   (CM)
    a. PESSIMISTIC IS EXPECTING BAD THINGS TO HAPPEN   (PR)
    b. PESSIMISTIC IS BAD   (PR)
    c. BAD IS DARK   (PM)

As can be seen above, the two decomposition accounts in (3) and (4) are not the same as those in (1) and (2). There is an important difference between them. In (3a) and (4a), which define the contents of the target concepts in question, although the valence terms GOOD and BAD also appear in the definitions, OPTIMISTIC and PESSIMISTIC are not defined in terms of them in the same way as are MORAL and IMMORAL in (1a) and (2a). In this case, OPTIMISTIC and PESSIMISTIC are not subcategories of GOOD and BAD as are MORAL and IMMORAL. Instead, OPTIMISTIC and PESSIMISTIC are only evaluated in terms of GOOD and BAD. In this case, because OPTIMISTIC IS EXPECTING GOOD THINGS TO HAPPEN (3a), so OPTIMISTIC IS GOOD (3b). Contrastively, because PESSIMISTIC IS EXPECTING BAD THINGS TO HAPPEN (4a), so PESSIMISTIC IS BAD (4b). Of course, GOOD and BAD are still key concepts in (3a) and (4a) that are responsible for the corresponding valence judgments we make on the target concepts in (3b) and (4b): namely, OPTIMISTIC IS GOOD and PESSIMISTIC IS BAD, and here the subject-predicate relationship between OPTIMISTIC and GOOD and between PESSIMISTIC and BAD is one of evaluation rather than definition as in (1a) and (2a). Together, what (3) and (4) mean is the following: given their definitions in (3a) and (4a), OPTIMISTIC IS GOOD (3b) and PESSIMISTIC IS BAD (4b), and if GOOD IS LIGHT (3c) and BAD IS DARK (4c), then OPTIMISTIC IS LIGHT (3) and PESSIMISTIC IS DARK (4).

With the differences between (1) and (2) on the one hand and (3) and (4) on the other, as pointed out above, the decomposition analysis of (3) and (4) can be illustrated with the two diagrams in Figure 6.2. As shown in Figure 6.2(a), OPTIMISTIC and GOOD are no longer two frames with one inside the other, but two separate frames linked together. In other words, OPTIMISTIC is not a subcategory of GOOD; instead, it is linked to GOOD because people with this mental attribute, namely those who tend to believe that good things will happen in the future, are judged as having a positive or "good" attitude in their mental outlook. Put differently, OPTIMISTIC and GOOD are linked in a subject-predicate relationship that is evaluative in nature. As shown in Figure 6.2(a), LIGHT and GOOD are linked together, with a line without arrowheads, as a result of a recurring correlation in our life experience. In this case, the experiential correlation gives rise to a primary metaphor GOOD IS LIGHT. As is shown in Figure 6.2(a), the source concept LIGHT maps directly to GOOD and indirectly to OPTIMISTIC as its target concepts. Figure 6.2(b) is interpreted in the same way.

Before we turn to another pair of examples involving the primary metaphors GOOD IS LIGHT and BAD IS DARK, we may want to ask a question: Why should the OPTIMISTIC and PESSIMISTIC metaphors only choose LIGHT and DARK, but not other visual concepts such as CLEAN and DIRTY, as their source concepts, while MORAL and IMMORAL metaphors can choose both? I believe the answer lies in the fact that, as suggested above, optimism and pessimism characterize that aspect of one's mental "outlook" in a way in which physical light is metaphorically evoked as a crucial factor that determines one's "view" or "vision" of things. That is, how things are seen depends overwhelmingly on the physical light they are in. On the other hand, the degree of cleanness and dirtiness, though part of one's visual experience, cannot affect one's "view", "vision", or "outlook" in a similar way.

(a)   (b)

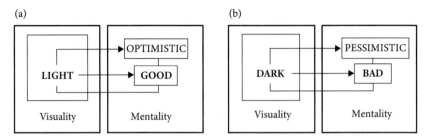

Fig. 6.2 A decomposition analysis of OPTIMISTIC IS LIGHT and PESSIMISTIC IS
DARK

Another pair of complex metaphors that may contain primary metaphors
GOOD IS LIGHT and BAD IS DARK as their components is INTELLIGENT IS LIGHT
(e.g., *a **bright** student, a **brilliant** idea*) and UNINTELLIGENT IS DARK (e.g., *a
dull student, a **dim-witted** idea*).[1] A possible decomposition analysis of them is
provided in (5) and (6) below. The interpretation of (5) and (6) should be quite
similar to that of (3) and (4). The diagrammatic illustration, which is omitted
here, should look very similar to Figure 6.2 as well, only differing in the target
concepts onto which LIGHT and DARK are mapped.

(5) INTELLIGENT IS LIGHT   (CM)
    a. INTELLIGENT IS HAVING GOOD MENTAL CAPACITY   (PR)
    b. INTELLIGENT IS GOOD   (PR)
    c. GOOD IS LIGHT   (PM)

(6) UNINTELLIGENT IS DARK   (CM)
    a. UNINTELLIGENT IS HAVING BAD MENTAL CAPACITY (PR)
    b. UNINTELLIGENT IS BAD   (PR)
    c. BAD IS DARK   (PM)

The advantage of the decomposition analysis proposed above is that we are
now not dealing with eight individual metaphors in isolation from one another, but a hierarchical network of metaphors that are unified by a single pair
of primary metaphors in opposition to each other. As illustrated in Figure 6.3,
the eight conceptual metaphors are related to one another in three different
ways: contrastive, coordinate, and hierarchical. The contrastive relationship is

---

[1] It is worth noting in passing that LIGHT and DARK are relational and relative concepts. That is, DARK
can mean "black", or just "darker" than the average in lightness. In English, for instance, PESSIMISTIC
IS DARK can be instantiated by such expressions as *a dim view* or *a dark view*. On the other hand,
UNINTELLIGENT IS DARK can be instantiated by *a dim-witted student* or *a dull student*, but not by *a
dark student*. Although DARK appears in the conceptual metaphor as a cover term for a range of "darker"
degrees in light, the word *dark* itself may not be used to instantiate this conceptual metaphor at the
linguistic level.

represented by lines with stealth arrowheads at both ends. With this relationship, metaphors form pairs of two whose source and target concepts are in polar opposition to each other, such as GOOD and BAD, and LIGHT and DARK.

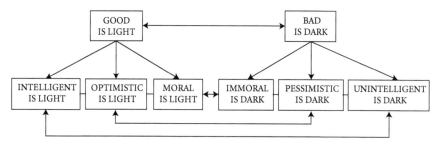

Fig. 6.3 A network of metaphors with contrastive, coordinate, and hierarchical relations

The coordinate relationship is represented by lines without arrowheads. As much as metaphors in contrastive relationship, metaphors with coordinate relationship exist on the same level of the hierarchical network, as "sisters" of each other. In Figure 6.3, the metaphors in this relationship have the same primary source concept, LIGHT or DARK; their targets are more complex concepts. Although they are different concepts, they share the same value in valence judgment (i.e., either GOOD or BAD).

The hierarchical relationship, represented by lines with a single stealth arrowhead, is held between metaphors existing at different levels of the hierarchical network, as reflected especially in the kinds of relationship forged between their target concepts. In Figure 6.3, there are only two levels in the hierarchy. On the higher level are two primary metaphors, whereas the ones on the lower level differ in the target concept, which may either inherit or incorporate the target concept of the primary metaphor at the higher level. Thus, MORAL can be considered a subcase of GOOD, and MORAL is also judged as possessing the positive valence GOOD for showing "good" behavior in social interaction. Both OPTIMISTIC and INTELLIGENT are judged as GOOD because they show "good" attitude in outlook or "good" capacity in intelligence. The source concepts LIGHT and DARK should be able to map to other target domains too, such as LEGALITY, where the distinction is made between LEGAL and ILLEGAL and GOOD and EVIL. In brief, with a decomposition analysis proposed here, we can pinpoint the kind of essential relationship held between metaphors, telling how they are related with one another, vertically and horizontally, to form a hierarchical network. That is exactly why and how we want to "formalize" CMT (Stickles et al. 2016; see also Dancygier and Sweetser 2014; Kövecses 2017a, 2020).

In the above, I argued that as target concepts of moral metaphors, MORAL and IMMORAL are not primary concepts because they are defined on the basis of GOOD and BAD as primary concepts. As such, for instance, MORAL IS LIGHT and IMMORAL IS DARK cannot be primary metaphors. At this point, I would like to ask a question: What about the concepts at Level 3 in the hierarchy? More specifically, are they primary or complex concepts? This is a difficult question for me to answer. In the above, I argued that Level-3 concepts hold a part-whole relationship with their superordinate concepts MORAL and IMMORAL. As parts, they do not occupy conceptual spaces as large as the latter, nor do they have conceptual structures as complex as the latter, since they all together constitute the totality of the latter. Yet, they still inherit the frame structures of the latter while focusing on their own structures that may be out of focus in the latter's basic frame structures. As a concrete analogy, for instance, a wheel of a car is not just any wheel but a car wheel, nor is a leg of a chair any leg but a chair leg. The wheel or leg can only be profiled against the base of a car or a chair.

On the other hand, however, parts are not equal in complexity or cruciality. The engine of a car is a car part, so is a bolt of a car. In a similar vein, my hypothesis regarding Level-3 moral concepts, as aspects (or parts) of MORAL and IMMORAL, is that they may vary in degree as complex or primary concepts. For instance, concepts such as HONEST and DISHONEST, CHASTE and UNCHASTE are intrinsically moral. On the other hand, concepts like EQUAL and UNEQUAL are not necessarily so; they have more basic meanings in physical domains. For example, there is no moral implication whatsoever when we say, "John and Tom are of **equal** height" or "The two halves of the apple are **equal** in size". This pair of concepts becomes moral, however, when it is extended into abstract social domains, as reflected in such terms as "social equality" or "gender equality". In other words, as social and moral concepts, EQUAL and UNEQUAL build metaphorically on their more fundamental physical senses.

To follow up on this hypothesis and line of reasoning, I will use two pairs of moral-spatial metaphors as examples to illustrate the decomposition analysis of moral metaphors with complex target concepts at Level 3. As will be seen, even though the two pairs of moral-spatial metaphors both have complex target concepts, their analyses may not be the same. The first pair of moral-spatial metaphors is MORAL IS UPRIGHT and IMMORAL IS SLANTED. The source concept UPRIGHT refers to a vertical axis (such as a human body standing straight up) that is perpendicular, namely, standing at right angles to the plane of horizon, whereas SLANTED refers to such a vertical axis that is leaning to one side (see version (a) of Figure 5.3). When the vertical axis is "upright", it maintains

balance. When "slanting" or "tilting" toward one side, this axis is off balance
to the extent of falling over depending on the circumstances. A decomposition
analysis of this pair of moral metaphors is provided in (7) and (8).

(7) MORAL IS UPRIGHT   (CM)
    a. MORAL IS GOOD FOR PUBLIC WELLBEING   (PR)
    b. MORAL FOR HONEST IS UPRIGHT   (CM)
    c.   UPRIGHT IS GOOD   (PR)
    d.   GOOD IS UPRIGHT   (P-M)

(8) IMMORAL IS SLANTED   (CM)
    a. IMMORAL IS BAD FOR PUBLIC WELLBEING   (PR)
    b. IMMORAL FOR DISHONEST IS SLANTED   (CM)
    c.   SLANTED IS BAD   (PR)
    d.   BAD IS SLANTED   (P-M)

As (7) shows, in the complex metaphor MORAL IS UPRIGHT, the target concept MORAL actually stands for HONEST in the target (7b), which is a WHOLE
FOR PART metonymy. That is, MORAL IS UPRIGHT (7) when MORAL STANDS FOR
HONEST (7b). In the target, HONEST and MORAL hold a part-whole relationship.
That is, HONEST is a particular aspect or part of MORAL as a whole. Note that
this part-whole relationship is distinguished from the category-subcategory
relationship that characterizes GOOD and MORAL. Category and subcategory
hold a "type-of" relationship. The "part-of" relationship that characterizes
HONEST and MORAL, however, is different (see the preceding discussion). In
this analysis, I consider HONEST a complex target concept describing a subjective judgment on the moral conduct or character of a person. On the other
hand, I treat UPRIGHT as a primary source concept on the ground that it
represents a basic category, in contrast with SLANTED, in our sensorimotor
experience with body posture or spatial orientation. This fundamental aspect
of sensorimotor experience is rooted in and represented by the BALANCE image
schema in Figure 5.3(a). In (7c), at the next level down (indicated by inden-
tion), the proposition characterizes a common sensorimotor experience with
an upright body (see section 6.6 below) or any other vertical axis in space
as being "good". The proposition in (7c) grounds the pre-metaphor GOOD IS
UPRIGHT in (7d).

Note that I am here being refrained from identifying (7d) as a full-fledged
primary metaphor. Instead, it is viewed as a "pre-metaphor", i.e., a "cognitive association" derived from experiential correlation (Grady and Ascoli
2017). Such pre-metaphors are well motivated by recurring correlations in
our everyday experience and, as such, should be psychologically real, but they
have not reached the full status of primary metaphors for lack of confirmed

linguistic or multimodal evidence for their "official" existence. In holding this view, I conservatively insist that the existence of a primary metaphor needs to be proven by sufficient identifiable evidence, linguistic or multimodal. Before that evidence is identified and confirmed, a primary-like metaphorical pattern remains (tentatively) a pre-metaphor. The decomposition analysis in (8) is similar to that of (7).

The formulaic version of the decomposition analysis is illustrated in Figure 6.4, which provides a diagrammatic counterpart. As seen in Figure 6.4(a), UPRIGHT is connected with GOOD as a pre-metaphor (see 7c and 7d), and its mapping onto MORAL (MORAL IS UPRIGHT) and HONEST (HONEST IS UPRIGHT) are complex metaphors since their targets are not primary concepts. In this case, MORAL stands metonymically for HONEST (i.e., WHOLE FOR PART) in the target. Figure 6.4(b), which illustrates DISHONEST IS SLANTED, is interpreted in the same manner.

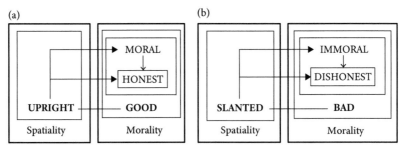

Fig. 6.4 A decomposition analysis of MORAL IS UPRIGHT and IMMORAL IS SLANTED

Just to mention in passing that the source concepts UPRIGHT and SLANTED may be mapped onto other pairs of moral concepts, such as IMPARTIAL and PARTIAL, UNBIASED and BIASED, and so on. All these metaphorical mappings are based on the BALANCE image schema, which has two possible cases with a vertical line in perpendicular relation with a horizontal line (see Figure 5.3(a) and (b)). In this particular case, as it seems, a moral person who is honest, impartial, or unbiased is one with a body that stands "upright" in good balance. Contrastively, an immoral person who is dishonest, partial, or biased is one with a body that stands "slanted" to one side and hence off balance.

Also note that MORAL IS STRAIGHT and IMMORAL IS CROOKED can be analyzed in a similar way as MORAL IS UPRIGHT and IMMORAL IS SLANTED, but they elaborate on different image schemas. The latter pair is based on the (a) version of BALANCE image schema, where a vertical line is perpendicular in relation to a horizontal line (Figure 5.3(a)). The question is whether the vertical line is "straight up" (in balance) or "slanted to one side" (off balance). In the former pair, namely MORAL IS STRAIGHT and IMMORAL IS CROOKED, however, only one line is involved, and the question is whether this line is "straight" or "crooked" (or "un-straight"), regardless of its orientation. The STRAIGHT image schema is represented by a simple straight line. A horizontal straight line is also what is used to represent the PATH image schema. The question remains open whether GOOD IS STRAIGHT and BAD IS CROOKED is a pair of primary metaphors or pre-metaphors. I would prefer to take them as pre-metaphors since I have not yet seen sufficient linguistic or multimodal evidence for their status as full-fledged primary metaphors. Regardless of their exact nature, they seem to be well motivated by experiential correlations and to be psychologically real as cognitive associations.

The second pair of moral-spatial metaphors to be discussed here is MORAL IS BIG and IMMORAL IS SMALL, of which a decomposition analysis is provided in (9) and (10).

(9) MORAL IS BIG   (CM)
    a. MORAL IS GOOD FOR PUBLIC WELLBEING   (PR)
    b. MORAL FOR GENEROUS IS BIG   (CM)
    c.   BIG IS GOOD   (PR)
    d.   GOOD IS BIG   (PM)

(10) IMMORAL IS SMALL   (CM)
    a. IMMORAL IS BAD FOR PUBLIC WELLBEING   (PR)
    b. IMMORAL FOR UNGENEROUS IS SMALL   (CM)
    c.   SMALL IS BAD   (PR)
    d.   BAD IS SMALL   (PM)

As shown above, the decomposition analysis of (9) and (10) is similar to that of (7) and (8). What is different with this pair is that GOOD IS BIG in (9d) and BAD IS SMALL in (10d) are analyzed as full-fledged primary metaphors because it is already well established as such in the literature. Figure 6.5 provides a diagrammatical illustration of (9) an (10). In version (a), GOOD IS BIG is a primary metaphorical pattern, as represented by the solid arrowhead, and it is well grounded in the experiential correlation between BIG and GOOD linked together by the arrowless line below them.

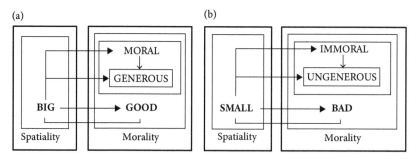

Fig. 6.5 A decomposition analysis of MORAL IS BIG and IMMORAL IS SMALL

In the above analysis of two moral-spatial metaphors, the two pairs of Level-3 target concepts, i.e., HONEST and DISHONEST, and GENEROUS and UNGENEROUS, are not considered primary concepts, as discussed above. Therefore, the metaphors with them as target concepts cannot be primary metaphors either. Besides, GOOD IS UPRIGHT (7d) and BAD IS SLANTED (8d) are taken as pre-metaphors even though their source and target are primary concepts. This is because, so far, there does not seem to be sufficient evidence, linguistic or multimodal, in support of their status as full-fledged primary metaphors. To me, there is ample evidence that UPRIGHT and SLANTED are used as source concepts for metaphors in the MORALITY domain (i.e., MORAL IS UPRIGHT and IMMORAL IS SLANTED, HONEST IS UPRIGHT and DISHONEST IS SLANTED) in both English and Chinese, but the evidence for their deployment in the VALENCE domain in general (i.e., GOOD IS UPRIGHT and BAD IS SLANTED) is yet to be found and confirmed.

6.3 The source concepts of moral metaphors

In the preceding section, I argued that in the moral metaphors such as MORAL IS LIGHT and IMMORAL IS DARK, the target concepts MORAL and IMMORAL are not primary concepts. Instead, they are more complex concepts with GOOD and BAD as key components combined with other elements. However, it was suggested that their source concepts, LIGHT and DARK, are indeed primary concepts. In this section, my questions are: What about other source concepts? Are they primary as well? These questions are, again, not easy to answer. This is because primary metaphors as mappings between primary concepts are characterized along six different dimensions: (a) basicness of concepts involved, (b) sensory vs. nonsensory concepts as source vs. target concepts,

(c) directionality of mappings between concepts, (d) correlation and covariation between concepts, (e) wide distribution across languages, and (f) bases for more complex conceptualization (Grady and Ascoli 2017: 29–37).

As I suggested earlier, citing prototype theory in categorization, concepts are distinguished in a particular category, for instance, basicness, by scalar differences along a continuum that is gradient in nature. While concepts located toward either end of the continuum can be unequivocally categorized one way or another, those located in the middle, the "gray" area, are not subject to clear and distinct categorization. Subsequently in this section, I will take the visual subsystem of moral metaphors as an example, because I believe there is less uniformity, and more variability, among the source concepts in this subsystem than those in the other two subsystems. I will show in this section that the source concepts in the visual subsystem are not "created equal" as basic concepts, but that some are more basic than others. As such, those that are less basic may depend on those more basic ones in meaning making. My central argument is therefore the following: the four pairs of visual source concepts are graded in their status as basic. Along the same line, their status as primary concepts may be gradient as well. It is worth remembering that well-motivated association between primary concepts grounded in universal aspects of human experience may not necessarily end up becoming primary metaphors manifested in productive linguistic patterns. They may remain as pre-metaphors (Grady and Ascoli 2017).

Before moving onto a decomposition analysis of the moral-visual metaphors, I first review the study of them in Chapter 4. There, I argued that the eight source concepts of visual nature form a network in an associative as well as contrastive way (see Figure 4.1). This network is divided into two halves, forming four contrastive pairs of opposite concepts across the two sides, i.e., LIGHT VS. DARK, CLEAN VS. DIRTY, CLEAR VS. MURKY, and PURE VS. IMPURE. Furthermore, the concepts on both sides are also associated with one another, directly or indirectly, within each half, i.e., LIGHT, CLEAR, CLEAN, PURE VS. DARK, MURKY, DIRTY, IMPURE. It is in this way of contrastive and associative relations among the source concepts that the moral-visual metaphors themselves are also connected into a network of metaphorical mappings, which I call "the visual subsystem of moral metaphors". In other words, these moral-visual metaphors form a subsystem because their source concepts are closely linked in one way or another.

In the preceding section, I argued that LIGHT and DARK form a contrastive pair of primary concepts, and for that matter, GOOD IS LIGHT and BAD IS

DARK form a contrastive pair of primary metaphors, playing a core role in the composition of a corresponding pair of complex metaphors, MORAL IS LIGHT and IMMORAL IS DARK. I believe that another pair of visual source concepts, CLEAN and DIRTY, is very similar to LIGHT and DARK in status. First, CLEAN and DIRTY, as much as LIGHT and DARK discussed above, have their intrinsic positive and negative values, meaning that something or somewhere is "without or with unwanted matter", where "unwanted matter", i.e., DIRT, means "matter out of place" (Lizardo 2012). As such, they are primary concepts as much as GOOD and BAD are. The MORAL IS CLEAN and IMMORAL IS DIRTY metaphors can undergo the same decomposition analysis in (11) and (12) as are MORAL IS LIGHT and IMMORAL IS DARK in (1) and (2).

(11) MORAL IS CLEAN   (CM)
    a. MORAL IS GOOD FOR PUBLIC WELLBEING   (PR)
    b. CLEAN IS GOOD   (PR)
    c. GOOD IS CLEAN   (PM)

(12) IMMORAL IS DIRTY   (CM)
    a. IMMORAL IS BAD FOR PUBLIC WELLBEING   (PR)
    b. DIRTY S BAD   (PR)
    c. BAD IS DIRTY   (PM)

Here, GOOD IS CLEAN (11c) and BAD IS DIRTY (12c) are again primary metaphors. In Yu (2009a: 303–305), I pointed out that these two primary metaphors are manifested in our everyday language and thought. For instance, a *clean* copy of a document is one free of errors that are considered "bad". A *clean* piece of work is a "good" job "well" done. A person who keeps a *clean* tongue is one that does not use "bad" language or "dirty" words. A ship with *clean* lines is one with a "good" design of its shape. Related to *clean* is the verb *cleanse* when it means "to remove something bad". Thus, for example, to *cleanse* one's mind means to remove "bad" thoughts from one's mind. Similar metaphorical thought is reflected in such phrases as *ethnic cleansing*, where those who do the cleansing believe that people from other ethnic groups are not as "good" or, rather, "bad". During the Cultural Revolution of China (1966–1976), a political movement was called a purification campaign, in which those who were considered "bad elements" (坏分子 *huàifēnzǐ*) were "cleared" out of their units in order to "clean up the class ranks". Note that the primary metaphors GOOD IS CLEAN and BAD IS DIRTY again entail, and are grounded by, their nonmetaphorical reversals, CLEAN IS GOOD (11b) and

DIRTY IS BAD (12b). Since the diagrammatic illustrations of (11) and (12) look the same except for having different source concepts, they are omitted here.

In Figure 4.1, the four visual source concepts located at the four corners of the conceptual network form two contrastive pairs: namely, CLEAR and MURKY, and PURE and IMPURE. They are placed in more peripheral positions because they are concepts, in my view, less basic than LIGHT and DARK, and CLEAN and DIRTY. In English dictionaries (*Merriam-Wester, Oxford Lexico, Longman*, etc.), therefore, they may be defined in terms of the latter, but not vice versa. While definitely less basic, these two pairs are still considered primary concepts in the analyses below for reasons to be explained.

Let us first look at PURE and IMPURE. There is no doubt that MORAL IS PURE and IMMORAL IS IMPURE, the two adjectival parametric versions of the nominal form MORALITY IS PURITY, are a pair of moral metaphors that takes a central position in the moral metaphor system. This does not mean, however, that their source concepts PURE and IMPURE are as basic as CLEAN and DIRTY to which they are directly linked (see Figure 4.1). While CLEAN and DIRTY are intrinsically positive and negative in valence, PURE and IMPURE are inherently neutral, meaning respectively "unmixed" and "mixed" with something else, but whether this "something else" is wanted or unwanted depends on specific cases. For instance, in English expressions ***pure** folly* and ***pure** terrorism* from the Corpus of Contemporary American English (COCA), *pure* is not positive in meaning. Also, if I do not like the tasteless pure water, I can squeeze lemon juice into it to make it impure, to my liking. Thus, PURE is positive only when it is equivalent to CLEAN or "unmixed with unwanted matter". Similarly, IMPURE is negative only when it is equivalent to DIRTY or "mixed with unwanted matter". This suggests that in moral metaphors PURE and IMPURE (i.e., "unmixed or mixed with unwanted matter") are less basic than CLEAN and DIRTY ("without or with unwanted mater"). It can be suggested that the moral sense of PURE, i.e., "free from moral fault or guilt", depends on its CLEAN sense "free from dust, dirt, or taint" (*Merriam-Webster*). The source IMPURE can undergo the same interpretation.

If, as suggested above, PURE and IMPURE as concepts are not as basic as CLEAN and DIRTY, a question that follows is: Are they primary concepts as are CLEAN and DIRTY? Intuitively, PURE and IMPURE represent a basic perceptual, especially visual, category in our everyday experience. I am therefore inclined to consider them a pair of primary concepts which are nonetheless less basic than CLEAN and DIRTY. Thus, I propose a decomposition analysis of MORAL IS PURE and IMMORAL IS IMPURE in (13) and (14).

(13)   MORAL IS PURE   (CM)
    a. MORAL IS GOOD FOR PUBLIC WELLBEING   (PR)
    b. PURE IS GOOD   (PR)
    c. GOOD IS PURE   (P-M)

(14)   IMMORAL IS IMPURE   (CM)
    a. IMMORAL IS BAD FOR PUBLIC WELLBEING (PR)
    b. IMPURE IS BAD   (PR)
    c. BAD IS IMPURE   (P-M)

The decomposition analysis in (13) and (14) is the same as the one offered in (11) and (12) with the exception that GOOD IS PURE (13c) and BAD IS IMPURE (14c) are not characterized as primary metaphors (PM), but as "pre-metaphors" (P-M). This is because, once again, there does not seem to be sufficient linguistic or multimodal evidence thus far to justify their status as full-fledged primary metaphors. Whether or not this is true awaits further research. There seems to be experiential correlation between PURE and GOOD, and between IMPURE and BAD, which may have given rise to our cognitive association between the two dimensions of experience. Cognitive association, however, is still at the stage of pre-metaphor (Grady and Ascoli 2017). That is to say, GOOD IS PURE and BAD IS IMPURE need the mediation and reinforcement of cultural and linguistic environments before they can develop into full-fledged conceptual patterns as primary metaphors, to be manifested in language and multimodality.

Figure 6.6 provides the diagrammatic version of the formulaic analysis in (13) and (14). In Figure 6.6(a), PURE is treated as a primary concept (hence in bold) which is correlated with GOOD. In this analysis, GOOD IS PURE is a potential primary-metaphor pattern, but at this time is still a pre-metaphor, as is represented by the bare straight line linking PURE with GOOD. Though a pre-metaphor, the cognitive association between PURE and GOOD can still provide experiential motivation grounding the complex metaphor MORAL IS PURE. That is, PURE as a primary source concept maps to the more specific target concept MORAL on Level 2, but its mapping does not apply to the more general target concept GOOD on Level 1. Just to mention in passing that PURE and IMPURE can map to Level-3 concepts CHASTE and UNCHASTE, resulting in a pair of complex moral metaphors CHASTE IS PURE and UNCHASTE IS IMPURE. In such a case, the target concepts MORAL and IMMORAL as wholes stand metonymically for CHASTE and UNCHASTE as parts (see (7) and (8) and Figure 6.4 for a similar case of analysis of MORAL IS UPRIGHT and IMMORAL IS SLANTED).

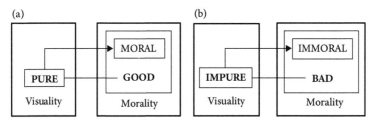

Fig. 6.6 A decomposition analysis of MORAL IS PURE and IMMORAL IS IMPURE

At this point, I would like to suggest the possibility that a pre-metaphor in one language and culture may be a full-fledged primary metaphor in another language and culture. This may be an area for cross-linguistic and cross-cultural variation. Another area for such variation is that a primary metaphor can have extensive manifestation in one language, but limited manifestation in another. For instance, DIFFICULTY IS SOLIDITY (i.e., DIFFICULT IS HARD and EASY IS SOFT) is manifested richly in English, but sparsely in Chinese. In Chinese, nevertheless, HARD and SOFT map onto many other target concepts than DIFFICULTY: for instance, people can be "hard" or "soft" in character, will, attitude, ability, or in social interaction, and things can be "hard" or "soft" in quality, need, or requirement (Yu and Huang 2019).

Now, let us turn to the next pair of moral-visual metaphors MORAL IS CLEAR and IMMORAL IS MURKY. As shown in Figure 4.1, CLEAR and MURKY are each linked with two of the more basic concepts: CLEAR with LIGHT and CLEAN, and MURKY with DARK and DIRTY. According to the major English dictionaries I consulted, the former is in fact defined in terms of the latter. That is, *clear* is defined with "light" and "clean", and *murky* with "dark" and "dirty", among others. In their morality-related senses, *clear* means "free from guile or guilt" (e.g., a ***clear*** *conscience*) whereas *murky* means "involving dishonest or illegal activities that are kept secret or not clearly known" or "morally questionable" (e.g., a *government minister with a **murky** past*). Based on this observation, I would suggest that CLEAR and MURKY are again less basic than those with which they are defined. This is because, in the physical world, whether a substance like water, for instance, is clear or murky depends on whether it is, primarily, in light or darkness and, secondarily, clean or dirty. In terms of frame relations (Stickles et al. 2016), it can be said, CLEAR and MURKY incorporate LIGHT and DARK as well as CLEAN and DIRTY as roles (see No. 4 in Table 2.2), whereas the latter two pairs have affordance of the former pair (see No. 5 in Table 2.2). That is to say, the frames of LIGHT and DARK as well as CLEAN and DIRTY exist at a higher and more basic level than the frames of CLEAR and MURKY, which inherit the frame structure of the former two pairs and add more elements to their own. As analyzed above, CLEAR and MURKY are less basic than either LIGHT and DARK or CLEAN and DIRTY.

Nonetheless, CLEAR and MURKY are here treated as primary source concepts because, again, they seem to represent a fundamental category of visual experience in our everyday life. Following this trail of reasoning, I propose the following decomposition analysis in (15) and (16) for the pair of moral-visual metaphors:

(15) MORAL IS CLEAR (CM)
    a. MORAL IS GOOD FOR PUBLIC WELLBEING (PR)
    b. CLEAR IS GOOD (PR)
    c. GOOD IS CLEAR (P-M)

(16) IMMORAL IS MURKY (CM)
    a. IMMORAL IS BAD FOR PUBLIC WELLBEING (PR)
    b. MURKY IS BAD (PR)
    c. BAD IS MURKY (P-M)

Here, (15) and (16) are interpreted in the same manner as (13) and (14). That is, (15c) and (16c) are both pre-metaphors instead of full-fledged primary metaphors. The diagrammatic illustration of (15) and (16), which should look similar to Figure 6.6, too, is omitted here.

It is worth noting that CLEAR and MURKY, as visual concepts, are mapped not only into the moral domain, but also into the mental domain. In effect, they are lexicalized in the mental domain to a much greater extent in English. For instance, the word *clear* can mean that something is easy to understand, impossible to doubt, or free from obscurity and ambiguity (e.g., a *clear* explanation, *clear* instructions, *clear* evidence). It can also mean that some person is capable of sharp discernment or free from doubt or confusion (e.g., a *clear* thinker, *clear* about what is expected, a *clear* understanding of the issues). On the other hand, *murky* means that something is difficult to understand or darkly vague or obscure (e.g., a *murky* explanation, a *murky* question, *murky* instructions, *murky* official rhetoric), or that some person is not clear in thinking (e.g., a *murky* thinker, quit thinking those *murky* thoughts). Obviously, these meanings involve metaphorical mappings between visuality and mentality. That is, things that are easy to understand are easy to "see" or "see through" (i.e., transparent), and a mind that is free from doubt or confusion is an eye that is sharp in "seeing" or "seeing through" things (i.e., KNOWING IS SEEING or UNDERSTANDING IS SEEING). The opposite is true of things difficult to understand and a mind full of doubt and confusion. As much as the case with morality, the conception of CLEAR and MURKY in the domain of MENTALITY is based on that of LIGHT and DARK, and CLEAN and DIRTY, in the domain of VISUALITY. A thorough analysis of the mappings involved in the MENTALITY domain deserves a separate study.

6.4 Complex conceptualization with primary metaphors

The sixth characteristic feature of primary metaphors is that they serve as bases for more complex conceptualization (Grady and Ascoli 2017). In this section, I will utilize just two pairs of moral-spatial metaphors as examples to show how primary metaphors can be combined into more complex conceptual structures. The first pair is MORAL IS HIGH and IMMORAL IS LOW. The two contrastive moral-spatial metaphors are decomposed in (17) and (18).

(17) MORAL IS HIGH   (CM)
    a. MORAL IS GOOD FOR PUBLIC WELLBEING   (PR)
    b. HIGH IS UP   (PR)
    c. UP IS GOOD   (PR)
    d. GOOD IS UP   (PM)

(18) IMMORAL IS LOW   (CM)
    a. IMMORAL IS BAD FOR PUBLIC WELLBEING   (PR)
    b. LOW IS DOWN   (PR)
    c. DOWN IS BAD   (PR)
    d. BAD IS DOWN   (PM)

In (17), the second proposition (17b) characterizes the source concept HIGH, which means "having a large upward extension", as oriented "up", describing a point on the upper half of an imaginary vertical axis. The third proposition (17c) displays a correlation in our daily experience in which UP is generally correlated with GOOD. For example, in sports competition, the podium for the championship winner is both in the middle (i.e., IMPORTANT IS CENTRAL) and higher up than the second and third place winners' (i.e., GOOD IS UP). Therefore, GOOD IS UP in (17d) is a primary metaphor widely deployed in our conceptual systems and, in this particular case, serves as the foundational stone of the complex metaphor MORAL IS HIGH. The decomposition analysis of (18) can be interpreted in the same way. As analyzed above, this pair of moral metaphors is based on the UP-DOWN image schema.

(a)   (b)

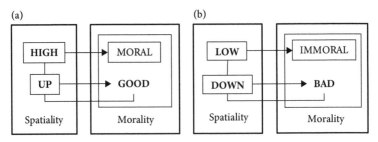

Fig. 6.7 A decomposition analysis of MORAL IS HIGH and IMMORAL IS LOW

Figure 6.7 presents the diagrammatic format of MORAL IS HIGH and IM-MORAL IS LOW. More specifically, they involve mappings from verticality to morality. In the source domain, UP and DOWN are treated as concepts more schematic and basic than HIGH and LOW although the latter are still considered primary concepts. In terms of lexical category, prepositions belong to the closed-class system, which is the most fundamental and schematic conceptual structuring system of a language (Talmy 2000). Thus, UP and DOWN are linked directly to GOOD and BAD. In contrast, HIGH and LOW are each encoded by an adjective which belongs to an open lexical category. With this analysis, therefore, HIGH and LOW as concepts are not as basic as UP and DOWN. That is also the reason why we have established primary metaphors such as HAPPY IS UP and SAD IS DOWN, instead of HAPPY IS HIGH and SAD IS LOW.

A decomposition analysis is also able to show how moral metaphors can interact with other metaphors in the construction of more complex conceptual compounds. As an example, Figure 6.8 shows the dynamic relations and interactions between conceptual metaphors that form a conceptual network in our conceptual system. This figure includes MORAL IS HIGH and IMMORAL IS LOW, as well as two primary metaphors from the Event Structure Metaphor (ESM) (see section 2.5). As a metaphor system, ESM has dual subsystems: Location Event Structure Metaphor (LESM) and Object Event Structure Metaphor (OESM).

Figure 6.8 contains Figure 6.7(a) and (b); in addition, it involves two more primary metaphors from LESM, i.e., STATE IS LOCATION and CHANGE IS MOVEMENT (or MOTION). MORAL and GOOD are states, but states are metaphorically conceptualized as locations, hence the primary metaphor STATE IS LOCATION in LESM. The same analysis can apply to IMMORAL and BAD. What it means in this case is that a MORAL STATE is conceptualized as a HIGH LOCATION, and an IMMORAL STATE is conceptualized as a LOW LOCATION. In the middle is another

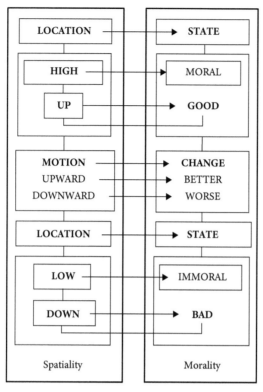

Fig. 6.8 A decomposition analysis of MORAL IS HIGH and IMMORAL IS LOW in combination with LESM

primary metaphor CHANGE IS MOTION, which exists in both LESM and OESM. Change for the better is "upward" movement; change for the worse is "downward" movement (see (4) in section 5.3.1). Hence, the metaphorical mappings BETTER IS UPWARD and WORSE IS DOWNWARD, which are the entailments of the combinations of the primary metaphors involved: STATE IS LOCATION, CHANGE IS MOTION, GOOD IS UP, and BAD IS DOWN. That is the reason why in language, for instance, we use, *rise* and *fall* to express change in moral status for better or worse, respectively (cf. 4a and 4b in section 5.3.1). This analysis shows how our moral cognition benefits from the spatial subsystem of moral metaphors that maps the relational structure and logic of space onto the abstract domain of MORALITY. In this case, the moral-spatial metaphors (MORAL IS HIGH and IMMORAL IS LOW), based on primary metaphors (GOOD IS UP and BAD IS DOWN) are also plugged into the ESM system (see also Cienki 1998). Thus, our moral cognition is constructed on the basis of metaphor systems with smaller building blocks. A decomposition analysis shows clearly how abstract concepts are basically conceptualized in terms of location, object, motion, force, and so on (Lakoff, 1993; Lakoff and Johnson, 1999; Yu 1998).

The next pair of moral-spatial metaphors to be discussed is MORAL IS LEVEL and IMMORAL IS UNLEVEL. This pair is different in that it focuses on morality at the societal rather than individual level. That is, it is concerned with whether a society is fair with its members or, more specifically, making efforts toward establishing social equity and equality for its members. In this case, therefore, MORAL as a whole again stands metonymically for EQUAL as its part, which is a particular aspect (or part) of MORAL concerning "fair and just". As discussed earlier in section 6.2, EQUAL as a social and moral concept is derived metaphorically from its more fundamental counterpart in a physical domain, which I regard as a primary concept in the following analysis. Moreover, an additional primary metaphor STATUS IS HEIGHT, with which the status of people is conceptualized as the height of their spatial location, is also included in the decomposition analysis in (19) and (20).

(19) MORAL IS LEVEL   (CM)
    a. MORAL IS GOOD FOR PUBLIC WELLBEING   (PR)
    b. MORAL STANDS FOR EQUAL   (MY)
    c. MORAL FOR EQUAL IS LEVEL   (CM)
    d. EQUAL IS HAVING SAME STATUS   (PR)
    e. LEVEL IS HAVING SAME HEIGHT   (PR)
    f. STATUS IS HEIGHT   (PM)
    g. EQUAL IS LEVEL   (PM)
    h. GOOD IS UP   (PM)

(20) IMMORAL IS UNLEVEL   (CM)
    a. IMMORAL IS BAD FOR PUBLIC WELLBEING   (PR)
    b. IMMORAL STANDS FOR UNEQUAL   (MY)
    c. IMMORAL FOR UNEQUAL IS UNLEVEL   (CM)
    d. UNEQUAL IS HAVING DIFFERENT STATUS   (PR)
    e. UNLEVEL IS HAVING DIFFERENT HEIGHT   (PR)
    f. STATUS IS HEIGHT   (PM)
    g. UNEQUAL IS UNLEVEL   (PM)
    h. BAD IS DOWN   (PM)

As listed in (19), MORAL as a whole stands metonymically for EQUAL as its part (19b), which is a particular aspect (or part) of MORAL concerning "fair and just". This WHOLE FOR PART metonymic relation is found in the target of the complex metaphor in (19c). At the next level down, (19d) and (19e) define literally what EQUAL and LEVEL mean, respectively. There, EQUAL refers to members of a society as "having the same social status" whereas LEVEL refers to a plane or line as "having the same spatial height". Finally, in (19f–h) are three primary metaphors, STATUS IS HEIGHT (19f), EQUAL IS LEVEL (19g), and GOOD IS UP (19h). A similar, symmetric analysis can be applied to (20).

The diagrammatic illustration of the decomposition analysis in (19) and (20) is provided in Figure 6.9. In Figure 6.9(a), STATUS IS HEIGHT is a primary metaphor. Its source, spatial HEIGHT, and its target, social STATUS, are connected respectively to LEVEL and EQUAL in a subject-predicate relationship, represented by the vertical lines. Their adjectival predicates also form a primary metaphor EQUAL IS LEVEL. Note that the source concept UP does not play a direct role in the focal primary metaphor EQUAL IS LEVEL. In this case, it is nonetheless linked indirectly to HEIGHT, which is the source concept of STATUS IS HEIGHT. When social status is conceptualized metaphorically as vertical height, which is a primary metaphorical mapping, the primary metaphor that goes with it is GOOD IS UP. While MORAL IS LEVEL is a complex metaphor, EQUAL IS LEVEL is a primary metaphor, but both are grounded in the BALANCE image schema (see Figure 5.3(b)). Figure 6.9(b), which illustrates IMMORAL IS UNLEVEL, is interpreted in the same manner.

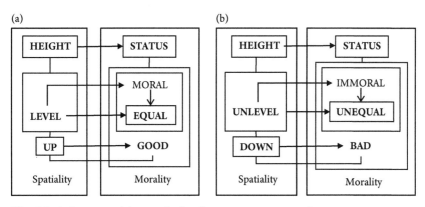

Fig. 6.9 A decomposition analysis of MORAL IS LEVEL and IMMORAL IS UNLEVEL in combination with STATUS IS HEIGHT

As a pair of moral-spatial metaphors, MORAL IS LEVEL and IMMORAL IS UNLEVEL are different from MORAL IS HIGH and IMMORAL IS LOW (see (17) and (18) above). In the latter pair, for instance, HIGH in (17) maps onto more general aspects of MORAL such as LOFTY, NOBLE, and GOOD (vs. EVIL) concerning both individual moral character and social ethical atmosphere, but LEVEL in

(19) maps onto more specific aspects of MORAL such as FAIR, JUST, and IMPAR-
TIAL in the narrower scopes of MORAL concerning human equality and social
equity. Besides, because one more key concept EQUAL is involved as the real
target in (19), it alters the internal structure, the level of complexity, and the
conceptual mappings engaged therein. As a consequence of the above differences, the complex metaphors in (19) and (20) are based on different primary
metaphors which employ different aspects of human experience. In (19) and
(20), GOOD IS UP and BAD IS DOWN are primary metaphors with wide application, but EQUAL IS LEVEL and UNEQUAL IS UNLEVEL are apparently less so as
they focus on fairness and justness at a social level.

It is worth noting at this point that in (19) and (20) GOOD IS UP and BAD
IS DOWN are highly relevant, operating in the background of the domain of
MORALITY. For instance, in the case of UNEQUAL IS UNLEVEL, people with different levels of politico-economic power and strength stand on different social
statuses with different heights. We can imagine that the more powerful and
stronger occupy "higher up" positions than those who are less so. This is because such metaphors as POWERFUL IS UP and AUTHORITATIVE IS UP are in
operation in our conceptual systems. The question that arises is: If those more
powerful and authoritative are "higher up" in the social hierarchy, are they
necessarily "good"? The answer is no. We can say that it is human nature for
people to want to go "up" rather than "down" on their life-journey since we
have such primary metaphors as GOOD IS UP and BAD IS DOWN in our conceptual system. A fundamental difference among people, however, is whether
they go "up" through a "straight" or "crooked" path. If it is the latter, then, they
are not good or "up" morally even if they are "higher up" socially. In (17) and
(18), GOOD IS UP and BAD IS DOWN are deployed in a moral context, and they
are relevant in (19) and (20) as well, but they are just out of the focus.

In sections 6.2 through 6.4, I conducted a decomposition analysis of some
moral metaphors. It so happens that these moral metaphors come exclusively
from the visual and spatial subsystems. None of the moral-physical metaphors
were analyzed. Remember that there are five pairs of moral metaphors in the
physical subsystem. There, the moral metaphors all have their source concepts
characterizing the wellbeing of physical entities, ranging from objects to human beings, with respect to their physical appearance, essence, or condition.
These source concepts are BEAUTIFUL and UGLY, STRONG and WEAK, SOUND
and ROTTEN, WHOLE and BROKEN, and HEALTHY and ILL. In my opinion, all
of them are primary concepts in light of Grady and Ascoli's (2017) characterization of the special traits of primary metaphors. This also means that these
source concepts have the potential to form primary metaphors. In the context

of moral metaphor analysis, the question then is whether they can combine with the target concepts GOOD and BAD to form primary-metaphor patterns. In other words, the question is whether these source concepts can mean "good" or "bad" more generally rather than just "moral" or "immoral" in the more specific domain of MORALITY.

To answer this question calls for further research, but my speculation at this point is that some of the source concepts can map onto GOOD or BAD in general. For example, a possible pair of primary metaphors may be GOOD IS BEAUTIFUL and BAD IS UGLY (see section 3.2 for the discussion on the bidirectional stereotypes "What is beautiful is good" and "What is good is beautiful"). Thus, for instance, the English adjective *beautiful* originally means "pleasing the senses or mind aesthetically", referring especially to physical beauty or beautiful looks (e.g., *She is a **beautiful** young woman*), but the word also has the more general sense "excellent" (e.g., *She spoke in **beautiful** English*), in addition to its more specific moral sense to refer to "moral beauty" (see section 3.3.1). By contrast, the antonym of *beautiful*, *ugly*, can mean broadly "very bad" (e.g., *Things could turn **ugly***; *an **ugly** situation*; *an **ugly** temper*), in addition to its moral sense "morally offensive or objectionable; morally repugnant" (e.g., *corruption—the **ugliest** stain of all*; *racism and its most **ugly** manifestations*) as well as its original visual sense (e.g., *People in school always told me I was **ugly***).

In Chinese, the counterparts of *beautiful* and *ugly*, 美 *měi* and 丑 *chǒu*, have parallel semantic extensions. Therefore, the former originally means "beautiful; pretty; handsome; attractive" in its visual sense, referring to the appearance of physical or human beings, e.g., 美女 *měinǚ* "beautiful woman"; 美景 *měijǐng* "beautiful scenery or landscape". It can also mean "good" more broadly, e.g., 美酒 *měijiǔ* "good wine" (lit. beautiful wine); 美言 *měiyán* "(put in) good words" (lit. beautiful words), aside from its moral sense, e.g., 美德 *měidé* "virtue; moral excellence" (lit. beautiful virtue); 心灵美 *xīnlíngměi* "noble character; high integrity" (lit. heart-soul-mind beautiful). As its antonym, 丑 *chǒu*, which originally means "ugly" in its visual sense, e.g., 丑相 *chǒuxiàng* "ugly features", 丑八怪 *chǒubāguài* "very ugly person", can also mean "bad" in general, e.g., 丑名 *chǒumíng* "bad reputation" (lit. ugly reputation), 脾气丑 *píqichǒu* "bad-tempered" (lit. temper ugly), and "wicked" in a moral sense, e.g., 丑秽 *chǒuhuì* "ugly and dirty affair", 丑恶行径 *chǒu'è xíngjìng* "wicked act" (lit. ugly and evil act).

Those examples in the above two paragraphs suggest that GOOD IS BEAUTIFUL and BAD IS UGLY are applicable in both English and Chinese as primary metaphors. If so, their decomposition analysis should be the same as that for GOOD IS LIGHT and BAD IS DARK provided in (1) and (2) and in Figure 6.1.

The status of the remaining pairs (i.e., GOOD IS STRONG and BAD IS WEAK, GOOD IS SOUND and BAD IS ROTTEN, GOOD IS WHOLE and BAD IS BROKEN, GOOD IS HEALTHY and BAD IS ILL) are yet to be determined. Good candidates should include, for instance, GOOD IS SOUND (e.g., *It's really **sound**, too good to be true! He's a **sound** bloke, solid and reliable.*) and BAD IS ROTTEN (e.g., *He's had **rotten** luck this year. She was a **rotten** cook. The year after an election is often **rotten** for stocks.*). For those physical source concepts whose connections with GOOD and BAD cannot be established as primary metaphors yet, such connections should still be grounded in experiential correlations, but the metaphorical mappings still stay in a pre-metaphor stage and may or may not become primary metaphors in a particular language in the future depending on the mediation and reinforcement from the linguistic and cultural environment.

Languages always have their own ecological environments. Such environments should foster both similarities and differences among languages. For example, the antonymous pair of English adjectives *good* and *bad* have a close equivalent in Chinese as 好 *hǎo* "good" and 坏 *huài* "bad". But the Chinese adjective *hǎo* "good" also overlaps in some sense with the English adjective *sound*, which is somewhat synonymous with *good*. As such, Chinese 好 *hǎo* "good", which is basically literal, has another metaphorical antonym 烂 *làn* "rotten" meaning "very bad" (cf. the definitions for 腐 *fǔ* "rotten" in Table 3.3; see also 31b and 31c in section 3.4.3). Thus, informally, things or people "(very) bad" can be 烂 *làn* "rotten" in Chinese: e.g., 烂点子 *làn diǎnzi* and 烂主意 *làn zhǔyi* both mean "(very) bad idea" (lit. rotten idea); 烂学校 *làn xuéxiào* "(very) bad school" (lit. rotten school); 烂人 *làn rén* "(very) bad person" (lit. rotten person). This means that the conceptual metaphor BAD IS ROTTEN does exist in Chinese, but 烂 *làn* "rotten" in these cases is used in contrast with 好 *hǎo* "good" as one of its possible antonyms.

In parallel, the common Chinese counterpart for the English adjective *broken* is 破 *pò* "broken", and informally it can also mean "(very) bad" in general: e.g., 破主意 *pò zhǔyi* "(very) bad idea" (lit. broken idea); 破学校 *pò xuéxiào* "(very) bad school" (lit. broken school); 破地方 *pò dìfang* "(very) bad place" (lit. broken place). Even though such collocations do not show in the Chinese language dictionaries, their usages are confirmed by the Chinese language corpora. This again means that the conceptual metaphor BAD IS BROKEN also exists in Chinese, but 破 *pò* "broken" in such cases are again used in contrast with 好 *hǎo* "good" as one of its possible antonyms. With 烂 *làn* "rotten" and 破 *pò* "broken" used as possible antonyms of 好 *hǎo* "good", these examples show that the existence of negative parametric metaphors (i.e., BAD IS ROTTEN and

BAD IS BROKEN) may not necessarily mean the symmetric existence of their positive parametric counterparts (e.g., GOOD IS SOUND or GOOD IS WHOLE). It simply takes extensive and comprehensive research to reveal the complex terrains on the landscape of metaphorical language and thought within and across linguistic boundaries.

In sections 6.2 through 6.4, I proposed various decomposition analyses of moral metaphors from the three subsystems. A summary of my analysis is in order at this juncture. Of these three sections, section 6.2 focused on the target concepts, using some moral-visual and moral-spatial metaphors as examples; section 6.3 on the source concepts, utilizing the moral metaphor from the visual subsystem as examples; and section 6.4 on the combination of primary metaphors into more complex metaphorical compounds, citing examples from the spatial subsystem, with additional discussions of examples from the physical subsystem.

As far as the target concepts are concerned, there are only two of them: MORAL and IMMORAL. My analysis, however, postulates a three-level hierarchical structure for the target domain of MORALITY. At the middle level are MORAL and IMMORAL, which are treated as complex concepts. Above them are GOOD and BAD, the valence values at affective level. These two values are treated as primary concepts because they are very fundamental concepts of generic or schematic nature. MORAL and IMMORAL are defined in terms of GOOD and BAD in the moral domain. The implication of this analysis is that affectivity always underlies morality and moral judgments are inevitably made on an emotional basis.

My analysis also covered some Level-3 target concepts, which, I argued, are constituent parts that comprise MORAL and IMMORAL as wholes. At this lower level, concepts such as HONEST vs. DISHONEST, GENEROUS vs. UNGENEROUS, and EQUAL vs. UNEQUAL, are considered specific aspects of MORAL and IM-MORAL, but their status, hypothetically, may vary in degree between complex and primary concepts. It takes further research to determine the exact nature of these moral concepts on Level 3.

With respect to the source concepts, they are all treated as primary con-cepts, because they represent fundamental categories of human sensori-motor experience. Nonetheless, they are not equal as primary concepts as some of them are more basic concepts than others and therefore the for-mer may play an underlying role in the understanding of the latter. Be-sides, the connections between primary source and primary target concepts that are well motivated by tight correlations in experience do not neces-sarily constitute primary metaphors. Instead, they may be "pre-metaphors", which represent cognitive associations built on the basis of experiential correlations. Pre-metaphors have not yet risen to the full status of primary metaphors. Full-fledged primary metaphors undergo a process at four different levels, experiential, cognitive, conceptual, and linguistic. First, they are initiated by experiential correlations. Second, they become cognitive associations or pre-metaphors resulting from experiential correlations. Third, with appropriate mediation and reinforcement from cultural and linguistic environment, they turn into conceptual patterns of primary metaphors. Fourth, they are manifested on the surface of language use (see Grady and Ascoli 2017).

6.5 Unity of the three subsystems

In Chapters 3 through 5, I analyzed the moral metaphors in the three subsystems, physical, visual, and spatial. My analysis showed that the moral metaphor system consists of three subsystems because the moral metaphors in each of these subsystems are linked together systematically by their source as well as target concepts. While the target concepts are moral in nature, those source concepts are primarily physical, visual, or spatial in character. In this section, I discuss the idea that, while the moral metaphors under study are linked together coherently by their source concepts within each of the three subsystems, they are also linked together with some coherence across the subsystems such that the three of them are connected and combined into a single unified moral metaphor system, revolving around a single pair of target concepts MORAL and IMMORAL.

In Chapters 3–5, I discussed how, in Chinese, compound words bring together two different source concepts, either from one subsystem (e.g., "dirty-murky", "upright-straight", "strong-big") or from two different subsystems (e.g., "clear-upright", "pure-upright", "high-clean"), pack them up through the morphological process of compounding, and transfer them to the target domain of MORALITY in metaphorical mappings. Those lexical items illustrate in Chinese how coherence and unity exist among the source concepts across three different subsystems as well as within a single subsystem.

Figure 6.10 illustrates how the source concepts are linked within and across the three subsystems to form the moral metaphor system as a whole. At the top of the figure, MORAL and IMMORAL are the single pair of target concepts in opposition to each other, as represented by the horizontal line with stealth arrowheads at both ends. Below them are the three subsystems of

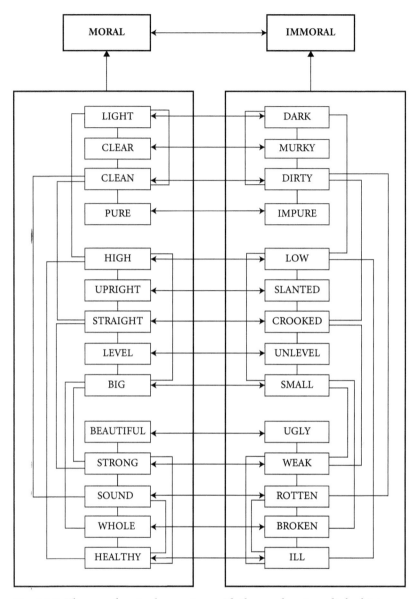

Fig. 6.10 The moral metaphor system with three subsystems linked into a conceptual network

source concepts divided into two symmetrical halves, left and right, mapping metaphorically onto their corresponding target concepts above them, represented by the two vertical lines with solid arrowheads indicating the direction of mapping.

On the left half are the source concepts with positive values, and on the right are the source concepts with negative values. They are divided within each half into three sections representing three subsystems, visual, spatial, and physical. All the source concepts with positive values are aligned contrastively with their counterparts with negative values. Their contrastive relationship is represented by the horizontal lines with stealth arrowheads at both ends. Within each of the left and right halves, the source concepts are linked by short vertical lines representing associations between them within each subsystem. For example, in the visual subsystem, LIGHT and CLEAR hold a relationship of association, in contrast with DARK and MURKY that hold a similar relationship. In addition, LIGHT is also associated with CLEAN, and this association between the two source concepts, which are not neighboring each other within a single subsystem, is represented by the inside line to their right. Symmetrically, the association between DARK and DIRTY on the opposite, negative side is represented by an inside line to their left.

Note, however, that the source concepts are coherent with each other not only within each subsystem, but also to some extent across the three subsystems. The cross-subsystem coherence is represented by the outside lines on both sides. Such coherence accounts for why the moral metaphors in the three subsystems constitute a single unified moral metaphor system, in addition to the fact that they all share a common pair of target concepts. Thus, on the left side, for instance, LIGHT in the visual subsystem and HIGH in the spatial subsystem are linked because, according to the common sense that light usually comes down from its natural or artificial sources, entities higher up in spatial location are likely to receive more light than those down low (see, e.g., Tolaas 1991). Similarly, there exists a correlation between spatial height and human health. Those who remain healthy are more likely to maintain an erect posture with a greater height than those who have "fallen ill" and had to "lie down" in the bed.

As shown in Figure 6.10, the visual concept CLEAN is simultaneously linked with two concepts, one spatial (STRAIGHT) and one physical (SOUND). We know from our everyday life experience that surfaces that are straight are less likely to collect dirt than those that are crooked and, when they do collect dirt, they are much easier to clean than those with corners. Also, entities that are clean are less likely to rot, and those that turn rotten may be dirty on their surfaces in the first place. Moreover, entities that are sound in essence usually have a clean look, and those that have decayed usually look dirty as well. As seen in the figure, the spatial concept STRAIGHT is also linked with STRONG in the physical subsystem. This is because entities that are able to remain straight under pressure or force are considered strong whereas those that are bent giving in to pressure or force are taken as weak. Finally, the spatial concept BIG is connected with two physical concepts, STRONG and WHOLE. Under normal circumstances, people who are stronger are bigger in stature as well, and vice versa. On the other hand, those entities that are whole are not necessarily big in size, but they are necessarily bigger than if they are broken; once broken, they will only turn into smaller pieces.

It is worth noting that the source concepts linked across the subsystems in Figure 6.10 should be seen as examples of how associative relations can exist among three separate subsystems. There may be other instances that are not overtly linked. For example, there can be some kind of association between CLEAN and HEALTHY on the one hand, and DIRTY and ILL on the other. That is, those who are cleanly are more likely to remain healthy, and less likely to become ill, than those who are not. A similar kind of association can be found between UPRIGHT and STRONG, and between SLANTED and WEAK. Keeping an upright bearing is seen as a sign of strength in physique or in character, whereas being slanted in body stance, namely with one's body leaning to one side or another, may be taken as a symptom of weakness, suggesting that the person is out of balance or without self-control, and may fall as a result.

In sum, the three subsystems are indeed coherent with one another to form a unified moral metaphor system, as can be seen from the linkages in Figure 6.10. The unity of the whole moral metaphor system lies in the conceptual coherence among its three subsystems more generally, and among the source concepts of the metaphorical mappings as constituent components of the three separate subsystems. It may be the case that many of those source concepts from different subsystems serve as frame elements or their values within the source-domain frames of the same conceptual metaphors. The concepts linked directly in such a way serve as access points. That is, one concept in one subsystem is linked to another concept in another subsystem, and the latter provides an access point via which the former is also linked indirectly with the other concepts in the same subsystem of the latter. In this way, the three subsystems are bound together, forming one integrated, unified moral metaphor system.

6.6 Visual or multimodal manifestation of moral metaphors

As a cognitive theory of metaphor, CMT argues that metaphor is "primarily a matter of thought and action", but manifests itself in language through verbal communication (Lakoff and Johnson 1980: 153). This important tenet of CMT means that "metaphors should appear not just in language but also in visuals, gestures, sounds, music, and in discourses that combine these modes"

(Forceville 2017: 26; see also Cienki and Müller 2008; Forceville and Urios-Aparisi 2009). In Chapters 3–5, I presented the linguistic evidence from both English and Chinese that points to the existence of underlying conceptual metaphors for morality in both languages. In this section, I look at visual or multimodal evidence for the moral metaphors under study. My goal here is not to provide a comprehensive analysis of visual or multimodal evidence, but to support my study in the preceding chapters from a different and additional perspective. The 10 images to be discussed in (21) were accessed via either Baidu Images (21a) or Google Images (21b–j).[2] In (21), I only provide a brief verbal description of the images, followed by an analysis pointing out what conceptual metaphors for morality are possibly involved. Due to copyright restriction, I am only able to provide three actual images (21b, i, and j) that I received permission or license to use here. Interested readers, however, can use the links in the relevant footnote to access all the images online.

(21) a. Image (a), named "Double-faced Buddha and Devil" (佛魔双面), displays a face image of which the left half is that of Buddha and the right half is that of a devil. The Buddha half looks "kind", "clean", and "beautiful" whereas the devil half looks "fierce", "dirty", and "ugly". The image presents the idea that "good" and "evil" are closely interrelated, combining halves of the Buddha and devil faces into a whole, involving visual mode only. The image therefore instantiates visually MORAL IS CLEAN VS. IMMORAL IS DIRTY, and MORAL IS BEAUTIFUL VS. IMMORAL IS UGLY.

   b. Image (b) shows a "dark" rock in contrast with a "light" diamond, and the two objects correspond to the two words above them, "Suppressing vs. Forgiving", which represent two immoral and moral acts, respectively (see Figure 6.11). The image thus manifests MORAL IS LIGHT and IMMORAL IS DARK in a multimodal (verbal and visual) manner.

---

[2] The original online sources of the images are provided below as they were last accessed through Baidu Images or Google Images in November 2021:

   (a) https://image.110go.com/upload/tpk/134118794.jpg
   (b) https://www.goasksuzie.com/true-forgiveness-false-forgiveness
   (c) https://calvinayre.com/wp-content/uploads/2016/01/us-sports-betting-poll.jpg
   (d) http://photographerstownsville.blogspot.com/2018/08/5-extremely-common-but-very-distasteful.html
   (e) http://troop21.scoutlander.com/MediaVaults/imagevault/g34jf72ey88130.jpg
   (f) http://alwaysonwatch2.blogspot.com/2010/04/obama-grovelbow-gauge.html
   (g) https://oneworldgifted.weebly.com/uploads/1/0/7/7/10779418/864011_orig.png
   (h) http://www.cartoonistgroup.com/store/add.php?iid=10735
   (i) https://coreybradshaw.files.wordpress.com/2016/11/slanted.jpg?w=300&h=218
   (j) https://lalinternadediogenes.files.wordpress.com/2011/03/thumbnail-aspx.jpg

Fig. 6.11 A multimodal example instantiating MORAL IS
LIGHT and IMMORAL IS DARK

Source: https://www.goasksuzie.com/true-forgiveness-false-forgiveness
With kind permission from Suzie Johnson at GoAskSuzie.com

c. Image (c) figures scales, "moral scales" that weighs "Good" vs.
"Evil". The two arms of the scales are "unlevel", inclined toward the
right, with "Good" being "higher" in space than "Evil", indicating
that "moral balance" is lost. The image is a visual and multimodal
instantiation of MORAL IS LEVEL and IMMORAL IS UNLEVEL, and
MORAL IS HIGH and IMMORAL IS LOW.

d. Image (d) also figures "moral scales", but this time we see "Ethics"
on the left and "Money" on the right. It also includes a verbal
caption "Unethical Business Practices". Again, the two arms of
the scales are "unlevel", inclined toward the right, with "Ethics"
being "higher" in space than "Money", indicating that "moral balance" is lost. In this image, however, "Ethics" looks much "larger"
than "Money". It is thus a visual and multimodal instantiation of
MORAL IS LEVEL and IMMORAL IS UNLEVEL, and MORAL IS HIGH
and IMMORAL IS LOW. In this example, furthermore, because
the word "Ethics" is represented in a much larger font size than
is "Money", which is a metonymy for unethical business practices, image (d) is also a visual instantiation of MORAL IS BIG and
IMMORAL IS SMALL (see, e.g., Meier et al. 2008). It is worth noting that in both images (c) and (d) the fact that the good side
is "outweighed" by the bad side (which only suggests the loss of
"moral balance") is no evidence against the point that they visually instantiate MORAL IS HIGH and IMMORAL IS LOW. It is because
the bad side is "heavier" than the good side that the former should
"stay lower" than the latter, and vice versa. It is interesting to see
that in image (d) "Ethics" looks much bigger and therefore should

"carry more weight" than "Money", but it is still "outweighed" by, and "stays higher" than, "Money". This is actually consistent with the observation that there is asymmetry between MORAL and IMMORAL as target concepts for moral metaphors grounded in our real-life experience. Thus, for instance, it is easier to make something clean dirty, than the other way around (see Chapter 4). It is more difficult to go up than to go down, to be upright than slanted, and there is only one way to be straight but indefinite number of ways to be crooked (see Chapter 5). Moreover, just to mention in passing, a search for "moral compass" in Google Images brought up a large collection of images of "moral compass". Almost all of them have "Good" on the "high" side in contrast with "Bad" or "Evil" on the "low" side.

e. Image (e) looks like a photo frame. The photo shows a healthy-looking Boy Scout taking the Boy Scout Oath, which is displayed verbally on the background (cf. 9a in section 5.3.4). He is standing "upright", his right arm extending "level" to the right, forming a "right" angle with the forearm that rises "straight up" in parallel with his body and head. The image of the Boy Scout figure is a physical embodiment of its oath to keep oneself "physically strong, mentally awake, and morally straight". It is a multimodal instantiation of MORAL IS UPRIGHT, MORAL IS STRAIGHT, MORAL IS STRONG, and MORAL IS HEALTHY. As will become clear, this image presents a sharp contrast in terms of body posture with image (f) below.

f. Image (f), a cartoon caricature, has the main caption "The Obama Grovel/Bow Gauge". It shows Obama "stooping so low" in a bow (cf. 11c in section 5.3.4), with an extremely skinny and ill-looking body.[3] In the cartoon, the background gauge is a 90 degree right angle divided by four other lines in between the "upright" and the "level" lines. The captions at the top end of each line beyond the curve say the following from the "highest" to the "lowest" position, respectively: (i) "Upright position"; (ii) "I apologize for that capitalist nation … America"; (iii) "I apologize for the very

---

[3] It so happened that President Obama was criticized by some in the U.S. for having bent his body too much in a "treasonous" bow when he met with the Japanese Emperor Akihito at the Imperial Palace in Tokyo in 2009. "How low will he go?" is the title of a blog post.

existence of America ...”; (iv) “No, seriously, I apologize for everything American ...”; and (v) “Take my country, please ...”. With his “stooping so low” posture, Obama’s head is positioned between (iv) and (v). This caricature apparently conveys a political message that President Obama is sacrificing the national interests of the U.S., which is of course perceived as “morally weak” according to the political view of the cartoonist. In stark contrast with (e), image (f) multimodally instantiates four moral metaphors: IMMORAL IS SLANTED; IMMORAL IS CROOKED; IMMORAL IS WEAK, and IMMORAL IS ILL. That is, as illustrated by images (e) and (f), the moral character, strong or weak, is “embodied” by the figure and posture of the body.

g. Image (g), which features two images side by side, illustrates what two abstract concepts, EQUALITY and EQUITY, mean with visual metaphors. The image on the left for “Equality” shows that three boys of different heights, tall, medium-height, and short, are each standing on a crate of equal size, trying to watch a baseball game over a fence. While the tops of the three crates on which they are standing are level at the same height, the three boys nonetheless have very different results watching the game. The tall boy has the best view as his head is way above the fence. The medium-height boy is also able to watch the game pretty clearly since his head is right above the fence. The short boy, however, is unable to watch the game at all because his head is below the top of the fence, which blocks his view completely. That is, although the three boys have “equal” standings, they end up having “unequal” results. In the image on the right for “Equity”, the tall boy is not standing on any crate at all, having given away his crate to the short body, who is now standing on the top of two crates instead of one. Now, the three boys are standing on different heights, the tall boy on the bare ground, the medium-height body on one crate, and the short boy on two crates, but their heads are all level at the same height, right above the top of the fence, and they are therefore having “equitable” views. Thus, the two images visually instantiate MORAL IS LEVEL and IMMORAL IS UNLEVEL (see sections 5.3.4 and 5.4.4), which can be decomposed into two pairs of primary metaphors, EQUAL IS LEVEL and UNEQUAL IS UNLEVEL, GOOD IS UP and BAD IS DOWN, plus another primary metaphor STATUS IS HEIGHT (see (19) and (20), and Figure 6.9 in section 6.4).

h. In image (h), Uncle Sam is clinging to the top of a skyscraper that appears tilted and that has "MORAL HIGH GROUND" written on it (cf. 1a and 1b in section 5.3.1), but he is being pulled down by the heavy loads of two large metal balls chained to the shackles on his feet. "IRAQ" and "GUANTANAMO" are written on the two metal balls. As shown in this image, Uncle Sam is in danger in two ways. First, the moral high ground, to the top of which he is clinging, is likely to collapse because the skyscraper is so tilted to one side and appears to have lost its balance. Second, the loads chained to his feet are so heavy that Uncle Sam is likely to lose his hold on the top of the skyscraper and to fall from the "moral high ground". This image multimodally instantiates two pairs of moral metaphors: MORAL IS HIGH and IMMORAL IS LOW; MORAL IS UPRIGHT and IMMORAL IS SLANTED.

i. Image (i) shows a politician speaking behind a podium with a row of reporters standing in front of him holding pens and note-books or recorders. Instead of standing "upright" in balance, the reporters all stand "tilted" or "slanted" toward their right at an angle of about 45 degrees (see Figure 6.12). The caption of the cartoon says, "SLANTED MEDIA COVERAGE" (cf. 6a and 6b in section 5.3.2). That is, the biased or unfair coverage of the media

Fig. 6.12 A multimodal example instantiating MORAL IS UPRIGHT and IMMORAL IS SLANTED
Licensed for use by CartoonStock Ltd.

is visually represented by the "slanted" body posture of those reporters. In other words, the loss of physical or bodily balance is
a metaphor for bias, partiality, and unfairness as a result of the
loss of "moral balance". The cartoon appears to be a multimodal
instantiation of MORAL IS UPRIGHT and IMMORAL IS SLANTED.

j. The last image, image (j), shows an "unlevel playing field" for football or soccer (see Figure 6.13; cf. 8a and 8b in section 5.3.3). The
side of the "WEST" is elevated so high that the whole field forms a
steep slope. The lower side of the field is the "REST" of the world.
The latter's disadvantage is multiplied by the fact that, while the
goal of the West appears to be a normal one, that of the Rest is exceptionally large, the distance between its two posts being almost
the width of the playing field. A referee-looking person standing
by the side of the field has "WTO" printed on his jersey. He is
thinking aloud to himself: "FANCY A GAME?" The message apparently is that WTO, i.e., the World Trade Organization, designs
"unfair" competition (on an "unlevel playing field") with game
rules "tilted" in favor of the West against the rest of the world. The
conceptual metaphors manifested multimodally here are MORAL
IS LEVEL and IMMORAL IS UNLEVEL, which can again be decomposed into a few primary metaphors (cf. the discussion on image
(g) above).

Fig. 6.13 A multimodal example
instantiating MORAL IS LEVEL and
IMMORAL IS UNLEVEL
© Gavin Coates; reproduced with
permission.

In sum, the analysis of the visual and multimodal evidence from the images analyzed in this section reinforces the analysis of the linguistic data in English and Chinese in the preceding chapters. In fact, the linguistic examples and the visual and multimodal examples, to a notable extent, mirror and reinforce each other. I will analyze more multimodal examples in section 7.2.3 when I discuss the influence of linguistic experience on cultural experience.

6.7 Summary

In this chapter, I have applied DAMCA in the examination of the moral metaphor system. The assumption of using DAMCA as a tool for metaphor analysis is that conceptual metaphors may be conceptual compounds comprised of literal propositions, metonymies, complex and primary metaphors, and pre-metaphors. My objective is to further develop my earlier argument (Yu 2015a, 2016; Yu, Wang, and He 2016) that moral metaphors analyzed in the preceding chapters are not primary metaphors, but complex metaphors. For that purpose, I first analyzed the target concepts MORAL and IMMORAL, arguing that they are more complex than primary concepts, staying on the middle level of a three-level conceptual hierarchy. At the top and generic level, GOOD and BAD are primary concepts. As such, they are basic and schematic in character, and their contrastive structure and valence values are inherited and elaborated by MORAL and IMMORAL at a lower level and in a more specific domain of MORALITY. Then, at the third level, the moral concepts such as HONEST and DISHONEST, GENEROUS and UNGENEROUS are specific constituent parts of MORAL and IMMORAL. My hypothetical proposal is to regard these concepts as varying in degree as complex or primary concepts.

If MORAL and IMMORAL are not primary concepts, then the moral metaphors with them as target concepts cannot be primary metaphors either, based on the assumption that primary metaphors are mappings between primary concepts. At this time, we really do not know how many primary metaphors there are. Lakoff (2014: 6) suggested, "There are hundreds, if not thousands, of primary metaphors structuring our conceptual system". With a more rigorous and restrictive means of categorization, my decomposition analysis implies a smaller number, perhaps hundreds rather than thousands. It is certainly desirable that metaphorical thought, however complex, can be constructed from a relatively small number of primary metaphors and pre-metaphors. It suggests more efficient operations of our conceptual system.

After the analysis of the target concepts, I turned to the source concepts. I regard most of the source concepts as primary concepts because, in my view, they represent basic categories of human experience along physical, visual, and spatial dimensions. Nevertheless, I do not see them as having equal statuses as primary concepts. Instead, I take up a prototype view of categorization so that the source concepts have gradient statuses along the dimension of their basicness. In my decomposition analysis, for example, GOOD IS PURE analyzed as underlying MORAL IS PURE is not a full-fledged primary metaphor, but a pre-metaphor. A pre-metaphor represents cognitive association based on experiential correlation, but it has not risen to the full status of a primary metaphor. A primary metaphor as a conventional conceptual pattern should manifest itself in language. Yet, GOOD IS PURE does not seem to have reached that level in English or in Chinese. Though PURE and IMPURE still represent contrastive values of a fundamental category of our perceptual experience, their metaphorical moral senses are based on the more basic pair of concepts CLEAN and DIRTY. Being a pair of concepts less basic than the latter perhaps hinders the former from entering into a wider scope of metaphorical application as primary metaphors.

The decomposition analysis, therefore, has shown how some of the moral-visual metaphors are more central than the others in the subsystem, and how they are related to one another in the cluster as a radial category. In this chapter, I have also shown, employing decomposition analysis, how primary metaphors can be combined, in conjunction with other components, to form more complex metaphorical conceptualizations. Thus, by taking complex metaphors apart, DAMCA can enable us to see in a metaphorical complex what component is metaphorical and what is literal, and what is metaphoric and what is metonymic, and what is a primary metaphor and what is yet a pre-metaphor. By digging deep into metaphorical compounds with DAMCA, we can be more specific about various motivations that ground metaphors, and about varied mechanisms and compositions of metaphors. In doing so, we are able to see constituent components of metaphors and how metaphors are linked with one another via those components into conceptual networks of metaphors at different levels of schematicity, and of metaphors at the same level with different kinds of interrelations. Needless to say, DAMCA as an analytical tool still has much room for development and refinement. It calls for, I believe, a more rigorous and comprehensive working definition of what constitutes a primary metaphor, a construct on which the whole analysis hinges.

Also in this chapter, I have shown that the source concepts of moral metaphors are coherent and linked with one another within each, and across all three, of the subsystems. Such conceptual coherence and linkage constitute the unity of one single moral metaphor system. Finally, in this chapter, I have analyzed some examples of visual or multimodal manifestation of moral metaphors. The visual and multimodal analysis reinforces the CMT claim for the existence of conceptual metaphors since they are manifested not only linguistically—although linguistically they manifest themselves to the fullest extent—but also multimodally. One interesting observation is that, as mentioned in section 6.6, we see a high degree of affinity between visual and linguistic metaphors in instantiating conceptual metaphors. A question to ask is: What is the relationship between visual, linguistic, and conceptual metaphors? I will come back to this question in the next and final chapter.

7

The moral metaphor system and beyond

As we begin this final chapter, there is a need to address a couple of the more general issues relating to and arising from the current study. The first concerns examining the moral metaphor system from a holistic perspective on the structures and mechanisms of its source and target frames together. The second relates to the relationship between language, culture, and body in metaphorical thought.

7.1 The moral metaphor system as a whole

As suggested by the title of this monograph, the goal of this book has been to study moral metaphors as a system. This moral metaphor system consists of three subsystems, physical, visual, and spatial, studied separately in Chapters 3–5. In those chapters, I analyzed how the moral metaphors in each subsystem are linked, in various ways, via their different source concepts as well as their common target concepts (MORAL and IMMORAL). In each of those chapters, I also presented a schematic representation of a general source frame, applicable to all the moral metaphors within their own subsystem (see Figures 3.2, 4.2, and 5.4). It turns out that all three source frames share exactly the same structure at a schematic level, with three core elements, HUMAN PERCEIVER, ENTITY PROPERTY, and AFFECTIVE VALENCE, which are linked by some sort of relation between them. That is, a human person perceives (i.e., becomes aware of) some salient property of a physical entity which, depending on the specific value of the property, evokes in the person an emotional response, either positive (good) or negative (bad) in valence. The three source frames differ only by the set of values feeding into the role of ENTITY PROPERTY. Thus, individual moral metaphors are distinguished by various property values that serve as their source concepts, and the three subsystems of moral metaphors are distinguished by the three different sets of property values that they have as their source concepts.

The Moral Metaphor System. Ning Yu, Oxford University Press. © Ning Yu (2022).
DOI: 10.1093/oso/9780192866325.003.0007

After discussions on how the source concepts are related to one another within each subsystem in Chapters 3–5. I also discussed how the three sets of source concepts are coherent with one another, to varied degrees, across the three subsystems (see section 6.5). That is, my focus has been up to this point on the source domains, with source frames and source concepts. I have not looked at the moral metaphor system as a whole. In my view, this whole moral metaphor system, with both source and target, and the mappings between them, can be presented schematically as in Figure 7.1. As a reminder, the lines with solid arrowheads indicate metaphorical mappings and those with stealth arrowheads, or no arrowhead at all, represent nonmetaphorical relations.

As in Figure 7.1, the target frame of all the moral metaphors in the system also contains three core elements that are linked in some relations. At the top, there is a MORAL JUDGER, who, after noticing some HUMAN BEHAVIOR (specifically, some person's social behavior), feels either positive or negative about it and therefore is compelled to make a judgment with MORAL VALENCE. The two possible alternative values of the moral valence are either MORAL or IMMORAL, which pair up and serve as the target concepts of all the moral metaphors in the system.

Note in Figure 7.1 that both target and source frames have a similar topological or image-schematic structure: three core elements, or roles, forming identical relations between them in a triangular fashion. In the source

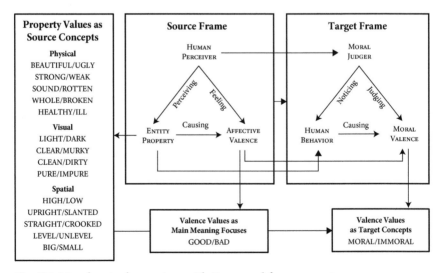

Fig. 7.1 Moral metaphor system with its general frame mappings

frame, pertaining chiefly to perceptual experience and emotional response, the perceiver feels either positive or negative, or good or bad, about a stimulus, i.e., a salient property of some physical entity, upon perceiving it. In this case, the stimulus is physical, and the response is affective, i.e., at a lower level of cognition, affective cognition. In the target frame, pertaining mainly to rational reason and moral judgment, the moral judger still feels positive or negative, or good or bad, about some stimulus, i.e., some human behavior, upon noticing it, but this time his or her notice of the behavior and the affective state arising from it push this sentient agent into making a moral judgment with either a positive or a negative moral valence (i.e., it is moral, or immoral, of the person to behave like that). In this case, the stimulus is social and the response is moral, i.e., at a higher level of cognition, moral cognition.

Moral cognition, however, is related to and based on affective cognition. "Judging" supersedes "Feeling". Both involve valence. Before anything else, valence, which pertains to the values of goodness and badness, is "a central component of all affective states" (Carruthers 2018: 658). Moral valence is derived from, and grounded by, affective valence in general. This is the exact reason why I argued that, as concepts, MORAL and IMMORAL are subcategories of GOOD and BAD (see section 6.2). In fact, my argument running through the whole of Chapter 6 is that, while GOOD and BAD as values of affective valence in general are basic and primary concepts, MORAL and IMMORAL are not. As such, the moral metaphors under study are not primary but complex metaphors.

As in Figure 7.1, the moral metaphors in the system map the triangular, image-schematic structure of the source frame onto the similar triangular structure of the target frame. Therefore, HUMAN PERCEIVER is mapped onto MORAL JUDGER, and ENTITY PROPERTY onto HUMAN BEHAVIOR. Of these two metaphorical mappings, the first, while both the source and the target refer to a human person, involves a cross-domain mapping from bodily function to mental function or, more generally, from body to mind, namely the MIND IS BODY metaphor. The second mapping is from some salient physical property (i.e., ENTITY PROPERTY) to some noticeable social behavior (i.e., HUMAN BEHAVIOR). Note, however, that the third connection is between AFFECTIVE VALENCE in the source and MORAL VALENCE in the target. In this connection, GOOD and BAD as values of AFFECTIVE VALENCE do not serve as source concepts that map metaphorically onto MORAL and IMMORAL as values of MORAL VALENCE (hence, the line with a stealth instead of a solid arrowhead). Rather, GOOD and BAD merely serve as the main meaning focuses carried over by the metaphorical mappings from the source to the target. After all, as I argued in section 6.2, GOOD and BAD and MORAL and IMMORAL, as two pairs of valence values, do not belong to conceptual categories of different kinds. Instead, they are related to each other vertically, staying at different levels of the same taxonomic hierarchy of concepts: GOOD and BAD as superordinate, more generic concepts on Level 1, and MORAL and IMMORAL as subordinate, more specific concepts on Level 2. As such, the latter inherit the structures and values of the former whereas the former encompass the latter as their subcategories in the domain of MORALITY (i.e., MORAL means "morally good" whereas IMMORAL means "morally bad"). If this is true, then moral judgment presupposes affective feeling, and affectivity grounds morality.

When we formulate conceptual metaphors for morality, we only utilize source and target concepts in the form of MORAL IS X and IMMORAL IS Y. The formulas of conceptual metaphors are merely a shorthand form for more complex mappings between frames. For that matter, the mappings between the source and target frame structures do not show themselves overtly in the conceptual formulas of the moral metaphors. Those formulas involve only the source and target concepts (or domains). For the moral metaphor system under study, there is just a single pair of target concepts, MORAL and IMMORAL, which, as shown in Figure 7.1, are the two possible opposite values that fill the role of MORAL VALENCE, resulting from the moral judgment in the target frame. Valence "provides the foundations for all human decision making" (Carruthers 2018: 676). In a moral context, the decision to be made is a moral one, a moral judgment.

As already discussed in the preceding chapters, the source concepts of the moral metaphors are the values that feed into the role of ENTITY PROPERTY in the source frame. Figure 7.1 packs up all three sets of them for the three subsystems in a single box. They carry values in opposition, representing the two polar ends of a particular dimension of human experience, be it physical, visual, or spatial. The polar values correspond to the values, GOOD and BAD, of valence as a central component of the affective state felt by the experiencer when perceiving the salient property. Also, as argued, the contrastive values of affective valence serve as the main meaning focuses of the moral metaphors, carried over by the mappings from the source to the target concepts MORAL and IMMORAL, which, as moral valence, is also derived from and grounded by general affective valence GOOD and BAD. Analyzed as such, the main meaning focuses, GOOD and BAD, serve the bridging function between the source and the target, and account for the aptness of the moral metaphors.

Specifically, when people make a moral judgment upon noticing some human behavior in the social world, that is, when they judge whether it is moral (i.e., morally good) or immoral (i.e., morally bad), their judgment builds primarily on their feeling good or bad about that behavior. It so happens that this affective component of their moral judgment overlaps the affective feeling they have, either good or bad, when they perceive the salient property of some physical entity in the physical world. It is then that affective feeling (good or bad) that serves the bridging link in the metaphorical mappings between bodily experience in the source domain and social and moral cognition in the target domain.

Note that the triangular structure in the source frame represents experiential correlation between two dimensions of experience: perceiving a salient, polarized property of a physical entity and feeling a valenced affective state. Experiential correlations constitute the experiential basis for, or embodied nature of, primary metaphors. Although there is a causative relationship between ENTITY PROPERTY and AFFECTIVE VALENCE, namely, the perception of the former causes the feeling of the latter, the two dimensions of experience are nonetheless perceived and conceived as cooccurring and correlated with each other. Since the two elements coexist in the same frame, the source frame, they also hold a metonymic relationship between them. This metonymic relationship is called in conceptual metaphor theory (CMT) the metonymic basis, metonymic motivation, or metonymic stage of conceptual metaphors based on experiential correlation (see, e.g., Barcelona 2000b; Kövecses 2013; Radden 2000). It accounts for the embodied nature of such metaphors.

As has been argued, the moral valence, with MORAL and IMMORAL as its alternative values, comprises an affective component with GOOD and BAD as its alternative values. While MORAL and IMMORAL as concepts are more complex in nature, GOOD and BAD are schematic and generic and, as such, are primary concepts. They are argued to be underlying the target concepts MORAL and IMMORAL of the moral metaphors in the moral metaphor system, as shown by the decomposition analyses conducted in sections 6.2 and 6.3. Moreover, those source concepts as values of the salient property perceived by the human perceiver are largely primary concepts. This means that GOOD IS X and BAD IS Y, where X and Y are any pair of source concepts of the moral metaphors, have the potential to be primary metaphors. Yet, some of them may still remain pre-metaphors, at least in the languages under study, as I argued in sections 6.3 and 6.4. The implication is that a conceptual metaphor being based on experiential correlation and its source and target being primary concepts are necessary conditions, but not sufficient conditions, of a primary metaphor. Pre-metaphors satisfy the necessary conditions, but are yet to meet the sufficient conditions in cultural mediation and linguistic manifestation before they can become full-fledged primary metaphors.

In brief, Figure 7.1 provides a "big picture" of the moral metaphor system under study. The picture exhibits the source and target frames, the source and target concepts, and the main meaning focuses, of the whole moral metaphor system. According to this analysis, the moral metaphor system maps the source frame structure onto the target frame structure. The frame structures of the source and target domains are comprised of their separate frame elements and relations, as well as the values of the two elements (or roles), one in the source frame (ENTITY PROPERTY) and one in the target frame (MORAL VALENCE). The values of these two elements serve respectively as the source and target concepts of the moral metaphors in the system. It is worth stressing that the mapping from the source frame to the target frame is partial, since one of the three core elements, AFFECTIVE VALENCE, in the triangular image-schematic (topological) structure of the source frame is not mapped metaphorically onto its counterpart, MORAL VALENCE, in the target frame (hence, the line with a stealth arrowhead). That target role, along its values, is retained in the metaphorical equation as the target concept.

More generally, my analysis supports an extended version of the Invariance Principle (Sullivan 2013), which emphasizes the crucial role that frame structures play in metaphor analysis. According to the standard version of the Invariance Principle, "Metaphorical mappings preserve the cognitive topology (that is, the image-schema structure) of the source domain, in a way consistent with the inherent structure of the target domain" (Lakoff 1993: 215). Sullivan (2013: 37) proposes an "extended" definition of "cognitive topology" so as to include frame structure as well as image-schema structure. With this extended definition, then, metaphorical mappings preserve not only image-schema structure, but also frame structure, of the source domain in a way consistent with the inherent structure of the target domain.

7.2 Body, culture, and language in metaphorical thought

What roles do body, culture, and language play in metaphorical conceptualization? This is an intriguing question. In Chapter 1, I addressed some of the issues involved. In this section, I follow up on them from a holistic perspective. According to CMT, metaphor involves three levels of phenomena, as illustrated by Figure 7.2, modified from Yu (2020: 13). As displayed in the figure bottom-up, the interaction between bodily and cultural experience in the experiential basis gives rise to conceptual metaphor (with mapping from source to target domain), which is instantiated by linguistic metaphor (with mapping from source to target expression). Put differently top-down, linguistic

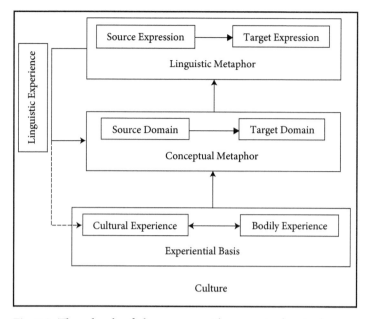

Fig. 7.2 Three levels of phenomena with conceptual metaphor

metaphor consists in a particular linguistic pattern that manifests the under-lying conceptual metaphor, which, in turn, is grounded in an experiential basis which can be defined broadly as the interaction between bodily and cultural experience. All three levels of phenomena, however, exist in the all-encompassing sphere of culture (see also Chapter 2). In this section, I address issues pertaining to the three levels.

7.2.1 Experiential basis with body and culture for conceptual metaphor

Figure 7.2 includes three kinds of human experience linked in some ways with conceptual metaphor: i.e., *bodily experience*, *cultural experience*, and *linguistic experience*. CMT deserves great credit for its claim and argument for the em-bodied nature of metaphors.[1] In his summary of the structure of conceptual

---

[1] It is worth noting that there are various kinds of metaphors, but what CMT is particularly inter-ested in, and focused on, are those conventional conceptual patterns that are motivated fundamentally by bodily experience, and manifested widely in everyday language, especially those that are catego-rized broadly as correlation-based metaphors (Grady 1999; see also Kövecses 2013), such as the moral metaphors studied in this monograph.

metaphor, Lakoff (1993: 245) stated that metaphorical mappings "are not arbitrary, but grounded in the body and in everyday experience and knowledge".
Since humans across various cultures share many basic embodied experiences, it follows that many conceptual metaphors grounded in those common
embodied experiences are potentially universal or widespread. The earlier
CMT views never ignored the role of culture in the emergence of conceptual
metaphors. For instance, as cited in section 1.2, Lakoff and Johnson (1980:
57) said the following in emphasizing the cultural nature of human experience which is inevitably embodied since we can only experience everything in
the physical world through our body:

> Cultural assumptions, values, and attitudes are not a conceptual overlay
> which we may or may not place upon experience as we choose. It would be
> more correct to say that all experience is cultural through and through, that
> we experience our "world" in such a way that our culture is already present
> in the very experience itself.

Lakoff and Johnson (1980: 19) also argued that it is "hard to distinguish
the physical from the cultural basis of a metaphor, since the choice of one
physical basis from among possible ones has to do with cultural coherence".
Nevertheless, earlier CMT placed more emphasis on universal rather than
culture-specific aspects of metaphors. Subsequent cross-linguistic and cross-
cultural studies led to more balanced views on the roles of body and culture
in metaphorical conceptualization (see, e.g., Brenzinger and Kraska-Szlenk
2014; Frank et al. 2008; Gibbs 1999; Kövecses 2005, 2015a; Kraska-Szlenk
2020; Maalej and Yu 2011; Sharifian et al. 2008; Yu 1998, 2009a, 2009b; Zeimke
et al. 2007). That is, "conceptual metaphors emerge from the interaction between culture and body" and "metaphors are grounded in bodily experience
but shaped by cultural understanding" (Yu 2008: 247). While humans across
cultures indeed share the basic structure of the body along with many basic aspects of bodily experience, their understandings of the body and bodily
experience may vary, shaped in differing molds of cultural models.

In Yu (1998), for example, I studied anger metaphors in Chinese in comparison with those in English (Lakoff and Kövecses 1987). It was found that anger
is conceptualized in terms of "heat" (i.e., rise of body temperature) and "internal pressure" (i.e., body as a container) in both English and Chinese, as a result
of embodied understanding of emotion. Hence, ANGER IS HEAT is applicable in
both languages. At a more specific level, however, English and Chinese display
both a commonality and a difference. They share the first subversion ANGER IS

FIRE, but differ in the second one: ANGER IS FLUID IN A HEATED CONTAINER in English vs. ANGER IS GAS IN A HEATED CONTAINER in Chinese. Why should Chinese select the GAS metaphor in contrast with the FLUID metaphor of English while both languages construe the body as a "container" with "internal pressure" increasing as a result of increasing "heat"? I proposed an account of the difference by referring to the *Yin-Yang* theory of ancient Chinese philosophy and traditional Chinese medicine, according to which heat and gas, as well as fire, are categorized with *Yang* whereas cold and fluid are categorized with *Yin*. It was argued that the *Yin-Yang* theory serves as an underlying cultural model in Chinese in the selection of the GAS over FLUID metaphor even though both metaphors are grounded in the bodily experience of increasing heat, and hence increasing internal pressure inside the body. That is, the interaction between cultural and bodily experience gives rise to a colorful spectrum of conceptual metaphors, of which some may be potentially universal or widespread whereas others are culture-specific.

7.2.2 Impact of linguistic experience on metaphorical conceptualization

In section 7.2.1, I discussed how body (bodily experience) and culture (cultural experience) interact to give rise to the emergence of conceptual metaphor in thought. This view disagrees with a purely usage-based theory of metaphors in thought, especially from a historical perspective, namely it is repeated use of metaphors in language that gives rise to metaphors in thought (Sanford 2012). While noting the importance of linguistic usages in the interaction between language and thought, Gibbs (2013b) points out that this theory does not accord with the findings of gestural and multimodal research on metaphor, which suggest that gestural, visual, or multimodal metaphors, as well as linguistic metaphors, emerge directly from conceptual metaphors (see, e.g., Cienki and Müller 2008; Forceville and Urios-Aparisi 2009). In their study of primary metaphors, Winter and Matlock (2017) argue that cultural reflections of primary metaphors in cultural artefacts and gestures feed back into the underlying conceptual patterns such that primary metaphors are not only embodied, but cultural as well.

In this subsection, the question I want to ask is: How does metaphorical language interact with metaphorical thought? Or more specifically, how is metaphorical conceptualization related to our experience of using language? According to standard CMT, conceptual metaphors are manifested linguistically when we talk about what we think and communicate in language.

Linguistic metaphors consist in particular linguistic patterns that manifest the underlying conceptual metaphors. When this happens, linguistic expressions, including lexical items and other linguistic units, which are primarily associated with source domains, are deployed to express target-domain concepts (Lakoff 1993). Prompted by the MIND IS BODY metaphor, for instance, body-part terms are utilized in the expression of more abstract states, processes, and traits associated with cognition, emotion, disposition, and so on. Thus, language serves as a window onto the mind, and systematic description and analysis of linguistic patterns can lead us toward the understanding of possible function, composition, and construction of our conceptual system that is otherwise hidden in the dark.

More recently, metaphor research, especially in the field of psychology, has arrived at the conclusion that the use of linguistic metaphors in a particular language may actually exert a causal influence on the development and formulation of conceptual metaphors in the minds of speakers of that language (see, e.g., Casasanto 2013, 2016, 2017). Through their repeated use, linguistic metaphors can potentially reinforce, modify, or even produce conceptual metaphors, especially through linguistic inheritance from a diachronic viewpoint, as Yu and Jia (2016: 177) suggested:

> It is worth noting that linguistic manifestations of conceptual metaphors in characteristic patterns in languages are not just a simple consequence of conceptual mappings in thought. Instead, characteristic linguistic patterns in a language influence its speakers' way of viewing the world and their experience in it. They constitute whole-sale packages that the speakers of the language inherit as part of their cultural and cognitive heritage. For that matter, they carry special weight on and for those who carry them.

The impact of linguistic metaphors on conceptual metaphors is consistent with a version of linguistic relativity, namely, people using different metaphors in their respective languages conceptualize the target the way they talk about it (Casasanto 2016). In Figure 7.2, such influence is represented by a line pointing from linguistic metaphor back to conceptual metaphor, as the impact of linguistic experience on metaphorical conceptualization.

Along this line, I conducted a corpus-based study of the relationship between language and thought in general and between linguistic and conceptual metaphor in particular, investigating evidence from relevant linguistic corpora (Yu 2020; see also Yu and Jia 2016). I report this study in detail here to make my point clearer. My central argument is threefold. First, salient features in linguistic patterns, both qualitative (types) and quantitative (tokens), may affect the underlying conceptual patterns of the language users. Second, native speakers of that language inherit their linguistic experience as part of their cultural and cognitive heritage. Third, it is possible that they inherit the underlying conceptual patterns through their linguistic experience learning and using salient linguistic patterns.

For my study, I focused on the Chinese terms for two body parts, the face (脸 liǎn "face"; 面 miàn "face") and the heart (心 xīn "heart"), which I regard as cultural keywords (Wierzbicka 1992, 1997) in the Chinese language because they are filled with rich Chinese cultural meanings and values. In traditional Chinese culture, the "social face" is an exceptionally important concept at the core of interpersonal relations and social interactions, and the heart is regarded as the cognitive and affective center of a human person, namely the "cognitive and affective heart". I had previously studied these two Chinese body-part terms qualitatively (Yu 2001, 2009a, 2009b, etc.), but this time I looked at them in a new light, using quantitative as well as qualitative data in the linguistic corpus, the Corpus of the Center for Chinese Linguistics (CCL). In doing so, I also looked at some English data in the Corpus of Contemporary American English (COCA), not for the purpose of comparison (since comparable they are not), but to establish a reference point. The capacities of the two corpora at the time of research (2017) are listed in Table 1.1, with more than 581 million Chinese characters for contemporary Chinese in CCL, and over 520 million English words for contemporary American English in COCA.

The first question I asked for the study of "face" is: What are the frequencies of the body-part terms for "face" in each corpus for both languages? The keyword searches led to the results in Table 7.1. Note that, as mentioned earlier, Chinese has two basic words for "face", so the total is the sum of two separate numbers. Here, the total frequency does not include another Chinese "face" word 颜 yán, which has other meanings not directly related to the face. As can be seen from this table, the Chinese "face" words' total frequency is over 4.7 times of that of English.

Table 7.1 Frequencies of the "face" words in COCA and CCL

Corpus	Term	Frequency	Total
COCA	*face*	183,490	183,490
CCL	脸 *liǎn* + 面 *miàn*	85,323 + 792,750	878,676

My next question is: To what extent do the Chinese body-part terms for "face" express metaphorical senses related to "social face"? To answer this question, I narrowed down my searches to some compound words that I know are commonly used in the relevant senses. The search results are in Table 7.2. "Total" refers to the total numbers of tokens retrieved, ranging from 536 to 3,773. I then manually went through just the first 100 tokens to see how many of them are used metaphorically in the senses of abstract "social face". The numbers so obtained also represent the percentages of tokens referring metaphorically to "social face".

Table 7.2 Chinese compounds with "face" meaning abstract "social face"

Compound	English gloss	English translation	Total	% in first 100
面子 *miànzi*	face-suffix	face; reputation; prestige	3,773	93
脸面 *liǎnmiàn*	face-face	face; self-respect; sensibilities; feelings	794	85
脸皮 *liǎnpí*	face-skin	face; feelings; sensibilities; sense of shame	785	93
颜面 *yánmiàn*	face-face	face; decency; sensibilities	536	41
情面 *qiánmiàn*	feeling-face	feelings; sensibilities	763	88
体面 *tǐmiàn*	body-face	face; dignity; prestige	2,385	72

My next step was to search for the frequencies of some common V+N collocations (as compounds or idiomatic expressions), where N stands for a Chinese "face" word used in its abstract social senses. There are 15 of them (i.e., types), with a total frequency of 3,769 relevant tokens, averaging 251 for each type. Table 7.3 lists the first four types as examples. Those omitted have the following distinct types of collocation as glossed in English: "like face", "love face", "give (sb) face", "leave (sb) face", "attend to (sb's) face", and "be hindered by (sb's) face".

Table 7.3 Frequencies of Chinese "face" compounds and collocations in abstract social senses

Expression	English gloss	English translation	Frequency
有脸 *yǒuliǎn*	have-face	have prestige; have face	435
没脸 *méiliǎn*	not have-face	be too ashamed (to do sth.)	273
要脸 *yàoliǎn*	want-face	have a sense of shame	579
丢脸 *diūliǎn*	lose-face	lose face; be disgraced	719

The last thing I did with "face" in CCL was to look at the variety of the "face" collocations. Particularly, I focused on 面子 *miànzi*, which is often used to refer to dignity and prestige as well as interpersonal feelings and sensibilities, namely "social face". As listed in Table 7.2, this word has a total frequency of 3,773 in CCL, and 93 per cent of them refers to the relevant senses of "social face". I looked through just the first 200 tokens, but found as many as 59 different types of relevant collocations (the complete list is left out here), such as "vie for face", "look for and recover one's face", "prop up one's face", "protect and hold one's face", "lay down one's face", and so on and so forth.

There is no comparison between the wide variety of types, and great number of tokens, of "social face" found in Chinese, and those for the English word *face* in this regard. As far as I know, only *lose face* and *save face* are relatively common, and *gain face* is rare. I searched for their frequencies in COCA, with the results provided in Table 7.4. I looked into the contexts of *gain face*, and found that, interestingly, two tokens occur in one academic journal article about Chinese politics and the other two occur in writings about Chinese culture. By the way, there were two more tokens of *gaining face*, but they were simply providing "noise" in the data because both of them occur in the same context in which the speaker, a man, was being humorous in saying that he was not losing hair, but "gaining face".

As shown in Table 7.4, although I did not attempt a real comparison between English and Chinese, we can see from what I did initially with the corpora that the magnitude of differences between the two languages is enormous both qualitatively and quantitatively. While the abstract "social face" exists in both languages, we see on the Chinese side very productive linguistic elaborations, extensions, and constructions which are virtually absent in English. Chinese shows a huge pyramidal structure. At the very tip are two basic "face" words, which combine with other elements into various compounds and idiomatic expressions (see Yu 2001) at the middle, which are then further elaborated, extended, and constructed into a gigantic base of collocations. These collocations are used frequently and repeatedly in daily communication in the Chinese language.

Table 7.4 Frequencies of English collocations with *face* meaning abstract "social face"

Collocation	Frequency	Collocation	Frequency	Collocation	Frequency
lose face	69	*save face*	245	*gain face*	2
loses face	6	*saves face*	7		
lost face	22	*saved face*	12	*gained face*	1
losing face	56	*saving face*	76	*gaining face*	1
Total	153		340		4

My second case study in Yu (2020) concerns the Chinese "heart", 心 *xīn*, which I argued is taken as the central faculty of cognition in traditional Chinese culture (Yu 2009a). The cultural belief that the heart is the center of mental as well as emotional life, in other words, "cardiocentrism" (see, e.g., Sharifian et al. 2008), is reflected in a great number of Chinese linguistic expressions (Yu 2009a). Experimental studies have confirmed that folk theory that the heart is an organ that governs aspects of mental life, or "cardiopsychism", is still very much alive, and that conventionalized "heart" expressions people use in everyday life might be responsible for its perseverance and persistence (Zhou and Cacioppo 2015).

I first searched the terms for "heart", "brain", and "head" in English and Chinese and the total frequencies for these terms are given in Table 7.5. The frequency for the "heart" is especially high in Chinese, over six times as many as that of *heart* in English, whereas the frequencies for the "brain" and "head" terms are about 2:1 between Chinese and English. I then went through the first 100 tokens for the "heart" terms in both languages, and found a remarkable difference, namely, in English 61 tokens (61%) refer to the physical organ compared with only two (2%) in Chinese.

Table 7.5 Total frequencies for "heart", "brain", and "head" in COCA and CCL

COCA			CCL		
Heart	Brain	Head	心 *xīn* "heart"	脑 *nǎo* "brain"	头 *tóu* "head"
111,184	47,490	234,599	689,611	93,158	428,033

In Chinese, the source concept of "heart" is mapped onto all cognitive and affective aspects of a human person, such as mental, intellectual, rational, moral, emotional, dispositional, and so on. In Table 7.6, the Chinese compounds provide just some examples to illustrate that in Chinese the "heart" is present in all aspects of inner life. Interestingly, while all Chinese compounds involve "heart" as one of the two components, none of the English translations contains its English counterpart *heart*. Further, many of these compounds have extremely high frequencies in CCL.

The last thing I did in CCL is that I went through the first 200 tokens of the "heart" keyword search, which brought up a total of 689,611 tokens (see Table 7.5). Among the first 200 tokens, there are 33 different types of compounds and idioms in which "heart" does not refer to the physical organ. In fact, there are only three in which "heart" refers to the internal organ. The remaining 164 are simply tokens of some of those 33 types. I then searched

Table 7.6 Examples of Chinese compounds referring to the "cognitive and affective heart"

Compound	English gloss	English translation	Frequency
诚心 *chéngxīn*	sincere-heart	sincerity	1,420
良心 *liángxīn*	good/fine-heart	conscience	3,766
知心 *zhīxīn*	knowing-heart	intimate; understanding (friend)	1,039
心想 *xīnxiǎng*	heart-think	think to oneself	6,484
心服 *xīnfú*	be heart-convinced	be genuinely convinced	942
心甘 *xīngān*	be heart-willing	be willing	1,032
好心 *hǎoxīn*	good-heart	good intention	3,134
成心 *chéngxīn*	establish-heart	on purpose	655
用心 *yòngxīn*	use-heart	with concentrated attention	4,531
决心 *juéxīn*	determined-heart	determination; be determined	21,971
违心 *wéixīn*	disobey/violate-heart	against one's will	408
恒心 *héngxīn*	constant-heart	perseverance; persistence	221
小心 *xiǎoxīn*	small-heart	be careful; be cautious	11,319
粗心 *cūxīn*	thick-heart	careless; thoughtless	624
焦心 *jiāoxīn*	scorch-heart	feel terribly worried	67
开心 *kāixīn*	open-heart	feel happy	4,964
心醉 *xīnzuì*	be heart-drunk	be charmed; be enchanted	405

the frequencies for each of them. Their frequencies range from 67 to 119,322. Specifically, four of them have frequencies up to 100 (67, 77, 88, 100), six of them up to 1,000 (159, 258, 308, 575, 681, 946), and the remaining 20 ranging from 1,261 all the way up to 119,322. On the other hand, the English word *heart* appears in their English translations only twice (bolded). Table 7.7 just lists nine instances out of the 33 types with over 10,000 tokens in frequency.

Table 7.7 Nine "heart" compounds out of 33 types with over 10,000 tokens in frequency

Compound	English gloss	English translation	Frequency
关心 *guānxīn*	enclose-heart	be concerned with; care for	36,207
决心 *juéxīn*	determined-heart	determination; be determined	21,971
小心 *xiǎoxīn*	small-heart	take care; be careful; be cautious	11,319
信心 *xìnxīn*	trust-heart	confidence; faith	27,283
内心 *nèixīn*	inner-heart	innermost being; inner self	12,974
心灵 *xīnlíng*	heart-soul/spirit	mind; **heart**; soul; spirit; psyche	11,890
心理 *xīnlǐ*	heart-principle	mind; mentality; psychology	35,868
核心 *héxīn*	core-heart	core; **heart** of the matter	24,332
中心 *zhōngxīn*	central-heart	center; main; key	119,322

As shown in the relevant tables above, each type of linguistic item with its token frequency in the corpus may not look significant in the sea of everyday language use. When the variety and frequency of them are added up, however, the magnitudes of types and tokens are tremendous. This is just the tip of the iceberg, though, considering that the 33 different compounds and idioms found were among just the first 200 "heart" tokens in the corpus, which holds a total number of 689,611 tokens.

At this point, I would like to elaborate on one compound word in Table 7.6 as it is particularly relevant to the study of moral metaphors in Chinese. In Table 7.6, the second item, 良心 *liángxīn*, which, literally meaning "good or fine heart", refers to one's conscience or moral sense (cf. 18b in section 4.4.3). This is because in Chinese culture the heart is traditionally held as the locus of one's moral sense or moral character (see, e.g., Yu 2009a: 78–81). According to ancient Chinese philosophy, therefore, it is crucial for people to "cultivate the heart" (修心 *xiūxīn*), to "cleanse the heart" (净心 *jìngxīn*; 清心 *qīngxīn*), and to "straighten the heart" (正心 *zhèngxīn*) (cf. section 5.4.2) so that they can foster and maintain a good sense of morality. It is interesting to note that the Chinese cultural conceptualization of the heart as the locus of one's moral sense and moral character has been preserved in the Chinese language to the present day. Therefore, conscienceless people are said to "lack the good heart" (没良心) because, for instance, it has become "rotten" (良心烂了) or "eaten by a dog" (良心让狗吃了). In fact, the heart being the locus of moral sense in Chinese is illustrated by many more commonly used compound words. Those in Table 7.8 are just some examples listed with their varying frequencies in CCL. See Yu (2009a: 195–203) for a more detailed discussion of the heart as the locus of moral sense and moral character in Chinese.

In sum, the Chinese cultural conceptualization of the heart as the cognitive and affective center of a human person (i.e., cardiocentrism) can be traced back to its deep roots in ancient Chinese philosophy and traditional Chinese medicine over 2,000 years ago in history (Yu 2009a: chapters 2–3). Therefore, the salient linguistic patterns centering on the "cognitive and affective heart" in Chinese, as discussed above (see also Yu 2009a: chapters 4–5), can be characterized as having arisen and grown from the underlying conceptual pattern. However, ordinary Chinese speakers are not really so conscious of this underlying cultural conceptualization, rooted so deeply in ancient Chinese philosophy and traditional Chinese medicine. This means that the culturally

Table 7.8 Compounds showing the heart as the locus of moral sense and moral character

Compound	English gloss	English translation	Frequency
善心 shànxīn	kind-heart	mercy; behnevolence	361
慈心 cíxīn	kind-heart	benevolent heart; kind-hearted	85
爱心 àixīn	love-heart	love; loving care; sympathy; compassion	5,969
孝心 xiàoxīn	filial-heart	filial love; love for and devotion to one's parents	400
狠心 hěnxīn	ruthless-heart	heartless; merciless; cruel	848
兽心 shòuxīn	beast-heart	the heart of a beast—ruthless; relentless; callous	53
贪心 tānxīn	insatiable-heart	greed; avarice; greedy; avaricious; insatiable	249
异心 yìxīn	different-heart	infidelity; disloyalty; apostasy	62
二心 èrxīn	two-heart	disloyalty; unfaithfulness; half-heartedness	173
变心 biànxīn	change-heart	change loyalties; break faith	258
负心 fùxīn	betray-heart	untrue (esp. in love); ungrateful; heartless	205
昧心 mèixīn	conceal-heart	(do evil) against one's conscience	122
心毒 xīndú	heart-poisonous	callous-hearted; evil-minded; malicious	46
心黑 xīnhēi	heart-black	evil; venomous; greedy; predatory	56
心狠 xīnhěn	heart-ruthless	ruthless; merciless	320

shared conceptualization has been acquired, subconsciously or unconsciously, through learning and using Chinese as their native language.

The linguistic usages involving the "face" and "heart" words are embodied in the sense that they express aspects of cultural cognition through parts of the body. They convey cultural conceptualizations through embodied cultural metaphors (Sharifian 2017). Embodiment manifests itself in varying linguistic patterns that entail differing linguistic experiences. Different strengths of linguistic patterns in linguistic experience would exert an impact on the cognitive status of the corresponding conceptual patterns as being either strong or weak in different languages and cultures. That would be an important reason why the abstract "social face" and "cognitive and affective heart" concepts are much stronger in Chinese-speaking cultures than are they in English-speaking cultures. That is, linguistic patterns are not mere linguistic manifestations of conceptual patterns, and the linguistic experience they constitute should in turn loop back to affect the conceptual system one way or another.

7.2.3 Impact of linguistic experience on cultural experience

In section 7.2.2, I outlined the linguistic patterns in Chinese related to "social face" and "cognitive and affective heart" in both qualitative and quantitative terms, comparing and contrasting these with usage in English. Such are the unique linguistic patterns experienced by native speakers of Chinese in everyday life that when those salient linguistic patterns repeat and expand themselves, there is a snowball effect in everyday linguistic usages, reinforcing the underlying patterns at a conceptual level. It can be argued that such linguistic patterns, among others, constitute a main driving force that helps fix the conceptual patterns in the minds of individual Chinese speakers as they grow up learning and using the various linguistic features. Since linguistic usage is a part of the cultural heritage passed down from generation to generation, each new generation of speakers inherits earlier conceptual patterns while learning and using the corresponding linguistic patterns. Thus, native speakers acquire the underlying conceptual patterns through their linguistic experience. The repeated use of linguistic expressions that form salient linguistic patterns are at least partially responsible for the corresponding elements in the conceptual systems of individual native speakers. The influence of linguistic patterns in affecting an individual person's underlying conceptual patterns cannot of course deny the fact that the interaction between culture and body has given rise to the conceptual patterns, shared by all native speakers, in the first place.

In this subsection, I discuss my latest modification in Figure 7.2. It is represented by the dash line as an extension of linguistic experience leading to cultural experience. What it means is that linguistic experience using linguistic metaphor can also affect cultural experience and, by extension, will influence conceptual metaphor in a larger loop.

To illustrate what this means, let me first refer to my studies on the cultural variation in conceptualizing life metaphorically in terms of the performing arts. The central metaphor in this regard is LIFE IS SHOW (Kövecses 2005), which however may have its source subcases, such as LIFE IS PLAY and LIFE IS OPERA, organized at different levels in a hierarchical structure. Yu and Jia (2016) argued that, while LIFE IS PLAY is a basic metaphor for life in English (Lakoff and Turner 1989), LIFE IS OPERA, in contrast, manifests itself most saliently in Chinese. In the Chinese context, "OPERA" refers to Chinese opera, with Beijing opera as its prototype (see also Yu 2011a). In Yu and Jia (2016), we supported our argument with ample linguistic evidence, both qualitative and quantitative. In Yu (2017), I moved a step further and showed how LIFE IS OPERA, as a cultural metaphor, is instantiated richly and diversely, citing multimodal evidence from such cultural artefacts as song lyrics, calligraphies, paintings, and photographs. I noted that all those artefacts revolve around a single four-character idiom in the Chinese language: 人生如戏 *rénshēng rúxì* "life is opera". In Chinese culture, I argued, this idiom prototypically instantiates the conceptual metaphor LIFE IS OPERA and, as "a motto-like expression ... filled with cultural values", it presents "the Chinese philosophical stances on or attitudes toward life" (Yu 2017: 69). For this reason, this idiomatic expression has turned into a popular theme in Chinese literary, musical, and visual arts.

Thus, for instance, keyword searches on Google and Baidu led to about 50 million results each. The same searches on Google Images and Baidu Images also result in large pools of visual and multimodal artefacts with this idiomatic expression as their central theme. To me, this is a good example showing how our linguistic experience using a salient linguistic expression can change our cultural experience with huge numbers of cultural artefacts resulting from it. It can be expected that change in cultural experience should also bring about change in the dynamics in the relationship between language, thought, and culture as a whole.

Now, let me turn to the examples of moral metaphors studied in this book. In section 6.6, I discussed some visual and multimodal examples of moral metaphors. According to CMT, visual and multimodal metaphors, as much as linguistic metaphors, are motivated directly by their underlying conceptual metaphors. However, there is evidence suggesting that at least some visual and multimodal metaphors found in cultural artefacts may be motivated by linguistic metaphors found in conventional linguistic expressions. So, most of the images discussed in (21) in section 6.6 found on Google Images seem to have corresponding English expressions that have either implicit or explicit presence in them. These types of expressions have various frequencies of tokens in COCA. Thus, images (21c) and (21d) display *moral scales* (explicit), which is a metaphorical instrument for measuring or weighing *moral balance* (implicit). Image (21e) corresponds to both *morally upright* (implicit; cf. 5a in section 5.3.2) and *morally straight* (explicit; cf. 9a in section 5.3.4) whereas image (21f) matches the idiomatic expression *stoop (so) low* (implicit; cf. 11c in section 5.3.4).

Further, images (21h) and (21i), as political cartoons, both have linguistic expressions rendered explicitly in them. Image (21h) shows Uncle Sam hanging onto the top of a skyscraper with *moral high ground* written on its side (cf. 1a in section 5.3.1). Since this is a common expression about morality, we see a sizable collection of political cartoons revolving around this theme. Image (21i) shows a politician speaking to a row of reporters standing slanted at about a 45 degree angle (see Figure 6.12). The caption of the cartoon reads *slanted media coverage* (cf. 6a and 6b in section 5.3.2). Given that this and similar expressions are used to criticize the unfairness and partiality of media coverage, it is probable that the linguistic expression gave the cartoonist the inspiration for the creation of the cartoon. The last image, image (21j), is also a cartoon showing a very tilted football or soccer field and presenting the theme that the World Trade Organization (WTO) is biased in favor of the West over the rest of the world (see Figure 6.13). It is very likely that this cartoon was motivated by the common English expression *level/unlevel playing field* (cf. 8a and 8b in section 5.3.3) even though the expression itself does not appear in it.

In all these cases, a legitimate question we can ask is: Are these images indeed motivated by the linguistic expressions, implicit or explicit in them, in the first place? Comparative searches on Google Images and Baidu Images seem to suggest that the answer is positive. It seems that, in both of these image databases, images with visual and multimodal metaphors are tied, to a considerable extent, to linguistic metaphors used in the respective languages. In other words, if in one language there exists a (salient) linguistic expression instantiating some conceptual metaphor, then corresponding visual and multimodal expressions instantiating that conceptual metaphor can be found in the image database in that language, and vice versa.

For instance, keyword searches using English expressions *moral scale* and *moral compass* result in large collections of images on Google Images, featuring either scales or compasses. In Chinese, there is a close equivalent to *moral scales* (道德天平 dàodé tiānpíng), but there is no counterpart for *moral compass*, as mentioned previously in section 5.5. Keyword searches for these two terms on Baidu Images led to very different results. The one for "moral scales" brought up a good collection of images featuring scales.

One example shows a purse (or wallet) on one pan, and the Chinese character for "virtue" (德 dé) on the other pan, of the scales. A small human figure is trying to climb onto the scales, reaching for the purse while thinking out loud of money, as represented metonymically by a Chinese 100-*yuan* banknote. As a result, the scales have tilted toward the side of purse, with moral balance lost. It is worth noting that, in this caricature, the Chinese character for "virtue" is given human attributes, having a pair of eyes staring at the human figure. Since morality is ascribed to the heart as one of its many cognitive and affective functions (Yu 2009a; cf. section 7.2.2), the character for "virtue" has the character for "heart" as one of its component radicals.

While the search for "moral scales" bore fruitful results including what has been discussed in the preceding paragraph, the search for "moral compass" turned out quite "dry". A few (six, to be exact) images of a compass turned out to be "foreign" or "imported", rather than produced natively in the Chinese context. The only "native" product consisted in 13 different images of the same book, shot from various angles in various "poses". Reading its front cover, I realized that the book is a Chinese translation of an English-language book titled *The Moral Compass*, written by an American author by the name of William Bennet. As such, then, the Chinese counterpart for "moral compass" here was a "loan translation", with no linguistic tokens at all in either CCL or BCC, the two major linguistic corpora in China.

The next example I would like to discuss in this subsection is the English idiomatic expression *level/unlevel playing field*, which is a linguistic instantiation of MORAL IS LEVEL or IMMORAL IS UNLEVEL. As I suggested above, this English expression, with its positive and negative form, would have motivated the creation of the cartoon in (21j) in section 6.6 (see Figure 6.13). That cartoon centers on the theme of unfair competition under the WTO between the "West" and the "Rest", featuring an unlevel football or soccer field tilted sharply downwards to the side of the Rest, putting the West in a "highly" advantageous position "over" the rest of the world. In fact, a good pool of cartoons on the theme of "fair or unfair competition" was sourced from searching for "level/unlevel playing field" on Google Images, and they are apparently motivated by the same linguistic expressions.

In contrast, because Chinese does not have a parallel linguistic metaphor with the same source (i.e., level or unlevel playing field) and target (i.e., fair or unfair competition) at the same level of specificity, I was unable to find comparable cartoons on Baidu Images. When I searched for the source (level or unlevel playing field), the result produced large numbers of photos of football fields and other ball game courses, with no noticeable trace of visual or multimodal metaphors being involved. When I searched for the target (fair or unfair competition), however, there was a large collection of cartoons produced in the relevant results. Those discussed below are just a few of these examples, which I will comment on one by one.

The first example is the most "Chinese-specific" one, an art clip featuring the Chinese compound word for "fair" consisting of two characters 公平 *gōngpíng* (lit. fair-level) (see Figure 7.3; and section 5.4.3, especially the examples in (22) and (23)). As can be seen in the art clip, the first character for "fair" looks in good balance between left and right, with two symmetric strokes on top

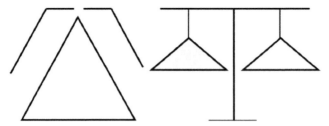

Fig. 7.3 A stylized representation of the Chinese compound word for "fair" (公平)

Note: This figure is my own drawing based on the idea of the original art clip, which can be seen via the following link: https://www.163.com/dy/article/DO7HNQ6O05129E3H.html (last accessed in November 2021). It is provided here in order to give the reader a better understanding of multimodal metaphors involved in the artistic representation of the two Chinese characters of the compound word for "fair".

of an isosceles triangle, its top being level with the top of the second character for "level". Artistically, the second character for "level" is styled in the shape of "scales", which again looks strictly symmetric, with two pans hanging on the horizontal bar on top of a vertical post. What the art clip designer is driving at is, obviously, the metaphorical idea that "fairness" is based on spatial "balance" and "levelness". The shapes of the two original Chinese characters already "embody" this idea, but the designer makes the embodiment look perfect.

The second example pertains to the theme of the local government getting involved in suppressing unfair market competition—offering unreasonable prices, either too low or too high—through its own purchases to "level" (i.e., to regulate) the market. The image features a steelyard, a traditional Chinese-style weighing instrument called 秤 *chèng*, still used by many private sellers in the market. Such a steelyard consists of three major components: a steelyard beam (actually made of special wood) on which gradations are marked, a pan on which things to be weighed are placed hangs close to one end of the beam, and a sliding weight made of pig iron hanging also on the beam (see Figure 7.4). When weighing the thing being sold, the seller holds the string close to the pan end on the steelyard beam and slowly moves the sliding weight away from the pan end until the steelyard beam is level. By reading the gradation marks on the beam where the sliding weight hangs, the seller finds out how much the thing being sold weighs. In the cartoon, the sliding weight is an official stamp, which metonymically stands for the governmental power. On the stamp is the caption "the government purchase price", in contrast with "the

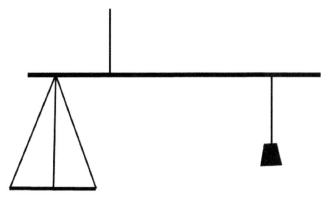

Fig. 7.4 An art clip of a traditional Chinese-style weighing instrument

market price" shown above the middle of the steelyard beam. That is, the government uses its (financial) power to make unfair competition fair. In this case, fair competition is depicted metaphorically in a visual and multimodal way, with an image in which a steelyard beam is being kept "level". This visual and multimodal representation is extremely culture-specific, but the underlying conceptual metaphors are exactly the same as those underlying (21j) in section 6.6, namely MORAL IS LEVEL and IMMORAL IS UNLEVEL (see Figure 6.13).

The third example is another caricature with the theme of "fair competition". In this one, two people metaphorically represent two business enterprises through the personification metaphor CORPORATE IS PERSON, as suggested by the captions on their bodies, which read "Enterprise A" and "Enterprise B". They are hand-wrestling at a table, on the top of which is the caption "the platform of competition". Since the top of the table is "level", it suggests that the competition between them is fair, open, and aboveboard.

The fourth and last example in this group is about "unfair competition", showing two people playing on a seesaw. On the higher side to the right, the person is shouting out "No subsidy, and we just want fairness!". In China today, there are three types of business: state-owned enterprises, people-managed companies, and foreign-capital companies. According to the caption on his body, the one on the higher side represents the second type. We do not know the identity of the one on the lower side since it is not revealed. One guess is that he represents state-owned enterprises, which receive more support from the government. In this case, "unfair competition" is represented visually, through a visual metaphor, with the fulcrum not being at the middle of the seesaw such that the one on the lower side has much more leverage against his competitor. This time, the theme of "unfair competition" is represented visually by the image of an unsymmetrical, unbalanced, and hence unlevel seesaw.

As discussed above, the four examples all involve visual and multimodal manifestation of the target concept FAIRNESS through the source concept LEVELNESS, namely, FAIR IS LEVEL and UNFAIR IS UNLEVEL, which are target subcases of MORAL IS LEVEL and IMMORAL IS UNLEVEL in the moral metaphor system. In this regard, they all share some commonality with example (21j) in section 6.6, the tilted football field (see Figure 6.13), at a schematic level, even though at a specific level there is no similarity among them at all. As I suggested earlier, the cartoonist who drew the cartoon of a tilted football field would have been motivated directly by the highly conventionalized idiomatic expression *level/unlevel playing field* in English. In effect, this English expression has given numerous artists inspiration for their artistic creations, as can be seen from the search results on Google Images.

At this point, we can ask a couple of questions. If the "tilted football field" cartoon is indeed motivated by an idiomatic expression in English, are the four Chinese cartoons discussed above motivated by some linguistics expressions as well? If yes, what are those linguistic expressions? I have to say that I cannot think of any metaphorical expressions in Chinese that can immediately account for the messages those cartoons convey. For instance, I am aware of a Chinese saying, "The masses have a beam of steelyard in their heart" (老百姓心里有杆秤), but it means that commoners (or the public) have good standards or criteria in their mind with which they are capable of "weighing", i.e., judging, the behavior of other people, especially the performance of government officials, "fairly". As such, it is not directly relevant to the message of the second example discussed above, although it still instantiates FAIR IS LEVEL.

If there are no linguistic expressions that immediately motivate the cartoons in the four examples, does that mean that they are directly motivated by the underlying conceptual metaphors FAIR IS LEVEL and UNFAIR IS UNLEVEL? Of course, I do not want to deny the ultimate role that underlying conceptual metaphors play in motivating linguistic metaphors. After all, that is what CMT is all about. What I am really driving at is the role of linguistic motivation in the artistic creation of specific products by individual artists. Then, it comes back to the question: What are the linguistic motivations for the Chinese cartoons under consideration? My answer to this question, which points to a fundamental difference between English and Chinese, lies in the first example discussed above (see Figure 7.3). That art clip displays the Chinese word for "fair", which is a compound consisting of two components represented by two characters. The first means "fair", and the second means "level", namely, FAIR IS LEVEL. That is to say, the conceptual metaphor was already underlying this Chinese compound when the word was first created. Once created and conventionalized, the word, which is used so often in daily communication, does not necessarily activate the conceptual metaphor behind it in the individual minds of native speakers. But that conceptual link is there, all the time, at the cultural and linguistic level, like the sediment under a body of water. When stirred, it will come up and become visible.

Up to this point, it has not been so difficult to tell the difference between English and Chinese in this respect, within the system of schematicity hierarchy. First of all, the pair of conceptual metaphors FAIR IS LEVEL and UNFAIR IS UNLEVEL is in play in both English and Chinese, and that is the reason why we can find its manifestation in both languages and cultures, regardless of whether it is instantiated linguistically, visually, or multimodally. The main difference, however, lies at the level of instantiation. In Chinese, the pair of conceptual metaphors manifests itself lexically in the formation of a compound word. The metaphorical mappings are there from LEVEL and UNLEVEL to FAIR and UNFAIR, but these mappings are at a schematic level, the level of image schema (cf. Figure 5.3(b)). They are implemented at the lexical level, between two components of a compound, which literally means "fair-level".

For this reason, the source frames that the metaphorical mappings evoke are very schematic, with minimum structures of elements and relations that are *not* filled with specific values at this level. Average Chinese speakers in everyday communication use the word to express the concept of "fairness", without noticing the underlying conceptual metaphors. Nevertheless, some speakers, be they writers, poets, fine artists, or simply speakers with a better understanding of their native language, are indeed aware of their existence and make use of them in their literary, poetic, or artistic creation, or in their rhetoric or stylistic composition, at the level of "mental space" (Kövecses 2020). What they do is to elaborate on the schematic frames, exploring lower-level subcases of the frames through their imagination. In doing so, they enrich the structures of the frames by adding to them more elements and relations and filling core and noncore elements and relations with special values. In language use, this is when seemingly novel linguistic metaphors come into play.

In the cases of the cartoons under discussion, it is likely that the cartoonists were conscious of the conceptual metaphors that they accessed via the compound word for "fair" (or "unfair"), and perhaps other like compounds (see section 5.4.3). In order to express their common theme of "fair or unfair competition", they explored, delving down into different source frame subcases that share the common schematic structure of the BALANCE schema (see Figure 5.3(b)), until they landed on their separate source frames: the level steelyard beam as a traditional Chinese-style weighing tool in the second example, the hand-wrestling contest on the level tabletop in the third example, and the unlevel seesaw with unequal levers on both sides of the fulcrum in the fourth example.

In sum, in these cases, even though there is not an immediate linguistic expression that motivates each of the cartoons, they all share a common source concept LEVEL VS. UNLEVEL at a high, schematic level, as represented by Figure 5.3(b) as one of the two versions of the BALANCE schema. It so happens that the spatial concept LEVEL VS. UNLEVEL is contained in the compound word that means "fair" or "unfair" and that expresses the common theme of the cartoons, "fair or unfair competition". My point is that the Chinese word for "fair" (lit. fair-level) can be the motivation for each of the Chinese cartoons from a higher schematic level, since more specific subcases at a lower level inherit the structure of their more schematic case at a higher level.

In contrast, as I argued earlier, the English cartoon in (21j) in Chapter 6 (Figure 6.13), as well as many similar ones in the collection of results found on Google Images, was motivated directly by a highly conventional idiomatic expression *level/unlevel playing field*. The phrase itself already establishes a source frame at a relatively specific level. It would be a sports competition, likely ballgames, especially international football or American football that is played on a large level field and is particularly popular in their own cultural settings. Once it is set in the frame of international football, its elements and relations can be deployed for entailed mappings. In (21j) of Chapter 6, for instance, the lower side of the football field also has an unusually large goal, and the referee who plays a crucial role in making the game fair is a Westerner who, with the "fancy" thought, will side with the West against the Rest, and so on (see Figure 6.13).

The linguistic metaphor, *level/unlevel playing field*, does not have to activate the source frame of a football game. For example, one cartoon in the pool shows three vertical posts of different lengths. While the tops of the posts are level at the same height, their bottoms are so unlevel because they are planted in the terrain of very different elevations. On the top of each post is a sign with "School A, B, or C" written on it. Three school kids are climbing the posts in a contest. The kid of School B appears to be highest on the post despite the fact that he has climbed the least distance from the ground because his post is located on the top of a highly elevated spot. The School A kid appears to be at the lowest height on the post even though she has climbed the greatest distance from the ground because her post is planted far below, at the bottom of what appears to be a huge hole. Two adults are standing far away watching the climbing contest behind yellow tape that says "Parents" on it, one speaking to the other, "School B gets the best result". The caption of the cartoon is "The Unlevel Playing Field". This cartoon again focuses on the theme of "unfair competition" among schools, but the source frame here is completely different from the preceding one, even though the cartoonist may have been motivated by the same linguistic metaphor, which is such a conventional and popular expression in Western discourse.

On the other hand, Chinese does not have a similar linguistic metaphor; no similar cartoons were found on Baidu Images either. As the English linguistic metaphor has to do with sports, I thought of a sports metaphor that I know is very popular in contemporary Chinese discourse, in speaking of being in a disadvantageous position when starting some kind of competition in life. The expression literally means "losing at the starting line" (输在起跑线). It is obviously a race metaphor, LIFE IS RACE (with, e.g., LIFE IS MARATHON as a source subcase), making use of LIFE IS JOURNEY. That is, it refers to a situation in which someone is already losing even before the race gets started. It is common sense in sports that it is difficult to win a race, especially a short-distance one, if the competitor is losing at the starting line. That is why athletes commit the mistake of "jumping the gun" even if they know that they will be disqualified if they repeat it.

I made a Baidu Images search, which brought up a good pool of relevant results. The cartoons to be discussed here are just three examples. In China today, competition for college education has been so severe and bitter that parents have to start the long process of getting their children prepared early on, when their kids are still in the kindergarten or nursery school, investing as much money and time as possible into it. "Don't let your child lose at the starting line" became a catchphrase among parents. They try their best to "open up" their children's academic and talent potentials. They are afraid that they will let their children "lose at the starting line" if they do not do the same as other parents do. The three examples are cartoons satirizing this state of affairs.[2]

---

[2] The three examples of cartoons can be accessed through the following links (last accessed November 2021):

(a) https://www.163.com/dy/article/CIU7U1510526EPS2.html
(b) https://www.jianshu.com/p/7ee94afe7a8b
(c) https://jingyan.baidu.com/album/c1a3101e8bfec2de656debf8.html?picindex=7

In the first example, a row of children and one adult are getting ready for a race at the starting line facing their separate track lanes. What the children are carrying represent metonymically what they are being burdened with in order for them not to "lose at the starting line": one big backpack full of books, two musical instruments, one painting brush pen, one book of Confucian classics, and one banner with "Olympics Math Class" written on it. The adult, a pregnant woman, is holding a guidebook for "Prenatal Conditioning of the Fetus" in her left hand and a microphone for singing Karaoke in her right hand.

The second example shows four kids getting set for a race at the starting line, each carrying a school backpack. However, their starting positions are not placed "level" along a straight line, but vary a lot with different gaps between them, depending on the amounts of money stacked behind them by their parents, who are obviously hyper-anxious (as illustrated by their facial expressions and drops of sweat), rooting for their own children. There are four yellow signs behind the four piles of cash on four different track lanes, showing how much money each of the parents have "invested" in their children in order for them to be more "advanced" at the starting line. The amounts shown on the signs are, respectively, 200,000 for the most "advanced", 120,000 for the second, 80,000 for the third, and 60,000 for the furthest "behind". In this situation, the more money the parents spend, the better schools their children can attend, since on the lanes there are two Chinese characters meaning "choose schools". Understandably, children are not happy with all this "fear" of losing the "race" early on in their life, neither are their parents. Many parents complain about it, but when the practice is an overwhelming social trend, they are worried about "letting their children lose at the starting line" if they do not follow suit. It is worth noting that the Chinese government is fully aware of the enormous negative social impact of all the "hype" surrounding "don't let your child lose at the starting line", so restrictions were recently placed on the "education and training industry" (教培行业) that has flourished in the past decades in providing all different forms of after-school education and training.

The third and last example in this group pertains to the same theme of "unfair competition", but it focuses on the situation in which young people are faced with social inequity as a result of the polarizing social divide between the rich and the poor. Two young men are set for a race (the journey of life) at the starting line. It is clear that this cannot be a fair race. A fat one, with a sinister grin on his face, is on top of the hood of a luxury car, his rich-looking parents are sitting inside, with his father in the driver's seat. By contrast, a thin one, wearing a college degree cap, and showing miserable sadness on his face, is yoked with ropes drawing a cart, sitting on which are his poor-looking parents. It is expected that the one riding on the car will be much faster than the one pulling the cart. That is the difference between having rich and poor parents. There is no social equity between the two, with one having a free ride and the other being hindered burdensomely. Again, the Chinese government is fully aware of the widening gap between the rich and the poor, and therefore a slogan of "common prosperity" (共同富裕) was recently put forward with the goal to narrow the gap.

As I said above, these three cartoons are just examples of a large number of Baidu images motivated by a linguistic sports metaphor, "losing at the starting line", which has become a vogue phrase in China. However, its English equivalent does not appear to be as popular a linguistic metaphor as *level/unlevel playing field*. I was curious as to what I would find if I searched for it on Google Images. I did find three relevant photographic images in the results, but they had all been originally produced in China. Looking into their sources, I realized that they all had come from a single online English article written by a Chinese or Chinese-heritage author and posted under "Rhetoric 2013" on a blog site "blogspot.com".[3] In this article titled "The myth of the starting line", the author, who had researched the subject, wrote about why and how "Don't lose at the starting line" or "Don't let your child lose at the starting line" became a popular slogan in China about three decades ago. Four photos and one cartoon were inserted into the article. Coincidentally, the cartoon, which is pertinent to social inequity "at the starting line", is the third example discussed in the preceding paragraph.

The four photos display the following images. The first one shows a naked little baby being set for a race at the starting line. The second image, according to the author, is an advertisement from a hospital, with a verbal message on it: "If your child has rhinitis, he loses at the starting line". It features a boy being set for a race at the starting line. The third image shows the front cover of a "how-to" book (also available on Amazon.com), the English translation of the original Chinese title being: *Don't Let Your Child Lose at the Starting Line: 30 Strategies to Raise Your Child's Intelligence* (translation my own, different from the article author's or the one on Amazon.com). The fourth image, not collected in the pool of results on Google Images, shows the lower body of a little baby in a diaper, and a piece of paper lying next to the baby says in Chinese: "Countdown: 6598 days, 17 hours, 10 minutes, and 10 seconds

---

[3] Here is the link to access these photos and cartoon: http://fsurhet2013.blogspot.com/2013/01/the-myth-of-starting-line.html (last accessed November 2021).

away from College Entrance Examinations". Satirically, the countdown for the college entrance exams starts with the birth of the baby.

In the above, I discussed some images from the Chinese context. My intent was to illustrate, with evidence from Google and Baidu Images, the point that visual and multimodal manifestations of some underlying conceptual metaphors may be motivated directly by linguistic metaphors that instantiate those conceptual metaphors. The evidence on which the finding is based is that, if both English and Chinese have an equivalent linguistic metaphor, corresponding visual or multimodal metaphors can also be found on both Google and Baidu Images. If a linguistic metaphor exists in one language but not in the other, corresponding visual or multimodal metaphors can be found only in one of the respective image databases. Exceptions turn out to be "imported" or "borrowed" from one database into the other database. In this sense, it is linguistic metaphors that mediate the connection between conceptual metaphors and visual or multimodal metaphors. Or, put differently, linguistic metaphors play a mediating role in the connection between conceptual metaphors and visual or multimodal metaphors.

This finding supports the newly added dashed extension line, which extends from the solid line of "Linguistic Metaphor" and points to "Cultural Experience", in Figure 7.2. The use of linguistic metaphor as part of "Linguistic Experience" leads to the creation of cultural artefacts as part of "Cultural Experience". Any change in "Cultural Experience" should influence its dynamics in interacting with "Bodily Experience", which should eventually affect "Conceptual Metaphor" accordingly.

7.3 Closing remarks

In closing, let me summarize what I have done and what I have found in this study, to bring the focal points into perspective. I have done a comparative study on moral metaphors between English and Chinese in this book, applying a CMT approach. With this approach, every metaphor is analyzed as a node in relation to other nodes in a cluster, and every cluster of nodes is analyzed in connection with other clusters in a network. Consistent with recent development in CMT, this approach treats moral conceptual metaphors as forming a moral metaphor system, which in turn can be divided into three subsystems depending on the kinds of source concepts involved in the metaphorical mappings: namely, the physical subsystem, the visual subsystem, and the spatial subsystem. In my treatment, the three subsystems comprise a total of 14 pairs of moral metaphors, with each pair involving two contrastive source concepts representing the two polarities of one dimension of embodied experience in the physical world. Thus, there are all together 28 individual moral metaphors which appear to be applicable in both English and Chinese. The list, comprising major moral metaphors from the bodily and physical domains, is of course not exhaustive. There will be others that could be added, depending on the languages and cultures being studied.

The three subsystems of moral metaphors were analyzed separately in Chapters 3–5. While seeing moral metaphors as constituting a system, I applied a general source frame structure to all three subsystems. This frame structure contains three core elements linked in particular relations: i.e., a "human perceiver" is sensing an "entity property", which causes the "human perceiver" to feel an "affective valence", either positive or negative. According to this source frame analysis, the differences between the three subsystems merely lie in the three different sets of values that fill the role of "entity property" and that serve as source concepts of moral metaphors, conditioned by two environmental or ecological factors: situation and culture. The pairs of source concepts, with polar values, are generally perceived as being related, positively or negatively, to human physical wellbeing or illbeing. That is the reason why they are also related to human feeling, as being either good or bad. Feeling good (positive) or bad (negative) is the two alternative values of "affective valence", which in my analysis serve as the main meaning focuses of the moral metaphors, carried over from the source frame to the target frame by metaphorical mappings.

In Chapter 6, I focused on the nature of moral metaphors, applying DAMCA, a decompositional approach to metaphor analysis. This analytical approach is based on the distinction between primary and complex metaphor. On the basis of my decomposition analysis, I argued that the moral metaphors are not primary metaphors, but complex metaphors, because their target concepts MORAL and IMMORAL are not primary concepts. Instead, they are more complex subcategories of the primary concepts GOOD and BAD. More specifically, MORAL and IMMORAL are the two alternative values of moral valence, which are GOOD and BAD, the two alternative values of general, affective valence, applied to the more specific domain of MORALITY. In my decomposition analysis, GOOD and BAD are generic values underlying the specific moral valence values MORAL and IMMORAL, overlapping the values of affective valence and metaphorical main meaning focuses carried over by metaphorical mappings from the source frame.

Simply put, primary metaphors are metaphorical mappings between primary source and primary target concepts based on experiential correlations, namely, correlations between sensorimotor experience and subjective experience. In my analysis, however, primary source concepts, as a category, show prototype effects, that is, some of them are more basic or fundamental than others as primary concepts. Primary concepts and nonprimary concepts form a continuum, those in the middle of the gray area are less primary or nonprimary than those at both ends. The decomposition analysis attempts to account for their subtle differences.

According to primary metaphor theory (PMT), primary metaphors are basic metaphorical mechanisms and components for the construction of more complex metaphors. More complex conceptualizations that are metaphorical in nature can be decomposed as containing primary metaphors. My decomposition analysis showed, however, that there may be "pre-metaphors", which have the potential to become full-fledged primary metaphors because they link two primary concepts based on some sort of experiential correlation. As such, they may still be underlying more complex metaphorical conceptualizations without independent linguistic or multimodal evidence for their status as primary metaphors. Besides, what is perhaps more commonly seen is that individual instances of linguistic metaphor can be analyzed as having emerged from different primary metaphors. There is a need for further research on these aspects. Chapter 6 also showed how the three subsystems of moral metaphors are coherent with one another and unify into one whole system. That chapter discussed visual and multimodal manifestations of moral metaphors as well.

In this final chapter, I first laid out the complete mappings between the source and the target frame. The target frame, as laid out in Figure 7.1, has a similar topological or image-schematic structure as the source. It also comprises three core elements linked in similar relations: i.e., a "moral judger" notices some "human behavior", which causes the "moral judger" to judge the behavior as being either moral or immoral. And MORAL and IMMORAL are the two alternative values of "moral valence", which serve as target concepts of moral metaphors. The general frame analysis characterizes the two frames as sharing the same topological or image-schematic structure. Moral metaphors map the source-domain frame structure onto the target-domain frame structure in a way that is consistent with the latter structure. What cannot be mapped from the source frame to the target frame is "affective valence", because affective valence (good and bad) and moral valence (moral and immoral) do not belong to different conceptual categories or domains; rather, the latter is a subcategory of the former. The target frame has to preserve MORAL and IMMORAL as target concepts of moral metaphors. This can be seen as CMT's Invariance Principle remolded in the frame analysis of conceptual metaphors, an extended version of Invariance Principle in which topological structure refers to not only image-schema structure but also frame structure.

In this final chapter, I have also looked beyond the moral metaphor system, addressing the issues concerning the three-level phenomena of conceptual metaphors (see Figure 7.2). The issues pertain to the relationship between the experiential level (i.e., body and culture constituting experiential basis), the conceptual level (i.e., conceptual patterns and structures in conceptual system), and the linguistic level (i.e., linguistic expressions and patterns in language use). CMT sees the relationship as a "one-way traffic" going bottom-up, i.e., the interaction between body and culture at the experiential level gives rise to metaphors at the conceptual level in the conceptual system, and conceptual metaphors are manifested by metaphorical expressions at the linguistic level of communication with language. I do not disagree about these general causal relations from experiential to conceptual to linguistic level. I believe that this general direction of causal development holds from a historical and evolutional perspective. Nevertheless, I want to emphasize "the other direction of traffic", though not as heavy, in the causal relationships, first, between language and thought, and, second, between language and culture. That is, language can actually influence thought and culture.

Specifically, in the first aspect, our language use does not just reflect, it also affects our thinking and understanding of reality and our experience in and with it. To demonstrate this, I have discussed two salient Chinese cases of cultural conceptualization as part of cultural cognition: the "social face" and the "cognitive and affective heart". The face is construed as the locus of dignity and prestige, and the heart as the cognitive and affective center of a human person. Undoubtedly, these two cultural conceptualizations are part of the cognitive heritage that has been passed down from generation to generation through the long history of Chinese cultural tradition, but the carrier of that heritage is the Chinese language. For individual Chinese speakers in each generation, they inherit that cognitive heritage by learning and using the Chinese language. My corpus-based study of qualitative and quantitative data—with regard to the variety of types and frequency of tokens, and with a reference point from English—strongly supports the claim that people think about reality the way they talk about it. That is, linguistic experience with salient linguistic patterns plays a crucial role in the formation of conceptual patterns in individual speakers' conceptual systems.

Indeed, the influence of language on thought may have been overlooked by CMT when it stressed linguistic manifestation of metaphorical thought. In talking about the complex relationship between metaphorical language and thought, Gibbs (2017: 145) argues that the reality of human experience suggests that "metaphorical cognition and communication are tightly coupled", and that we should not neglect "the guiding force of metaphorical language" in metaphorical thought or "the mutuality between thought and language" in general. There has been growing attention to the possibility of conventional conceptual patterns being inherited, from generation to generation, through the inheritance of conventionalized linguistic patterns, as well as the role of speakers' linguistic experience, in conjunction and interaction with their bodily and cultural experience, in metaphorical conceptualization and human cognition. My corpus-based study adds more weight to this view.

The second aspect that I have studied about "two-way traffic" is the influence of language on culture, or the influence of linguistic experience on cultural experience. In this chapter, I have studied how linguistic expressions can motivate and inspire the creation of cultural artefacts. Comparative searches in two image databases, namely English-based Google Images and Chinese-based Baidu Images, led to the following initial findings. First, parallel relations were found between popular linguistic expressions and visual or multimodal images in both databases. Second, if equivalent linguistic expressions exist in both languages, corresponding visual or multimodal images can be found in both databases. Third, if a particular linguistic expression exists in one but not in the other language, corresponding visual or multimodal images exist in the database of that language, but not in the database of the other language. Fourth, exceptions tend to be "borrowings" imported from one database into the other. These findings, while in need of further research for confirmation, suggest that linguistic experience using popular linguistic expressions can cause changes in cultural experience with the creation of cultural artefacts. Since cultural experience and bodily experience both participate in the formation of conceptual patterns, change in culture, resulting from language use, should eventually affect metaphorical thought as well.

As shown in Figure 7.2, there are two loops in the circular relationship between language, thought, and culture, a smaller one and a larger one. The smaller one goes up from thought to language and comes back down to thought. The larger one goes from the interaction between body and culture up to thought, and then from thought further up to language, and then comes back down to culture. Such are the dynamics of the interaction between body and culture, and language and thought, and their crossover. How to measure the forces in one way or another is a matter for further research.

References

Abdel-Raheem, Ahmed. 2014. The JOURNEY metaphor and moral political cognition. *Pragmatics and Cognition* 22(3): 373–401.

Adams, Francis M. and Charles E. Osgood. 1973. A cross-cultural study of the affective meanings of color. *Journal of Cross-Cultural Psychology* 4(2): 135–156.

Aksan, Yeşim and Dilek Kantar. 2008. No wellness feels better than this sickness: Love metaphors from a cross-cultural perspective. *Metaphor and Symbol* 23(4): 262–291.

Aldokhayel, Reyadh. 2008. *The Event Structure Metaphor: The case of Arabic.* Doctoral dissertation, Ball State University, Muncie, Indiana.

Arcimavičienė, Liudmila. 2007. Moral strength metaphor in Lithuanian virtual political discourse. *Respectus Philologicus* 11(16): 136–144.

Austin, Sue. 2013. Spatial metaphors and somatic communication: The embodiment of multigenerational experiences of helplessness and futility in an obese patient. *Journal of Analytical Psychology* 58(3): 327–346.

Banerjee, Pronobesh, Promothesh Chatterjee, and Jayati Sinha. 2012. Is it light or dark? Recalling moral behavior changes perception of brightness. *Psychological Science* 23(4): 407–409.

Barcelona, Antonio (ed.). 2000a. *Metaphor and metonymy at the crossroads: A cognitive perspective.* Berlin: Mouton de Gruyter.

Barcelona, Antonio. 2000b. On the plausibility of claiming a metonymic motivation for conceptual metaphor. In Antonio Barcelona (ed.), *Metaphor and metonymy at the crossroads: A cognitive perspective*, 31–58. Berlin: Mouton de Gruyter.

Basson, Alec. 2011. The path image schema as underlying structure for the metaphor *Moral Life is a Journey* in Psalm. *Old Testament Essays* 24(1): 19–29.

Baumeister, Roy F. and Julie Juola Exline. 1999. Virtue, personality, and social relations: Self-control as the moral muscle. *Journal of Personality* 67(6): 1165–1194.

Baumeister, Roy F. and Julie Juola Exline. 2000. Self-control, morality, and human strength. *Journal of Social and Clinical Psychology* 19(1): 29–42.

Bennardo, Giovanni and Victor C. de Munck. 2014. *Cultural models: Genesis, methods, and experiences.* Oxford: Oxford University Press.

Berdayes, Vicente, Luigi Esposito, and John W. Murphy (eds.). 2004. *The body in human inquiry: Interdisciplinary explorations of embodiment.* Cresskill, NJ: Hampton Press.

Bougher, Lori D. 2012. The case for metaphor in political reasoning and cognition. *Political Psychology* 33(1): 145–163.

Bourk, Michael and Kate Holland. 2014. From silos to flows: Spatial metaphor and communication responses to the Christchurch earthquakes. *Australian Journal of Emergency Management* 29(2): 35–41.

Bradshaw, Cleo. 2011. *Soul-shaping: Spatial metaphors in the development of subjectivity in Plato.* Doctoral dissertation, York University, Toronto.

Brandt, Mark J., Hans IJzerman and Irene Blanken. 2014. Does recalling moral behavior change the perception of brightness? A replication and meta-analysis of Banerjee, Chatterjee, and Sinha (2012). *Social Psychology* 45(3): 246–252.

Brenzinger, Matthias and Iwona Kraska-Szlenk (eds.). 2014. *The body in language: Comparative studies of linguistic embodiment*. Leiden: Brill.

Bromme, Rainer and Elmar Stahl. 1999. Spatial metaphors and writing hypertexts: Study within schools. *European Journal of Psychology of Education* 14(2): 267–281.

Brown, Michael. 2006. A geographer reads *Geography Club*: Spatial metaphor and metonym in textual/sexual space. *Cultural Geographies* 13(3): 313–339.

Burgard, Peter J. 1987. Lessing's tragic topography: The rejection of society and its spatial metaphor in *Philotas*. *Deutsche Vierteljahrsschrift für Literaturwissenschaft und Geistesgeschichte* 61(3): 441–456.

Cady, Duane L. 2005. *Moral vision: How everyday life shapes ethical thinking*. Lanham, MD: Rowman & Littlefield.

Cameron, Lynne and Graham Low (eds.). 1999. *Researching and applying metaphor*. Cambridge: Cambridge University Press.

Cameron, Lynne and Graham Low. 2011. Metaphor and social world: Introduction to the first issue. *Metaphor and the Social World* 1(1): 1–5.

Campbell, Courtney S. 2013. Metaphors we ration by: An interpretation of practical moral reasoning. *Soundings: An Interdisciplinary Journal* 96(3): 254–279.

Carruthers, Peter. 2018. Valence and value. *Philosophy and Phenomenological Research* 97(3): 658–680.

Casasanto, Daniel. 2008. Similarity and proximity: When does close in space mean close in mind? *Memory & Cognition* 36(6): 1047–1056.

Casasanto, Daniel. 2009a. Embodiment of abstract concepts: Good and bad in right- and left-handers. *Journal of Experimental Psychology. General* 138(3): 351–356.

Casasanto, Daniel. 2009b. When is a linguistic metaphor a conceptual metaphor? In Vyvyan Evans and Stéphanie Pourcel (eds.), *New directions in cognitive linguistics*, 127–145. Amsterdam: John Benjamins.

Casasanto, Daniel. 2010. Space for thinking. In Vyvyan Evans and Paul Chilton (eds.), *Language, cognition, and space: The state of the art and new directions*, 453–478. London: Equinox.

Casasanto, Daniel. 2013. Development of metaphorical thinking: The role of language. In Mike Borkent, Barbara Dancygier, and Jennifer Hinnell (eds.), *Language and the creative mind*, 3–18. Stanford, CA: Center for the Study of Language and Information Publications.

Casasanto, Daniel. 2014. Bodily relativity. In Lawrence Shapiro (ed.), *The Routledge handbook of embodied cognition*, 108–117. New York: Routledge.

Casasanto, Daniel. 2016. Linguistic relativity. In Nick Riemer (ed.), *The Routledge handbook of semantics*, 158–174. New York: Routledge.

Casasanto, Daniel. 2017. Relationships between language and cognition. In Barbara Dancygier (ed.), *The Cambridge handbook of cognitive linguistics*, 19–37. Cambridge: Cambridge University Press.

Casasanto, Daniel and Roberto Bottini. 2014. Spatial language and abstract concepts. *Wiley Interdisciplinary Reviews: Cognitive Science* 5(2): 139–149.

Casasanto, Daniel and Katinka Dijkstra. 2010. Motor action and emotional memory. *Cognition* 115(1): 179–185.

Chen, Rui, Jiao Sai, Qi Zhu, Renlai Zhou, Peng Li, and Shunchao He. 2018. Horizontal spatial metaphor for morality: A cross-cultural study of Han Chinese students and ethnic minority Hui students in China. *Frontiers in Psychology* 9: 1145.

Chiou, Wen-Bin and Ying-Yao Cheng. 2013. In broad daylight, we trust in God! Brightness, the salience of morality, and ethical behavior. *Journal of Environmental Psychology* 36: 37–42.

Chow, Rosalind M., Larissa Z. Tiedens, and Cassandra L. Govan. 2008. Excluded emotions: The role of anger in antisocial responses to ostracism. *Journal of Experimental Social Psychology* 44(3): 896–903.

Cienki, Alan. 1998. STRAIGHT: An image schema and its metaphorical extensions. *Cognitive Linguistics* 9(2): 107–149.

Cienki, Alan and Cornelia Müller (eds.). 2008. *Metaphor and gesture*. Amsterdam: John Benjamins.

Coeckelbergh, Mark. 2010. Engineering good: How engineering metaphors help us to understand the moral life and change society. *Science and Engineering Ethics* 16(2): 371–385.

Conrad, Peter. 1994. Wellness as virtue: Morality and the pursuit of health. *Culture, Medicine and Psychiatry* 18(3): 385–401.

Courte, Lisa J. 1998. *Engaging the moral imagination through metaphor: Implications for moral education*. M.A. thesis, McGill University.

Craddock, Susan. 1995. Sewers and scapegoats: Spatial metaphors of smallpox in nine-teenth century San Francisco. *Social Science and Medicine* 41(7): 957–968.

Crawford, L. Elizabeth. 2009. Conceptual metaphors of affect. *Emotion Review* 1(2): 129–139.

Crawford, L. Elizabeth, Skye M. Margolies, John T. Drake, and Meghan E. Murphy. 2006. Affect biases memory of location: Evidence for the spatial representation of affect. *Cognition and Emotion* 20(8): 1153–1169.

Croft, William and D. Alan Cruse. 2004. *Cognitive linguistics*. Cambridge: Cambridge University Press.

Cronin, Kieran. 1995. Illness, sin and metaphor. *Irish Theological Quarterly* 61(3/4): 191–204.

Csordas, Thomas J. (ed.). 1994. *Embodiment and experience: The existential ground of culture and self*. Cambridge: Cambridge University Press.

Cuccio, Valentina. 2015. Embodied simulation and metaphors: On the role of the body in the interpretation of bodily-based metaphors. *Epistemologia* 38: 97–112.

Cuervo, Hernán and Johanna Wyn. 2014. Reflections on the use of spatial and relational metaphors in youth studies. *Journal of Youth Studies* 17(7): 901–915.

D'Andrade, Roy G. 1989. Cultural cognition. In Michael I. Posner (ed.), *Foundations of cognitive science*, 795–830. Cambridge, MA: MIT Press.

Damasio, Antonio R. 1994. *Descartes' error: Emotion, reason, and the human brain*. New York: Putnam.

Dancygier, Barbara and Eve Sweetser. 2014. *Figurative language*. Cambridge: Cambridge University Press.

Daniel, Amanda Cooksey. 2010. *Immorality-blackness associations and the moral-purity metaphor in African Americans*. M.S. thesis, Tennessee State University.

David, Oana, George Lakoff, and Elise Stickles. 2016. Cascades in metaphor and grammar: A case study of metaphors in the gun debate. *Constructions and Frames* 8(2): 214–255.

Davies, Catherine. 2004. Spanish-American interiors: Spatial metaphors, gender and modernity. *Romance Studies* 22(1): 27–39.

Deignan, Alice. 2005. *Metaphor and corpus linguistics*. Amsterdam: John Benjamins.

Denham, Alison E. 2000. *Metaphor and moral experience*. Oxford: Clarendon Press.

Denke, Claudia, Michael Rotte, Hans-Jocken Heinze, and Michael Schaefer. 2016. Lying and subsequent desire for toothpaste: Activity in the somatosensory cortex predicts embodiment of the moral-purity metaphor. *Cerebral Cortex* 26(2): 477–484.

De la Fuente, Juanma, Daniel Casasanto, Antonio Román, and Julio Santiago. 2015. Can culture influence body-specific associations between space and valence? *Cognitive Science* 39(4): 821–832.

De Vega, Manuel, Arthur M. Glenberg, and Arthur C. Graesser (eds.). 2008. *Symbols and embodiment: Debates on meaning and cognition*. Oxford: Oxford University Press.

Diekema, Douglas S. 1989. Metaphors, medicine, and morals. *Soundings: An Interdisciplinary Journal* 72(1): 17–24.

DiMaggio, Paul. 1997. Culture and cognition. *Annual Review of Sociology* 23(1): 263–287.

Dion, Karen, Ellen Berscheid, and Elaine Walster. 1972. What is beautiful is good. *Journal of Personality and Social Psychology* 24(3): 285–290.

Dirven, René and Ralf Pörings (eds.). 2002. *Metaphor and metonymy in comparison and contrast*. Berlin: Mouton de Gruyter.

Dirven, René and John R. Taylor. 1988. The conceptualization of vertical space in English: The case of *tall*. In Brygida Rudzka-Ostyn (ed.), *Topics in cognitive linguistics*, 379–402. Amsterdam: John Benjamins.

Dodge, Ellen. 2016. A deep semantic corpus-based approach to metaphor analysis: A case study of metaphoric conceptualizations of poverty. *Constructions and Frames* 8(2): 256–294.

Dodge, Ellen, Jisup Hong, and Elise Stickles. 2015. MetaNet: Deep semantic automatic metaphor analysis. In Ekaterina Shutova, Beata Beigman Klebanov, and Patricia Lichtenstein (eds.), *Proceedings of the third workshop on metaphor in NLP*, 40–49. Stroudsburg, PA: Association for Computational Linguistics.

Dodge, Ellen and George Lakoff. 2005. Image schemas: From linguistic analysis to neural grounding. In Beate Hampe (ed.), *From perception to meaning: Image schemas in cognitive linguistics*, 57–91. Berlin: Mouton de Gruyter.

Dong, Ping, Xun Huang, and Chen-Bo Zhong. 2015. Ray of hope: Hopelessness increases preferences for brighter lighting. *Social Psychological and Personality Science* 6(1): 84–91.

Eagly, Alice H., Richard D. Ashmore, Mona G. Makhijani, and Laura C. Longo. 1991. What is beautiful is good, but...: A meta-analytic review of research on the physical attractiveness stereotype. *Psychological Bulletin* 110(1): 109–128.

Efrain, Michael G. and E. W. J. Patterson. 1974. Voters vote beautiful: The effect of physical appearance on a national election. *Canadian Journal of Behavioral Science / Revue Canadienne des Sciences du Comportement* 6(4): 352–356.

El-Sawad, Amal. 2005. Becoming a lifer? Unlocking career through metaphor. *Journal of Occupational and Organizational Psychology* 78(1): 23–41.

Erickson, Thane M. and James L. Abelson. 2012. Even the downhearted may be uplifted: Moral elevation in the daily life of clinically depressed and anxious adults. *Journal of Social and Clinical Psychology* 31(7): 707–728.

Evans, Vyvyan. 2019. *Cognitive linguistics: A complete guide*. Edinburgh: Edinburgh University Press.

Feldman, Jerome A. 2006. *From molecule to metaphor: A neural theory of language*. Cambridge, MA: MIT press.

Ferentzy, Peter and Nigel E. Turner. 2012. Morals, medicine metaphors, and the history of the disease model of problem gambling. *Journal of Gambling Issues* 27: DOI: http://dx.doi.org/10.4309/jgi.2012.27.4

Fesmire, Steven. 1999. Morality as art: Dewey, metaphor, and moral imagination. *Transactions of the Charles S. Peirce Society* 35(3): 527–550.

Fesmire, Steven. 2003. *John Dewey and moral imagination: Pragmatism in ethics.* Bloomington, IN: Indiana University Press.

Feyaerts, Kurt. 2000. Refining the Inheritance Hypothesis: Interaction between metaphoric and metonymic hierarchies. In Antonio Barcelona (ed.), *Metaphor and metonymy at the crossroads: A cognitive perspective*, 59–78. Berlin: Mouton de Gruyter.

Fillmore, Charles J. 1975. An alternative to checklist theories of meaning. *Proceedings of the first annual meeting of the Berkeley Linguistics Society*, 123–131. Berkeley, CA: Berkeley Linguistics Society.

Fillmore, Charles J. 2006. Frame semantics. In Dirk Geeraerts (ed.), *Cognitive linguistics: Basic readings*, 273–400. Berlin: Walter de Gruyter.

Fishbach, Ayelet and Aparna A. Labroo. 2007. Be better or be merry: How mood affects self-control. *Journal of Personality and Social Psychology* 93(2): 158–173.

Forceville, Charles. 2011. The journey metaphor and the source-path-goal schema in Agnès Varda's autobiographical gleaning documentaries. In Monika Fludernik (ed.), *Beyond cognitive metaphor theory: Perspectives on literary metaphor*, 281–297. London: Routledge.

Forceville, Charles. 2017. Visual and multimodal metaphor in advertising: Cultural perspectives. *Styles of Communication* 9(2): 26–41.

Forceville, Charles and Thijs Renckens. 2013. The GOOD IS LIGHT and BAD IS DARK metaphor in feature films. *Metaphor and the Social World* 3(2): 160–179.

Forceville, Charles and Eduardo Urios-Aparisi (eds.): 2009. *Multimodal metaphor.* Berlin: Mouton de Gruyter.

Frank, Roslyn M. 2015. A future agenda for research on language and culture. In Farzad Sharifian (ed.), *The Routledge handbook of language and culture*, 227–239. London: Routledge.

Frank, Roslyn M., René Dirven, Tom Ziemke, and Enrique Bernárdez (eds.). 2008. *Body, language and mind: Sociocultural situatedness* (Vol. 2). Berlin: Mouton de Gruyter.

Fuller, Robert C. 2000. *Stairways to heaven: Drugs in American religious history.* Boulder, CO: Westview Press.

Fusaroli, Riccardo and Simone Morgagni (eds.). 2009. Conceptual metaphor theory: Thirty years after. [Special issue]. *Cognitive Semiotics* 5(1/2).

Gallagher, Shaun. 2005. *How the body shapes the mind.* Oxford: Oxford University Press.

Gallese, Vittorio and George Lakoff. 2005. The brain's concepts: The role of sensory-motor system in conceptual knowledge. *Cognitive Neuropsychology* 22(3/4): 455–479.

Gattis, Merideth (ed.). 2001. *Spatial schemas and abstract thought.* Cambridge, MA: MIT Press.

Gattis, Merideth. 2002. Structure mapping in spatial reasoning. *Cognitive Development* 17(2): 1157–1183.

Geeraerts, Dirk and Hubert Cuyckens (eds.). 2007. *The Oxford handbook of cognitive linguistics.* Oxford: Oxford University Press.

Gibbs, Raymond W. 1994. *The poetic mind: Figurative thought, language, and understanding.* Cambridge: Cambridge University Press.

Gibbs, Raymond W. 1999. Taking metaphor out of our heads and putting it into the cultural world. In Raymond W. Gibbs and Gerard J. Steen (eds.), *Metaphor in cognitive linguistics*, 146–166. Amsterdam: John Benjamins.

Gibbs, Raymond W. 2006. *Embodiment and cognitive science*. Cambridge: Cambridge University Press.

Gibbs, Raymond W. 2007. Why cognitive linguists should care more about empirical methods. In Monica Gonzalez-Marquez, Irene Mittelberg, Seana Coulson, and Michael J. Spivey (eds.), *Methods in cognitive linguistics*, 2–18. Amsterdam: John Benjamins.

Gibbs, Raymond W. (ed.). 2008. *The Cambridge handbook of metaphor and thought*. Cambridge: Cambridge University Press.

Gibbs, Raymond W. 2009. Why do some people dislike conceptual metaphor theory? *Cognitive Semiotics* 5(1/2): 14–36.

Gibbs, Raymond W. 2011. Evaluating conceptual metaphor theory. *Discourse Processes* 48(8): 529–562.

Gibbs, Raymond W. 2013a. Walking the walk while thinking about the talk: Embodied interpretation of metaphorical narratives. *Journal of Psycholinguistic Research* 42(4): 363–378.

Gibbs, Raymond W. 2013b. Does conceptual metaphor emerge from metaphorical language? *Journal of Cognitive Science* 14: 319–334.

Gibbs, Raymond W. 2014. Conceptual metaphor in thought and social action. In Mark J. Landau, Michael D. Robinson, and Brian P. Meier (eds.), *The power of metaphor: Examining its influence on social life*, 17–40. Washington, DC: American Psychological Association.

Gibbs, Raymond W. 2015. Counting metaphors: What does this reveal about language and thought? *Cognitive Semantics* 1(2): 155–177.

Gibbs, Raymond W. 2017. *Metaphor wars: Conceptual metaphors in human life*. Cambridge: Cambridge University Press.

Gibbs, Raymond W. 2020. My great life with "Metaphor and Symbol". *Metaphor and Symbol* 35(1): 1.

Gibbs, Raymond W. and Herbert L. Colston. 1995. The cognitive psychological reality of image schemas and their transformations. *Cognitive Linguistics* 6(4): 347–378.

Gibbs, Raymond W., Jessica J. Gould, and Michael Andric. 2006. Imagining metaphorical actions: Embodied simulations make the impossible plausible. *Imagination, Cognition and Personality* 25(3): 221–238.

Giessner, Steffen R. and Thomas W. Schubert. 2007. High in the hierarchy: How vertical location and judgments of leaders' power are interrelated. *Organizational Behavior and Human Decision Processes* 104(1): 30–44.

Gillan, Douglas J. 1995. Visual arithmetic, computational graphics, and the spatial metaphor. *Human Factors* 37(4): 766–780.

Glucksberg, Sam and Matthew S. McGlone. 1999. When love is not a journey: What metaphors mean. *Journal of Pragmatics* 31(12): 1541–1558.

Gow, Gordon. 2001. Spatial metaphor in the work of Marshall McLuhan. *Canadian Journal of Communication* 26(4): 63–80.

Gozli, Davood G., Penelope Lockwood, Alison L. Chasteen, and Jay Pratt. 2018. Spatial metaphors in thinking about other people. *Visual Cognition* 26(5): 313–333.

Grady, Joseph E. 1997a. *Foundation of meaning: Primary metaphors and primary scenes*. Doctoral dissertation, University of California at Berkeley.

Grady, Joseph E. 1997b. THEORIES ARE BUILDINGS revisited. *Cognitive Linguistics* 8(4): 267–290.

Grady, Joseph E. 1999. A typology of motivation for conceptual metaphors: Correlations vs. resemblance. In Raymond W. Gibbs and Gerard J. Steen (eds.), *Metaphor in cognitive linguistics*, 79–100. Amsterdam: John Benjamins.

Grady, Joseph E. 2005. Primary metaphors as inputs to conceptual integration. *Journal of Pragmatics* 37(10): 1595–1614.

Grady, Joseph E. and Giorgio A. Ascoli. 2017. Sources and targets in primary metaphor theory: Looking back and thinking ahead. In Beate Hampe (ed.), *Metaphor: Embodied cognition and discourse*, 27–45. Cambridge: Cambridge University Press.

Grady, Joseph E. and Christopher Johnson. 2002. Converging evidence for the notions of *subscene* and *primary scene*. In René Dirven and Ralf Pörings (eds.), *Metaphor and metonymy in comparison and contrast*, 533–554. Berlin: Mouton de Gruyter.

Graf, Eva-Maria. 2011. Adolescents' use of spatial TIME metaphors: A matter of cognition or sociocommunicative practice? *Journal of Pragmatics* 43(3): 723–734.

Gross, Alan E. and Christine Crofton. 1977. What is good is beautiful. *Sociometry* 40(1): 85–90.

Haggerty, Donald F. 1997. Friendship: A metaphor for moral advancement? *New Blackfriars* 78: 291–300.

Haidt, Jonathan. 2001. The emotional dog and its rational tail: A social intuitionist approach to moral Judgment. *Psychological Review* 108(4): 814–834.

Haidt, Jonathan and Selin Kesebir. 2010. Morality. In Susan T. Fiske, Daniel T. Gilbert, and Gardner Lindzey (eds.), *Handbook of social psychology* (Vol. 2), 797–832. Hoboken, NJ: John Wiley & Sons.

Haidt, Jonathan, Silvia Helena Koller, and Maria G. Dias. 1993. Affect, culture, and morality, or Is it wrong to eat your dog? *Journal of Personality and Social Psychology* 65(4): 613–628.

Haidt, Jonathan, Paul Rozin, Clark MaCauley, and Sumio Imada. 1997. Body, psyche, and culture: The relationship between disgust and morality. *Psychology and Developing Societies* 9(1): 107–131.

Halloran-Bessy, Marianne. 2009. Spatial metaphors and identity formation in Pham Van Ky's Frères de Sang. *The French Review* 82(4): 762–772.

Hampe, Beate (ed.). 2005. *From perception to meaning: Image schemas in cognitive linguistics*. Berlin: Mouton de Gruyter.

Hampe, Beate (ed.). 2017. *Metaphor: Embodied cognition and discourse*. Cambridge: Cambridge University Press.

Hanne, Michael. 2015. Diagnosis and metaphor. *Perspectives in Biology and Medicine* 58(1): 35–52.

Hargett, James M. 2006. *Stairway to heaven: A journey to the summit of Mount Emei*. Albany, NY: SUNY Press.

Harley, David N. 1993. Medical metaphors in English moral theology, 1560–1660. *Journal of the History of Medicine and Allied Sciences* 48(4): 396–435.

Harms, Peter D. and Seth M. Spain. 2015. Beyond the bright side: Dark personality at work. *Applied Psychology* 64(1): 15–24.

Haser, Verena. 2005. *Metaphor, metonymy, and experientialist philosophy: Challenging cognitive semantics*. Berlin: Mouton de Gruyter.

Hassin, Ran and Yaacov Trope. 2007. Facing faces: Studies on the cognitive aspects of physiognomy. *Journal of Personality and Social Psychology* 78(5): 837–852.

Heine, Bernd. 1997. *Cognitive foundations of grammar*. Oxford: Oxford University Press.

Helzer, Erik G. and David A. Pizarro. 2011. Dirty liberals! Reminders of physical cleanliness influence moral and political attitudes. *Psychological Science* 22(4): 517–522.

Hill, Patrick L. and Daniel K. Lapsley. 2009. The ups and downs of the moral personality: Why it's not so black and white. *Journal of Research in Personality* 43(3): 520–523.

Holland, Dorothy and Naomi Quinn (eds). 1987. *Cultural models in language and thought.* Cambridge: Cambridge University Press.

Holman, Mirya R. 2016. Gender, political rhetoric, and moral metaphors in state of the city address. *Urban Affairs Review* 52(4): 501–530.

Howe, Bonnie. 2006. *Because you bear this name: Conceptual metaphor and the moral meaning of 1 Peter.* Leiden: Brill.

Howell, Mark, Steve Love and Mark Turner. 2005. Spatial metaphors for a speech-based mobile city guide service. *Personal and Ubiquitous Computing* 9(1): 32–45.

Huang, Zhenwei, Wenwen Zheng, Xuyun Tan, Xiaoxiao Zhang, and Li Liu. 2016. Polluted air increases perceived corruption. *Journal of Pacific Rim Psychology* 10: e13 (pp. 1–11). DOI:10.1017/prp.2016.10

Hyatt, Betty Delay. 1984. *The functions of spatial metaphors in three narrative works by Nathalie Sarraute.* Doctoral dissertation, Ohio State University, Columbus, OH.

Ibarretxe-Antuñano, Iraide. 2002. Mind-as-body as a cross-linguistic conceptual metaphor. *Miscelánea: A Journal of English and American Studies* 25(1): 93–119.

Ignatow, Gabriel. 2009. Culture and embodied cognition: Moral discourses in internet support groups for overeaters. *Social Forces* 88(2): 643–669.

IJzerman, Hans and Gün R. Semin. 2010. Temperature perceptions as a ground for social proximity. *Journal of Experimental Social Psychology* 46(6): 867–873.

Inkson, Kerr. 2002. Thinking creatively about careers: The use of metaphor. In Maury Peiperl, Michael Bernard Arthur, Rob Goffee, and N. Anand (eds.), *Career creativity: Explorations in the remaking of work*, 15–34. Oxford: Oxford University Press.

Inkson, Kerr. 2004. Images of career: Nine key metaphors. *Journal of Vocational Behavior* 65(1): 96–111.

Jäkel, Olaf. 2002. Hypotheses revisited: The cognitive theory of metaphor applied to religious texts. *Metaphorik. de* 2(1): 20–42.

Janoff-Bulman, Ronnie, Sana Sheikh, and Sebastian Hepp. 2009. Proscriptive versus prescriptive morality: Two faces of moral regulation. *Journal of Personality and Social Psychology* 96(3): 521–537.

Jin, Lingxia. 2011. *Second language acquisition of spatial metaphors in English and Chinese writings: Insights from native and learner language corpora.* Doctoral dissertation, University of Arizona, Tucson, AZ.

Johnson, David J., Felix Cheung, and M. Brent Donnellan. 2014. Does cleanliness influence moral judgments? A direct replication of Schnall, Benton, and Harvey (2008). *Social Psychology* 45(3): 209–215.

Johnson, Mark. 1987. *The body in the mind: The bodily basis of meaning, imagination, and reason.* Chicago, IL: University of Chicago Press.

Johnson, Mark. 1993. *Moral imagination: Implications of cognitive science for ethics.* Chicago, IL: University of Chicago Press.

Johnson, Mark. 1995. Introduction: Why metaphor matters to philosophy. *Metaphor and Symbolic Activity* 10(3): 157–162.

Johnson, Mark. 1996. How moral psychology changes moral theory. In Larry May, Marilyn Friedman, and Andy Clark (eds.), *Mind and morals: Essays on cognitive science and ethics*, 45–68. Cambridge, MA: MIT Press.

Johnson, Mark. 2007. *The meaning of the body: Aesthetics of human understanding.* Chicago, IL: University of Chicago Press.

Johnson, Mark. 2014. *Morality for humans: Ethical understanding from the perspective of cognitive science.* Chicago, IL: University of Chicago Press.

Johnson, Mark. 2017. *Embodied mind, meaning, and reason: How our bodies give rise to understanding.* Chicago, IL: University of Chicago Press.

Johnson, Mark and Tim Rohrer. 2007. We are live creatures: Embodiment, American pragmatism and the cognitive organism. In Tom Ziemke, Jordan Zlatev, and Roslyn M. Frank (eds.), *Body, language and mind: Embodiment* (Vol. 1), 17–54. Berlin: Mouton de Gruyter.

Kennedy, John M., Chang Hong Liu, Bradford F. Challis, and Victor Kennedy. 2003. Form symbolism across languages: Danish, Slovene, and Japanese. In Cornelia Zelinsky-Wibbelt (ed.), *Text, context, concepts*, 221–239. Berlin: Mouton de Gruyter.

Kertész, András and Csilla Rákosi. 2009. Cyclic vs. circular argumentation in the Conceptual Metaphor Theory. *Cognitive Linguistics* 20(4): 703–732.

King, Robert Thomas. 1988. Spatial metaphor in German causative constructions. In Brygida Rudzka-Ostyn (ed.), *Topics in cognitive linguistics*, 555–585. Amsterdam: John Benjamins.

Klaassen, Johann Albert. 1998. *Moral emotion and moral understanding: Guilt, shame, regret, and the metaphor of moral taint.* Doctoral dissertation, Washington University in Saint Louis, MO.

Koller, Veronika. 2005. Critical discourse analysis and social cognition: Evidence from business media discourse. *Discourse and Society* 16(2): 199–224.

Kövecses, Zoltán. 2000. *Metaphor and emotion: Language, culture, and body in human feeling.* Cambridge: Cambridge University Press.

Kövecses, Zoltán. 2005. *Metaphor in culture: Universality and variation.* Cambridge: Cambridge University Press.

Kövecses, Zoltán. 2006. *Language, mind, and culture: A practical introduction.* Oxford: Oxford University Press.

Kövecses, Zoltán. 2008. Conceptual metaphor theory: Some criticisms and alternative proposals. *Annual Review of Cognitive Linguistics* 6(1): 168–184.

Kövecses, Zoltán. 2010. *Metaphor: A practical introduction* (2nd ed.). Oxford: Oxford University Press.

Kövecses, Zoltán. 2013. The metaphor-metonymy relationship: Correlation metaphors are based on metonymy. *Metaphor and Symbol* 28(2): 75–88.

Kövecses, Zoltán. 2015a. *Where metaphors come from: Reconsidering context in metaphor.* Oxford: Oxford University Press.

Kövecses, Zoltán. 2015b. Surprise as a conceptual category. *Review of Cognitive Linguistics* 13(2): 270–290.

Kövecses, Zoltán. 2017a. Levels of metaphor. *Cognitive Linguistics* 28(2): 321–347.

Kövecses, Zoltán. 2017b. Conceptual metaphor theory. In Elana Semino and Zsótia Demjén (eds.), *The Routledge handbook of metaphor and language*, 13–27. London: Routledge.

Kövecses, Zoltán. 2020. *Extended conceptual metaphor theory.* Cambridge: Cambridge University Press.

Kövecses, Zoltán, Laura Ambrus, Dániel Hegedűs, Ren Imai, and Anna Sobczak. 2019. The lexical vs. corpus-based method in the study of metaphors. In Marianna Bolognesi, Mario Brdar, and Kristina Despot (eds.), *Metaphor and metonymy in the digital age: Theory and methods for building repositories of figurative language*, 149–173. Amsterdam: John Benjamins.

Kraska-Szlenk, Iwona (ed.). 2020. *Body part terms in conceptualization and language usage.* Amsterdam: John Benjamins.

Krois, John Michael, Mats Rosengren, Angela Steidele, and Dirk Westerkamp (eds.). 2007a. *Embodiment in cognition and culture.* Amsterdam: John Benjamins.

Krois, John Michael, Mats Rosengren, Angela Steidele, and Dirk Westerkamp. 2007b. Introduction. In John Michael Krois, Mats Rosengren, Angela Steidele, and Dirk Westerkamp (eds.), *Embodiment in cognition and culture,* xiii–xxii. Amsterdam: John Benjamins.

Lakens, Daniël. 2011. High skies and oceans deep: Polarity benefits or mental simulation? *Frontiers in Psychology* 2: 21. DOI: 10.3389/fpsyg.2011.00021

Lakens, Daniël. 2012. Polarity correspondence in metaphor congruency effects: Structural overlap predicts categorization times for bipolar concepts presented in vertical space. *Journal of Experimental Psychology* 38(3): 726–736.

Lakens, Daniël, Daniel A. Fockenberg, Karin P. H. Lemmens, Jaap Ham, and Cees J. H. Midden. 2013. Brightness differences influence the evaluation of affective pictures. *Cognition & Emotion* 27(7): 1225–1246.

Lakens, Daniël, Gün R. Semin, and Francesco Foroni. 2011. Why your highness needs the people: Comparing the absolute and relative representation of power in vertical space. *Social Psychology* 42(3): 205–213.

Lakens, Daniël, Gün R. Semin, and Francesco Foroni. 2012. But for the bad, there would not be good: Grounding valence in brightness through shared relational structures. *Journal of Experimental Psychology: General* 141(3): 584–594.

Lakoff, George. 1986. A figure of thought. *Metaphor and Symbolic Activity* 1(3): 215–225.

Lakoff, George. 1987a. *Women, fire, and dangerous things: What categories reveal about the mind.* Chicago, IL: University of Chicago Press.

Lakoff, George. 1987b. Foreword. In Mark Turner, *Death is the mother of beauty,* vii–x. Chicago, IL: University of Chicago Press.

Lakoff, George. 1993. The contemporary theory of metaphor. In Andrew Ortony (ed.), *Metaphor and thought* (2nd ed.), 202–251. Cambridge: Cambridge University Press.

Lakoff, George. 1996. *Moral politics: What conservatives know that liberals don't.* Chicago, IL: University of Chicago Press.

Lakoff, George. 2004. *Don't think of an elephant! Know your values and frame the debate.* White River Junction, VT: Chelsea Green Publishing.

Lakoff, George. 2006a. *Whose freedom? The battle over America's most important idea.* New York: Farrar, Straus and Giroux.

Lakoff, George. 2006b. *Thinking points: Communicating our American values and vision.* New York: Farrar, Straus and Giroux.

Lakoff, George. 2008a. The neural theory of metaphor. In Raymond. W. Gibbs (ed.), *The Cambridge handbook of metaphor and thought,* 17–38. Cambridge: Cambridge University Press.

Lakoff, George. 2008b. *The political mind: Why you can't understand 21st-century American politics with an 18th-century brain.* New York, NY: Viking.

Lakoff, George. 2012. Explaining embodied cognition results. *Topics in Cognitive Science* 4(4): 773–785.

Lakoff, George. 2014. Mapping the brain's metaphor circuitry: Metaphorical thought in everyday reason. *Frontiers in Human Neuroscience* 8: 1–14.

Lakoff, George. 2016. Preface. *Constructions and Frames* 8(2): 131–132.

Lakoff, George and Mark Johnson. 1980. *Metaphors we live by.* Chicago, IL: University of Chicago Press.

Lakoff, George and Mark Johnson. 1999. *Philosophy in the flesh: The embodied mind and its challenge to western thought.* New York: Basic Books.

Lakoff, George and Mark Johnson. 2003. Afterword. In George Lakoff and Mark Johnson, *Metaphors we live by* (with a new afterword), 239–276. Chicago, IL: University of Chicago Press.

Lakoff, George and Zoltán Kövecses. 1987. The cognitive model of anger inherent in American English. In Dorothy Holland and Naomi Quinn (eds.), *Cultural models in language and thought*, 195–221. Cambridge: Cambridge University Press.

Lakoff, George and Rafael Núñez. 2000. *Where mathematics comes from: How the embodied mind brings mathematics into being.* New York: Basic Books.

Lakoff, George and Mark Turner. 1989. *More than cool reason: A field guide to poetic metaphor.* Chicago, IL: University of Chicago Press.

Landau, Mark J. 2017. *Conceptual metaphor in social psychology: The poetics of everyday life.* London: Routledge.

Landau, Mark J., Brian P. Meier, and Lucas A. Keefer. 2010. A metaphor-enriched social cognition. *Psychological Bulletin* 136(6): 1045–1067.

Landau, Mark. J., Michael D. Robinson, and Brian P. Meier (eds.). 2014. *The power of metaphor: Examining its influence on social life.* Washington, DC: American Psychological Association.

Langacker, Ronald W. 1987. *Foundations of cognitive grammar: Theoretical prerequisites* (Vol. 1). Stanford, CA: Stanford University Press.

Langacker, Ronald W. 1991. *Foundations of cognitive grammar: Descriptive application* (Vol. 2). Stanford, CA: Stanford University Press.

Lee, Spike W. S. and Norbert Schwarz. 2010. Dirty hands and dirty mouths: Embodiment of the moral-purity metaphor is specific to the motor modality involved in moral transgression. *Psychological Science* 21(10): 1423–1425.

Lee, Spike W. S. and Norbert Schwarz. 2011. Wiping the slate clean: Psychological consequences of physical cleansing. *Current Directions in Psychological Science* 20(5): 307–311.

Lee, Spike W. S. and Norbert Schwarz. 2012. Bidirectionality, mediation, and moderation of metaphorical effects: The embodiment of social suspicion and fishy smells. *Journal of Personality and Social Psychology* 103(5): 737–749.

Leeman, Richard W. 1995. Spatial metaphors in African-American discourse. *Southern Journal of Communication* 60(2): 165–180.

Lemay, Edward P., Margaret S. Clark, and Aaron Greenberg. 2010. What is beautiful is good because what is beautiful is desired: Physical attractiveness stereotyping as projection of interpersonal goals. *Personality and Social Psychology Bulletin* 36(3): 339–353.

Levinson, Stephen C. 1996. Relativity in spatial conception and description. In John J. Gumperz and Stephen C. Levinson (eds.), *Rethinking linguistic relativity*, 177–202. Cambridge: Cambridge University Press.

Li, Heng and Yu Cao. 2017. Who's holding the moral higher ground: Religiosity and the vertical conception of morality. *Personality and Individual Differences* 106: 178–182.

Little, Anthony C., D. Michael Burt, and David I. Perrett. 2006. What is good is beautiful: Face preference reflects desired personality. *Personality and Individual Differences* 41(6): 1107–1118.

Littlemore, Jeannette. 2019. *Metaphors in the mind: Sources of variation in embodied metaphor.* Cambridge: Cambridge University Press.

Liu, Chang Hong. 1997. Symbols: Circles and spheres represent the same referents. *Metaphor and Symbol* 12(2): 135–147.

Lizardo, Omar. 2012. The conceptual bases of dirt and cleanliness in moral and non-moral reasoning. *Cognitive Linguistics* 23(2): 367–393.

Lomas, Tim. 2019. The spatial contours of wellbeing: A content analysis of metaphor in academic discourse. *The Journal of Positive Psychology* 14(3): 362–376.

Lorenzo, Genevieve L., Jeremy C. Biesanz, and Lauren J. Human. 2010. What is beautiful is good and more accurately understood: Physical attractiveness and accuracy in first impressions of personality. *Psychological Science* 21(12): 1777–1782.

Lu, Zhongyi, Lining Jia, and Dongxue Zhai. 2017. The mapping for vertical spatial metaphor of the moral concepts: Bidirectional and unbalanced. *Acta Psychologica Sinica* 49(2): 186–196.

Lynott, Dermot and Kenny Coventry. 2014. On the ups and downs of emotion: Testing between conceptual-metaphor and polarity accounts of emotional valence–spatial location interactions. *Psychonomic Bulletin and Review* 21(1): 218–226.

Maalej, Zouheir A. 2004. Figurative language in anger expressions in Tunisian Arabic: An extended view of embodiment. *Metaphor and Symbol* 19(1): 51–75.

Maalej, Zouheir A. 2008. The heart and cultural embodiment in Tunisian Arabic. In Farzad Sharifian, René Dirven, Ning Yu, and Susanne Niemeier (eds.), *Culture, body, and language: Conceptualizations of internal body organs across cultures and languages*, 395–428. Berlin: Mouton de Gruyter.

Maalej, Zouheir A. and Ning Yu (eds.). 2011. *Embodiment via body parts: Studies from various languages and cultures*. Amsterdam: John Benjamins.

Maasen, Sabine and Peter Weingart. 2000. *Metaphors and the dynamics of knowledge*. London: Routledge.

MacKay, Donald G. 1986. Prototypicality among metaphors: On the relative frequency of personification and spatial metaphors in literature written for children versus adults. *Metaphor and Symbolic Activity* 1(2): 87–107.

Martin, John Neil. 2008. The lover of the beautiful and the good: Platonic foundations of aesthetic and moral value. *Synthese* 165(1): 31–51.

Massengill, Rebekah Peeples. 2008. Prayers of the people: Moral metaphors in the right-to-life and faith-based labor movements. *Poetics* 36(5/6): 338–357.

May, Joshua. 2014. Does disgust influence moral judgment? *Australasian Journal of Philosophy* 92(1): 125–141.

McAdams, Dan P., Michelle Albaugh, Emily Farber, Jennifer Daniels, Regina L. Logan, and Brad Olson. 2008. Family metaphors and moral intuitions: How conservatives and liberals narrate their lives. *Journal of Personality and Social Psychology* 95(4): 978–990.

McGlone, Matthew S. 2007. What is the explanatory value of a conceptual metaphor? *Language & Communication* 27(2): 109–126.

Meier, Brian P. and Adam K. Fetterman. 2020. Metaphors for god: God is high, bright, and human in implicit tasks. *Psychology of Religion and Spirituality*. Advance online publication. http://dx.doi.org/10.1037/rel0000324

Meier, Brian P., David J. Hauser, Michael D. Robinson, Chris Kelland Friesen, and Katie Schjeldahl. 2007. What's "up" with God? Vertical space as a representation of the divine. *Journal of Personality and Social Psychology* 93(5): 699–710.

Meier, Brian P. and Michael D. Robinson. 2004. Why the sunny side is up: Associations between affect and vertical position. *Psychological Science* 15(4): 243–247.

Meier, Brian P. and Michael D. Robinson. 2005. The metaphorical representation of affect. *Metaphor and Symbol* 20(4): 239–257.

Meier, Brian P., Michael D. Robinson, and Andrew J. Caven. 2008. Why a big Mac is a good Mac: Associations between affect and size. *Basic and Applied Social Psychology* 30(1): 46–55.

Meier, Brian P., Michael D. Robinson, and Gerald L. Clore. 2004. Why good guys wear white: Automatic inferences about stimulus valence based on brightness. *Psychological Science* 15(2): 82–87.

Meier, Brian P., Michael D. Robinson, L. Elizabeth Crawford, and Whitney J. Ahlvers. 2007. When "light" and "dark" thoughts become light and dark responses: Affect biases brightness judgments. *Emotion* 7(2): 366–376.

Meier, Brian P., Martin Sellbom, and Dustin B. Wygant. 2007. Failing to take the moral high ground: Psychopathy and the vertical representation of morality. *Personality and Individual Differences* 43(4): 757–767.

Menéndez-Viso, Armando. 2009. Black and white transparency: Contradictions of a moral metaphor. *Ethics and Information Technology* 11(2): 155–162.

Moore, Kevin Ezra. 2017. Elaborating time in space: The structure and function of space-motion metaphors of time. *Language and Cognition* 9(2): 191–253.

Murphy, Gregory L. 1996. On metaphoric representation. *Cognition* 60(2): 173–204.

Nazar, Lonardo. 2015. Metaphor in language, discourse, and history: *Gieldan* and *Paien* in the medieval English religious use of the moral accounting metaphor. *Metaphor and the Social World* 5(1): 42–59.

Noonan, John T. Jr. 1988. The metaphors of morals. *Bulletin of the American Academy of Arts and Sciences* 42(2): 30–42.

Ortiz, María J. 2011. Primary metaphors and monomodal visual metaphors. *Journal of Pragmatics* 43(6): 1568–1580.

Pacilli, Maria Giuseppina, Stefano Pagliarot, Federica Spaccatini, Ilaria Giovannelli, Simona Sacchi, and Marco Brambilla. 2018. Straight to heaven: Rectitude as spatial representation of morality. *European Journal of Social Psychology* 48(5): 663–672.

Palmer, Susan J. 1989. AIDS as metaphor. *Society* 26(2): 44–50.

Panther, Klaus-Uwe and Günter Radden (eds.). 1999. *Metonymy in language and thought*. Amsterdam: John Benjamins.

Panther, Klaus-Uwe and Linda L. Thornburg (eds.). 2003. *Metonymy and Pragmatic Inferencing*. Amsterdam: John Benjamins.

Panther, Klaus-Uwe, Linda L. Thornburg, and Antonio Barcelona (eds.). 2009. *Metonymy and Metaphor in Grammar*. Amsterdam: John Benjamins.

Parret, Herman. 2011. On the beautiful and the ugly. *Trans/Form/Ação* 34(SPE2): 21–34.

Paunonen, Sampo V. 2006. You are honest, therefore I like you and find you attractive. *Journal of Research in Personality* 40(3): 237–249.

Peltola, Henna-Riikka and Tuija Saresma. 2014. Spatial and bodily metaphors in narrating the experience of listening to sad music. *Musicae Scientiae* 18(3): 292–306.

Persich, Michelle R., Jessica L. Bair, Becker Steinemann, Stephanie Nelson, Adam K. Fetterman, and Michael D. Robinson. 2018. Hello darkness my old friend: Preferences for darkness vary by neuroticism and co-occur with negative affect. *Cognition and Emotion* 33(5): 885–900.

Persich, Michelle R., Becker Steinemann, Adam K. Fetterman, and Michael D. Robinson. 2018. Drawn to the light: Predicting religiosity using "God Is Light" metaphor. *Psychology of Religion and Spirituality*. Advance online publication. http://dx.doi.org/10.1037/rel0000216

Petruck, Miriam R. L. 2016. Introduction to MetaNet. *Constructions and Frames* 8(2): 133–140.

Pfann, Gerard A., Jeff E. Biddle, Daniel S. Hamermesh, and Ciska M. Bosman. 2000. Business success and businesses' beauty capital. *Economics Letters* 67(2): 201–207.

Price-Chalita, Patricia and Tuija Saresma. 1994. Spatial metaphor and the politics of empowerment: Mapping a place for feminism and postmodernism in geography? *Antipode* 26(3): 236–254.

Quinn, Naomi and Dorothy Holland. 1987. Culture and cognition. In Dorothy Holland and Naomi Quinn (eds), *Cultural models in language and thought*, 3–40. Cambridge: Cambridge University Press.

Radden, Günter. 2000. How metonymic are metaphors? In Antonio Barcelona (ed.), *Metaphor and metonymy at the crossroads: A cognitive perspective*, 93–108. Berlin: Mouton de Gruyter.

Reed, Gail S. 2003. Spatial metaphors of the mind. *Psychoanalytic Quarterly* 72(1): 97–129.

Reeder, Stacy, Juliana Utley, and Darlinda Cassel. 2009. Using metaphors as a tool for examining preservice elementary teachers' beliefs about mathematics teaching and learning. *School Science and Mathematics* 109(5): 290–297.

Ritchie, L. David. 2013. *Metaphor: Key topics in semantics and pragmatics*. Cambridge: Cambridge University Press.

Rohrer, Tim. 2006. Three dogmas of embodiment: Cognitive linguistics as a cognitive science. In Gitte Kristiansen, Michel Achard, René Dirven, and Francisco J. Ruiz de Mendoza Ibáñez (eds.), *Cognitive linguistics: Current applications and future perspectives*, 119–146. Berlin: Mouton de Gruyter.

Rohrer, Tim. 2007. Embodiment and experientialism. In Dirk Geeraerts and Hubert Cuyckens (eds.), *The Oxford handbook of cognitive linguistics*, 25–47. Oxford: Oxford University Press.

Ross, Alison. 2011. Moral metaphorics, or Kant after Blumenberg: Towards an analysis of the aesthetic settings of morality. *Thesis Eleven* 104(1): 40–58.

Rowlands, Mark. 2010. *The new science of the mind: From extended mind to embodied phenomenology*. Cambridge, MA: MIT Press.

Royzman, Edward and Robert Kurzban. 2011. Minding the metaphor: The elusive character of moral disgust. *Emotion Review* 3(3): 269–271.

Rozin, Paul, Jonathan Haidt, and Katrina Fincher. 2009. From oral to moral. *Science* 323: 1179–1180.

Rozin, Paul, Laura Lowery, Sumio Imada, and Jonathan Haidt. 1999. The CAD triad hypothesis: A mapping between three moral emotions (contempt, anger, disgust) and three moral codes (community, autonomy, divinity). *Journal of Personality and Social Psychology* 76(4): 574–586.

Rozin, Paul and Edward B. Royzman. 2001. Negativity bias, negativity dominance, and contagion. *Personality and Social Psychology Review* 5(4): 296–320.

Ruppenhofer, Josef, Michael Ellsworth, Miriam R. L. Petruck, Christopher R. Johnson, and Jan Scheffczyk. 2016. *FrameNet II: Extended theory and practice*. Mannheim: Institut für Deutsche Sprache, Bibliothek.

Saban, Ahmet. 2006. Functions of metaphor in teaching and teacher education: A review essay. *Teaching Education* 17(4): 299–315.

Sanford, Daniel R. 2012. Metaphors are conceptual schemata that are emergent over tokens of use. *Journal of Cognitive Science* 13(3): 211–235.

Schaefer, Michael, Michael Rotte, Hans-Jochen Heinze, and Claudia Denke. 2015. Dirty deeds and dirty bodies: Embodiment of the Macbeth effect is mapped topographically onto the somatosensory cortex. *Scientific Reports* 5: DOI: 10.1038/srep18051

Schnall, Simone. 2011. Clean, proper and tidy are more than the absence of dirty, disgusting and wrong. *Emotion Review* 3(3): 264–266.

Schnall, Simone, Jennifer Benton, and Sophie Harvey. 2008. With a clean conscience: Cleanliness reduces the severity of moral judgments. *Psychological Science* 19(12): 1219–1222.

Schnall, Simone, Jonathan Haidt, Gerald L. Clore, and Alexander H. Jordan. 2008. Disgust as embodied moral judgment. *Personality and Social Psychology Bulletin* 34(8): 1096–1109.

Schnall, Simone and Jean Roper. 2012. Elevation puts moral values into action. *Social Psychological and Personality Science* 3(3): 373–378.

Schnall, Simone, Jean Roper, and Daniel M. T. Fessler. 2010. Elevation leads to altruistic behavior. *Psychological Science* 21(3): 315–320.

Schneider, Iris K., Bastiaan T. Rutjens, Nils B. Jostmann, and Daniël Lakens. 2011. Weighty matters: Importance literally feels heavy. *Social Psychological & Personality Science* 2(5): 474–478.

Schubert, Thomas. 2005. Your highness: Vertical positions as perceptual symbols of power. *Journal of Personality and Social Psychology* 89(1): 1–21.

Schubert, Thomas, Sven Waldzus, and Steffen R. Giessner. 2009. Control over the association of power and size. *Social Cognition* 27(1): 1–19.

Semino, Elena. 2008. *Metaphor in discourse*. Cambridge: Cambridge University Press.

Shanahan, Murray. 2010. *Embodiment and the inner life: Cognition and consciousness in the space of possible minds*. Oxford: Oxford University Press.

Shands, Kerstin W. 1999. *Embracing space: Spatial metaphors in feminist discourse*. Westport, CT: Greenwood Publishing Group.

Shannon, Micheal L. and C. Patrick Stark. 2003. The influence of physical appearance on personnel selection. *Social Behavior and Personality: An International Journal* 31(6): 613–623.

Shapiro, Lawrence. 2011. *Embodied cognition*. London: Routledge.

Sharifian, Farzad. 2008. Distributed, emergent cultural cognition, conceptualization and language. In Roslyn M. Frank, René Dirven, Tom Ziemke, and Enrique Bernárdez (eds.), *Body, language, and mind: Sociocultural situatedness* (Vol. 2), 109–136. Berlin: Mouton de Gruyter.

Sharifian, Farzad. 2009. On collective cognition and language. In Hanna Pishwa (ed.), *Language and social cognition: Expression of social mind*, 163–182. Berlin: Mouton de Gruyter.

Sharifian, Farzad. 2015. Cultural Linguistics. In Farzad Sharifian (ed.), *The Routledge handbook of language and culture*, 473–492. London: Routledge.

Sharifian, Farzad. 2017. *Cultural linguistics*. Amsterdam: John Benjamins.

Sharifian, Farzad, René Dirven, Ning Yu, and Susanne Niemeier (eds.). 2008. *Culture, body, and language: Conceptualizations of internal body organs across cultures and languages*. Berlin: Mouton de Gruyter.

Shayan, Shakila, Ozge Ozturk, Melissa Bowerman, and Asifa Majid. 2014. Spatial metaphor in language can promote the development of cross-modal mappings in children. *Developmental Science* 17(4): 636–643.

Sheikh, Sana, Lucia Botindari, and Emma White. 2013. Embodied metaphors and emotions in the moralization of restrained eating practices. *Journal of Experimental Social Psychology* 49(3): 509–513.

Sherman, Gary D. and Gerald L. Clore. 2009. The color of sin: White and black are perceptual symbols of moral purity and pollution. *Psychological Science* 20(8): 1019–1025.

Sherman, Gary D., Jonathan Haidt, and Gerald L. Clore. 2012. The faintest speck of dirt: Disgust enhances the detection of impurity. *Psychological Science* 23(12): 1506–1514.

Shore, Brad. 1998. *Culture in mind: Cognition, culture, and the problem of meaning.* Oxford: Oxford University Press.

Silvera, David H., Robert A. Josephs, and R. Brian Giesler. 2002. Bigger is better: The influence of physical size on aesthetic preference judgments. *Journal of Behavioral Decision Making* 15(3): 189–202.

Sinha, Chris. 1995. Introduction to the special issue on "Spatial Language and Cognition 1". *Cognitive Linguistics* 6(1): 7–9.

Sinha, Chris and Enrique Bernárdez. 2015. Space, time, and space-time metaphors, maps, and fusions. In Farzad Sharifian (ed.), *The Routledge handbook of language and culture,* 309–324. London: Routledge.

Sinha, Chris and Lis A. Thorseng. 1995. A coding system for spatial relational reference. *Cognitive Linguistics* 6(2/3): 261–309.

Slingerland, Edward. 2004. Conceptual metaphor theory as methodology for comparative religion. *Journal of the American Academy of Religion* 72(1): 1–31.

Slingerland, Edward. 2011. Metaphor and meaning in early China. *Dao* 10(1): 1–30.

Sontag, Susan. 1978. *Illness as metaphor.* New York: Farrar, Straus and Giroux.

Spencer, Albert R. 2013. The dialogues as dramatic rehearsal: Plato's *Republic* and the moral accounting metaphor. *The Pluralist* 8(2): 26–35.

Steen, Gerard J. 2011. The contemporary theory metaphor—now new and improved. *Review of Cognitive Linguistics* 9(1): 26–64.

Stefanowitsch, Anatol and Stefan Th. Gries (eds.). 2006. *Corpus-based approaches to metaphor and metonymy.* Berlin: Mouton de Gruyter.

Stewart, Dianne M. 2005. *Three eyes for the journey: African dimensions of the Jamaican religious experience.* Oxford: Oxford University Press.

Stickles, Elise, Oana David, Ellen Dodge, and Jisup Hong. 2016. Formalizing contemporary conceptual metaphor theory: A structured repository for metaphor analysis. *Constructions and Frames* 8(2): 166–213.

Stites, Lauren J. and Şeyda Özçalişkan. 2013. Developmental changes in children's comprehension and explanation of spatial metaphors for time. *Journal of Child Language* 40(5): 1123–1137.

Stokes, Patrick. 2007. Kierkegaard's mirrors: The immediacy of moral vision. *Inquiry* 50(1): 70–94.

Strathern, Andrew. 1996. *Body thoughts.* Ann Arbor, MI: University of Michigan Press.

Sullivan, Karen. 2013. *Frames and constructions in metaphoric language.* Amsterdam: John Benjamins.

Sullivan, Karen. 2016. Integrating constructional semantics and conceptual metaphor. *Constructions and Frames* 8(2): 141–165.

Suojanen, Mika. 2016. Aesthetic experience of beautiful and ugly persons: A critique. *Journal of Aesthetics and Culture* 8(1): DOI: 10.3402/jac.v8.30529

Sweetser, Eve E. 1990. *From etymology to pragmatics: The mind-body metaphor in semantic structure and semantic change.* Cambridge: Cambridge University Press.

Sweetser, Eve E. 1992. English metaphors for language: Motivations, conventions, and creativity. *Poetics Today* 13(4): 705–724.

Talmy, Leonard. 2000. *Toward a cognitive semantics* (2 vols.). Cambridge, MA: MIT Press.

Taub, Sarah F. 1990. Moral accounting. Manuscript, University of California, Berkeley, CA.

Taub, Sarah F. 2001. *Language from the body: Iconicity and metaphor in American Sign Language.* Cambridge: Cambridge University Press.

Tobia, Kevin Patrick. 2014. The effects of cleanliness and disgust on moral judgment. *Philosophical Psychology* 28(4): 556–568.

Tolaas, Jon. 1991. Notes on the origin of some spatialization metaphors. *Metaphor and Symbol* 6(3): 203–218.

Tsukiura, Takashi and Roberto Cabeza. 2011. Shared brain activity for aesthetic and moral judgments: Implications for the Beauty-is-Good stereotype. *Social Cognitive and Affective Neuroscience* 6(1): 138–148.

Turner, Joan. 1998. Turns of phrase and routes to learning: The journey metaphor in educational culture. *Intercultural Communication Studies* 7(2): 23–36.

Turner, Mark. 1987. *Death is the mother of beauty.* Chicago, IL: University of Chicago Press.

Turner, Mark. 1991. *Reading minds: The study of English in the age of cognitive science.* Princeton, NJ: Princeton University Press.

Tversky, Barbara. 2011. Visualizing thought. *Topics in Cognitive Science* 3(3): 499–535.

Tversky, Barbara. 2015. The cognitive design of tools of thought. *Review of Philosophy and Psychology* 6(1): 99–116.

Ungerer, Friedrich and Hans-Jörg Schmid. 2013. *An introduction to cognitive linguistics* (2nd ed.). London: Routledge.

Vallet, Guillaume T., Lionel Brunel, Benoit Riou, and Nicolas Vermeulen. 2016. Dynamics of sensorimotor interactions in embodied cognition. *Frontiers in Psychology* 6: 1929.

Van Acker, Wouter and Pieter Uyttenhove. 2012. Analogous spaces: An introduction to spatial metaphors for the organization of knowledge. *Library Trends* 61(2): 259–270.

Varela, Francisco J., Evan Thompson, and Eleanor Rosch. 1991. *The embodied mind: Cognitive science and human experience.* Cambridge, MA: MIT Press.

Vervaeke, John and John M. Kennedy. 1996. Metaphors in language and thought: Falsification and multiple meanings. *Metaphor and Symbol* 11(4): 273–284.

Violi, Patrizia. 2003. Embodiment at the crossroads between cognition and semiosis. *Recherches en Communication* 19: 199–217.

Violi, Patrizia. 2008. Beyond the body: Towards a full embodied semiosis. In Roslyn M. Frank, René Dirven, Tom Ziemke, and Enrique Bernárdez (eds.), *Body, language, and mind: Sociocultural situatedness* (Vol. 2), 53–76. Berlin: Mouton de Gruyter.

Wa Thiong'o, Ngugi. 1986. *Decolonizing the mind: The politics of language in African literature.* London: James Currey.

Wang, Jing, Tiansheng Xia, Liling Xu, Taotao Ru, Ce Mo, Ting Ting Wang, and Lei Mo. 2017. What is beautiful brings out what is good in you: The effect of facial attractiveness on individuals' honesty. *International Journal of Psychology* 52(3): 197–204.

Wang, Tingting, Lei Mo, Ce Mo, Li Hai Tan, Jonathan S. Cant, Luojin Zhong, and Gerald Cupchik. 2015. Is moral beauty different from facial beauty? Evidence from an fMRI study. *Social Cognitive and Affective Neuroscience* 10(6): 814–823.

Weiss, Gail and Honi F. Haber (eds.). 1999. *Perspectives on embodiment: The intersections of nature and culture.* New York: Routledge.

Wierzbicka, Anna. 1992. *Semantics, culture, and cognition: Human concepts in culture-specific configurations.* Oxford: Oxford University Press.

Wierzbicka, Anna. 1997. *Understanding cultures through their key words.* Oxford: Oxford University Press.

Wilcox, Phillis Perrin. 2000. *Metaphor in American Sign Language.* Washington, DC: Gallaudet University Press.

Wilson, Nicole L. and Raymond W. Gibbs. 2007. Real and imagined body movement primes metaphor comprehension. *Cognitive Science* 31(4): 721–731.

Winter, Bodo. 2014. Horror movies and the cognitive ecology of primary metaphors. *Metaphor and Symbol* 29(3): 151–170.

Winter, Bodo and Teenie Matlock. 2017. Primary metaphors are both cultural and embodied. In Beate Hampe (ed.), *Metaphor: Embodied cognition and discourse*, 99–115. Cambridge: Cambridge University Press.

Winter, Steven L. 1995. A clearing in the forest. *Metaphor and Symbolic Activity* 10(3): 223–245.

Wolter, Sibylla, Carolin Dudschig, Irmgard de la Vega, and Barbara Kaup. 2015. Musical metaphors: Evidence for a spatial grounding of non-literal sentences describing auditory events. *Acta Psychologica* 156: 126–135.

Wurzbach, Mary Ellen. 1999. The moral metaphors of nursing. *Journal of Advanced Nursing* 30(1): 94–99.

Xie, Jiushu, Yanli Huang, Ruiming Wang, and Wenjuan Liu. 2015. Affective valence facilitates spatial detection on vertical axis: Shorter time strengthens effect. *Frontiers in Psychology* 6: 277. DOI: 10.3389/fpsyg.2015.00277

Yu, Ning. 1998. *The contemporary theory of metaphor: A perspective from Chinese*. Amsterdam: John Benjamins.

Yu, Ning. 2001. What does our face mean to us? *Pragmatics and Cognition* 9(1): 1–36.

Yu, Ning. 2003. Chinese metaphors of thinking. *Cognitive Linguistics* 14(2/3): 141–166.

Yu, Ning. 2008. Metaphor from body and culture. In Raymond W. Gibbs (ed.), *The Cambridge handbook of metaphor and thought*, 247–261. Cambridge: Cambridge University Press.

Yu, Ning. 2009a. *The Chinese* HEART *in a cognitive perspective: Culture, body, and language*. Berlin: Mouton de Gruyter.

Yu, Ning. 2009b. *From body to meaning in culture: Papers on cognitive semantic studies of Chinese*. Amsterdam: John Benjamins.

Yu, Ning. 2011a. Beijing Olympics and Beijing opera: A multimodal metaphor in a CCTV Olympics commercial. *Cognitive Linguistics* 22(3): 595–628.

Yu, Ning. 2011b. A decompositional approach to metaphorical compound analysis: The case of a TV commercial. *Metaphor and Symbol* 26(4): 243–259.

Yu, Ning. 2012. The metaphorical orientation of time in Chinese. *Journal of Pragmatics* 44(10): 1335–1354.

Yu, Ning. 2013. The body in anatomy: Looking at "head" for the mind-body link in Chinese. In Rosario Caballero and Javier Diaz-Vera (eds.), *Sensuous cognition—explorations into human sentience: Imagination, (e)motion and perception*, 53–73. Berlin: Mouton de Gruyter.

Yu, Ning. 2015a. Metaphorical character of moral cognition: A comparative and decompositional analysis. *Metaphor and Symbol* 30(3): 163–183.

Yu, Ning. 2015b. Embodiment, culture, and language. In Farzad Sharifian (ed.), *The Routledge handbook of language and culture*, 227–239. London: Routledge.

Yu, Ning. 2016. Spatial metaphors for morality: A perspective from Chinese. *Metaphor and Symbol* 31(2): 108–125.

Yu, Ning. 2017. LIFE AS OPERA: A cultural metaphor in Chinese. In Farzad Sharifian (ed.), *Advances in Cultural Linguistics*, 65–87. Singapore: Springer.

Yu, Ning. 2020. Linguistic embodiment in linguistic experience: A corpus-based study. In Iwona Kraska-Szlenk (ed.), *Body part terms in conceptualization and language usage*, 11–30. Amsterdam: John Benjamins.

Yu, Ning and Jie Huang. 2019. Primary metaphors across languages: Difficulty as weight and solidity. *Metaphor and Symbol* 34(3): 111–126.

Yu, Ning and Dingding Jia. 2016. Metaphor in culture: LIFE IS A SHOW in Chinese. *Cognitive Linguistics* 27(2): 147–180.

Yu, Ning, Lu Yu, and Yue Christine Lee. 2017. Primary metaphors: Importance as size and weight in a comparative perspective. *Metaphor and Symbol* 32(4): 231–249.

Yu, Ning, Tianfang Wang, and Yingliang He. 2016. Spatial subsystem of moral metaphors: A cognitive semantic study. *Metaphor and Symbol* 31(4): 195–211.

Zhai, Dongxue, Yaling Guo, and Zhongyi Lu. 2018. A Dual mechanism of cognition and emotion in processing moral-vertical metaphors. *Frontiers in Psychology* 9: 1554. DOI: 10.3389/fpsyg. 2018.01554

Zhang, Xiaobin, Bin Zuo, Kendall Erskine, and Tao Hu. 2016. Feeling light or dark? Emotions affect perception of brightness. *Journal of Environmental Psychology* 47: 107–111.

Zhong, Chen-Bo, Vanessa K. Bohns, and Francesca Gino. 2010. Good lamps are the best police: Darkness increases dishonesty and self-interested behavior. *Psychological Science* 21(3). 311–314.

Zhong, Chen-Bo and Julian House. 2014. Dirt, pollution, and purity: A metaphoric perspective on morality. In Mark J. Landau, Michael D. Robinson, and Brian P. Meier (eds.), *The Power of metaphor: Examining its influence on social life*, 109–131. Washington, DC: American Psychological Association.

Zhong, Chen-Bo and Geoffrey J. Leonardelli. 2008. Cold and lonely: Does social exclusion literally feel cold? *Psychological Science* 19(9): 838–842.

Zhong, Chen-Bo and Katie Liljenquist. 2006. Washing away your sins: Threatened morality and physical cleansing. *Science* 313(5792): 1451–1452.

Zhong, Chen-Bo, Brendan Strejcek, and Niro Sivanathan. 2010. A clean self can render harsh moral judgment. *Journal of Experimental Social Psychology* 46(5): 859–862.

Zhou, Haotian and John T. Cacioppo. 2015. More than a blood pump: An experimental enquiry of the folk theory of the heart. In David C. Noelle, Rick Dale, Anne S. Warlaumont, Jeff Yoshimi, Teenie Matlock, Carolyn D. Jennings, and Paul P. Maglio (eds.), *Proceedings of the 37th annual meeting of the cognitive science society*, 2823–2828. Austin, TX: Cognitive Science Society.

Ziemke, Tom, Jordan Zlatev, and Roslyn M. Frank (eds.) 2007. *Body, language and mind: Embodiment* (Vol. 1). Berlin: Mouton de Gruyter.

Zinken, Jörg, Iina Hellsten, and Brigitte Nerlich. 2008. Discourse metaphors. In Roslyn M. Frank, René Dirven, Tom Ziemke, and Enrique Bernárdez (eds.). *Body, language and mind: Sociocultural situatedness* (Vol. 2), 363–385. Berlin: Mouton de Gruyter.

Zwaan, Rolf A. 2008. Experiential traces and mental simulations in language comprehension. In Manuel de Vega, Arthur M. Glenberg, and Arthur C. Graesser (eds.), *Symbols and embodiment: Debates on meaning and cognition*, 165–180. Oxford: Oxford University Press.

Zwaan, Rolf A. 2009. Mental simulation in language comprehension and social cognition. *European Journal of Social Psychology* 39(7): 1142–1150.

Zwaan, Rolf A. 2014. Embodiment and language comprehension: Reframing the discussion. *Trends in Cognitive Sciences* 18(5): 229–234.

English dictionaries

Hard-copy dictionaries

CODCE. 1976. *The concise Oxford dictionary of current English*. Oxford: Oxford University Press.

LDCE. 1978. *Longman dictionary of contemporary English*. Harlow and London: Longman.

WNCD. 1977. *Webster's new collegiate dictionary*. Springfield, MA: G. & C. Merriam.

Online dictionaries

Longman dictionary of contemporary English. https://www.ldoceonline.com/
Merriam-Webster. https://www.merriam-webster.com/
Merriam-Webster learner's dictionary. http://learnersdictionary.com/
Oxford lexico. https://www.lexico.com/

Chinese dictionaries

Hard-copy dictionaries

HYDCD. 2000. 汉语大词典 [*Grand dictionary of Chinese language*]. Shanghai: Grand Dictionary of Chinese Language Press.

XDHYCD. 2002. 现代汉语词典 [*Contemporary Chinese dictionary* (Chinese-English ed.)]. Beijing: Foreign Language Teaching and Research Press.

XDHYCD. 2005. 现代汉语词典 [*Contemporary Chinese dictionary* (5th ed.)]. Beijing: Commercial Press.

XDHYCD. 2012. 现代汉语词典 [*Contemporary Chinese dictionary* (6th ed.)]. Beijing: Commercial Press.

XDHYCD. 2016. 现代汉语词典 [*Contemporary Chinese dictionary* (7th ed.)]. Beijing: Commercial Press.

XSDHYDCD. 2004. 新时代汉英大词典 [*New age Chinese-English dictionary*]. Beijing: Commercial Press.

XXDHYCD. 1992. 新现代汉语词典 [*A new dictionary of modern Chinese language*]. Haikou, Hainan: Hainan Press.

Online dictionaries

HYDCD. 汉语大辞典 [*Grand dictionary of Chinese language*]. http://www.hydcd.com/
ZXHYCD. 在线汉语词典 [*Online Chinese dictionary*]. http://www.ichacha.net/hy/

Chinese and English corpora

BCC. Corpus of Beijing Language and Culture University Corpus Center. http://bcc.blcu.edu.cn/

CCL. Corpus of Center for Chinese Linguistics (Peking University). http://ccl.pku.edu.cn:8080/ccl_corpus/

COCA. Corpus of Contemporary American English (Brigham Young University). https://www.english-corpora.org/coca/

Online databases and resources

Baidu Images. https://image.baidu.com/

FrameNet. The International Computer Science Institute in Berkeley, California. https://framenet.icsi.berkeley.edu/fndrupal/

Google Images. https://images.google.com/

MetaNet Metaphor Wiki. The International Computer Science Institute in Berkeley, California. https://metanet.icsi.berkeley.edu/metanet/

Wikipedia. https://en.wikipedia.org/wiki/Main_Page

Index